4352

940   Bruce, Colin John
.54   War on the ground / Colin John Bruce. --London :
0941   Constable, 1995.
Bru   318 p. : ill. ; 25 cm.

712242   ISBN:0094724903

1. World War, 1939-1945 - Personal narratives,
British. I. Title

327   95OCT26   3559/he   1-394023

WAR ON THE GROUND

WAR ON THE GROUND

Colin John Bruce

Constable · London

First published in Great Britain 1995
by Constable and Company Limited
3 The Lanchesters, 162 Fulham Palace Road, London W6 9ER
Copyright © 1995 Colin John Bruce
ISBN 0 09 472490 3
The right of Colin John Bruce to be
identified as the author of this work has been asserted by him
in accordance with the Copyright, Designs and Patents Act 1988
Set in 11pt Linotype Sabon by
Rowland Phototypesetting Ltd
Bury St Edmunds, Suffolk
Printed in Great Britain by
St Edmundsbury Press Ltd
Bury St Edmunds, Suffolk

CIP catalogue record for this book
is available from the British Library

For Rose and Alex

Contents

List of Illustrations

All illustrations are reproduced by kind permission
of the Imperial War Museum, London

Acknowledgements

This book was compiled from a selection of the conversations and correspondence I conducted over the course of two years. There is not space to acknowledge everyone generous enough to relive their wartime experiences for me, but I would particularly like to thank the following, without whose unstinting help this book would not have been possible:

Messrs E.C. Annis and G.W. Bainbridge, Rev. A.W. Barrah, Mrs D. Bradley, Messrs J. Bradley, F.S. Brown, A.W. Card, J.A. Cowley, M. Crossley and C.E. Daniels, Rev. H.L.O. Davies, Messrs A.R. Day, H.A. Dean, A.V. Domoney and B. Duffy, Mrs E. Eaton, Mrs I. Eden, Messrs W.D. Edwards, A.G. Frampton and Z.R. Gasowski, Rev. G.A.W. Gold, Mr E. Hamilton, Mrs P. Hoare, Messrs H. Hodgson, E.H. Holland and W.G. Hornsby, Dr W.S. Hossack, Messrs J. Jefferis, A.T.J. Lamb, H.M. Lowry, D.W. Marshall, R. Masterton, R. McKay and J. McRobie, Mrs P.M. Morris, Messrs J.H.B. Munro, S. Oliver, R. Payling, R.A. Perry, E. Raspison, S.L. Relidzinski, T.B. Ridley, J. Russell, W. Scully, A.W. Sheppard, A. Silver, E. Simpson and S.W. Squires, Ms A.E.M. Taylor, Messrs M. Thomas, J.A. Waller, A. Ward, M. Wartalski and H.D. Webber, Mrs H. Whitehouse, Messrs J.H. Whitelee, S. Wicks and J. Wise.

1

INTRODUCTION

In the years between the First and Second World Wars the British Army was the Cinderella of the three armed services.

Unpopular, underfunded and overstretched, its role was basically that of an Imperial peacekeeper, the deployment of whose units around the world was still governed by the Cardwell system of 1881.

Named after the progressive Secretary of State for War Edward Cardwell, whose package of reforms had also included finally outlawing the sale of commissions for cash, this stated that one infantry battalion should be maintained at home for every battalion overseas. Since the strengths of the other arms were adjusted accordingly, this meant that roughly half of the Regular Army would be serving abroad at any given moment. Anyone choosing an Army career could therefore expect to spend several years at a time in one of the foreign garrisons, especially the larger ones in the Middle East and India.

Movement between these was by troopship, with the vessels and crews being provided on a contract basis by civilian shipping companies. In the inter-war period the two British firms which virtually monopolized 'trooping', as it was called, were the Bibby Line and the British India Steam Navigation Company. Two of the latter's purpose-built troopships, the 12,556-ton *Dilwara* and her sister the *Dunera*, had the distinction of being the first to provide bunks for other ranks, although hammocks remained more common. Life on board was just as regimented as in barracks ashore, with formal inspections of the troop decks, and officers being obliged to wear mess kit at dinner.

Despite the lure of foreign travel, however, recruiting remained low. Enlistment into the Army was voluntary, and recruits signed on for an initial period of twelve years, normally split between actual service with the Colours and service in the Reserve – seven years and five years respectively in the case of the infantry, for example. This could be followed by nine more years, at the end of which a pension was payable. But the fact that the Army was the service most closely associated with the horrors of the First World War resulted in a deep-rooted distrust of a military career, and one striking illustration of the Army's unpopularity was the fact that even during the 1930s, a decade of mass unemployment and hardship, it was unable to attract sufficient recruits to maintain its authorized strength. Indeed, by April 1937 the Regular Army had fallen 27,300 below its nominal establishment of 221,000.

For those who did sign up, the inter-war period was frequently one of frustration. With the Army very much the poor relation of the Royal Navy and the RAF when it came to funding, there were shortages of equipment as well as of manpower.

Even so, not everyone disdained the Army life.

This blue form is my attestation paper, from when I joined the Army, which was 20th November 1930. See, it gives my date of birth as 18th November 1912, but that's a lie, that. I was born the year after, in May. So I was really seventeen, and the bloke said, 'You can't join till you're eighteen.' I said, 'I'm eighteen tomorrow!' He said, 'Well, come back tomorrow, then.' [Laughs.]

Was there a lot of falsification going on?

Oh, some put a year on to their age. I didn't go that far, I added six months, which isn't a lot. Well, they were very short in them days. It was entirely volunteers, and they weren't getting particularly good class people.

So where did you actually sign on?

In Liverpool. It was a recruiting office at 92 London Road, which is in the city centre. You were wheeled in, and the officer swore you in and all that. They didn't bother with birth certificates. They just checked that you were a responsible person. You had to give an employer's certificate. If you couldn't get your parents' permission, and I couldn't, you got permission from your boss, which I could. I told me mum the day after, and she done her nut.

Where were you working at the time?

I worked in a furniture store in Liverpool, the Renown Furniture Store. He was a good boss, actually. And the reason why he signed was that he was going to close down the next year. Close the business down.

Because the firm was in difficulties?

Yes, this was the time of the Great Depression, of course. So he decided to do a favour for me, otherwise I'd have been out of work. So it worked out well. I was living in Liverpool then, with me stepfather. He wasn't particularly sorry, because it took a burden off his shoulders, didn't it?

So away you went, and the Army looked after you after that.

That's my paybook. You always had that in your top right-hand pocket. They marked off your inoculations, your medical inspections, some of the times you went on leave, any bits and pieces about yourself.

The peacetime Regular Army was pretty good, pretty good. Plenty of sport. More sport than enough; that was to keep you occupied, and keep you fit. We got plenty of football, cricket, tennis, anything you liked to go for. There weren't all that many places to do it, but places where there were, you could. And you always got time off. If you were any good at it they worked on you.

In those days they had what they called regimental depots. Liverpool's one was just on the outskirts, a place called Seaforth Barracks. It's gone now, been demolished a long time ago. And that was the central place where you had to go to. Wherever the different battalions of the regiment were stationed, the HQ was always that depot. So you knew exactly where to go to. That's what we all had to do, report to the depot of the King's Regiment (Liverpool) at Seaforth Barracks.

So how long did they keep you at the depot?
Six months.

And at the end of that time they regarded you as fully trained?
At the end of six months you were fully trained. Then you were posted to whichever battalion was nearest. At that time it was the 2nd Battalion, at Aldershot. The 1st Battalion were a bit further away – they were in Egypt. So after you'd done a couple of years with the home battalion, you went out to the abroad battalion. That filled another five years of your time. So eventually most of them did seven years, and then came out. And if anything broke loose, like the war, you went in again. That's exactly what happened to me.

Did you get leave from abroad?
No, what they used to do to make up for that was they used to give you six weeks' leave, or if they thought it was going to be a long absence they'd give you eight weeks' leave, before you went. And that covered the time you were away, then, near enough. When you were discharged at the end you got another month's leave, or six weeks' leave, on discharge. So you eventually got all your leave, all in one lump. Because in those days they didn't send you home from abroad. Malta was the furthest one they sent you home from. But all the others further out, Egypt, India or any of them, you didn't.

Must have been a long haul, away for five years.

Oh, yes. Especially if you were a married man, though there weren't many – they didn't encourage soldiers to marry in them days. It was expensive for the Army. The few married men in the battalion were mostly those that'd *had* to be married because they'd had a baby; they were compelled to get married.

And did they take their wives abroad with them?

If there was room. They had a fixed number, so many wives. And once you got over that . . .

Like a quota?

That's it. They had a waiting list, and after a period of time you were sent with your husband.

So if you were at the end of the queue . . .

Might not see her for five years. During the war that happened all the time. The only way you could get out of it was a thing called compassionate leave. If your wife was sick, or going to have a baby, they'd send you home. Course, if she was going to have a baby and you'd been abroad for eighteen months . . . you got a bit suspicious! [Laughs.] It happened. They still had them go home, though. Just to sort it out. Caused a bit of friction, I should imagine.

So, as I say, I went to the 2nd Battalion at Aldershot. You went down in groups of about thirty, with a couple of NCOs in charge. And when you got there they lined you all up, and sorted you out into the different units you were going to go to in the battalion. They used to have a big party the first night you were there, an introduction party. And you got to know all your new mates. A battalion in those days was only about 500 men. It should have been nearer 800, but they were always under strength. Particularly the home battalions, because they tried to keep the numbers in the abroad battalions up. 500 men spread over a big barracks, you'd hardly notice them.

Aldershot was a big place. Only snag was that there was no girls there. Or very few. 'Cos the local inhabitants kept away from us, knowing what soldiers are. In any case we didn't have a lot of money, so there was no question of girls living on us – we had no money to live on! We only got, what, two shillings a day. Two old-fashioned shillings, equivalent to about 5p nowadays.

What time off did you get? Did you have your evenings to yourself?

Oh yes, nights off, yes. Weekends. You could go places if you wanted. If you lived near enough, you could go home on weekend leave. Most of them went home about once a month, on a weekend leave. But the fare from Aldershot to Liverpool in those days was about thirty bob, I think, which was two weeks' pay. So I only managed that about once in three months.

They had cinemas which were run by the Army, and which you didn't have to get dressed up to go to. They had about three of them, small cinemas, one in each area. So you went to the movies most nights. Television hadn't come in then. The farthest one was about a twenty-minute walk, there was one within ten minutes, and there was one just outside the barracks. You could go to the town cinemas if you liked, and pay the full prices, but they would be expensive. Whereas the Army ones were about a penny, I think, something like that. You got older films, but it didn't matter to us.   ·

After about two years you expected to see your name in the list – the list that used to go up, every year, of who was getting posted. On the notice-board – 'The following personnel have been selected for draft to the such-and-such Battalion, as from a certain date.' Then as the day got nearer they had a thing called the waiting list. The men selected were first to go, and the ones on the waiting list used to go if someone had run away, deserted, or just didn't turn up. You went up the list. So one day, a parade's called in the morning, eight o'clock, or nine o'clock. And they read out the list of names, then there's a big blank space, then they work through the also-rans. You were all listening hard, to see if your name was called. Then they'd say, 'List full, closed.' I had that twice, that.

Some people didn't like the idea of going abroad?

Oh, they were quite comfortable staying at home. They didn't want to go abroad where you had diseases, and fighting, and all that kind of nonsense! [Laughs.] So they just skipped.

We were stationed right outside what we called the Glasshouse, the big punishment centre that Aldershot had. And the prisoners, Army prisoners, used to go there. No civilians, only Army. It was quite a rough outfit too, I'll tell you. They used to have to scrub their equipment white, instead of putting that green stuff on it – green blanco. When you'd been in detention you had white equipment, and stood out a mile. It took a long time to get it green again, but that was part of the punishment.

When your name came up on the drafting list, you were marched straight off. You didn't go back to barracks, you'd go straight out with the unit. Off by train to the docks, and they'd go through all the ceremonials, 'Should old acquaintance . . .' and all that. Quite a heart-breaking party at the docks. Southampton they used to go from. And all the wives left behind crying their eyes out. Terrible.

I missed Egypt. Our 1st Battalion'd just moved from Egypt to

India. So when I went out through the Suez Canal it was to go straight through, round to Bombay.

You got welcomed by what they called a regimental friend, for each soldier, and he told you what was happening, all the battalion rules and regulations and all that kind of thing.

Were there differences between the two battalions?

Oh yes. Definitely a difference. The crack battalion was the 1st. They regarded themselves as far above the 2nd Battalion. The different battalions of a regiment would only meet on rare occasions. Our two Regular battalions had last met in Malta, in 1927. They had a big sports meeting to celebrate. That was very rare. What happened was, I think the 2nd Battalion was on its way home from Iraq, and the 1st Battalion was stationed in Malta, so they happened to cross on the way. So they had a sports meeting – which ended up an honourable draw! [Laughs.]

I got to India in 1933, when the 1st Battalion was at Jubbulpore. We had some trouble with the natives, which wasn't their fault, it was *our* fault. Somebody got murdered. Must have been . . . let's see . . . 1935.

Our company wasn't involved, I'm glad to say. It was all a real cock-up, to tell you the honest truth. The village that they attacked was the one that rescued the man that was beaten up. They were all Irishmen. Turned up at the wrong village. They obviously couldn't read maps, either. And killed the wrong villager. The first man, the white man, that got into trouble had been chasing women. And this woman had objected, quite naturally, to being raped. So the villagers attacked him, which was quite right and proper. That's what started it. And these other nutters went out to avenge their mate. In the end a bloke got life imprisonment, I think. He was lucky he didn't hang. 'Cos in those days they had hanging.

In fact the punishments were quite strict. For striking a native, a British soldier could have got five years. It was as strict as that. Whereas in England you got a twenty-bob fine, or forty-bob fine. In India you got five years in prison, and no messing about. Partly to protect the natives, and partly to maintain the prestige of the British troops. And they let it be known that that would always happen; they'd always get heavy sentences.

So after we got into this fracas with this lot it went worse after that. They sent us up to the North-West Frontier, to Landi Kotal, which guarded the Khyber Pass, on the border between Afghanistan and British India.

It was a good place for a fighting soldier. There was bullets whizzing round all over the place. 'Cos what they used to do in their spare time was they used to shoot people in the fields. Fire over our camp, and shoot the people on the other side of the ridge. The local tribesmen had always been at it. They haven't stopped ever. They never stopped when the Karachi government took over. They used to carry arms all the time. Rifles, and ammunition. Even hand grenades. No question of disarming them. We used to see them in the streets there with their rifles. And every now and again they'd whip it up and fire up in the air. As long as they fired up in the air we left them alone. It's only when they started firing at people that we started getting interested. Landi Kotal. That was the very farthest outpost of the Empire in them days.

But I was only there about three months. And I got out of the Army then. I was discharged from there, actually. My time was up. I'd been in the Army seven years, and I'd been in India about five years. Just on five years.

They bring you back, that's part of the agreement. The only time you have to foot the bill is if you leave for your own reasons, then you have to pay your own fare home. If for any reason you got bought out, or you got fed up with the Army. Took a train down from Landi Kotal. Well, we had to get four trains actually. A mountain railway down from the frontier, then another one, then another one, then another one. By the time you got to the coast about ten days had gone past. And then a troopship back to England, twenty-one days. We had Christmas Day at sea that year, Christmas of 1937.

Did you have to go back to the depot?

No, you got discharged on the docks. And then you could go straight home from there. Then later on you got all your papers that told you what to do. I went on a, what do you call it? Vocational training course. Training for a job in civvy street. I went to be a painter and decorator. I wasn't very good at it.

How did you feel about leaving the Army after seven years?

Well, bit lost actually. Very lonely. Because thirty of you used to live in one room sometimes. Usually at least fifteen. So when you got home and had to live on your own ... And I had no brothers and sisters, or anything like that. I had a *terrible* time trying to fit in.

So did you move back to Liverpool?

No, never. Never been back since. Or rather only once, when I was called up, when the war broke out.

You see I was still a Reservist, so when the war broke out I had to go back to Liverpool. That's how the system worked. A call-up notice came.

Had things changed quite a bit when you rejoined?

Oh, they had. Different guns, different techniques, different everything. You had to learn it all over again. We were old men to the youngsters. We were twenty-six-year-olds, whereas they were eighteen. (*Mr Silver*)

Apart from the Regular Army's own Reservists, and what was called the Supplementary Reserve (mainly composed of civilians with useful trade or professional skills, who signed up to do the same jobs in the Army in time of war), the bulk of the immediately available reinforcements came from the Territorial Army. Although few of the TA's units could have been described as combat-ready in September 1939, and although its members were often jokingly disparaged as 'Saturday Night Soldiers' because of their part-time service, they nevertheless formed a vital pool of men – and, from 1938, women – possessing basic military training.

My regiment was the Essex Yeomanry, which had been my father's regiment before me. When I was born, during the First World War, I was given the names of the CO, the second-in-command, and one of the squadron commanders!

By the time I joined them, at the time of the big expansion of the TA in April 1939, they'd been converted from a mounted unit into artillery.

Was the deteriorating situation on the Continent a factor in your decision, or would you have joined anyway, do you think?

I had no reason to think that there would be a war, though my father felt for certain there would be. In fact we were both in Scotland in August 1939, and he smelt the air and said, 'I'm going home – I've got jobs to do.' And I thought, There can't possibly be another war, I'll stay here until the end of my holiday. Of course a few days later I had to go home too. He was chairman of the local council, that was the main duty to which he had to return.

I'd passed my OTC certificates before I joined up – there was the School Officers Training Corps, and you got Certificate 'A' there. Which wasn't very difficult. And then I joined the Cambridge University Officers Training Corps and got Certificate 'B'.

Did these involve sitting exams?

A practical exercise of some sort – a 'Tactical Exercise without Troops'. And a written examination as well. It guaranteed you a commission, if you joined the Army.

Was the OTC popular at university? I ask because of course only in February 1933 the Oxford Union had had their famous debate and had voted under no circumstances to fight.

I don't think numbers were really very high – it was mostly people like me. I didn't meet any pacifists. I didn't move in those circles. [Laughs.]

Did everyone sit the certificate exams?

I should think it was the minority who actually sat Certificate 'B'. I took it fairly seriously, because I was that sort of person.

What were you reading at Cambridge?

I went up with the intention of being a medical student. But I changed my mind, and I in fact got a degree in Geography and Economics.

Which college did you go to?

Trinity. Which was, and still is, very big. I enjoyed my three years there very much. So, I think, did all my contemporaries.

And then you joined the TA at the time the government ordered it to double its size.

That's right. I joined our new second-line regiment, the 147th (Essex Yeomanry) Regiment, Royal Horse Artillery.

This must have been a period of considerable disruption for the existing regiment.

It was indeed. They had to send officers from the first-line to the second-line, to help in setting it up. And of course they all got promotion, one step up. The same with a few senior NCOs; not very many.

I was told that I would go to the battery recruited in Colchester. I remember going with my brother, who joined at the same time, and what you might call 'sitting in' while recruits were being sworn in by the battery commander, Major Turner. A very large proportion of our men in the Colchester Battery came from the town council. When we were embodied [called out for active service] it must have absolutely denuded the council offices.

We had, I think, two officers who had fought in the First World War and one Warrant-Officer, but those were the only ones, really, with practical experience.

Our battery commander had come from the first-line regiment. He was a chartered surveyor by profession. A very able man indeed. And he used to lecture to us on the technical side of artillery. Ballistics, and allowances for height, heat, and weather, and so on. We didn't actually think he was divine, but he was pretty high on the pedestal towards being Almighty. [Laughs.] And it wasn't for about four months that we discovered there was a book called *Field Artillery Training*, or something like that, and he was reading up the chapters, you see, and then lecturing to us on them the next day! Eventually somebody was sent on a course, and they were introduced to *Field Artillery Training*, or whatever it was called, and we learned that it could be found in a book! And the God fell off his pedestal!

I think most of my generation who had my background would have all joined up, either Regular or Territorial. A lot of them went into the Regulars, and of course a lot of them were killed, because the first phases of the war like Dunkirk were very expensive in young officers. It was the obvious thing to do; I don't think there were any second thoughts about it. (*Rev. Gold*)

But the bulk of the mass citizen Army needed for another world war had no such previous training, and the Regulars and the TA – the distinctions between which were effectively suspended for the duration of hostilities – formed the absolutely essential foundations on which to build.

For many pre-war soldiers, promotion in the burgeoning Army was rapid.

It was a strange feeling wondering what the situation would be on becoming an Officer Cadet under training when one had been a Warrant-Officer virtually running an infantry company.

It meant saying farewell to my friends in the ranks and stepping into the unknown, from being someone of note as a depot instructor to becoming a nonentity at an Officer Cadet Training Unit – OCTU – and having been then married for fifteen months, having to leave my wife to her own devices and go to live in bachelor accommodation in barracks.

In retrospect I now realize that the depot staff – mostly young NCOs – were all being named for officer training, and as an Acting Company Sergeant-Major I was selected, with three Sergeants, for the first batch for OCTU. I was twenty-four at the time.

The staff at the OCTU were an indifferent assembly of Regular officers, Reservists, university cadet officers and a few Regular NCOs. Those NCOs recalled from the Reserve were, through no fault of their own, not familiar with the latest weapons or techniques. But there's no doubt that the OCTU course was most instructive as regards battalion and brigade training. And mixing with cadets from other arms of the service gave me a knowledge of artillery, transport and administration.

166 OCTU was at Colchester. The cadets had an operational role to fulfil in addition to their training, and assisted the Regular

Army in the defence of West Mersea, carrying out night patrols, sea defences, mine-laying and fire-watching. There was little time for relaxation.

The four-month training period passed quickly and I was gazetted [commissioned. The term 'gazetted' comes from the practice of publishing officers' appointments in the pages of the *London Gazette*] as a Lieutenant, with orders to report to the Adjutant at the depot of the Queen's Royal Regiment (West Surrey).

Rejoining the regiment, in which I had served as an other rank since 1933, as an officer I was rather apprehensive at first. But then I found I was accepted by those officers who knew me, and respected by WOs and NCOs who had served with me previously. There was no embarrassment on my or their part.

The accepted procedure on joining was to report to the Adjutant, be conducted to the officers' mess and introduced to anyone not known previously, and then be allocated accommodation and a batman [personal servant]. The following day one was posted to a company. In view of my previous service in the ranks I was gazetted as a full Lieutenant, and in actual fact was placed in command of one of the companies [normally a Major's post].

Most commissions granted from 1940 onward were Emergency or Temporary, but I never experienced any difference between Regular and Emergency commission officers. In the Queen's Royal Regiment you were judged on your merit and ability. In Italy I alternated commanding the 2/7th Battalion in action with the CO, who was a TA product. I was then the second-in-command of the battalion. I served under four COs who were TA officers and they were all first class, as were the Regular COs I served with. Many TA were excellent officers and did sterling work in the field. One of those I served under was a double DSO and MC winner, and rose to the rank of Brigadier.

So far as you can judge there was no real distinction among those who served. (*Mr Domoney*)

There also seems to have been less prejudice against the civilians drawn into the Army for the duration of the war than there was against such 'outsiders' in, say, the Royal Navy. Undoubtedly one reason for this was simply that the Army expanded so enormously, leaving the pre-war officers and other ranks dispersed throughout a vast number of units composed almost entirely of newcomers.

The instrument of this transformation was conscription, introduced by the Chamberlain government while the country was still at peace. The first 34,500 young men were called up for their compulsory six months with the Colours in July 1939, and were known in the Army as 'Militiamen'.

> I joined as a Regular. I remember that one afternoon in August of 1939 we were on the barrack square and our instructor was a Squadron Quartermaster Sergeant from the Royal Horse Guards. He was drilling us for sword drill. And there was a group of yobbos outside the railings trying to take the mickey. This drill instructor said, 'Don't take any notice of them, because they'll soon be in here, where you are.' (*Mr Day*)

When the Second World War broke out this limited liability was immediately broadened, as was the age range to which the provisions applied. The fact that the system of call-up was already in place when war was declared on 3rd September meant that the Army's expansion could proceed at a much more measured pace than in 1914.

> All those between the ages of eighteen and forty were liable. It was interesting to note that as it would take time to medically examine and provide clothing and equipment, the call-up would be in groups.
>
> Eventually a letter arrived from the War Office, asking if I would like to take up an interesting occupation with His Majesty's Forces or, as I was in agriculture, would I prefer to dig more furiously to provide food for the nation.
>
> My hobby at this time was radio, and now I thought would be a golden opportunity to learn the thing properly. Having made up my mind I wrote back, thinking they would jump at the chance of employing me, and indicating that if I could join as a radio mechanic I could start right away. This apparently was too complicated for the War Office, for they replied with identical forms asking the same old questions.
>
> My initial enthusiasm evaporated immediately. (*Mr Wicks*)

While enlistment was voluntary the choice of which branch of the Army a recruit joined had been entirely up to him, and if his first choice happened to be full he quite often decided not to join at all.

Now things were different. On the very first day of the war Parliament had passed the Armed Forces (Conditions of Service) Act, which allowed the Army to make this decision, not the individual.

> The Selection Officer was elderly – obviously brought out of retirement to do the job. He tried hard to interest me in the various

corps, but I held out that I wanted my county regiment, the Royal Berkshire Regiment.

However, we had already supplied information about education and background, and some weeks later I was told that I would be joining the Royal Corps of Signals. This did not please me very much. It was an early lesson in the ways of the forces and official-dom, and there was, of course, a lot more to come in the future.

I was sent a railway warrant and told to report to the 3rd Signal Training Centre at Ossett, Yorkshire before 23.59 hours on Thursday. I didn't plan my route correctly, and finally detrained at Ponte-fract. I reached Ossett by bus via Wakefield. I reported and was checked in at the guardroom and was then directed to the dining hall, where bread, cheese and cocoa were available. Once a group of new arrivals had assembled we drew bedding and made our first acquaintance with a palliasse – which *wasn't* a friendly don-key! This had to be filled with straw and was, in fact, a somewhat primitive mattress. We were then led to our first Army billet, the Green Chapel, which was furnished with closely spaced rows of wooden bunks, and very little else. Toilet facilities were basic – there was one cold water tap in the yard outside the side door. The elements did not help, as it hardly rose above 32° Fahrenheit during our sojourn in Ossett.

During working hours we were marched everywhere, including to and from the dining hall. During Friday and Saturday we drew our kit, including rifle, and we received our first inoculations. We discovered that there was a good canteen in the town.

On Sunday morning we were assembled in a hall and given various written tests to complete. We were then told to study the various trades available in the corps. These were prominently dis-played on the end wall, and meant nothing at all to most of us. This was, laughingly, called our 'free choice of trade'. We had to choose the one which we thought would suit us, and to make a second choice in case there were no vacancies for training in our first one. So far, so good. I selected 'DR' and 'Lineman'. However, the nigger in the woodpile now appeared in the form of the Trades Allocation Officer – a Major – who informed me that I would be trained to be an OWL [Operator, Wireless and Line]. I objected strongly but was told that that was my free choice. (*Mr Holland*)

Even for those with no strong preferences, the spectre of trench war-fare made the Royal Navy and the RAF seem the more attractive alternatives.

I didn't relish going into the Army, being well aware of the terrible suffering in the trenches of Flanders in the Great War, 1914–1918. I had an uncle killed at Ypres in 1916.

Within a couple of days I was off to Uxbridge to volunteer for the RAF. The Interviewing Officer asked me only two questions. One – could I type? I answered no. Two – could I do shorthand? No.

'Sorry,' he said, 'you'll have to go in the Army.' (*Mr Squires*)

I knew Dad was disappointed. He had been through the First World War, wounded twice and gassed, to be discharged totally disabled. Mother seemed to hide her fears. My going made it that two of her sons were leaving home within four days. After the war she told me she couldn't go into our bedroom for many weeks, her upset was so great. Our family now had three sons and four sons-in-law serving in His Majesty's Forces. We were fortunate. They all came home.

Everything the Army issued seemed to be for the discomfort of the soldier. The blankets were very rough after lovely sheets at home. Uppermost in my mind was the uniform issued, never the right size, and the smell of the mysterious powder which we presumed was a delousing agent. It took many weeks to get used to the rough, stiff collar which rubbed and chafed one's neck, and the heavy boots with the fifteen studs in each sole. Two pairs, with one pair to be 'best'. Many hours spent polishing the toes so they became mirror-like. Each soldier using his own method, but we found that Kiwi brand polish applied and rubbed hard with the handle of a toothbrush and plenty of spit gave a perfect shine approved by any RSM.

Many young men were experiencing homesickness for the first time, and many tears flowed.

We received the princely sum of two shillings per day – fourteen bob a week. But seven shillings was taken from our pay for one reason or another, so each pay-day some of the men would start a card game – Brag, or Crown and Anchor – to try to increase their purchasing power. If your mum could send you a half-crown postal order now and again this did help.

The very hard decision was how to spend wisely to fill the stomach somehow. I recall we could purchase from the lovely ladies of a Church of Scotland mobile canteen a jam fritter, one per person at a penny each as long as the jam lasted. The fritter was a slice of bread spread with jam, folded in half then dipped in batter and dropped into hot fat. I found them delightful. One could no longer purchase many things with a high sugar content, as most of this was imported. Other things more essential had priority.

A normal day's meals in the Army would be breakfast at 7 a.m., maybe 4 inches by 2 inches of bacon or liver, of course the inevitable porridge, two slices of bread. This lasted one till noon. Midday meal always spuds, cabbage, carrots, meat and gravy. During this meal the Orderly Officer made his appearance with his retinue, asking, 'Are there any complaints?' This was never answered! Then came sweet, usually semolina; very occasionally we had our popular favourite spotted dick, with the thin custard sometimes 'burned'. Remember in the early years cooks were 'volunteers' – 'You, you and you!' Kitchen help were men doing 'jankers' for some misbehaviour. Teatime was at 5 p.m., usually two slices of bread with about 2 ounces of cheese, maybe a piece of seed cake, but they always put the 7-pound tin of Ticklers jam on the table, of course 'Plum and Apple'. Supper was hit and miss; sometimes if the cooks hadn't gone out on an evening pass they would dish up any pudding left from midday. This was always cold, but then what could be better than cold pudding and a mess tin of unsweetened cocoa, and so off to bed, if you had no night duties.

To go on leave once every six months was a highlight of living. Though some chaps who had no family to go to would spend their leave at a services club in one of the big cities, sometimes glad to get back to the comradeship of pals in their unit.

The travelling by train in those war years was energy-sapping. On every railway station crowds of troops from all corners of the world. After a couple of years one learned to recognize cap badges at a glance. On occasion whilst in Scotland I had to catch an evening train. The journey from Edinburgh to Leeds would take about six hours; there would be no night connection to Manchester – at night goods trains had priority – so with several hundred more bodies one would try to sleep on the floor. The ladies in the refreshment room served tea. It was really vile, but it was warm and wet. If one was lucky there might be a milk train to Manchester in the early hours.

The trains themselves were an ordeal. Everyone seemed to smoke cigarettes, so one's mouth tasted like the proverbial sewer. No water on in the train washrooms. To go to the toilet was nigh impossible owing to corridors covered with wall-to-wall bodies sleeping in impossible positions. Not to forget the very low lighting in the carriages. Blinds were down because of black-out regulations, so when the train pulled into a station it was up to the porters to shout out the town's name. But at the end of the journey the lovely luxury of getting into a bed with real white sheets was just marvellous, after those rough Army blankets. After a good sleep the next job was to give your mum your food coupons issued by the Army, then plan for a great evening with the lads, only to find they had all been called up. (*Mr Hamilton*)

Regardless of the arm of service, basic training contained much the same elements for everybody. 'The object seemed to be to knock you down till you felt you were nothing, then to build you up again the way they wanted,' as one embittered conscript put it.

Many, though, retain humorous memories along with the unpleasant ones.

I can't say that I was really enthusiastic about soldiering, but though most tasks in training tended to be boring it did have its funny side, and a sense of humour helped enormously.

I remember one bitterly cold morning, we'd been issued with two pairs of long johns, made of thick wool. I put them on, hoping to turn April weather into June. We were to have our first introduction to the barrack square. I was taken aback somewhat, because I was enlisted as a driver. We formed up in columns of three and were put through a routine by a Drill Sergeant, who was so disappointed by our performance he broke down and cried into his handkerchief, telling us how, when he was a boy, his parents bought him a full platoon of tin soldiers and how they were lost in transit when they moved house. His 'tache quivering with rage, he said that he had just found his soldiers and that he felt suicidal. 'To punish you lot I am taking you for a little stroll on Salisbury Plain. The distance will be about 12 miles to start with.' And off we went. We'd done about 3 furlongs when my long johns started to sag, and every pace I took got shorter and shorter. Being in the rear rank the squad went on without me. By this time my knees looked like plant pots, stuffed by long johns. The squad was called to halt and the Sarge bellowed, 'What the hell's the matter, lad, have you shit yourself or are you trying to desert?' (*Mr Bainbridge*)

One of the first things they did was divide our intake of seventy-two into three troops of twenty-four. This was done by the very simple expedient of getting all seventy-two of us to line up shoulder to shoulder, tallest on the right, shortest on the left. So on the extreme right would be the tallest individual, and on the extreme left the shortest. So we sorted ourselves out by moving to the left or right as the case might be. Three NCOs supervised that process. Then they counted off the first twenty-four – the tall; the middle twenty-four – the medium; and finally the remaining twenty-four – the short. And then the three NCOs each took over a troop.

That's how our three troops were arrived at. Thus we remained for those first six weeks. One troop to each of the three barrack rooms. I was in the medium height troop – I'm 5 foot 9 inches – so our particular NCO was Sergeant Brear. Our opinion of him at the start was that he was the worst possible sadist. At the end of the six weeks our initial view was unchanged, but we all agreed that he was by far the best tutor and were glad to have been in his troop.

A new intake of about seventy-two recruits arrived at fortnightly intervals. Thus there would be ten or twelve groups training at any one time. Mine was called 46 Troop.

We had a fellow in 46 Troop named George. He unfortunately had two left feet, and if anyone could be guaranteed to step off on the wrong foot or to do the wrong thing it was him. He was quite well educated and bright in many ways, but he could *not* do simple things. Indeed there were times when we wondered whether he did it deliberately. He used to cut himself shaving, put his left webbing gaiter on his right ankle. *Anything* which could be done the wrong way George would demonstrate. Sergeant Brear was a man who never smiled, and had a harsh manner. We used to help George dress himself properly and cover up for him as best we could, but there were times when he really did stupid things – like losing his compass on the moors. Sergeant Brear one morning was very impatient – one man was missing from the early morning parade. It was, of course, George. While we waited, Brear asked us, 'Is he really as bad as he seems, or is he deliberately stringing me along?' We assured him that George was always the same.

Somehow he got through the first six weeks and survived with the rest of us for about a month, when we joined the 58th Training Regiment, Royal Armoured Corps. Then it was decided that he should be 'retarded' – the Army expression for being given extended training – to 48 Troop. That meant that the powers that be considered he was falling behind the rest of us. He was put back one month.

About a whole year later, when my regiment was on a gunnery course at Castle Douglas, I was surprised to see Sergeant Brear there. He said he'd been posted there from Bovington. I was quite pleased that the 'sadist' was quite human after all, and even remembered me, albeit vaguely. I asked him whatever happened to George, and he said in effect that he was permanently assigned to cookhouse duties, peeling spuds and so on.

As a sort of last fling to finish off our training, we recruits were given a 60-mile march in full kit, carrying rifles. We were taken in lorries from Bovington Camp to set points spread out in an arc. Six of us were dropped off at each point, separated by several miles from the next so that separate routes like a spider's web would take each group back to Bovington, with each party on a different road. The idea was that it would involve 60 miles at least back to camp – in fact to a battle area for the final test, which was a mock battle.

The rules were simple. Nobody was to have a penny in his pocket. No hitch-hiking allowed. We were dropped off between say two and two thirty on a Saturday afternoon, and the rendez-vous was to be ten o'clock on Monday morning. If you made an average of 3 miles per hour and sustained that for the 60 miles it worked out at 20 hours needed. That was the theory, but it didn't occur to us to do such estimates.

The point was that the six of us were left to our own initiative. We had a couple of maps between us, but no one was officially in charge.

Our first mistake was to notice, from our drop-off at a cross-roads, an RAF camp about 2 miles distant but in the wrong direc-tion. We'd been issued only with some very basic packed sandwiches in our packs. One bright spark had the notion that we could scrounge a free cooked meal from the RAF. So we walked 2 miles there and 2 miles back – 4 extra miles which only brought us back to the start point. We did get a meal, having pitched some yarn at the cookhouse. That was fine, but we had stupidly delayed our start. It must have delayed us by an hour and a half.

In the event we set off, and what I remember was that we covered 12 miles only and arrived at the Somerset town of Chard. We probably got along at a bit better than 3 miles per hour on that first leg. Anyway, it was by then seven or seven thirty. Three of us were in favour of pushing on right away, but the other three fancied going to a dance they'd seen advertised. So when we reached some sort of wayside barn three of us sat around while the others went to the dance. We knew it was ill advised, but that's what happened.

What time those three returned I can't remember clearly, but it was late. Evidently an officer called Lewis spotted the three at the dance and warned them about the need to be at Bovington by Monday morning.

Sunday morning came, after a night of resting in that barn, and the next problem we had was getting the three defaulters 'on the road'. We were anxious to make a very early start, but in the end it was after eight. We had 48 miles in all to go.

Lieutenant Lewis came along on a motor cycle and told us that our section was well behind all the others. His job was of course to check on progress.

Well, we managed 38 miles that day, and to add to our problems one fellow's legs virtually seized up with severe cramp about half-way through the day. We had to support him hobbling between two of us, taking turns. Somebody else carried his rifle with theirs and somebody else his big pack. The result was that we were handicapped. The weather was hot. At intervals we sat down on the grass verge with our feet upwards against the hedge. There was no traffic of any kind. We tried at several cottages *en route* to beg a cup of water, but nobody even answered the door when we knocked. Very, very late at night we turned in at a farm where the farmer let us indoors. His wife at least boiled some very small potatoes for us, but could offer nothing else.

On the Monday morning we had 10 miles left to go. We set off *very* early, and anyway we made it in time for the mock battle, but were very footsore.

But I'm not criticizing this at all, even though I may have felt none too happy at the time. There were for example things we had to learn by sheer rote, like what immediate action to take if your tank gun 'stops' [fails to fire]. There was a series of routine fault-finding steps to be memorized. Yet under fire, when the heat is on, one recalls those steps without flapping or getting flustered.

Regimental history was also very important. In some ways this was written into such things as why we, the 15th/19th the King's Royal Hussars, wore a split lanyard.

Most regiments issued lanyards, which basically consisted of a length of cord which was attached to one's uniform at one end and to one's revolver at the other – or sometimes to a whistle, or for certain individuals to a bugle. The idea is akin to a watch chain – the item of equipment is tethered to one's person to prevent it getting lost.

In the days of horses in the regiment the story is that the bit in the mouth of the Colonel's horse broke, and an enterprising soldier spliced a lanyard to be used in place of the bit. Thus the braided lanyards in different colours commonly worn by soldiers on their shoulders are invariably solidly braided and slip under the shoulder epaulette, but nor ours. In our regiment the epaulette had to be threaded through a section in the middle where the six strands were left unplaited, three remaining visible on the top side of the epaulette. So we carried a permanent reminder of our regimental history, and everyone was expected to know why.

Believe it or not, soldiers of other regiments used to enquire of us – say in a railway compartment – 'Why do you wear a split lanyard?' I remember being able to recite, 'Raised in the year 1759 as the 15th Light Dragoons . . .' et cetera, et cetera.

Regimental anniversaries were also important, such as the annual celebration of Sahagun Day on 21st December. During the Peninsular War a British force was sent to Spain to assist the Spaniards against the French, and on 21st December 1808 the 15th Hussars confronted a whole French brigade drawn up on a plain near Sahagun. The bugler was ordered to sound the Charge, and the regimental history records, 'But the Frenchmen, thinking their attackers were Spaniards who never charged home, took the charge at the halt.' So we recall how a single regiment charged a whole brigade and routed it.

Sahagun Day celebrations began on Sahagun Day but tended to spill over to Christmas. It took the form of a holiday – officers waited on the men with a slap-up dinner, similar to Christmas. Various football and other games were held. There were barrels of beer on tap, and volunteers from each barrack room ventured out to replenish bottomless jugs. I recall being among the few who couldn't become involved because we were nominated for night guard duties. But apart from such essential routine duties Sahagun was a memorable day.

In fact there is an Army List of regiments in order of precedence in descending order, listed regiment by regiment. I know for a certainty that Colonels of regiments jealously guard their regiments' order of precedence. During the war I heard that Colonels complained like mad if some official letter circulated to all the units in a division or in a brigade listed them in the wrong order. 'You have listed my regiment below the Cheshires' – or whatever. 'Please get the order correct next time'! (*Rev. Barrah*)

This feature, of primary group loyalty being to an individual unit rather than to the service as a whole, was something peculiar to the Army. Whereas members of the Royal Navy and the RAF expected to be moved around frequently from ship's company to ship's company and from squadron to squadron, the Army shifted people from regiment to regiment only in the case of dire necessity.

I was called up into the King's Own (Royal Lancaster Regiment), but was subsequently transferred to the 5th Battalion of the Highland Light Infantry, to help bring it up to strength.

My new battalion was part of the 52nd (Lowland) Division, and was engaged in heavy fighting in Holland. I remember when our platoon commander was killed we got one posted to us from the Royal Inniskilling Fusiliers. He refused to change his shoulder flashes, right up to the time when he himself was wounded. Our battalion once lost fifty-two men in one day, just a fortnight before the end of the European war. Some of course were just light shrapnel wounds, but all the same it meant they couldn't remain in the field.

After the war finished, I asked my Commanding Officer at Maryhill Barracks in Glasgow if I could now return to my old regiment, the King's Own . . .

You would have thought that I'd insulted his wife, by the way he carried on. He just could *not* understand anyone wanting to leave the regiment. Years later I hear he resigned his commission in protest at plans to amalgamate the HLI with another of the Scottish regiments. (*Mr Simpson*)

Despite its idiosyncrasies, most people found Army discipline to be fair. But there were, inevitably, exceptions.

I was the senior Corporal in our main improvised 'barrack room' which held about fifty men, who slept on thinly filled straw mattresses on the floor. At ten minutes to 9 a.m. the main bully, a very big Sergeant with a swank stick, shouted out for everyone to stand to attention for kit inspection. He ordered the senior Corporal – me – to double up to him, which I did. I was told to assist him in the inspection. With his stick he scattered the kit of a nervous soldier in all directions, then, as usual, ordered me to collect them and told the 'wretched man' to set them out correctly.

I quietly told the Sergeant that I was no longer prepared to be his 'retriever'. He glared at me and in a loud voice stated that I was on a charge for refusing to obey an order. Quietly I told him that I was not refusing to obey an order, but was refusing to obey a senior rank who was deliberately abusing his authority. He then swore at me, played to the gallery by loudly ridiculing my stance, and put me on another report for insubordination.

At the adjudication he said it was I who swore – which has never been part of my nature – and he lied about what he had done.

When I told the adjudicator that there were plenty of witnesses he refused to hear them.

It was only a minor affair, but the thin end of the bullying wedge. (*Mr Webber*)

On the Army's part, the fact that the Royal Navy and RAF usually had first pick from the manpower pool meant that it got more than its share of 'King's hard bargains'.

With so much of its strength concentrated in the UK from 1940 to 1944 the problem of absence without leave, for example, was a particularly acute one. Technically, a period of up to twenty-one days constituted absence without leave. Any more than that and the offence became the much more serious one of desertion, which up until 1930 had carried the death penalty.

In many cases, however, the Army acknowledged that such men could still be an asset if handled properly, and was prepared to treat them with more leniency than a peacetime Regular could have expected.

I was married in April 1941 and my wife was expecting our first child in May 1942. Although I'd requested a delay in my call-up it wasn't granted, and I felt a little upset – although I'd already been deferred through work.

We had a period of intense training; marching, saluting, weapons training, fieldcraft, sending and receiving Morse code, wireless in general, and driving 15-cwt and 3-ton lorries.

My first weekend leave was a disaster, as I received my pass on the Saturday morning instead of the Friday evening, and I decided to stay the extra day and reported back on Tuesday Reveille instead of Monday. I was confined to barracks for seven days and deducted a day's 'Royal Warrant' from my pay, and this was recorded in my Pay Book in red ink.

On completion of training I was posted. We went on an exercise to Annan, Scotland for a fortnight, and were given a weekend leave – 50 per cent the first weekend and 50 per cent the second weekend. I was fortunate enough to get the first weekend, and then decided to take the second weekend without a pass, as it would have meant hanging around camp on the Saturday afternoon and Sunday, and my wife and baby daughter – born on 27th May 1942 – were on their own.

I realized on the train, in my haste to get away I had failed to transfer my Pay Book from my working denims, and had spent my last penny on the rail fare. I knew my wife would pay for my return fare.

Unfortunately I was arrested by Military Police on the station exit in Nottingham. They escorted me to Nottingham Castle where I was locked up – with several other offenders – in one of the entrance gates until being collected by my regiment on the Monday morning. I was not permitted to get in touch with my wife whilst under arrest.

My Commanding Officer Major MacDiarmid was very understanding and set my punishment at another seven days confined to barracks and one day's pay deducted 'Royal Warrant', entered in red ink in my Pay Book.

After serving the seven days' CB I was transferred to another unit, where I was able to obtain a sleeping-out pass when I found accommodation in a farm for my wife and daughter. (*Mr Marshall*)

Most people saw their service as a necessary evil. They wanted to get on with the job, win the war, and then pick up their lives again. But not everyone, of course, joined reluctantly.

I was a PC in the Metropolitan Police, so we weren't allowed to join up until 1941–42, when they said that volunteers would be accepted for the Commandos or for flying duties with the Royal Air Force. I fancied my feet on the ground, so I joined the Commandos. And I went directly *into* the Commandos, and didn't go to a unit first, although officially I was a Royal Fusilier. That was the Army number I carried. 6482228 – I remember the number now! And I wore the Royal Fusiliers cap badge, even although I never went to the Royal Fusiliers Depot.

So you never had any connection with the regiment?

None whatsoever. I went directly to Achnacarry [the Commando training centre] and spent thirteen weeks there. But I was no stranger to being under fire, of course. The devastation caused by that City bomb in Bishopsgate [detonated by the IRA in April 1993] was nothing compared with one night's bombing raids on the City of London or down in the East End. The general public were most remarkable. I never understood how they stood up to it, really. Most remarkable. They sang songs, in their shelters, and they came out in the morning and their homes had disappeared.

The best-known incident was probably the Café de Paris, in Coventry Street between Piccadilly Circus and Leicester Square. It was a Saturday night [8th March 1941], and the place was packed. The bomb came down the well in the centre of the building – the night-club was in the basement. And it exploded, well, actually on the dance floor, I suppose. People were sitting at tables, dead.

Ken 'Snakehips' Johnson was the band leader. Everybody says Al Bowlly the singer was killed with 'Snakehips', but he wasn't – he wasn't there that night.*

It was uncanny, really. They were sitting there at the tables with shards of glass sticking in them, and knives and forks sticking in them. And they were dead. They were just sitting there dead. Blast. It all happened so quickly.

That was the only bomb incident I was at where they had martial law. They called out the Army to control the looting. Because the people downstairs – there were several hundred people downstairs in the Café de Paris – were all of the wealthy class, and they were bejewelled, and they had all their money and furs with them. So they called out the Army from Chelsea Barracks, because the police couldn't control it. (*Mr Bradley*)

Conscription for women did not get into its stride until 1941, yet large numbers volunteered prior to this. One specialization in which the Army had traditionally employed women even in peacetime was nursing, and during the war Queen Alexandra's Imperial Military Nursing Service, together with its Reserve and the Territorial Army Nursing Service, expanded fourteen-fold.

I was a nurse in civilian life. I trained at St Olave's Hospital in Lower Road, Rotherhithe, in London, and I'd completed my training when war was declared. Soon afterwards I joined the Queen Alexandra's Imperial Military Nursing Service Reserve, which involved filling in numerous documents and attending interviews, then buying my own uniform for home and abroad, and equipment for overseas. Though when we got to the Desert we had to wear khaki battledress tops, trousers and shirts anyway. Not fine khaki like our off-duty uniform, but rough. Some of the sisters rebelled at first over wearing trousers, but they had to give in eventually and conform. In those days it wasn't fashionable for trousers to be worn by women, as it is today.

The only military nursing I did in England was at Catterick for a few months, then I was posted to the Middle East, sailing on the *Otranto* with No. 3 General Hospital.

In the Middle East we were under canvas in a place called Buseili near Abu Qir Bay, where there was an RAF base. The airmen often

---

* In fact Bowlly survived his friend by only a little over a month, being killed at his flat in Duke Street by another German bomb on 16th April.

had social evenings to which we were invited. Someone would call for us and take us to their mess. The aircrews used to fly Sunderland Flying Boats, and on their missions they sometimes flew low over the hospital to say hello to us. Happy memories, but also very sad, as some never returned.

Part of my time was spent nursing prisoners of war. The tented wards for the POWs were surrounded by a security fence, like a compound, and guards were posted at the entrance. My most vivid memory of this time was that when Rommel and his army were approaching Alexandria some of the German wounded were sent to No. 3 General Hospital, and they already had passes made out for some leave in Alex. How confident they were of success. Before our victory, No. 3 General Hospital was evacuated to the Suez Canal area, but after El Alamein we returned to Buseili again.

A general hospital was a self-contained unit with maybe sixty nursing sisters, and the rest were Royal Army Medical Corps – surgeons, doctors, pathologists and a dentist. Then there were the NCOs and other ranks. The RAMC other ranks, or orderlies, had had medical training, so were on duty on the wards with a sister in charge. Although we were regarded as officers, the RAMC other ranks didn't need to salute us. We didn't have a personal batman either, but one was always available, as they were allocated duty to the sisters' mess. There was Army discipline in the hospital, and we underwent inspections by the Colonel. He was escorted round the ward with his entourage by the Matron – a Regular in the QAIMNS – and the sister in charge of the ward, to answer any questions regarding the patients. The 'up patients' stood at attention at the foot of their beds.

The more mobile ones used to help in the wards, serving meals and so on, and were very good to the bed patients.

Our hours of duty were erratic, as convoys used to arrive day or night, and when they did all hands were very busy. The Regular QAs were inclined to be a bit snooty with the Reserves, but in an emergency all that disappeared and we worked as a team. (*Mrs Eaton*)

Even at home, training hundreds of thousands of young men to operate machinery and to handle weapons for the first time in their lives meant that accidents were an ever-present danger.

Trying to recall the worst war memory is very difficult, I mean each time something bad happened, then at that time it was 'the worst'. But I think the first time I was really shocked and shaken was the worst; and that happened in England.

I was a Corporal in the Royal Engineers, in Chemical Warfare. A lot of our time was taken up in practising 4.2-inch mortar shoots way out in open country, but with high explosive mortar bombs instead of gas. The 4.2 was a *very* big mortar, by the way, and I never saw it used after leaving Chemical Warfare.

The mortar consisted of a base plate, a tripod and a barrel, and was calibrated in degrees for lateral and vertical adjustment. On a shoot the mortars were spaced out in a line with about 5 yards' distance between them. When they were set up, each NCO in charge set the direction and elevation he'd been given and called out in turn, 'No. 1 gun on,' 'No. 2 gun on,' and so forth.

On this live shoot occasion we got set up with No. 1 and No. 2 mortars close to a copse of trees – I was No. 2 mortar commander – and the remainder spread out in a line. After firing one round, each NCO reset and called out, 'Gun on,' and waited.

Then a new elevation was given and set, and we waited again until the order was given, 'No. 1 gun fire!'

There was no order for No. 2 gun to fire, because the whole world seemed to explode in deafening noise and confusion, with bits of metal and debris clattering off my helmet and shoulders for what seemed for ever. Then there was a stunned silence for a while, and then a high-pitched wailing cry started that came from the mortar right at the end of the line.

One of the two Sappers had lost a kneecap, and the other a foot, though the NCO was OK. What had happened was that the new elevation was an increase, and the mortar bomb hit a tree branch just overhead and detonated. Why the people directly underneath – including me – were still alive is difficult to understand.

I remember one of the Sappers was Joe Binney, but I can't remember the name of the other one.

The war had caught up with them before they were ready. (*Mr Ridley*)

But for most, being posted overseas marked the beginning of the real discomforts and dangers. With shipping at a premium, particularly once the entry of Italy into the war had effectively closed the Mediterranean to troop convoys and had begun forcing them to sail 'the long way round' via South Africa, every available vessel was pressed into service. Even Cunard's luxurious *Queen Mary* found herself painted drab grey and fitted out as a trooper.

We could see this big ship, with three funnels, painted grey. And we went on these lighters, about twenty blokes at a time, straight across to this ship, which was out in the middle of the Clyde. And we went through some big doors in the side.

Lot of blokes got bunks, I think, but as it turned out I was in the Forward Smoking Room. Hundred of us, on the floor; they gave us new single mattresses, on the floor, and sheets, pillows, and a new towel with 'Cunard White Star' on.

Once we'd got settled down in the Forward Smoking Room, we went on deck and we saw the ship's name on the bell – *Queen Mary*! We didn't know until then. (*Mr Sheppard*)

My first feeling of being uncomfortable was about 4 a.m. on a Thursday morning. We were in the Irish Sea, a few days before Christmas. I think I was among the first at the ship's side, being violently seasick. From 4 a.m. that Thursday morning I just kipped down on the deck. About three days elapsed before it got back to normal, but in that time I watched the other troopers – *Orontes*, *Orion*, *Leopoldville* – wallowing in the high seas.

It's one thing seeing it in newsreels at cinemas, but it's another when it's real life and there's actual heavy spray coming aboard.

And then, just before arriving in Bombay, I always remember looking out through a porthole and seeing the Indian fishing boats just as the sun was rising. (*Mr Duffy*)

Once abroad, the inequalities in the risks run by different individuals tended to be brought into sharp focus. A large proportion of the Army was made up of rear area services and support units, whose work was vital but often entailed no greater danger than many civilians faced.

The people who I feel have never been mentioned are the tea planters of the Darjeeling and Kalimpong districts who stuck it out with their families, providing wonderful leave accommodation for some of us at great risk to themselves. If the Japanese had broken through at Imphal and Kohima those planters had no retreat other than into Nepal – which at the time was forbidden territory – or Sikkim, which was equally difficult. At 7000 to 8000 feet above sea level and with the great mass of the Himalayas in front of them they knew that capture was inevitable if the Japanese swarmed through North Bengal. (*Mr Annis*)

I actually found myself doing the same job in the Army that I'd done before I was called up.

Since 1935 I'd worked for a firm of pork butchers, in the cutting-up room. I used to prepare the meat for the window, and work on the made-up dishes like brawn, cooked meats, bacon and pork pies.

I was called up in 1939, and after my six weeks' basic training as a soldier they posted me to the 11th Field Butchery, Royal Army Service Corps.

The only thing I didn't have any experience in was slaughtering, but I learned this in Egypt when we were sent out there. We eventually finished up at a place in the Desert by the Sweet Water Canal, where a slaughterhouse had been built by the Royal Engineers, and where we had a corral where cattle were kept awaiting slaughter. Our job was to provide fresh meat for troops in the Canal Zone. Our Sergeant-Major was a slaughterman in civvy street, and I soon learned from the local slaughtermen who were employed by a gaffer responsible to our officer-in-charge. Being as this was Egypt we had to conform to the religious way of doing things. A rope was put over the horns, then through an iron ring set in the floor. The beast was then pulled to the concrete floor, turned on its back – often easier said than done – and two people held the loose skin and simply cut its throat. Then it was left until all the blood had been pumped out by the heart. A very messy job, but that's what happened until we found a method of stunning that conformed to the laws in Egypt.

After slaughtering the place had to be swilled clean, ready for the next day. Meanwhile the carcasses were split and hung on runners, so they could be pushed out of the slaughterhouse on rails and into the bay where we used to weigh and issue to the base supply depots, whose lorries came to collect. The lorries were sheeted and tied down when loaded, and returned to their bases to issue to the units around them. (*Mr Payling*)

Such a life was very different to that experienced by the infantrymen and others at 'the sharp end'.

On top of these inequalities, certain battle-hardened units were asked to bear what they saw as a disproportionate share of the burden. After the end of the war in North Africa, for example, some of the Desert veterans were brought home to participate in the invasion of Normandy as well. Many Desert men resented this deeply, believing that the divisions which had stayed in the UK while they were fighting a long and tiring campaign in Africa should now be bearing the brunt of the fighting, and that they had 'done their bit'.

We ran into a dummy minefield and he [the enemy] set his artillery on the column. I was a Lance-Corporal, and our section was in the cooks' truck. A near miss and we were all thrown about, and as we were in battle order all wearing helmets I had two fingers chopped with a steel helmet landing on them. In the blast of the shell and swerve of the truck there was equipment flying everywhere. It was the bren-gunner's helmet actually. At that time slight wounds were strapped up and the boys carried on. My hip also gave me trouble off and on long after.

I was hospitalized in Bougie then Philippeville rest camp after the North African campaign finished, so I missed the invasion of Sicily and rejoined the battalion (*the 5th Battalion, the Queen's Own Cameron Highlanders*) on the island, when they were near Mount Etna.

The 51st (Highland) Division came home from Sicily in 1943 – we were never in Italy. We arrived in Hertford and after leave started training for D-Day. Again I was lucky, and was picked for LOB. It was usual procedure when a battalion went into action to leave a certain amount of officers, NCOs and other ranks behind to reinforce, or to make up a new battalion if it was destroyed. LOB – Left Out of Battle.

As first-line reinforcements we rejoined the battalion in Normandy, and what a shock we got. Dozens of new faces – replacements from English regiments, young boys, the battalion near wiped out. It was never the same after the reckless way the division was thrown in at Colombelles and Ste Honorine la Chardonerette. Our CO, Big Sandy Monro, drove into Brigade HQ and hammered the Brigadier for the mistakes he was making. They were both relieved of their jobs, but Big Sandy was right. That was France all over. Mistake after mistake. We attacked again at 'The Triangle' [a feature named after a triangle of roads on the map, east of Ste Honorine] – same again; picked off left, right and centre. Could never see them. They had it all in their favour.

Then in August was the big night attack down the Falaise road, 2nd Canadian Division to the right of it, 51st (Highland) Division to the left. Our platoon arrived on the objective just before daybreak and started to dig in, when all hell broke loose. 88s mainly. The shell-burst first, the scream of the shell, and last the report of the gun – that's close. Willie Greer, eighteen, joined us for the attack, killed. Corporal Andrews, left arm off. I was wounded again, in the neck and left arm.

Word was sent back and my old friend Bert, ex-Desert too, came flying up. I got Joe aboard the jeep, and off, bumping and dodging all over. Regimental Aid Post first – labels and bandages and into an ambulance. Joe – Corporal Andrews – on a drip and down to the Advanced Dressing Station then into theatre, and I was sent on down. Pretty hazy now. I was very upset when I rejoined the battalion to hear that Bert on returning for more wounded was killed that morning.

I was shipped over and into hospital at Chester-le-Street, Durham. I was in good company, it was nearly all Camerons. After hospital, leave. And then a month's intensive training at Banbridge, Northern Ireland, and back to the battalion in Holland.

Then the biggest trial of them all, the Reichswald Forest. Three weeks of creeping, crawling, no sleep, a sniper's dream. Sergeant Mackenzie was wounded there. We were encircled at the time and couldn't get the wounded out. Gangrene set in. Another great pal, Hughie Clearie, was killed there. Another Desert man.

I was made up to Lance-Sergeant in the Forest. Shows you how short they were getting of men.

The Rhine crossing was next. Outboard motors, trenches dug in the bund wall, our side's mortar barrage. Six of the platoon had to be left – they wouldn't come out for the crossing. No idea what happened to them. We crossed in darkness. No trouble apart from mortars, not too heavy. The fireworks started at daybreak. Camerons leading, my platoon first. We advanced a mile or so inland, single file in a ditch, bypassing the farms and houses. Sergeant Ronnie Whyte, who was in front of me, left our pal Alec Frood to cover me, at a low point in the ditch. A sniper got him. Another Desert man and a great friend.

We hit a strongpoint and were held up. Some bloody fool sent up two amphibious tanks – they didn't stand a chance. I crawled up the ditch with the stretcher bearers as the light was going, and got two of the boys in, terribly burnt – the tanks had 'brewed up'. Jerry was still firing at them, and a ricochet, or it could have been a mortar splinter, tore my knuckle, left hand, clean off.

I went back down later that night, taking prisoners – walking wounded. Crossed over the Rhine, arrived eventually in Brussels. Two nights there, then a Dakota to England, Derby Hospital and then Dr Gray's in Elgin. All for a few shillings a day.

I was one of the lucky ones.

I can't get to sleep at nights now – some memory or other comes back. I know the memories will never leave me. Especially the boys who fought for so long. Some wounded twice or three times. Men who'd fought at Alamein, killed in the Reichswald, and the Rhine crossing. (*Mr Russell*)

42

2

ATS

Like the Royal Navy and the RAF, the British Army had dispensed with its non-nursing service for women – Queen Mary's Army Auxiliary Corps – in the inter-war period.

On the evening of 27th September 1938, however, an announcement following the BBC nine o'clock news suddenly revealed the government's intention of forming a successor to the QMAAC, to be known as the Auxiliary Territorial Service, or ATS.

This had been largely precipitated by the Munich crisis, with the result that there were chaotic scenes up and down the country as eager women besieged recruiting centres caught unawares by the suddenness of the announcement.

Girls from all walks of life were attracted to the ATS, and those from more privileged backgrounds, like *Pam Hoare*, sometimes found Army life quite a shock.

> I had two special friends, Anne and Joy. One day after a long walk along the banks of the River Deben we said, 'Wouldn't it be fun to join something?' Of course, we thought, there won't really be a war – there couldn't – but let's get ourselves into something, just in case.
>
> There were the VADs [Voluntary Aid Detachments of the Red Cross], the ATS, the WRNS [Women's Royal Naval Service] and FANY [Women's Transport Service, originally the First Aid Nursing Yeomanry – now providing drivers rather than medical staff]. We rather liked the idea of the latter – a smart, officer-like uniform complete with Sam Browne belt – but it didn't come free, and our mothers refused to pay. Harwich wasn't a naval port, so we couldn't be Wrens. So what about the ATS? Only twelve drills a year, and we could go to the pictures in Ipswich afterwards. Also there was a summer camp. It all sounded rather fun, and so we blithely signed away our lives for an ill-fitting uniform and a few well-meant words of advice.

The drills were a farce. No one seemed to know or care what we were meant to do. The worst thing was the medical. We had to strip to the waist in front of a young doctor with whom we'd danced and played tennis. Goodness knows what he was thinking. As embarrassed as we were, I expect.

We were a mixed lot – the girl from the County Library, one or two parlour maids from houses we knew, several shop girls, a few from offices, one or two older ones from our sort of background, and two veterans from the last war, always telling us what they did in 1915. In all, there were about thirty of us.

So the year 1939 slid by. We dutifully attended our drills in Ipswich, and went to the cinema afterwards, merry as crickets.

Then came the summer camp. It was outside Canterbury, where we arrived one hot day in June 1939. There were rows of tents in a large field midway between the Buffs' [Royal East Kent Regiment] barracks and a lunatic asylum, with a right of way between. In those days it was fashionable to be completely unmilitary and not to have the faintest idea how to do anything, or to know what anything meant, and I was no exception; we had no conception of camp life.

However, to begin with, Anne, Joy and I wanted to make our tent look nice for the forthcoming inspection. We thought we were pretty ingenious and handy, as we square-lashed coat-hangers up on the tent poles over our suitcases, and as a final touch we picked white marguerites from the field. Having arranged these artistically in a jam jar, we stood to attention outside, feeling very pleased with ourselves.

The entourage approached, led by the head of the ATS, Dame Helen Gwynne-Vaughan. She was tall and very imposing. Gazing at our display she barked out, 'What is all this? Nothing is to be showing in your tent at all. Take down those coat-hangers and remove those flowers. Everything is to be inside your suitcases. You're in the Army now!' She swept on, while we militarized our house as best we could, muttering imprecations, and feeling cross and sullen.

Miseries followed thick and fast. We slept on straw palliasses, consisting it seemed of three straws and a few twigs, on bare boards through which the red ants marched like Soviet troops. All night long the boards creaked, the ants tickled, and the rough Army blankets scratched. Outside the sheep cropped the damp grass and the rain trickled down on our canvas roof.

Then at 7 a.m. we were woken and up went the dreaded order to prepare for PT.

Scrambling for our crumpled clothes in the half-light of the tent, we staggered outside. We spent the next hour knees bending and arms raising, toes touching and circling from the waist, all in the wet grass, praying for an earthquake or a tornado to bring it all to an end. How funny we must have looked – all shapes and sizes, half naked. I wince to think of it.

At last it was all over. We stood to attention and were told to dismiss.

Grabbing our towels we joined the rush for the wash house – a dreary grey corrugated shack with tin washbowls and no light.

The final horrors were the latrines. I had heard of them vaguely, and knew you had them in Guides and Scouts, but I never thought I should ever have to use one. Actually, I never did. We three pushed through the hedge to the golf club nearby, where we also got a free read of *Country Life* thrown in, with a proper wash and all the facilities.

Breakfast was congealing bacon and soggy fried bread eaten off tin plates, sitting on benches in the long, low mess tent. We had a good look at our fellow creatures – the long, the short, the fat and the thin, but they all merged into more or less of a khaki blur.

Then we had a route march which caused us undying shame.

Through the Kentish lanes we strode, with urchins running behind shouting, 'Berlin or bust' and other derisive remarks. And then the final degradation! We were ordered to sing – 'Tipperary' and 'Pack up your troubles' – like the troops in 1914. We felt we ought to take it all seriously, but how could we?

Finally we arrived back exhausted and hot, to fall upon and devour great hunks of bread and jam, and drink hot sweet tea out of thick pottery mugs.

We had to take it in turns to be Orderly. This meant sitting in a tent with an in-tray and an out-tray with very little in either, and a telephone that gave no promise of ringing. I surreptitiously did *The Times* crossword, sucked pieces of grass, and somehow the two boring hours passed.

Free time we spent in Canterbury in the haven of the cathedral, or browsing in second-hand bookshops.

We begged baths in one of the hotels, and got some sympathy from the manager. Oh, the luxury and bliss of those baths, soaking our board-bruised bones and ant-eaten flesh, running more and more hot water, lying wreathed in steam.

One bright spark was when we bought the *Sunday Times*, to

find I'd won the crossword competition and could choose £3 of books. £3 went a long way in those days.

One evening we went into Fordwich and found a lovely inn overlooking the water. Ducks and swans swam through the reeds, and the bridge was shadowed darkly in the clear stream. I had the feeling that something was slipping away with the swans as they slid by – a feeling of regret, and a sort of yearning; for what one wasn't quite sure, and I soon forgot it.

Later we were sitting in the evening sun eating bowls of strawberries and thick yellow cream – none of the pasteurized whitewash you get now – and we bought and ate more strawberries and cherries cheaper than we'd ever had before.

Another day we wandered round the cathedral thinking of Thomas à Becket, and putting off the evil moment of returning to the raucous camp, the PT and the clanking food tins.

The lunatics from the asylum and the Buffs from the barracks made use of the right of way through our field, and our Commandant, Miss Robinson, a rotund little woman with a baby Austin, drove furiously around the tents at night, chasing intruders real or imaginary, making sure that no licentious soldiery or madmen were molesting her girls.

Long after dark we'd hear that little car grunting round on its duties of guarding the innocent maidens in their virgin bowers.

At last the week came to an end. But awful things when shared can be very funny. I knew my parents would laugh their heads off when I described what we'd endured. They would probably say it was good for us, too.

The news on the radio got worse. At the last tennis party I went to the day was hot and humid, and we all played rather feebly. As we pushed our damp hair off our foreheads the sky darkened and a few drops of rain fell.

Someone came out of the house and said that Hitler's troops had marched into Poland, so our 'if' became 'when', and the tennis folded up rather abruptly.

That evening returning home I found a letter telling me to report to Ipswich station, in uniform, the following Sunday morning, 3rd September – two or three days' time, I think – I'm not sure.

Eight thirty we had to be there, and the letter also sternly said we should only bring 'hand luggage' containing 'necessary articles'. What should I take? I telephoned Anne and Joy and we discussed the matter. In the end we took our biggest cases and packed everything. Tennis racquets, bathing suits, gramophone records, dance dresses, books – well, we didn't know where we were going, and goodness knows when we'd get home.

The Sunday morning dawned, fine and fateful. I put on my appalling uniform and took a last look round my bedroom with my four-poster bed, my books and pictures, and said goodbye to the maids and the dog. I was driven to the station by my mother, who was full of doom and gloom – she was Dutch, and the Dutch are rather given to predicting the worst. She was convinced we were off to Poland – where else?

We arrived at Ipswich station. There they all were, all thirty of them – looking, I'm glad to say, as awful in their uniform as I did. We clustered together fearfully discussing our mysterious destination. No one knew, and I could tell my mother nothing. I could only promise to write.

It occurred to me that my buttons looked rather peculiar, like fungus or verdigris – of course they hadn't been cleaned. I rubbed them with my hanky and hoped for the best, as we were about to be inspected by Miss Robinson. Later we were issued with button-sticks, with a groove along the middle – soldiers all had them – and you sat the buttons along the groove and thus you cleaned them without messing up the khaki.

Terrified of being separated, Anne and Joy and I stuck doggedly together. At last we were all herded into a train, all chattering hard, and off we went. Useless to read – people were apprehensive and yet excited, as no one knew where we were going, in spite of questioning. Eventually we arrived at Liverpool Street in London. It was now that those of us who had brought everything cursed our heavy cases, for in double file we had to march all the way to Fenchurch Street. We prayed for red lights at the crossings to allow us to draw breath and drop the cases on the pavement. London was quiet, with only ourselves, a stray cat, the pigeons and a few idlers on the street corners. At last we reached the station, and as we stood on the platform looking for the train to our mystery destination, a siren wailed its mournful up-and-down notes on the morning air.

Trust the Germans to be quick off the mark, we thought, war having been officially declared at 11 a.m. – not that we'd actually been informed then.

We were bundled down the subway feeling rather foolish as we stumbled along trying to appear nonchalant, and disinterested.

There were giggles, tears, and heavy breathing; someone mislaid her gas mask container and started shrieking, and another fainted. We three sat stolidly pretending we weren't really there. And then the All Clear went. We learnt later that it was one small private plane dutifully heading for home.

At last we came to a full stop. It was a place I'd never heard of, called Shoeburyness, on the Thames estuary. But how well I was to know it before I'd finished!

Arriving outside the sunny station we found our little Commandant dipping and curtsying to a tall officer in shirt-sleeves. As we were all Privates – with two or three exceptions – he seemed a radiant and Olympian being. A mixture of God and Nanny, and he amicably told us to file into a waiting lorry.

Driving through the streets with only a late Sunday milkman and a cat, we eventually drew up in a sort of square, and were told to disembark. We were then lined up in the road ready to be divided up to go to the billets that had been allocated us.

Anne and Joy and I stuck close together and prayed that the dividing process wouldn't separate us. Miss Robinson moved inexorably down the line. 'You and you,' she intoned, reading from a list, and parting people with a sweep of her arm. My mouth was dry. The person behind me was rather smelly and I would move heaven and earth not to share any place with her. Help! The arm swept aside Anne and Joy and left me. I gazed piteously at this forger of our destinies – I am sure I had some very unmilitary tears in my eyes as I said, 'Please, please could we be together? Couldn't I stay with them – we are such old friends?' Which, knowing the services as I do now, would be the one reason to keep us apart, for fear we formed a Mafia or something perhaps.

She scanned her list. 'Mrs White, Roselen, Church Road – she can take three more. Yes, you may remain together.' I choked my thanks. In company together, whatever life held for us would be bearable. We could at least all go down together, and maybe we'd find something to laugh at too.

Roselen, in Church Road, was a one-time boarding house, so there was plenty of room. Mrs White, a good soul, had some of her family there – two daughters, and two sons on leave from the Merchant Navy.

Upstairs we trooped and were shown our rooms. Eight ATS were to be billeted here, with our Sergeant, Mrs Glasspool, in charge. We three were shown a really rather nice airy room with lots of lace mats and texts on the walls, white candlewick bedspreads, and *Dignity and Impudence* over the mantelpiece.

Then we realized that there were only two beds, and there were three of us.

'Mrs Glasspool, oh Mrs Glasspool, there's a mistake. Not

enough beds. What shall we do?' But there was no mistake, and we had to decide who was to share the one bed, which was only slightly larger than an ordinary single one.

We'd decided to take *The Times*, mainly for the crossword, the correspondence, the third leader, and partly to have some link, however slender, with any of our friends who might give birth, marry or die.

So we arranged a scheme whereby we would take it in weekly turns to share the bed, and whoever was enjoying the luxury of the single bed should have the chore of paying for *The Times*.

It was high tea at Mrs White's. A stout brown teapot, piles of bread and butter, ham and salad, or sausages and mash, or toad in the hole, etc. Ham and salad this evening, and after it we went for a walk along the beach of the Thames estuary and looked at the sunset. It was magnificent; a fiery red over the sea fading to pink, heliotrope and grey over London, to lose itself in the smoky fog hanging there.

And so to bed. I with Joy, head to tail and a bolster between us, and the alarm clock set for seven thirty.

Now we had to be found jobs. Most of the girls had been working. They could cook, do shorthand and typing, and so on. We, with our expensive boarding school education, could actually do damn all. I felt like a crab without a shell, and rather depressed at my lack of usefulness and being so unfitted to cope with the outside world.

Anne was turned into a waitress – or orderly – for the officers' mess. She was put into a drab brown overall and marched to work every morning by a fierce Mrs Parker, who had been head housemaid at a place well known to us.

Joy was one of those sensible girls – a rock upon whom I often leant rather heavily – and she got a pretty good job running the clothing store. She reigned in a huge sort of warehouse, surrounded by bales of khaki uniforms and stacks of boots. She seemed to have all sorts of exciting contacts with swanky Sergeants, and of course the recruits who had to be kitted out.

Shoeburyness was really a garrison town, with a large barracks and all the accompanying facilities, such as playing fields and tennis courts, and a garrison church. It also had an Experimental Gunnery Establishment known as the XP. All kinds of secret work went on there, but we only knew that they fired shells out into the estuary, and at low tide went down to collect them. We used to watch the horse-drawn hooded wagons, like those of the old Voortrekkers, as they trundled down to the sands, swaying and rattling as they went. The XP men looked gay and dashing, with their white trousers tucked into black wellington boots, blue blazers and caps piped with scarlet.

The soldiers exercising the horses bareback used to clatter past our office windows of a morning, and I was very envious. I should like to have ridden them too, but not a hope.

For myself, I was a problem, having no qualifications barring my wits, such as they were. But after a day of wandering around feeling unloved and unwanted, I was sent off to an office marked cryptically 'DOCS'. Could it be a surgery? But no – it stood for Documents. Documents and Records to be exact.

There were three tables, some shelves, pigeon-holes, chairs, and a Major. Recruits were going to pour in to sign on, we were assured, and we were all going to win the war.

It was our job to keep all their papers in order and filled in up to date with all their particulars – which included their 'physical peculiarities' – supplying information in detail, and sending these papers with them, with the appropriate forms filled in, when they went off to their various postings. Duplicates had to be sent to Army Records, Foots Cray, Sidcup, Kent. The address is graven on my soul. My life was ruled by lists of names, and they multiplied like the begats in the Bible. We had a special pigeon-hole for the Smiths alone.

I was to work with two others. Myra, a postman's daughter, and Barlee – can't remember her Christian name, we always just called her Barlee. Her father was a judge. She had an Eton crop, and said she was always being thrown out of the loos when her head was seen over the partition – if she'd tried the men's, she'd have been thrown out if they saw her skirt!

Myra reminded me of Rembrandt's portrait of his maid Hendrickje Stoffels, parting the bed curtains and peeping out. He married her after his wife Saskia died. I explained all this to Myra and she was rather pleased.

We learnt all sorts of things about the young men we packed up and sent off, including their medical histories of mostly childish ailments, and, as I said, their 'physical peculiarities'.

One had a girl sitting on a crescent moon tattooed on his chest, and another, inexplicably, had his 'tongue slit an inch from the end'.

Couldn't he have had it repaired? I was dying to see it, but no luck. We mused over it for days.

Having access to all the men's documents and records, I naturally was in a position to know a good deal about them. Without wishing to cast aspersions on the British soldier, some of them weren't always what they appeared to be.

Somebody already possessing a perfectly good wife and family would think nothing of more or less proposing marriage to a little ATS girl, and then disappear to another posting, leaving her bewildered and forlorn. Irreparable damage might have been done, and sometimes was.

Thus I found myself established as a sort of private detective agency, and frequently some doubting girl would ask me to 'turn up Gunner X and make sure he's all right'. I only exposed two or three fiends, but it did give some measure of security against would-be bigamists.

One man was quite unashamed and kept a mistress nearby. Nobody seemed to mind — neither did his wife apparently, judging by the letters to the office about money and such matters.

But one day he went home and left later with the bath towels. Then the storm broke. His wife didn't mind about the other woman; she didn't mind if he was rude to the neighbours, or even when he took some of the housekeeping money, but when he went off with the bath towels that was the last straw and she wanted a separation!

The room was pretty dull, though. In spite of the lessons learnt at the camp we dared to stick a picture or two on the walls, and I bought a cyclamen in a pot for the window sill. Miraculously we were not asked to remove them.

We were refreshed by occasional visits from our 'Scarlet Major', a dynamic Latin type with whom it was always 'imperative' that something was done. He seemed pretty fierce, but underneath he was really rather a dear. The word 'imperative' passed into our vernacular, and we amused ourselves copying his very distinctive signature and perfecting it. We could have forged cheques on him with ease.

One young Captain we called Kate. He was rather short, and used to work in his shirt-sleeves with braces holding up his trousers, which came nearly up to his chest, just like the little boys in the Kate Greenaway illustrations in those Victorian children's books.

There were some fantastic rules. How we grumbled at them.

To begin with, we were not supposed to have anything to do with a member of the opposite sex other than on strictly service matters, but that soon died a natural death, and quite right too.

We had to be in at 9.30 p.m., to wear uniform at all times and in all places, and not to be seen with anyone of superior rank except on business.

When a friend of ours came from Suffolk on a course and we hailed him with joy we were reprimanded, and our simple request for all four to go to the cinema was refused. I became rebellious and wrote home in scarlet ink to express my outraged feelings. Having left school five years previously I felt I was surely far beyond the reach of rules. After all, I'd spent such a long time waiting to grow up. Now it was being snatched away, and I was back at school again.

Later on I began to see some of the method in their madness, and it is more agreeable to have initially tight rules slackened later – as they were – instead of the other way round. The ATS was in its teething stage, and we gave it no benefit of the doubt.

But often we were given seemingly idiotic instructions, and were never told the reason.

Our Nanny, when asked 'Why?' always answered, 'Because I say so.' The military with equally unfailing monotony would reply, 'You're in the Army now,' and gave no reason for anything.

Our Commandant Miss Robinson, now known as Puffin, we discovered used to teach in a lunatic asylum, and we thought she could hardly differentiate between us and her past charges, the way she treated us.

Once Anne and I had been invited to dine and dance at the Palace Hotel in Southend by those of superior rank. Having each only one rather scruffy uniform, we secretly changed into civilian dresses, covered ourselves up in our greatcoats and sneaked off to the car waiting round the corner.

We spent a delightfully civilized evening, dining well and dancing to a jazz band, but two weeks later when I put in for a Sunday off to go to London – and to which I was entitled – I was refused.

On being granted an interview with Puffin, I was told that the reason was that I had been 'seen dining and dancing with officers at the Palace in civilian clothes', and hadn't actually come and confessed that I had done so. Thus my application was turned down. But how childish! Why not send for us when the crime was reported? We felt bitter and furious, and there seemed no one to whom we could turn for sympathy.

Gradually the strangeness wore off. We got to know people. The soldiers and others with whom one came into contact in the regimental office became characters and took on real personalities.

The Monk was a special friend. He'd been one of the Pères Blancs in Belgium; a tall bespectacled young man who had suddenly decided to cast off his cassock and sail to England to take up arms against the foe. He was now a Pay Sergeant. He spoke beautiful French with a slight Cockney accent, and read learned books on theosophy. Once he took me to a service at his Catholic church. He was innocent and unworldly. He didn't drink or smoke, but the Pères Blancs never reclaimed him, as he later married an ATS girl and by now he probably has a large family.

The two Welsh orderlies, Taffy and Dopey, were like pantomime characters. They clattered about in enormous boots doing odd jobs – taking the post, making tea, fetching books and papers, or just sitting about, hands splayed out on their knees, big boots set wide apart.

Sergeant-Major Faraday used to hurtle into the office like a thunderbolt, slam the door, and with his cane under his arm, bellow a request – more of a demand really – for somebody's documents, creating for the moment a minor panic.

The Regimental Sergeant-Major was a great dandy. He used to come in and talk about nothing at all, licking his little finger and smoothing his eyebrows in our mirror – a trick that with familiarity soon became irritating. 'Oh God, here comes the RSM . . .' and we'd dive into our work and pretend to be extra busy.

The Adjutant, Jock Murray, was a great charmer. He looked in from time to time, to find out who would play a game of mixed hockey and to tell us yet again something that happened 'when I was in Srinagar', in India.

Then there was little Gunner Marsden from Yorkshire, who would say at 4 p.m., 'Tea's mashed' with a beaming smile. He was always losing his respirator, and regaled us with horror stories of his crazy sister. They were all kind and cheerful, though I think that they resented us quite a bit at first.

The work was easy. You just had to be accurate. I had nightmares of names and of being lost in a jungle of alphabetical trees, though it was a bonus to come across names like Gotobed and Bummick. We worked long hours at first getting acclimatized and organized, but gradually things got going. Our main interests seemed to be the post, food and a good book.

Mrs White's food was all right, but there was never enough of it, and we were always sneaking into the kitchen looking for something to pick up. The Merchant Navy sons were getting bored waiting for berths, so they ironed our clothes for us after we'd washed them. It started with khaki shirts, but it gradually got down to the smalls, which they liked. The pinker and frillier the better.

The Army really gave us little peace. Even on Saturdays when we knocked off at midday we had 'road drill' for an hour.

I hated to see women marching. I'd never wanted to be a wilting vine, but there's something quite ridiculous about girls drilling. During the last five minutes of a march it was 'On respirators!', and round we tramped snuffling and sweating like a lot of porkers on their way to the abattoir.

At last would come the longed-for 'Dismiss', and off we three would rush, either to the bus for Southend to sink into the plush seats of the Alhambra cinema, or lie on our beds reading or sleeping.

On Sunday mornings we had Church Parade but were free for the rest of the day, unless of course one was on orderly duty, which meant sitting in a cell with a telephone which never rang except to make sure someone was actually there.

Our bed scheme was working nicely. The White family were more than amiable. We were free from military authority when off duty, though Mrs Sergeant Glasspool did her best to be menacing. I went to London on a Sunday eventually, for a Queen's Hall concert, was exceedingly late getting back and had to throw stones at the window loud enough to wake Anne or Joy but not loud enough for anyone else to hear – and certainly not Mrs G.

We had our bicycles too, and used to go off and explore up the River Crouch, a relief from the streets and a change from the grey sea.

After a time we had to leave cosy Roselen and move into soldiers' married quarters in the barracks, but mercifully Anne, Joy and I were able to stay together. We were allowed no transport for our removal, and had to lug our things about a quarter of a mile as best we could. We had to drag our cases along the ground several times, and we arrived at the little house allotted to us hot, dirty and very cross with the unfeeling Army.

On getting in and unpacking, I found a pot of raspberry jam which I'd snuggled cosily in had smashed among my clothes. Of course the mess was indescribable.

Imagine six little brick houses all along a barracks road. A back garden, a kitchen turned into a bedroom, two other bedrooms upstairs and, thank God, a bathroom. We had not a stick of furniture. Just three beds, narrow as ironing boards, with three square mattresses called 'biscuits' – shaped just like dog biscuits. We had one chair and a green vertical tin box that was supposed to be a wardrobe. And that was all.

We were not allowed to make our beds till lunchtime – I suppose to air them – and we had to go through an evolution called 'barracking', that is, placing the bedclothes in a symmetrical and perfect square at the end of the bed, on top of the three biscuits. This was duly inspected and then we made the damn things.

On the other side of the barracks road was a big house called The Grove, where the Colonel used to live. Here were now our asylum-trained Commandant, two junior officers and the rest of the ATS, amongst them the more unruly ones who had to be kept an eye on. We fed there, and did orderly duties.

There was also a common room with a tinny piano and admonitory notices all over the walls. We three went there as little as possible. It was usually in a state of pandemonium and chaos, and we'd rather sit in our little room in our house. We crammed beds for all three of us in there, for comfort and company, lying under our quilts, brewing cocoa on our primus, reading and playing our gramophone.

I only had two records. One was a nostalgic Austrian song which was all the rage in Kitzbühel when I was there in August 1937. I played it incessantly, in spite of the German words. The other one was Gigli singing 'Che Gelida Manina' from *La Bohème*. His voice was heart-rending. Anne had a Mozart and Joy two Brahms, and we made do with these.

Realizing the bleakness of our state, we went into Southend to improve things. After much haggling with a dirty little man in a dirty little shop, we acquired two chests of drawers, a table and a couple of looking-glasses, all bought with our own money. I asked my parents for a bit, which they sent, as did the others.

We sent home for a rug, eiderdowns, a couple of pictures, and we painted our lavatory seat scarlet.

None of us had ever lived away from home before, and it was quite fun getting our little nest together and being independent.

But at nine thirty nightly we had to rush across to The Grove and have our names ticked off on a list to say we were in, and then we could go back and get into bed.

Some of the girls used to leave any swains they'd acquired lurking in the bushes while they ticked themselves off, only to creep out again. This practice, however, was soon discovered and the disconsolate ones would be marched to their rooms by a Sergeant, who would then ruthlessly turn the key in the door and pocket it.

At least weekend leave offered a period of freedom, however brief, from the constraints imposed by authority.

One time I had a rather gilded two days with my old Suffolk friend Patricia in London. She dealt in Guards officers mostly, and we were to meet a couple at the Guards Club in Brook Street and dine at Quaglino's in Bury Street, the rather 'in' place at the time. Sunday we were going down to Maidenhead to have lunch at Skindles and go on the river. All rather a change from my present life-style.

On Saturday morning I set off for the station. I'd put on a scarlet suit under my greatcoat and silk stockings under my beastly khaki ones, and decent shoes in my haversack instead of my gas mask, with my gloves and bag. I hugged the greatcoat to me lest a peep of red should appear, and jumped into the train. Seven minutes between Shoeburyness and Southend gave me time to peel off my khaki stockings and change my shoes.

On arrival at Fenchurch Street station I bundled up my coat and dumped everything in the cloakroom, emerging as a civilian. Oddly enough, later on, although I still didn't like myself in khaki – it really is a fatal colour – I cared less and less to appear in civilian clothes, and never did, except on leave.

I even hoped I wore the uniform with a certain air, specially in hotels, where one often saw young women in furs and with red nails, who probably got away with doing a couple of days a week in a canteen.

Well, it was rather a glamorous weekend, I suppose. Beautiful chaps at the Guards Club, a jolly good dinner at Quaglino's, and then on to the Coconut Grove where we danced till 2 a.m. Sunday, down to Maidenhead, lunch and a row on the river.

It doesn't sound very warlike, does it? But then there wasn't much war going on just then, and people could still have a good time.

The days moved on into November and it got even colder. Certain songs were in fashion, and the recruits marching under our window would wake us up bellowing 'Roll out the barrel', 'The Quartermaster's Stores' or 'South of the Border'. Men's voices are quite stirring as they come nearer and nearer, and then fade and die away.

Perhaps these recruits weren't quite as happy as they sounded, but it was amazing how they smartened up and improved their appearance in quite a short time.

We used to watch them trooping down to Joy's clothing store to be kitted out, some rough and unkempt, others the exact opposite in coats with vast shoulders and pointed shoes.

Perhaps they hadn't envisaged the rough khaki battledress, the black heavy boots, and the voice on the square shouting, 'Like it or lump it!'

One had been a BBC singer and was always in full voice whenever he got the chance. No concert was complete without him, and when a rather weak but kindly concert party came to entertain the troops they were shouted off the stage with, 'We want Hughie – we want Hughie.' Hughie eagerly dashed on stage and finished the entertainment. The poor concert party must have felt very hurt, and there was CB [confined to barracks] for the shouters.

Life wasn't all that marvellous at first. The seemingly foolish rules; the ill-fitting, badly cut khaki uniforms. Some of us decided to shorten and narrow our shapeless skirts, but a skirt parade was called for. One of our officers frog-hopped down the line with a tape measure, and our skirts had to come down by at least 2 inches. You really couldn't do a thing with those uniforms, not even the prettiest and slenderest of us.

For the first three months we only got a meagre 9/4d a week, handed out to us at very solemn pay parades, where one could be carefully scrutinized. The keen eye of Miss Robinson swept over us from crown to toe, lingering unnecessarily at the buttons. I usually only breathed on mine and gave them a cursory rub.

As for the respirator – they didn't call them gas masks – I really did get a backache from carrying it 'at all times and in all places' as the rules said. I solved that one by removing the actual thing and stuffing my haversack with a couple of copies of the *Daily Mirror*. I arranged them so that they bulged convincingly; what my fate would have been had a gas attack materialized, I didn't think.

After three months on 9/4d our pay rose to 13/6d. This was called proficiency pay. How people managed who had no other source of income, I can't imagine. I had £4 a month from my parents, paid into my account, and I couldn't have done without it.

You know, before the war no girl like me would have dreamt, or been expected, to pay for herself anywhere!

The Army was really father, mother and general provider to us all. We were issued with combs, toothbrushes, shoebrushes, underclothes, in fact everything that was essential to female needs.

For a while I spurned the awful salmon pink vests and pants and produced them pristine and unworn at each monthly inspection. But as it grew colder I was jolly glad of them!

There's a lot to be said, we decided, for having few expenses and not having to make any decisions. Also a good case for being roped into a service at the very start of the war. Other people I knew, who had bided their time, were eventually called up and whisked away to a job they would never have chosen had they taken an earlier plunge.

We made the best of it by laughing at most things, and seeing to a few little comforts for ourselves. We wrote for more things from home such as cushions, lamps and a little rug, and we planted hyacinths in pots.

Regimental dances on Saturday nights were terribly popular. We loved them, and we nearly always went. But we weren't, as you know, allowed out of uniform, and with the black-outs up and the skylights closed it could be unbearably hot. Troops opened their top buttons and were reprimanded. I hauled off my jacket one night in a rage, and was sent off to bed!

This was the period of the 'Phoney War', when both sides were content to confine matters to skirmishes at sea or in the air.

We loved the beach at Shoeburyness. The evening air would be fresh and salty, and we used to watch the convoys assembling, counting the ships daily as they collected.

Then one misty morning they would be gone and the sea would be calm and blandly innocent of the armada that had so recently gathered there.

But the convoys were also a major target, and on the evening of 22nd November a German attempt to deploy one of their latest high-technology mines misfired with far-reaching consequences.

I was with Anne and Joy, out walking on the golf course after supper, when we saw two planes fly upriver. It was a clear night and the gunners on the golf course opened fire on the planes, which we could clearly see. Tracer bullets licked across the sky and the battery on Canvey Island was firing too. A machine gun rattled and we thought we'd better move off, out of the way.

We heard the leading plane was eventually shot down off Southend pier, and the other one got away after laying a magnetic mine. Perhaps the first plane was a decoy, attracting the gunfire up the river while the other one slipped in, dropped the mine and made off. But he didn't reckon with the tide in the Thames estuary, and when it ebbed, there sat the mine, high and dry on the beach just below the officers' mess of the XP.

Great excitement ensued all next day, though we weren't quite sure what exactly it was all about, as we weren't properly told.

In fact a team of specialists from the Navy's torpedo and mining establishment, led by Lieutenant-Commander John Ouvry, had been sent to examine this first intact example of the new weapon.

> While we spent our spare time gossiping, asking questions and getting misleading answers, brave Commander Ouvry was calmly sitting there on the sands pulling the mine to bits, and calling out his actions as he went along, to the other experts nearby.
>
> After removing everything metallic on his person, and using non-magnetic tools, he took several hours to dismantle it. It was this example of cool nerve that enabled our scientists to protect ships with degaussing apparatus [which reduced their magnetic signature] thus rendering these infernal machines quite innocuous.
>
> We saw the evil object, shrouded in white, being carted away on the back of a lorry, and we were cautioned not to write home about it in our letters.

Ouvry, who died in February 1993, was awarded the first naval DSO of the war for rendering the mine safe and allowing its precious secrets to be unlocked.

> In early spring 1940 I emerged, like a butterfly from a chrysalis, out of my school pyjamas and we cast aside our heavy greatcoats. They had been long and warm, but the weight was only just worth the warmth. I stuck a crocus in my buttonhole, which I was promptly told to remove.
>
> Anne, Joy and I cultivated our garden very earnestly as spring was turning into summer. We had about 500 square feet with a brick path down the middle, and on our two sides were five more exactly the same. We had to get interested in something other than the Army, and we felt gardening was the best thing to do, as well as being productive.
>
> We dug, raked and planted. We made another path from a pile of discarded bricks we found, and gardening became a mania. We had plenty of flowers, mostly easy ones like marigolds, antirrhinums, sweet williams begged from Joy's father, forget-me-nots, nasturtiums and eschscholtzias.
>
> We even grew carnations from seed, which was a real triumph. We ate our own vegetables – peas, spinach and lettuce – cooked on a primus, and got off church once or twice by saying we had arrears of work, but in fact we were grubbing about in the garden.
>
> Anne and I would go up to the office, fill in a form, address an

envelope, drink a cup of coffee with the orderly Sergeant, and post haste back to the soil.

It was all very matey, leaning over our fence discussing greenfly or the week's gossip with our next-door neighbours.

But as the weather improved, so the fortunes of war deteriorated. We stuck pins in a map on the wall, and all had anxious moments.

The first day we played tennis, France fell.

We were all convinced there would be an invasion by the Germans. Frightful fates loomed ahead for us.

The best we could do was to make jokes. The plainest and dullest would be sent to work in factories or down the mines. The blonde ones would be packed off to a stud farm and do their duty by raising stock for future German armies. Joy – tall, rosy and buxom – would probably be one of these. Anne, with a rather more delicate air, might still be in an office or perhaps a 'girlfriend' for a German officer. As for me, we thought I'd end up washing dishes.

We made more invasion jokes and laughed at the doubtful usefulness of the concrete barricades and barbed wire being set up along the coast roads.

3

BEF

The British Expeditionary Force which had been sent to France had included virtually all of the home-based Regular Army, together with a large proportion of the Territorial Army.

In contrast to the Regulars, many of the Territorial soldiers, like *Ronald McKay*, were relative newcomers who had never even been to annual training camp, let alone to war.

In the spring of 1939 I was living in Macduff, in the north-east of Scotland, working in my father's fish business, when the government brought out this militia scheme. It was advertised in the papers, and on the radio, that all men would serve for six months in the services when they reached a certain age. I don't think at this stage anyone really thought a war was coming, but it was a government order and nobody questioned it.

The majority of the people from here were put to the Gordon Highlanders, because that was the local regiment. Now, as I am – or was at that time – about 6 foot 2 inches tall and a bit skinny with it, I never fancied wearing a kilt. So the only way of getting out of it was we had a local Territorial unit here, of the Royal Artillery. The government said that if you were a Territorial you could do your six months' training with whatever regiment you were in at the time, so I thought rather than be put into the Gordon Highlanders I would sooner join the Royal Artillery, and do my six months' training with them.

The establishment of the TA had, of course, just been doubled overnight, with most of its units being required to form a brand-new duplicate of themselves in as short a time as possible. Ronald's regiment, the 65th (Highland) Medium Regiment RA, was one such duplicate, raised as the 'double' of the existing 56th (Highland) Medium Regiment RA.

61

With twice as many units to support, entrance standards could hardly afford to be stringent.

Our local drill hall was in Banff, our county town, so some of my pals and I went across and joined. We had a fairly basic medical examination at our own doctor's and that was it. We were all passed A1. I never heard of *anybody* who didna pass their medical, so I can only assume that either the examination was pretty perfunctory or we were all pretty fit!

We did training across in the drill hall in Banff, and out the back in the field. Once a week we had to go across and do two hours' training – I think it was seven o'clock till nine – which consisted of marches, foot drill, gun drill for the gunners, signalling – Morse code and that sort of thing – for the signallers, and driving for the drivers, of which I was one. As we only had two trucks, though, it was mostly maintenance.

Most of us were very, very raw recruits, with no idea of marching or drill of any kind, and one episode sticks in my memory.

We had a Sergeant-Major who was English. He was very English-spoken, and sometimes very difficult to pick up. And I can remember one night in particular we were all marching through this field in single file, when the drill Sergeant shouted out an order. He was quite a fair distance away from us, and being that he had this bit of an English accent, none of us were very sure what he had said! So the whole thing turned into a complete shambles, with some people going into twos, others going into threes, others going into fours, some about turning . . . and there was general confusion. And of course we always got an audience of spectators round about the field, so there was a sort of general idea, well, if this was what the country was relying on, thank God we had a Navy.

This Sergeant-Major, he was a Regular?

Yes, he was a Regular, and he was the instructor based in the drill hall. He was there long before I started taking an interest in the Territorials, and I suppose he'd just been posted there. He lived in the flat above the drill hall with his wife, and I think he had some family. So he had been there for quite a long time. He was the only one who was actually based in the drill hall. The officers were like us, they were only part-time as well.

So when the war came, how were you called out?

Well, I heard it on the radio. My kit was already packed, because we were going off to camp the following day, 2nd September, which was a Saturday.

Where was this to be?

At Barry, beside the firing range at Buddon Ness, which is between Carnoustie and Monifieth on the east coast above Dundee.

But we were actually called up on the Friday night. It came over the wireless that all Territorials had to report to their units, and war broke out at eleven o'clock on the 3rd. So it turned out to be a long 'camp' – in my case almost six years!

So it was just a case of picking up my kit and getting across to Banff to sign on, as it were. Some of us were kept in the drill hall to stay, but I was put up to the junior school in Banff. We were issued with two blankets each, that was all. And we slept on the hard floor.

As it was a rushed operation they got one of the local bakers, the late Mr Bowman of Whitehills, and he took in hand to do the catering for us. He used to take all the food in, from Whitehills – he must have done it in his bakehouse, I suppose – he took the meals in in his van and dished them up. Breakfast, dinner and then tea at night. And I must say that this was about the finest food that we got actually in the Army – when it was being done by an outside source and not the Army cooks.

I can remember I was actually on guard at eleven o'clock in the morning, on the day war broke out. It was lashing down with rain. We had no greatcoats, the only thing we had was a groundsheet, and a steel helmet. And I was told to march up and down the entrance to the school with a bamboo cane. This was the only thing I had to defend myself against the might of the German Army. However, as luck would have it none of them appeared, so that was all right.

But I was actually on guard at eleven o'clock when somebody came out and said, 'It's come over the wireless that we are now at war with Germany.'

We were in the school at Banff for about a month, and then we moved to Peterhead to meet up with some more of the regiment. Then about a month later to Aberdeen. We came from a fairly wide area – in addition to the HQ from Banff we had 'C' Troop at Fraserburgh, 'D' Troop at Peterhead, 'B' Troop from the Montrose area and 'A' Troop from Aberdeen. Each troop had four 6-inch howitzers which had been used in the First World War.

That's in addition to your bamboo canes?

In addition to the bamboo canes. [Laughs.] The 6-inch howitzers had wooden wheels with iron tyres – we could only do a maximum of 15 miles an hour while they were being towed.

We had, oh, maybe a month in Peterhead, billeted in the drill hall – now demolished – down beside the Crosse and Blackwell factory. There we continued doing mainly route marches, because I think we had maybe two vehicles, that was all. By this time it would be November, I suppose. We then went from Peterhead to Aberdeen, where we met up with the rest of the troops, and we stayed in Aberdeen until February 1940. Continued doing drills. Practically all we did was route marches. I was supposed to be a driver, but as we had no transport I didna do any driving. The gunners got gun drill, though they didna get to actually fire them.

We then went down to a place called Charfield, down in Gloucestershire. And I then made the first of many mistakes I made while I was in the Army. They asked for volunteers for an advance party. I was getting a bit fed up of Aberdeen by this time, so I was one of the people who volunteered. There was about twenty of us went down, I think, in this advance party to prepare for everybody else coming along. Everybody else got a weekend leave; we got no leave. So I made up my mind there and then that the only thing I would volunteer for from then on would be an extra helping of duff, or something like that, from the cookhouse. I thought, that's the end of *my* volunteering.

Now we were in this village – Charfield, just a little wee village. We were billeted in the village hall. They had taken all the chairs which had been in the hall and had stacked them up on the stage at one side, and there was a big stove right in the middle of the hall. We had no fuel of any kind, so we disposed of the chairs at a rate of about two every night we were there. This we thought was very good until after we left we got a bill for barrack room damages which just about ruined the lot of us!

So we stayed there until probably it would have been about March, when we went down to Southampton. By this time we had got vehicles, and of course there was a mad rush to get everybody through their driving test. I passed my driving test, which was very simple – if you could sorta move backwards and forwards you were in – and I got presented with a 15-cwt Bedford truck, which was known as a signal truck – Monkey 3, or M3. Our job was to lay the telephone line from the gun post out to the observation post at the front [from where an officer would direct the fire of the guns]. So we had quite a long bit of line to put out. And this was my job.

So we were taken to Southampton, put on a ship, and we landed at Cherbourg. We had a couple of days at Cherbourg and then we were moved.

What were the washing and shaving arrangements like at these camps?

Cold water and outside. In fact that was a very, very severe winter, the winter of '39–'40. It was the first time I had ever seen telephone lines so thick with frost that they were down to about a foot off the ground. Shaving water was absolutely frozen. And one thing I always remember was being as we had quite a few young lads with us, some of them only shaved once a week. However, the powers that be put up a notice on the notice-board saying that 'All ranks will shave every day *whether they need it or not.*' Which I came to regard later on as being typical Army mentality. We had no access to hot water. In fact some mornings there was no water at all, because everything was frozen up, so we could neither wash nor shave.

We got to Cherbourg, and we were there in a transit camp for two or three days. My main recollection of Cherbourg is that they had about twenty great big boilers there, and they had tins of what was known as M&V – this was Maconochie's Meat and Vegetable rations. And they had about twenty men with tin openers, opening these tins and emptying them into these big boilers. And this was our sole diet, this M&V, and hard biscuits. This was all we ever saw in Cherbourg. And there was a veritable *mountain* of empty tins lying round about, where these boilers were.

After we'd been two or three days there we were moved up to a place called La Bassée, where we were billeted in an old disused cinema, and then we were moved again to another place, where we were a few miles outside the town, billeted in a barn at a farm.

We usually just had palliasses filled with straw, and a couple of blankets and a straw-filled pillow. The facilities were again fairly primitive; just a cold water pump for washing and then a queue for breakfast outside wherever the cookhouse happened to be. And very often eaten outside unless you could find some shelter.

Once a week we were taken in open trucks to the nearest pithead baths for a shower, but I'm afraid by the time we got back to camp we were as bad as when we set out.

Despite this being the 'Phoney War' we were kept busy on exercises and so on, so we never got the chance to get bored.

At the time it didna really feel as if we were in a war zone, and we didna see much of any other units of the BEF, or the French either.

The area of north-east France you were in, of course, had been the one fought over by the First World War BEF.

That's right. We were taken to see the war memorial on Vimy

Ridge, and visited the cemeteries. In fact we were very moved and pleased that they were kept so well.

Funnily enough there was a Macduff man there who was keeper of a cemetery. Of course at that time our letters were all censored and we werna allowed to say where we were, but it was known in Macduff where the cemetery was that this man kept, so we all wrote home and said we had met in with this man at his work, and everybody at home knew where we were! The censors never picked that up.

We were there for quite a while. Our guns were to be taken down to the south of France, to be fitted with rubber tyres. However [laughs], Hitler must have got word of this, because he decided, there and then, to come round the side of the Maginot Line, and we were thrown into action with the guns as they had been originally.

The BEF, having spent months building up its defensive positions, was now called upon to abandon them and to advance into Belgium to meet the anticipated main thrust by the Germans.

When the Germans attacked I was the driver of Monkey 4, and our job, me as driver and three signallers, was still to lay the telephone line to the OP. I had to drive as far as possible paying out the cable from reels mounted on the back of the truck, then the signallers finished it off by hand.

We'd been out all night with the line-laying truck, the three signallers and myself, and going down the back of what we would normally term a row of council houses, we were tying the line up to the telephone poles. And the boys in the truck said to me, 'See if you can see any chance of getting a cup of coffee,' because we'd had hard tack biscuits, but that was all we'd had to eat and we'd had nothing to drink.

So a woman came out of the back door, and I said to her in my best Scottish Belgian French, '*Café au lait, madame?*', you see. And she sorta looked, and then she went back into the house again, so I thought no luck there. Then, about a couple of minutes later, a man came out. And of course I thought that the man had maybe thought that we were trying to get off with his wife or something, so we were a wee bit concerned. However, he came down to the bottom of the garden where we were, and he said, 'Is it coffee you want?' And I then discovered that this man, who again looked after one of the British war cemeteries from the First World War, had married a Belgian and settled down there. He asked me where

I came from and I told him, and it turned out that he had actually been born in Garden Street in Macduff, and his folk had moved to Dundee when he was about four years old.

Quite a coincidence, meeting a second expatriate who knew Macduff.

A very great coincidence, being as there was a whole row of houses and I could have picked any one of them, and I just happened to pick this particular one.

I often remember about this man. He said to us, 'What do you think'll happen?' And of course we, being as we thought we were invincible, said, Oh, you're safe enough. We're here.

I think about a week later the place was blown to bits.

Did you ever know what the regiment was firing at?

Not really. Our guns fired miles and miles, and since our job was to lay the telephone line from the gun post out to the observation post at the front, we were at the other end from the guns when they were being fired. Mind you, that was just as well, because they were a bigger danger to us than they were to the Germans. We had never fired these guns – never mind in anger; we had *never* fired them. At all. The gunners had no idea what was going to happen when they pulled the lanyard. In some cases bits fell off! But we seldom knew the intended target.

In fact we seldom knew very much at all, as either our officers didna know themselves or else they didna tell us. We knew very little about what was going on.

What was going on was that the BEF's situation was becoming increasingly perilous. The main German thrust had come not in Belgium but further south, and the French defences there had proved unable to cope.

We got orders one night at twelve o'clock to get on to our vehicles. We'd no idea what this was for; nobody told us. As I said, I had a 15-cwt truck. We were told to leave the small trucks and go aboard the big trucks, and everybody – the drivers, signallers, gunners, everybody – was loaded on to the big trucks. I went with a friend of mine who was a driver on a 3-ton truck, and I actually did the driving.

We left about the back of midnight and drove for about an hour and a half, couple of hours, and this friend of mine said to me, 'I think we're going the wrong way!', because we seemed to be getting *nearer* the flashes and the noise of battle.

German armoured columns, pouring through the gap in the French line, had already reached the Channel coast.

The BEF was cut off.

> We got orders to stop, and then we got orders to turn round in the middle of the road. It was a pretty narrow kind of road, and one vehicle went into the ditch. Now this in the Army meant somebody would have been put on a charge straight away; however, we were told to leave it and the men that were in that truck were just spread out amongst the other trucks.
>
> We then drove on through the night. We had no idea what we were doing or where we were going – nobody had ever told us. And then somebody said we were making for a place called Dunkirk.
>
> A few kilometres from Dunkirk the regimental police were there, and they came along, ordered us to put the lorries into a field, and we were told we had to walk the last bit to the town. We got there about three o'clock in the afternoon, to the beaches up above Dunkirk, and we saw all these men in long lines, in the water, boats taking them off.
>
> So we were then told that we were to be evacuated. There was no hope of getting off at the beaches, but we could maybe get off at Dunkirk itself. The men more or less flatly refused to walk any further, so six of us drivers were told to go and commandeer vehicles. We got some lorries which had just been dumped at the side of the road and that, came back to where the men were, and drove the men down to Dunkirk. I think I would have done two journeys, maybe three, before everybody got down, because we just had half a dozen trucks.
>
> We got down to Dunkirk, the mole – a long jetty leading out into the harbour. The men were queued up there about ten deep, right the way out. And we were then told to take the trucks and smash them up any way we could, so we took them across to a bit of waste ground maybe a mile away and put pickaxes into the tanks, let out the petrol, smashed up the distributor heads and the sparking-plugs, which was about all we could really do to make them unserviceable. We then had to walk back to Dunkirk, where we discovered that the entire regiment – officers, NCOs and men – had gone! We were the only ones that were left! [Laughs.] Of our regiment, that is, along with hundreds of other people.
>
> So we were just left to our own devices to get out any way we could. So we gradually got in this queue out this mole, and by about four o'clock in the morning there was a destroyer came along, and we were taken aboard, given bully beef sandwiches and

hot mugs of cocoa – which was the first food we had tasted for at least twenty-four hours. And it was certainly the first bread that we had seen for at least a couple of months. We'd been living on hard tack biscuits.

The Navy landed us at Ramsgate, where we were put on a train, all mixed up. There was only the six of us from our regiment. Other people from all kinds of units. And we were taken then up to beside Reading, to an Army camp there. During the time we were on that train, every station we stopped at members of the WVS [Women's Voluntary Services] were there, dishing us out cups of tea, cakes of chocolate, biscuits, sandwiches and God only knows what, and it was the best food we'd had for quite a long time.

One funny instance was that a friend of mine – Ronald Porterfield – was in the same regiment as I was, but he wasn't one of the drivers. He was off the day before. And when I got to, I think, Reading station, we stopped there for some time and, being as my father was a fish merchant and was accustomed to receiving telegrams, I gave somebody some money to go and send a telegram to say that I had arrived home. Because by this time we realized the seriousness of the situation. We only realized how bad things were when we got to Ramsgate and bought newspapers and saw the arrows – where the Germans were, and where we had been, and all the rest of it. And it was only then that we really realized how bad things really were. Because the Army believed in keeping you in ignorance and telling you very little.

Anyway, as I say, I sent off this telegram, which my father got that day. He went along to this friend of mine, Ronald Porterfield's, people to say he'd got word from me and had they got word. And they said no, they had had no word. Now, my friend's mother was inclined to be a wee bit hysterical-kind, and she said, oh well, if I was in this country and their son wasna with me then he must have been killed in action. Subsequently he sent home a postcard, which of course since the mail was in a pretty bad state at that time they didna receive for about four or five days, by which time his mother had gone into deep mourning, convinced that he was dead. In actual fact [laughs] he had arrived the day before me, because he got off with the earlier lot with everybody else. So that was one funny thing that happened there.

Well, we got to this camp near Reading. And we led the life of Reilly for about a week. We went about, we were the heroes and all the young recruits that were there were sorta looking up to us, because we had seen action, and all the rest of it. But then one night we were walking up from the local village pub, and when we got to the gate the Sergeant in charge of the guard said, 'Right, get yer hands out yer pockets, get yer collars done up, get yer hats on — yer back in the Army now!' End of the honeymoon.

So we were then all collected together. The rest of the regiment had more or less all landed at one place apart from the Sanitary Orderly, who for some queer reason or other had landed in Wales.

Can you describe the function of a Sanitary Orderly?

The Sanitary Orderly was the man who removed the . . . ehm . . . outside the barracks we had big buckets, which were used for urinating in through the night. And the Sanitary Orderly's job was to remove the contents of them and dispose of them in the morning, and also the latrines. He had to empty the buckets of the latrines and dispose of the contents of them as well.

Was the Sanitary Orderly a volunteer, or a pressed man?

Oh, a pressed man.

Any idea how he was chosen?

I think 'You'll do it' and that's that. [Laughs.] He might have been, shall we say, slightly sub-standard — without being nasty — intelligence-wise, and this was the only job they could get him to do. He would probably have gotten the whole Army mixed up if they'd put him on anything else, so they put him on that.

He was about the last one to rejoin us.

So then we went to Northumberland, to a place called Newbiggin-by-the-Sea, beside Ashington, where we reformed and were put on coastal defence. We had no transport again apart from [laughs] I was given a baker's van, as I drove a Major. If we had anybody else with us they just had to sit in the back.

If Hitler had had any sense and had come across at that particular time . . . well, that would have been the end of us. Because we had *nothing*.

4

REBUILDING

The bulk of the British troops, many of them bewildered and dispirited, had at least been saved from the disaster in France.

But their equipment had not. 63,879 motor vehicles had been wiped off the Army's inventories at a stroke, along with 2472 out of 2794 artillery pieces and 657,566 tons of ammunition, petrol and other stores.

There was simply nothing left with which to make good these staggering losses.

As the country braced itself for invasion there was an emergency acceleration of the call-up rate. But the best that could be done with the new recruits was to create a mass of infantry, bereft of heavy support.

The need for a new tank, and new production lines to build it, was particularly urgent. Vauxhall Motors at Luton, which already made Bedford vehicles for the Army and which had been working on a new tank engine, was an obvious choice for expansion.

Bertie Dean was the head of Vauxhall's Experimental Department, having joined the company over twenty years earlier.

My whole working life, in fact, was spent at Vauxhall Motors. I first joined them in April 1919 on a four-year premium apprenticeship, after training at the City and Guilds Technical College. The weekly output back then was twenty-six cars and there were about 1000 employees, the majority of whom I knew by their first names.

Vauxhall's would have been an independent firm in those days?

Oh yes, absolutely. It was in 1925–26 – my apprenticeship was finished in 1923 – when I was working at our Great Portland Street showroom in London that they suddenly told us that we'd been bought up by General Motors.

What did people think about the take-over?

Oh, several people decided they weren't going to stay. They couldn't stand the thought of being taken over by the Americans!

While the new owners were easing Vauxhall into the volume car market Bertie was moving back to Luton to become their Sales Manager, at the age of twenty-seven.

But then Harold Drew, Vauxhall's Assistant Chief Engineer, offered me a job in the V Block Engineering Building. Harold said to me, 'Since you're so damned critical of the product, you had better join us and criticize it in the early stages!' [Laughs.] I was good friends with Harold and his American wife Rosemary – he and I used to go sailing together [indicates the photo of a yacht on the wall behind him]. By the late 1930s I was Experimental Manager, concerned with the building, test and development of prototype Vauxhall cars and Bedford commercial vehicles.

In 1939, as with most car manufacturers, car design and development came to an abrupt halt when the war broke out, and we were asked to concentrate on truck production for use by the services.

Also, at that time a new heavy infantry tank called the A20 was being worked on by the War Office and Harland and Wolff, the Belfast engineering firm. We were first asked to design a suspension system for it, then to design a new, more powerful engine than the Meadows one originally fitted. It had to be a petrol engine, be of a size and shape to be accommodated and serviceable in the existing space [the maximum dimensions of new tanks were dictated by the railways, since all had to be capable of being transported by rail without danger to bridges, etc.], and develop 350 brake horsepower at around 2200 revs per minute. Our biggest Bedford engine developed 72 b.h.p., so a completely new engine had to be designed, and prototypes built, in the shortest possible time. We were given the OK to go ahead with the design and building of two engines on 15th March 1940.

Our engineers, and those at all our suppliers of castings and components, worked day and night, weekends and holidays, and unbelievably the first prototype engine was running under its own power on 11th June, just eighty-nine days later. By the 121st day 350 b.h.p. at 2100 revs per minute had been recorded. It was a flat twelve – twelve cylinders, in two banks of six, horizontally opposed.

However, the A20 project was cancelled in favour of an all-new specification called the A22. It was this vehicle which would eventually receive the big 21-litre engine just completed by Vauxhall, who were now asked to proceed with the design and construction of the whole tank.

This was a prodigious undertaking for a firm geared to the production of cars and trucks, but the country was in dire straits. Mr Churchill explained that our problem as a nation was to produce, as quickly as possible, the maximum number of tanks – new tanks, of a sufficiently powerful kind, for home defence.

Normally it took at least four years to design, build, test and develop a new tank. But in this urgent situation, with the threat of invasion by Hitler, no such time was available. So Dudley Perkins took over the Experimental Department, and I was switched to the development of the A22, soon renamed the Churchill.

We had advice and suggestions pouring in from many quarters. So many, in fact, that Harold Drew [still Assistant Chief Engineer at the Luton plant], who was most directly involved in Churchill design, had to perform a lot of weeding out. That prompted this cartoon drawn by one of our draughtsmen, Dick Shortland. [Shows me a copy of the cartoon, which consists of various versions of the finished product based on the demands of the different factions. In the 'Fighting Equipment Group' version gun barrels protrude from every conceivable location: the 'Suspension Group' version is all suspension; the 'Production Department' version is made entirely of angular blocks of wood, roughly nailed together.]

One of the most interesting features of the design was its Merritt-Brown combined gearbox and steering mechanism. Previously, to steer a tank the driver braked the inside track, thus losing power. But the Churchill had an epicyclic gearbox/steering system which enabled one track to move faster than the other, so when one brake drum was locked the other brake drum doubled its rate of speed through the differential. The effect of this difference in speeds on the output epicyclic was governed through the main power train from mainshaft to layshaft, so the turning radius depended on which gear you were in. The smallest turning radius was obtained in the first speed ratio and the largest in fourth, with gear changes often essential to negotiate tight turns. The actual turning radii were 11 feet in first gear, 30 feet in second, 57½ feet in third and 96 feet in fourth.

Not only that, but steering in neutral made one track go one way and the other in the totally opposite direction, so the tank turned almost in its own length, making it very manoeuvrable.

Were you involved in the design work with Harold Drew?

No [laughs], I was only really interested in making it go!

Five hundred Churchills were ordered off the drawing board on 1st July, forgoing the usual procedure of waiting until a prototype had been built and tested.

In the life of any automobile engineer there are plenty of examples which illustrate the need for an adequate development period, and the Churchill was no exception. We as development engineers pressed for this before production commenced, but Winston in no uncertain terms said that he doubted Hitler would leave us sufficient time for refinements!

The price to be paid came in the form of endless teething problems with the production vehicles.

All sorts of troubles showed up. Tracks broke, engine gaskets blew, hydraulic systems failed, bogie wheels came off their spindles.

But gradually reliability improved – 50 miles on the road without failure became 100, then 500. We drove them day and night to build up these mileages. Sometimes my wife Helen would come along at midnight with coffee and sandwiches for the crews.

Were you driving them on public highways?

Very often, yes. All round the area. I took one home once on a test run, as I had always done with cars. [Laughs.] My wife came back – she was working with the ambulances during the war – and wondered why there were all these tank tracks in our road.

Did you have any accidents?

Occasionally you'd knock a lamp-post down, or something of that sort. But the roads were very quiet, of course. Very different to now.

Was the factory ever targeted by the Germans?

Oh yes, very much so. The worst bombing was the day I wasn't there – the afternoon of 30th August 1940. A bomb splinter tore a jagged hole through the centre drawer of my desk, and my secretary was one of the thirty-nine Vauxhall employees killed.

Off-road testing was conducted on the estate of a nearby country house.

We also needed a large private testing ground adjacent to the factory, and were fortunate in that the Ministry of Supply arranged with Sir Harold Wernher for us to have exclusive use of a large portion of Luton Hoo Park. We built a wide concrete road from our Park Street entrance up to the house.

The Army Sappers [Royal Engineers] enjoyed themselves

producing some really large shell holes by means of suitable charges of explosive. Trenches and ditches were dug, vertical walls and other anti-tank obstacles were built, and we gradually overcame problems with engines, tracks, steering and transmission. The works fire brigade pumped water from the River Lea and used it to saturate a large area, which we churned up into deep mud with our tanks. We soon found that the tracks tended to throw tons of mud all over the tank and turret, so the gunners couldn't see what to fire at. This meant designing complete mudguards for the tracks. Then the mud collected between the tracks and the mudguards, forcing them off, so we countered this by fitting mud or snow ploughs behind the rearmost bogie.

In the early stages of production we demonstrated this new monster to a number of interested VIPs. Two recollections stand out in my mind.

The first is that before having his trial run at Luton Hoo, Winston Churchill was examining the tank in company with the Minister of Supply and Major David Raikes, who was on loan to us from the War Office. Winston, smoking a cigar, pointed with his stick at the little 2-pounder gun on this enormous tank, and said to the Minister, 'Why has it got that 2-pounder and not the new heavy gun?' The Minister replied that the department responsible had not yet had time to develop the new gun (*the 6-pounder, the 2-pounder's replacement*). To my surprise, David Raikes commented that they had had as much time as Vauxhall had had to produce the whole tank! I felt I might next see Major Raikes out of uniform wearing a bowler hat!

The second is of the visit of His Majesty King George VI, who I had the pleasure of driving for. The tanks got very dusty in dry weather, so we provided white coats for special occasions and VIPs. His Majesty had taken the hull gunner's seat alongside my driving position when our Managing Director, Charlie Bartlett, wearing his usual cap, spoke to me. The King said, 'What did Mr Bartlett say?' I said, 'Mr Bartlett was offering you his cap to keep yours clean.' The King smiled and replied, 'No thank you, I have another one at home!' [Laughs at the memory.]

What was he like?

Very shy man. Though he didn't stutter so much when he was talking to me as I know he did when he was speaking in public.

Did you drive for Winston too?

No, one of my men did. I was just watching on that occasion. I got to speak to him, but not very much because he was very occupied with David Raikes.

As the tanks began to roll off the production line one of Bertie's other hobbies, photography, was pressed into service to help with the Churchill's problems.

> Quite early on in the Churchill development programme I felt the need for a cine camera, partly for recording particular tests so they could be seen by engineers not actually present, and partly to observe the behaviour of certain components in slow motion. We used this camera quite extensively during the war. [Later I have a chance to watch some of this footage, converted by Bertie to video format, showing Churchill testing at the Luton Hoo obstacle course.]
>
> It did get me into trouble, though. One of our early production models was sent to the Tank Testing Establishment at Farnborough, for their assessment. One of their criticisms was that the suspension was causing the tank to pitch, making it difficult for the gunners to keep on target. So with two colleagues I drove to Farnborough and took some slow motion cine pictures through the sliding roof of my car, while travelling alongside and behind, to help our design engineers find a cure.
>
> That evening on the way home coming past Ascot, driving fairly fast with nothing on the road, an Army sentry suddenly dived out in front of me, making me brake hard and swerve to avoid him. I looked through my mirror, and to my horror saw him quickly getting his rifle off his shoulder, so I braked hard to a stop and then backed up and started ticking him off for that method of stopping traffic. A Sergeant appeared on the scene and asked me to come to the guardroom. I explained I didn't want to make a formal complaint, but he insisted we should go with him. He then phoned the Adjutant and said, 'We've got the car, sir – CMJ 708 – and the three occupants.' That altered things, and I apologized for criticizing the sentry when he was in fact looking for a particular registration number. Some well-meaning person had obviously reported seeing a civilian photographing a secret tank, and the whole countryside was looking for us. It took several hours of interrogation and phone calls to get us out!
>
> In addition to this sort of development work, we were also asked to find out how to waterproof the whole tank so that it could wade ashore in 6 feet of water from a tank landing craft, for invasion purposes. This involved not only protecting the working components from sea water, but fitting tall extension ducts to the air inlets and outlets, and putting sealing fabric around the turret. This all had to have explosive or other devices to enable it to be

jettisoned as soon as the tank got ashore. I was present at a trial in which eighteen Churchills were loaded on to tank landing craft and sailed round from Burry Port to Pendine Sands. All but one successfully reached the shore. The unfortunate one knocked off his air intake extension when leaving the LCT, with the result that the tank rapidly filled with water and the crew made a hurried appearance on top of the turret!

Churchills equipped with wading modifications were the first to see action, in the disastrous Dieppe Raid of 19th August 1942. The engineers were able to learn few lessons from this because the Germans were left in possession of all the tanks, but when two brigades of Churchills landed in North Africa the following year the opportunity arose of checking their battleworthiness at first hand.

In May 1943 Harold Drew, Maurice Platt and I went by special arrangement with the War Office and Ministry of Supply on a fact-finding visit. We intended to visit the battlefields to see Churchills that had been in action, and to have what might be called service conferences with the officers and men who had crewed them. It was all very hush-hush.

We went by train to an airfield the whereabouts and name of which were not disclosed. The three of us were kitted out with brand-new flying boots, Mae Wests, etc., so I remarked that apparently the last poor devils hadn't got back. 'Oh no, sir,' said the storekeeper, 'this is an experimental route and you are the first to fly it.'

'What plane are we flying in?' I queried.

'An Albemarle, sir.'

'An Albemarle? I've never heard of it.'

'Well sir, you see, it isn't used in action any more; only for transport. It catches fire too easily . . .'

We had a safe but sick-making flight, as not only were there no seats in the plane but auxiliary fuel tanks had been installed in the fuselage to give it more range. The stink of petrol was appalling.

We touched down at an American air base in intense heat at Fez, Morocco, at 10 a.m., and were given breakfast in the officers' mess — a plate of very greasy American bacon accompanied by a large dollop of jam. However, we survived and the discussions were most informative. [Shows me the detailed photographs they took.] We also found plenty of evidence in the form of knocked-out German tanks of the effectiveness of British anti-tank weapons.

I remember, too, the rather eerie feeling when pitching our tents at night by the roadside, knowing that the ground adjoining the roads hadn't been too well cleared of German land-mines.

In addition to building the tanks themselves, Vauxhall also acted as 'parent' company to the other ten firms of the Churchill Tank Group, answering questions of design and production and ensuring a smooth flow of the necessary components.

> Obviously one factory couldn't produce enough tanks quickly enough, so it was necessary to 'parent' other factories throughout the war, and see that they received a steady flow of materials. With their co-operation, a total of 5640 Churchills were produced, many of them converted for special purposes like bridge-laying and flame-throwing.
>   It really was a team effort, in celebration of which on 19th December 1945 [shows me his souvenir menu] we gave a dinner at the Dorchester Hotel for our leading suppliers and for the Army and Ministry of Supply people. The occasion was called 'We worked together: the Churchill Tank Dinner', and was attended by thirty-three guests and twenty-three Vauxhall staff.

But it was not just the traditional engineering industries which found themselves working for the Army. Even the most inoffensive of trades, like furniture making, had a role to play.

The audacious German airborne operations of 1940 had impressed the British greatly, and spurred them to establish a force of parachute and glider troops of their own. The gliders for the latter, such as the Airspeed Horsa, were built of wood, and were seen as perfect for subcontracting to civilian furniture concerns up and down the country.

Ivy Eden and *Daphne Bradley* worked for the biggest of these – the Harris Lebus factory at Tottenham, North London.

> *Did the two of you know each other?*
>   *Ivy*: Well, we did as children, because we belonged to a dancing troupe together, but we didn't meet each other at Lebuses. It was such a big place.
>   *Were you both local girls?*
>   *Ivy*: Yes, born in Tottenham, both of us.
>   *So was it natural to go into the factory? Was there a range of things you could have done?*
>   *Daphne*: Well, everybody had to do war work. They had to do essential work unless they were in the services. And unless they

were with young children. First of all I worked for a photographer, on Ministry of Information photographs – aircrews and things like that. You had to sign the Official Secrets Act, because you weren't allowed to divulge any information unless the government wanted you to! And then I heard – I don't know how Ivy heard about it – that Lebuses were paying big money. Although it was twelve hours a day you worked. I was earning eight pounds a week there, which was a lot of money in those days. And of course you got bonuses and everything else. Harris Lebus was, before the war, the biggest furniture manufacturer in the country. And because they had to do essential work they went over to making Horsa gliders for the Army, which were practically all made of wood.

I went there first of all as a progress checker, which I didn't like very much. And then I went into the Drawing Office, looking after the De Havilland [which had taken over Airspeed in 1940] drawings. If anybody borrowed a De Havilland drawing I had to keep tabs on it, because they didn't want them to get lost. There were little drawing offices dotted all over the factory, and you had to go round and chase up the draughtsmen and see that you brought the drawings back, because we had to account for them. If after a certain amount of time they hadn't come back, I would have to go and see what had happened to them. David Kossoff was one of our draughtsmen. You know, David Kossoff the illustrator? He was a draughtsman at Lebuses. And it was *such* a vast place – as Ivy will tell you – I mean, at the end of the day our poor feet . . . ! And they were all concrete floors. Really you had to be quite fit. We used to have an hour for lunch, and we worked seven days a week, didn't we? And then we had a day and a half off – at least I did. And then we worked another seven days. Every other month we had to do night work, which was seven o'clock in the evening until seven o'clock in the morning. And then we used to have to go up to the canteen and try and eat something, and next door there was a slaughterhouse where they killed horses. And the smell! I mean, they used to serve you up swede in the middle of the night, you know, and all the sort of horrible things that you had during the war – which you didn't ask too much what they were. And there was this horrible smell of horses cooking . . .

Ivy: Yes, it was horrible.

Daphne: And then of course you had to go home in the morning and try and get some sleep. I lived opposite the Castle public house in Church Road, and every Wednesday they used to get a delivery. And it used to be put down, you know, in the cellars on the pavement. No way did I get any sleep! In fact in the end I started fainting, and I had to go to the surgery and they put me on sun-ray treatment.

So the draughtsmen were on shifts as well?

Daphne: Oh yes, everybody was working shift work. You see, it was 24-hour-a-day production. And of course if there was an air raid warning they used to have a tannoy system, and there used to be lights. There used to be a spotter on the roof, and if the siren went there'd be a light come up with 'Alert'. And if you saw the alert you just carried on working. Then all of a sudden, perhaps if enemy planes were overhead, you had a light that said 'Take cover'. So *then* you had to turn everything off and go to the concrete shelters – they weren't underground, they were just concrete shelters within the shops. Then the men used to get their cigarettes out and play cards until the All Clear, anything from ten minutes to two hours or more. And then you'd get the notice up – they were everywhere, these lights – with 'All clear'. And then of course in the mornings – was it eleven o'clock? – we used to get 'Music while you work'.

Ivy: Eleven o'clock in the morning and three o'clock in the afternoon.

Daphne: For half an hour each. This was relayed by the BBC, so people at home listened to it as well.

This was coming over the tannoy system?

Daphne: Yes, over the tannoy. And one day we had Geoffrey De Havilland give us a talk about how important our work was.

Ivy: That's right.

Daphne: He was a test pilot, Geoffrey De Havilland.

Ivy: Of course sometimes you couldn't hear it, could you? Or *you* might have, but where I was was so noisy. I was in the machine shops.

What kind of machines were you working on?

Ivy: In our department we cut and drilled the joints for the gliders, all different shapes. When I started I was on this big machine. The men used to feed it with these long members of wood, and the women would take them off and stack them. Then I went on to the electric drills; you know, you had bits of wood about that size and there were about six drills at a time.

Drilling screw holes?

Ivy: That's it. Not a very interesting job, still. And I got my finger with it once. Then I went on circular saws.

Sounds even more dangerous!

Ivy: Oh, it was, and you had to be accurate – right down to a thousandth of an inch. You measured the wood first, and then worked to a template, after which the piece had to be passed by an inspector before progressing.

Did you get more money for the circular saw?

Ivy: No, you didn't get any more money, you were on the same rate. In fact, though, you were on a bonus, for the amount you did, but on the circular saw you were *scared* of going too quick!

Did you have protective gloves or anything?

Ivy: No, nothing. Not in those days.

Daphne: Yes [nodding], every one of the machinists had fingers missing. They did!

Ivy: It was very dusty with sawdust, which mostly got in your hair. The smell of wood was something you got used to, but we could have done with more ventilation. You had to wear overalls, and we were provided with heavy cotton ones, light khaki in colour, which were changed once a week. Also a kind of cap, to keep your hair from catching in the machines. That was because of Veronica Lake [the Hollywood actress] – Veronica Lake and the peek-a-boo hair-style. She was asked to change her hair-style because so many women were copying her, which she did.

What was the proportion of men to women in the workforce – was it largely men with just a few women?

Daphne: Oh, it was lovely! [Laughs.] Being a young girl, you know.

Presumably a lot of the men had been there since before the war, when they were still making furniture?

Ivy: Yes, the young men, as they got to the call-up age, they went off to the services. But most of the older men were only too pleased to be out of it and earning big money. I mean, the services didn't get much, did they?

Daphne: In the morning we used to get the tea trolley come round. You used to get ten minutes' break in the morning. And if you were very lucky they used to have slices of bread and dripping, which was a penny a slice, the old money. Of course everything was rationed, so if you were lucky enough to get bread and dripping you really thought you were on to a good thing! [Laughs.] The tea was horrible stuff, wasn't it, from an urn.

Ivy: The men used to have these old enamel mugs . . .

Daphne: . . . which they never washed. It was thick all round the edges. And they were all chipped . . .

Ivy: That's right. And in the afternoon they brought cakes round. Of course the quality of cakes during the war . . . God knows what was in them. And then we had entertainment. We used to have shows; Max Bygraves and those sort of people, who were just starting out, would come and give shows.

Where would they put them on?

Daphne: In the canteen.

Were these free concerts, or did you have to pay for them?

Ivy: Oh, free, yes. Though I remember there was a children's party once at Lebuses and Wilfred Pickles – who had quite a big name – wouldn't come unless they paid him.

Daphne: When I finished work – I'd be working all day – my friend and I would go to the ladies' washroom; we would have a general clean-up, then we'd get a bus outside Lebuses which would take us to Manor House station. We'd go from there to Covent Garden. There was a dance hall at Covent Garden which was taken over by Mecca during the war, and we would dance until eleven o'clock at night. After a twelve-hour day! And then you had to be home as soon as the dance finished, because you had to be at work at seven o'clock the next morning. But you had to have some sort of recreation. We didn't do that every night, because we had to do fire-watching. And my friend, she joined the Fire Service, which was part-time. I mean, you just couldn't get away with it, could you? You had to do these things.

Was fire-watching voluntary?

Daphne: No, they made you do it. And it was quite scary if you were a young girl, to have to do these things.

Was the factory ever hit?

Daphne: I don't remember it being, no. Which is surprising, 'cos it was such a vast place. You know where it was, do you, in Ferry Lane?

Ivy: The river ran alongside of it. The wood used to come up on barges – I think it was 11 Shop where they used to collect it all.

Daphne: There was lots of damage round about, though. I can remember going to work, seeing a land-mine – because they used to come down on parachutes – caught up on a chimney. The police were there, and you *had* to go past it because you had to go that way to work. And nobody realizes, do they, unless they lived through it, the *glass* that was everywhere. And there'd be great big craters in the ground, and unexploded bombs, and gas mains that'd been broken . . .

But we were young. I think to have been elderly, or perhaps to have had children, it may have been quite traumatic. First of all having to evacuate them, and then when nothing happened, bringing them back. And of course when we used to go dancing you'd come back on the Tube, and there were all these people sleeping in the stations. First of all they used to sleep on the platforms, but then as time went on so the government provided bunks for them. And then of course it was more organized. But you still had to step over the people, sleeping in the Tube. And how they ever slept I don't know, because some of them had to go to work the next morning, and trains were still going through until – I think the last train used to go at ten past eleven at night from where we went, Covent Garden. And I remember there were toilets there; they were buckets – you know, like dry toilets – and they used to put up sacking round them. And if you were caught and you wanted to go to the toilet, if a train came in the sacking used to blow aside! It was most embarrassing.

It's little things like that that you remember.

5

CHAPLAINS

Events in Europe seemed a very long way away from the British garrisons in the Far East, who were still on more or less a peacetime footing.

H.L.O. Davies was Chaplain to one of the Regular battalions stationed in China.

I was ordained into the Church of England in . . . let me see . . . Advent 1932. I had two and a half years in a parish in Newport, Monmouthshire, and then I joined the Army in 1935.

You may ask *why* I joined the Army; well, I was in an industrial parish, and there was a lot of unemployment then – this was, as I say, the early 1930s – and one Sunday the vicar gave out, 'The collection today is for the curate's stipend.' Well, I thought, by Jove, I'll go somewhere where I'm paid by the State. And that's the one thing that made me turn my mind to the Army! [Laughs.]

Did your family have any Army connections before that?

I had an uncle who was in the First World War in the Royal Army Medical Corps, but that's the only connection.

And who did you contact about joining the Army?

Well, I suppose somebody must have told me, because I wrote up to the Royal Army Chaplains' Department at the War Office. Then I was called for an interview, and the Chaplain-General said, 'Well, you seem acceptable – when can you join us?' So I joined within a few months. I had to report to Bulford, and I was three years as a Junior Chaplain at Bulford Camp, near Salisbury, on Salisbury Plain.

When I joined the Army, Chaplains still had to pass an equitation course as we were supposed to be mounted. So I did mine with the Gunners – Royal Horse Artillery. I'd ridden a horse when I was a boy, because an uncle of mine was a farmer, so I wasn't unfamiliar with it. And afterwards I could always get a horse from the lines and hunt twice a week with the harriers.

So this was quite a departure from the existence you'd led before.
Oh yes it was, from being in a parish, yes.
And was it quite a pleasant life?
Yes. You were dealing with men more, which suited me really.
Instead of having Mothers' Union and all that stuff.

I got a Regular commission, and then having done three years
I was due to go overseas, and my first station overseas was Tientsin,
in China, just to the south-east of Peking.
What did we have there at the time?
There was a single infantry battalion, the 1st Battalion, the
Durham Light Infantry. We always had a battalion there, protect-
ing the British trade interests. And there were supporting units like
RAMC and RASC, and so on.

It took me six weeks to get there, because then you didn't fly –
you went by boat. So it was a month to Hong Kong, and then
another fortnight up the coast calling at the ports. I spent a night
in Shanghai when the ship put in there – the British Chaplain in
Shanghai invited me to stay the night with him and his wife at
their flat.

When I got to Tientsin I'd spent all my pocket money on the
ship, so the first thing I did was go along to the Chartered Bank
in Tientsin. I introduced myself to the manager; I said, 'My name's
Davies, I'm the new Army Chaplain. Has my agreement come
through from Newport? I want to cash a cheque.' And he said,
'Now don't worry about your money,' he said, 'there's a meeting
of the Welsh Society here tonight.' [Laughs.] I never looked back!
He came from Llantwit Major. And the cashier came from Devil's
Bridge, Aberystwyth.
So were you the only Chaplain for the Tientsin area?
Oh yes. There was a priest who looked after the Roman
Catholics, but he was a civilian and worked in that area.

When I got to Tientsin I thought I'd be there three years, so I
got a Chinese to teach me Mandarin. And this Catholic priest, he
said, 'You've got a fellow teaching you Chinese? How long are
you here for?' I said I'd be there three years at the most. 'Pack it
in,' he said, 'I've been here thirty years, and I've only just mastered
it. It's a waste of money!' [Laughs.] So I took his advice!
*So what were your duties? Looking after the general welfare of
the men?*
Yes, that's right. Taking the services for the Durham Light Infantry and other people, and visiting the hospitals, and so on. When
I went there was a British community in Tientsin, business
people, and they had their own church and their own chaplain, a

civilian. I'd only been there a few weeks when his tour of duty expired – he'd been there three or four years – and so he went home and they asked me. So I ran the civilian church as well.

We always had a company of troops on embassy duty in Peking, and I had to go up once a month to visit them.

How did you get from Tientsin to Peking?

Oh, on the railway, which was quite efficient. So I've walked along the Great Wall of China, which is near there. And I did step down once, when nobody was about, into [Japanese occupied] Manchuria – just a few yards! [Laughs.]

I was up at Tientsin the whole of 1939, and then I went down to Hong Kong in 1940. I *would* have been up in Tientsin for three years, but the garrison was closing down, you see. After the outbreak of war the battalion was withdrawn from Tientsin, and I hadn't done my three years in China, so they simply moved me to Hong Kong.

Was that very different from Tientsin?

Well, in Tientsin we were in the British Concession – there was then a British Concession, and a French Concession – whereas in Hong Kong it was all British, of course. Different climate, too. In Tientsin in the winter we were wearing fur caps. But in Hong Kong it was more a problem of keeping cool. The best time in Hong Kong is probably around December, if you have reasonable weather. It isn't too hot then, November–December. But in May, the *humidity* . . . I'd come down in tropical evening dress, and before I got to the bottom of the stairs I'd have to go back and change, because I was soaking!

Were you still the only Army Chaplain?

Oh no, there were quite a number of us. Plus there was a Roman Catholic Chaplain, and as there was a Scottish battalion among the garrison – the 2nd Battalion, The Royal Scots – there was a Church of Scotland minister as well.

I was then the Chaplain to the 1st Battalion, the Middlesex Regiment. And I became engaged to a QA [an Army nurse, from Queen Alexandra's Imperial Military Nursing Service] stationed in Hong Kong, Sister Mary Currie.

As for the war – that was still something we read about in the newspapers.

It was, however, about to get a lot closer. On 8th December 1941, a few hours after their fleet had attacked Pearl Harbor, the Japanese sent their troops into Hong Kong. They quickly overran the New Territories and Kowloon, and then stormed Hong Kong Island itself.

The Japanese attack must have been a bolt from the blue.

Oh, it was, it was. We were overwhelmed. And we surrendered on Christmas Day, 1941.

Had they been able to evacuate any of the families and people like that?

Yes, a lot of the families had been evacuated to Australia over the previous months, before the Japs suddenly invaded.

But your fiancée wasn't among them, being an Army nurse?

No. When the war started, our RAMC took over a convent called St Albert's, which was on the Island. And that became an auxiliary hospital. And my fiancée was made the Matron there.

During the fighting a Japanese officer was wounded, and he was taken into St Albert's and put in a bed, but died. Then the next day the Japs came in force, and we surrendered. So my fiancée went down to meet them at the door, you see. And they made them sit down, and started hitting them about the head, and so forth, and my fiancée said then to one of the Japanese officers who spoke English, 'Why do you treat us like this – one of your officers was brought in last night and we tended him. He unfortunately died, but he's laid out upstairs.' 'Oh,' he said, 'take me to see him.' So they took him up, and there he was, laid out decently. The Japanese officer was very impressed, and he called his troops off the hospital, and kept them outside.

Well, in the other parts of Hong Kong the Japanese, they'd raped all the nurses, you see. But through that act St Albert's was saved.

In the wake of the defeat, the surviving service personnel and European civilians were herded into prisoner of war camps, a number of which were hastily established in different parts of the Colony.

There was a big camp where the men went, Sham Shui Po, on the Kowloon side. This had been a barracks occupied by two Canadian battalions, who had only just arrived before the Japs struck. But my fiancée was in Stanley, in the civilian camp. All the European civilians were interned there, on the Island.

Then they took over St Teresa's Convent in Kowloon as a hospital to take the very severe cases from Sham Shui Po. British nurses, of course, in this extra hospital, looked after the severely ill. And the Matron there asked that I come and take Communion and a service – this would have been Easter 1942. And so I had my Communion set ready on Easter Day. I'd taken services in the camp, and I was waiting then. I'd almost given up hope. Early in the afternoon, when I thought, well, they're not going to take me out to take the service, they finally sent for me. And I went down with my Communion set. And the Japs said, 'Where's your kit?' I said, 'Well, I'm coming back.' 'Get your kit.' And I was taken up to this auxiliary hospital at St Teresa's, and remained there until the middle of August, when I went back to Sham Shui Po.

What sort of accommodation did you have?

Well, St Teresa's had been a convent, so it was much better than Sham Shui Po. There were proper beds and sanitation. The only sanitation left in Sham Shui Po consisted of earth buckets. And Sham Shui Po was appallingly overcrowded. As I say, in peacetime the barracks had accommodated two battalions, but for most of 1942 there must have been 4000 of us there. Although the numbers were progressively reduced as they sent drafts off to the work camps in Japan, when each draft left the wire perimeter was made smaller, and the feeling of claustrophobia was made worse.

Were the Japanese quite orderly in how they treated the prisoners, or was there a degree of arbitrariness about their behaviour?

Arbitrariness, definitely. They could be quite brutal at times if something went wrong, or anything like that.

Two friends of mine, 'Dolly' Gray of the RAF and Dougie Ford, a Captain in the Royal Scots who I shared a room with on my return to Sham Shui Po, tried passing notes to Colonel Newnham [prior to 1940 the CO of the 1st Battalion, the Middlesex Regiment; a staff officer at HQ, China Command at the time of the surrender] in the officers' camp at Argyle Street. They were passing notes and planning an escape. I don't know why they did it.

They entrusted these notes to go from our camp to the officers' camp to the Chinese who were doing the rations. Well, the Japanese got suspicious and they got hold of these notes that they were passing. And the result was that 'Dolly' Gray, Dougie Ford and Colonel Newnham were all executed. Because they were planning an escape. Now in Germany they'd have been punished with solitary confinement, but the Germans would never have done a thing like that, you see. Just *planning* an escape.*

Was this unusual on the part of the Japanese?

Oh no, typical of them. It wasn't done publicly, but it was a nasty business. Brave men.

Where had they hoped to escape to?

---

* All three, Flight Lieutenant Hector Bertram Gray, Captain Douglas Ford and Colonel Lanceray Arthur Newnham, were posthumously awarded the George Cross for gallantry.

Overland, I suppose.

Actually when Hong Kong surrendered, there were a few days of confusion before they put us all in the camps, and three or four of our men escaped. One of them was a fellow called Jacobs, RAMC Private, who in peacetime was in and out of jug. He was always a bit of a menace. [Laughs.] He made his way — and he had a Military Medal for it — cross country for hundreds of miles and got to Chungking. By a strange coincidence my sister was also nursing in the Army, and she was then at Imphal in India. And she was going on night duty one evening and the sister she was relieving said, 'Look here, there's a fellow called Jacobs arrived — he's already hit one orderly. He's a bit odd. He's escaped from Hong Kong, so treat him gently and humour him.' So my sister went on duty, and saw Jacobs there, and she said, 'Jacobs, you escaped from Hong Kong. Did you know a Padre Davies there?' He said, 'Oh yes, I knew him well — he used to visit me when I was in jug,' so she asked, 'Well, is he alive?' Because we'd all been reported missing when Hong Kong fell. And the first news that she had that I was still alive was from this rogue, you see.

He'd made his way all that distance cross country, a few others with him. It was a marvellous feat. He was quite a character.

Even communicating through the permitted channels held its own perils.

As I say, my fiancée was interned in Stanley, on Hong Kong Island, and I was on the mainland, in Kowloon. Occasionally we were allowed to write one card, limit fifty words, to keep in touch. And about the beginning of 1944 I sent my card, and I wrote on it at the end, 'Hoping this year will see us together.'

A few days later I was sent for by the interpreter, and there was my card on his desk, so I thought, Hello, what's happened now? And he said, 'You're a priest, aren't you?' I agreed that I was. 'And you speak the truth, don't you?' I said I hoped so. 'Now,' he said, 'if you tell me where you got the information that the war's going to end this year,' he said, 'I shan't punish you.' [Laughs.] I gasped, you see. 'Well, hope springs eternal in the human heart,' I said. 'It's got to end sometime — I'm hoping.' He said, 'You've got some information. Where did you get it?' After about ten minutes of this arguing he got up and gave me a crack across the face, and he said, 'You are a liar. We shall watch you. Get out.'

How suspicious they were.

What was the treatment like generally?

89

Well, there were no medicines. And it was starvation. And in, I think, October 1943 we had an epidemic of diphtheria in the camp. There were no medicines, and with the starvation rations ... [Shakes head.] On some of those awful days I was burying five or six men a day.

Because of course their resistance would have been so low.

Due to the diet, yes. Some of them, big men, were 45 pounds in weight when they died.

At its worst, the diet in camp was basically rice and 'green horror' twice daily. Green horror was boiled chrysanthemums, or else a coarse watercress the Chinese normally fed to animals. At one time they gave us boiled seaweed. Your stomach rebelled and it came back up again. The doctors said, 'Now, you must keep it down – there's iron in it.'

Some men went almost completely blind in the camp, from vitamin deficiency.

But of course you had to keep cheerful. People were relying on you.

Regardless of how you yourself felt?

Yes. I think if I ever cut any ice as a Chaplain, perhaps I cut it then. Whatever you felt, you had to keep the morale of the troops up.

Did morale have highs and lows?

Yes, it had its lows. Things were low when the rations were low. There was a blockade of submarines around Hong Kong, and the Japanese had difficulty in getting food to the Colony, because Hong Kong couldn't feed itself – nothing grew there much. So when things were tight, morale dropped. And I remember one of the Canadian Chaplains saying to me, 'Look here, Davies, do you notice the attendance at church on a Sunday's increasing?' Because things were getting tight, you see. And the tighter things got, the bigger the attendance. I suppose it's human nature – when things are going well you don't bother about God.

I kept a diary in Hong Kong, and hid it under the false bottom of a table, because there were all these searches going on. They never found it. [Passes me the complete transcript he has had typed up, which runs from 25th February 1942 to 12th August 1945. Within its neat pages are entries like: 'Tuesday March 10th, 1942. Chinese shot on bamboo pier – a young Chinese was brought into camp by some Japanese soldiers. He was made to kneel on a small bamboo pier which jutted out on to the harbour. After lunging at him a few times with bayonets, he fell into the harbour bleeding profusely. Then they put a bullet through his head.' 'Monday July

20th, 1942. Double funeral. The graves were flooded due to heavy rain and the whole thing amused the Japs. We all got drenched through.']

Quite a few entries mention playing chess.

Yes, you played a lot of chess, those of us that played chess, to pass the time. And we had quiz nights, and whist drives, that sort of thing. At one time I would practise the piano, but I had to give that up because the starvation diet made it too difficult to concentrate. And some of us used to spend time at night star-gazing. There were no lights, and usually clear skies at night, free of cloud.

We also had to be counted at two parades a day, on the square. We had to keep ranks but were allowed to sit down, as each parade took three-quarters of an hour to two hours, or sometimes even longer. The Middlesex used to say the Japs were so short they had to count the number of feet and divide by two, and they couldn't do it! [Laughs.] But it was tedious on those parades.

Other than that, in Hong Kong before the war there was the Hong Kong Club, which everybody belonged to, and it had a very fine library. And we persuaded the Japs to bring this library to Sham Shui Po, which was an absolute godsend, you see. So we had books to read, and things.

And how much did you know about what was going on outside? Very little presumably?

That's a good question. Actually we used to have a fair idea. The Japanese used to publish a paper in English – the *Hong Kong News* – and our ration bringers used to get hold of this occasion-ally, and this gave us a very good idea of what was going on. We could tell when things were going our way in the war.

By reading between the lines of the news reports?

That's right. And another indicator was that when things were going our way, the Japanese got more nasty.

So you could actually gauge from how they were treating you how the war was going?

Yes.

So things became more unpleasant as the tide was turning against them towards the end of the war?

Yes. But, as you say, reading between the lines of this local paper we could tell things were going our way. And we'd get information from the fellows working the rations.

Was there any way to get back at your Japanese captors, or was it too risky to bait them in the way that prisoners in German camps sometimes did?

No, it was just too dangerous. One kept one's distance from them as much as one could. Like that one that hit me. If I'd have hit him back he'd have cut my head off with his sword.

Colonel Stewart [the CO after Colonel Newnham], he was of the old school. 'Padre, the Japanese, they're straight from the trees,' he said, 'and not a gentleman amongst them!' [Laughs.] His summing up! I won't repeat what our troops called them.

So from your own point of view, what was the worst thing about your captivity?

Not knowing when it would end. If you're in prison normally you at least know when you're going to get out. But we didn't know. And not knowing whether one was going to make it. Towards the end, with the American blockade all around, you see, we wouldn't have lasted another six months. Because things were so low. We were starving.

So it's just as well the Japanese surrendered when they did?

Oh, absolutely, yes. I don't think we could have made it more than six months at the most.

So what was your first contact with the outside world, after the Japanese suddenly surrendered?

A Royal Navy cruiser came in. Some of us were invited to come on board ship and have a decent meal one evening. And I remember going on to this cruiser, and there was a Naval Chaplain there, and he said, 'Would you like me to take you on a tour of the ship?', you see. And I said, 'Not particularly, thank you, I've been over one of these ships before. But,' I said, 'I've never been on a submarine' – a submarine had docked as well – 'so if you could take me over that submarine . . .' He looked a bit glum, and he said, 'Well, to tell you the truth, I haven't been on a submarine either myself. Because the sailors reckon if a Chaplain goes on board he'll be a Jonah and they'll sink!' [Laughs.] Superstition!

So when were you reunited with your fiancée?

We were reunited in Hong Kong, a few days after the surrender. And after the war I'm happy to say she became my wife.

We were all gathered in Manila, in the Philippines, and we didn't know what to believe. We'd gone on the *Empress of Australia* from Hong Kong to Manila, which was pretty rough and ready, as the ship was overcrowded. Then we'd been there a few days and the ship was going back to the UK. You had to consent to go – it was so rough, you see. And damn me, two days after we'd left the rest of the people, who'd chosen not to go on the ship, they went home via Canada. And my wife was amongst that lot. You didn't know what to believe. And I've always kicked myself that I missed that trip around the world.

But the thing was to get home, actually. I'd been abroad six years. My normal tour of duty would have ended just about the time I was captured.

By the time we landed in England it was November, and I remember saying to myself, Have I lived through this dismal weather and climate and never realized how awful it is? After the sunshine of Hong Kong!

But it was not only the weather at home which proved to be an unpleasant surprise.

As I say, I came back in November 1945. And while I was in London for a few days I went to Alkit's [Alkit Ltd, Outfitters] to get a new uniform, and I ran into a Chaplain who'd been a prisoner in Singapore. I ran into him in the shop, and he said to me sadly, 'Davies, you're finished, you know.' I said, 'What do you mean?' He said, 'Well, I've been to see the Chaplain-General; he's got no use for us, we've been out of the war.'

So I went along to see Freddie Hughes, the new Chaplain-General, and I said to him, 'How do I stand?' 'Well, Davies,' he said, 'you've been out of the war. I have to look after the Chaplains who've been through the war with me.' He never asked me did I take services in the camp, did I give Christian burial, nothing. He just said I'd been out of it. I was appalled.

Not even to ask could you take a service and help the morale of the men. I was disgusted with it. You almost felt a deserter.

So when he said he had to look after the people who had been with him, presumably he was already looking to the cuts in the size of the Army now the war had ended?

Yes, exactly.

Did this colour your views of the Army in general?

Well, it wasn't the outlook of the Army. It was really just Freddie Hughes. There were a lot of people in my position.

But as it turns out they didn't get rid of me, and I didn't retire until I'd done my twenty-five years.

Have you ever been back to the Far East?

No. I like the Chinese. They've got a sense of humour. But not the Japs.

So you've no desire to visit Hong Kong again?

I don't think so, no. Of course, now they fly out in about twelve hours, don't they? Little Kai Tak aerodrome I gather's a colossal airport now. When I was there Kai Tak was much smaller than it is now, but even then it was a difficult place to land. You had to fly between the hills.

Yes, and almost between the skyscrapers nowadays as well.

Well, when I was there there was only one skyscraper – the Hong Kong and Shanghai Bank. Somebody showed me a photograph of Hong Kong a few months ago, and I'd never seen anything like it. I didn't recognize the place with all those skyscrapers.

Looking back after all this time, do you think that anything good came out of your years in Japanese hands?

I was friendly with the Regimental Sergeant-Major of the 1st Battalion, the Middlesex Regiment, RSM Challis.

A few months before the surrender he said to me one day, 'Padre,' he said, 'you don't believe all that stuff you give out on a Sunday in church, do you?' And I said, 'Well, oddly enough I do, otherwise I wouldn't be here.' And I said, 'What about you?' He said, 'Oh, God's all right for women and kids,' he said, and laughed at it.

And then a few months later the Japanese invaded. I remained in Hong Kong. A lot of prisoners were taken up to Japan. Colonel Stewart said to me, 'The troops are going, and you're not coming.' 'Well,' I said, 'I volunteer for nothing, but if it's my duty to come with the battalion, I'll come.' He said, 'It's your duty, and you'll be on the ship with the rest of us.'

But he came along to my bunk at midnight and he said, 'They won't *touch* you in Japan, they won't have a Chaplain there.' And so, possibly by the Grace of God, I didn't go, because the ship was the *Lisbon Maru*, and the Americans torpedoed her off Shanghai with the loss of 843 of the prisoners.

So, I mentioned this fellow Challis, the RSM. He made it to Japan. And after the war we were all collected together, the prisoners in the Far East, in Manila. And I ran into him one day in the camp there. And as we were chatting together over a glass of beer I said to him, 'Challis, are you of the same opinion of God as you were when we were in Hong Kong?'

And he said, 'Padre, no man could have been through what I've been through,' he said, 'and *not* believe in God.'

6

RASC

Between the fall of France and the entry of the Japanese into the war a year and a half later, the only theatre in which the British and their enemies faced each other across a land frontier was in the Middle East.

Here, in the Western Desert of Egypt, began a campaign characterized by its rapid movement and wild swings of fortune. The beaten side in any engagement was frequently chased for hundreds of miles, in what the British wryly referred to as 'the Benghazi Handicap'.

The campaign in North Africa also brought into sharp focus the importance of logistics to a modern Army. With little or no infrastructure, literally everything the front-line troops needed on a daily basis – water, food, ammunition, 'POL' (petrol, oil, lubricants) for their vehicles – had to be carried by the trucks of the Army's supply and transport organization, the Royal Army Service Corps.

Jim Cowley was one of the drivers sent to work in this 'tactician's paradise and quartermaster's hell'.

> The sorting out after Dunkirk was quite good. At first I thought, However can this motley shower get back to being viable units again, but the people handling the job did it really well. Units like ours with half the men missing – we numbered around 250 men at that time, out of 480 who went to France – were destined to be broken up.
>
> The next year and a half I spent delivering ammo to AA gun sites, making coal dumps, clearing the bomb debris at Hull and taking the rubble to Aldbrough Cliffs and Spurn Head to make gun emplacements.
>
> Eventually I was shipped out to Egypt in early April 1942. That was an experience all of its own. Fully dressed and life jacket on for the first seven days. After leaving Freetown the threat of subs diminished, so life on board the *Monarch of Bermuda* fell into an easy-going pattern and passed quite pleasantly as far as Cape

Town. While we were in port I got word that my brother was also there – in fact the ship he was on was tied up at the next pier! We had a few days together, then I was taken off the boat and sent out to a camp. I stayed there for a month, then I was put on board an old boat, the RMS *Scythia*.

This old ship kept breaking down, and finally off Madagascar the convoy left us on our own. It took six weeks for us to reach Aden. The heat was intolerable – 120° in the shade, if you could find any!

Then into the Red Sea. I found out then how it was so named. It was tranquil as a mill pond, and covered with a film of red sand.

We disembarked at Port Taufiq and boarded a train for Geneifa base camp. During my stay there my brother-in-law came to see me. He was a Royal Marine, stationed on the Great Bitter Lake, a couple of miles away.

My spectacles had got damaged, so I had to stay at base camp when my friends were all posted 'up the blue', as the Desert was called.

What happened to your spectacles?

They got bent whilst on board ship. We slept in hammocks, and we used to roll out and land feet first on the deck. One morning my specs landed before I did, and my feet did the rest!

But after a few weeks I too was posted. I was taken to Tel-el-Kebir [just to the west of the Canal Zone], given a tank transporter loaded with a truck and put in a convoy to Amiriya, 20 miles from Alexandria [on the other side of the Nile Delta] – quite a drive!

Had you handled a tank transporter before?

Well, I had received training at Heckmondwike in Yorkshire on tank transporting, loading and unloading, on flat-backed six-wheeled trucks. Which by the way were quite useless – they tipped over because of the high centre of gravity.

But this one was a Diamond T tractor unit and trailer. The trailer was a hook-on low loader, two axles at the front, two at the rear. Each axle, or set as we called it, had eight wheels, thirty-two in all. They were American, and real good units. The tractor had ballast boxes fitted, in which 12 tons of concrete blocks were stowed. This was to give good traction when loaded. They could be varied according to load, but time wasn't wasted doing this. They were easy enough to drive once you had sorted out all the gear levers. There was a five-speed gearbox, a gear divider to make it ten, a rear winch and a forward winch. They were very powerful and reliable, and of course diesel.

The tank transporter job was a one-off. The transporters were needed up the front, so were we, so two jobs became one. After delivering the unit and load to Amiriya, we were sent to a transit camp nearby. The following day I was posted to 127 (General Transport) Company, RASC. They were camped about 10 miles further west.

The first thing when I reported was to be sent to a platoon, and have another driving test. When the wagons [trucks] returned from convoy I was allocated to one as second driver. Most of the lads were quite sociable, and I fitted in with all ... except the driver I was with. He was morose and *un*sociable, but I just had to put up with that.

After parrying a thrust from the enemy at the start of July, the British Eighth Army had launched a series of attacks of its own during the rest of the month. Neither side, however, had the strength to break through the El Alamein position, to which the British had been forced back after a string of previous defeats. The then commander of the Eighth Army, Auchinleck, was forced to halt the attacks in order to gather strength and to accumulate stocks. His opposite number, Rommel, did likewise.

When the Germans were stopped near Ruweisat Ridge, the thought of total collapse seemed to evaporate.

There followed a month of convoys with ammunition, petrol, food and Royal Engineers supplies to El Hammam, making large dumps. The railhead [the point of transfer from rail to road transport] was also pushed forward to El Hammam, around 30 miles from El Alamein.

While we were on a convoy to Burg-el-Arab, a few miles back, German aircraft bombed the forward dumps. A lot was destroyed, and we worked day and night to replace it. The trucks we had were American, six-wheeler 10-ton diesel Macks. We carried 10–12 tons each wagon each time.

Around this time Monty* was put in charge of the Eighth Army. Almost overnight the whole of the Army seemed to find a new spirit, a new awareness. The trouble with the old Eighth Army was the lack of coherent planning and priorities. Monty left no one in doubt as to what was about to happen – the bunch of men I came out with had all been through Monty's fitness and training programme on the Yorkshire Moors through the winter of '41–'42.

---

* Lieutenant-General Bernard Montgomery, later a Field Marshal and 1st Viscount Montgomery of Alamein.

Monty was always dashing around giving pep talks, telling the ordinary soldier what he had to do and how we were going to do it. The difference he made to morale had to be experienced to actually believe it.

As I say, we were building dumps to the rear of Alam Halfa in the area of El Hammam, Burg-el-Arab and around El Alamein station.

Did you know what was going on in the front line?

Yes, we knew what was going on, and we could hear it. In Desert conditions it was quite close, and we used to 'get the griff' as we went about our business. Someone always knew 'the latest'. We weren't told the date of the new offensive, but we knew it was close.

And what form did your cargoes take? Did you have to sign for them?

We had to sign for all loads. The cargoes of food were mostly of bully beef and biscuits at this stage. Later we added jam, tinned bacon and soya sausages. The ammo was in steel boxes up to 25-pounder, then the shells and charges were loose for the 4.5-inch and 5.5-inch. Small arms ammo and grenades in wooden boxes.

Our weight to carry was 10–12 tons of food or ammo, or 2000 gallons of petrol or diesel in 'flimsies' [square, thin-metal containers employed before the reusable 'jerrican' was copied from the Germans], or drums of high octane aero fuel. The latter was the worst to carry, and the most dangerous. Due to the rough terrain the cans and drums would puncture, and wagons were known to blow up.

One particular night we were allowed to go to the cinema in Amiriya, but nowhere else in case we were needed. Half-way through the film the call came, everyone back to camp. Shortly before getting back we saw the gun flashes and then the sound of the Alamein barrage. We knew we were in for it.

To the ammo dump to load – I had 25-pounder – and then we set out in the dark to take it to the guns. No lights to show where any other wagon was; you kept station by the gun flash illuminations. The sound of the guns was terrific. A Redcap [Military Policeman] stopped us and the Sergeant told him our load and unit. He told us to follow a white tape that led us to the guns, where we unloaded and got the hell out of it as soon as we could. The din, the smell and the shrapnel were horrific.

We did this run every night for a week, and our daytime runs as well. We didn't look forward to it, but luckily we never had a casualty.

We loaded one morning and were told to report to El Alamein railway station. This was a bus shelter type of building at the side of the single rail line. We were split up and, according to our loads, sent to various units waiting in the area. I had 2000 gallons of petrol on board, and was sent to an armoured car unit. Later in the day we were told that within, the next forty-eight hours the German line would be broken and that we would pour through the gap and take Fuka airfield.

That night it rained, and all the following day too. By the evening it was realized that the majority of vehicles were only rear wheel drive, and couldn't move in the powdery sand that had turned to slithery mud, so the chase was called off. We were all very glad we hadn't been forced to drive 2000 gallons of petrol or 12 tons of ammo through the fighting that we would have encountered.

On the day the Battle of El Alamein finished we had been stood down unable to move, so we went forward to the positions to see what it was like.

It was beyond description, and to make it all the more poignant a piper was playing a lament on the pipes. It was a cross between a charnel house and a burning scrap yard, with hundreds of dead – some burning, some so maggot-ridden that at first you thought they were alive, the bodies moved that much.

The memory of that time with all the dead lying about, and the burial parties going about their duties, affected me greatly. I still have that feeling now. From where I stand today it was never worth it, but of course that is after it all, which is always another story. The only consolation that I have is that all this was in the Desert with no civilians involved apart from the odd Bedouin, and very few of them.

We eventually reached El Daba two days later, and were given the job of clearing through Italian dugouts. We only found dead ones, but found plenty of livestock – they were all flea-ridden, and we all had to have our uniforms, blanket and kit fumigated. At the petrol depot at El Daba I found a stock of new, unused jerricans. They were rubberized inside, so I thought – water! I took twenty-five of them. At 5 gallons a can that meant 125 gallons of water to drink!

The pursuit was on; from dawn to dark we were on the road, seven days a week. We often caught up with the enemy rearguards, and regularly transported the German prisoners on our return journey. German prisoners were always guarded, unlike the majority of the Italians.

The coast road, the only one, melted in the sun and was sticky. Mostly we used tracks. Sometimes, as at Sollum, these were rocky; in other places firm sand, and at others soft sand that shifted and blew in clouds. You had to really drive in that kind of circumstance, reading the surface and being in the right gear for the conditions. Otherwise you were stuck and holding up the column, which made it more open to air attack than when it was moving. Of course we had the usual few who on a regular basis turned their wagons over and got stuck. They were mostly moved off driving, to cookhouse duties and so on.

We made camps at Mersa Matruh and one or two more places, but never stayed. We moved up all the time. During this part of the campaign we never had tents. It was OK when the wagons were empty, but to sleep on top of a load of petrol or ammo continuously was quite hair-raising.

One night we were to rendezvous at Buq Buq, but a sister company – 286 Company – were leaguered there, so it was decided we'd move on 20 miles or so, and in doing so we'd get up to the bottleneck of the Halfaya and Sollum Passes in front of 286. When we made the stop we were told no hot food because of air attack, but as we looked across the Desert we could see dozens of little brew can fires, so we prepared to do the same. But before most of us could, we heard aircraft, then bombs, and all the little fires snuffed out as if by a switch. We found out in the morning that 286 had copped it. Three wagons and crews burned to hell. We were more circumspect with regard to fires after that.

The ascent of Sollum Pass was very nerve-racking – 180° turns every few hundred yards, and the edges of the cliff had been blown so we had to shunt three times to get round them. Only a few inches from the edge, and nothing to stop you going over except by keeping your nerve. But we reached the top OK, and headed for Fort Capuzzo [just over the border into Libya].

At this point the Military Police stopped us and rerouted half the convoy via the Trigh Capuzzo [the track which paralleled the coast road and led to El Adem, level with Tobruk]; this was to reduce congestion on the coast road. We took the track and we rolled on, but unfortunately our rear torque rod came adrift so we stopped to fix it.

Some of the drivers and a Corporal had an argument over whether we should stop and make camp or carry on in the dark. The Corp said carry on, but after an hour we had to stop anyway as we couldn't see a thing.

We got to El Adem the following morning at ten thirty. The

road convoy hadn't arrived, so we found the position of the Field Maintenance Centre and offloaded, and waited for them.

Field Maintenance Centres were the supply hubs from which the front-line divisions drew their daily essentials. While the distance from front line to FMC was kept constant – usually no more than 45 miles – to ensure an uninterrupted stream of supply forward to the front-line troops, the distances covered by the units like Jim's in their efforts to keep each FMC fully stocked rose enormously as the Army advanced.

It turned out they had turned off the road in the dark right into the middle of a minefield, and didn't find out till it was daylight. A Corporal noticed a round tin with a lump on top next to where he had slept. On looking around he could see a lot more! It was decided that as they had got in without exploding any they could safely reverse out in the same tracks.

Most of the trucks got out, but one driver veered a little, turned the front wheels to correct it and passed over a mine, which promptly exploded. The driver was unhurt, though shocked, but Corporal George Whitehead received severe wounds. He was taken to a CCS [Casualty Clearing Station] and I never saw him again until we got back to England. One other wagon ran over another mine, so they had to wait for the Royal Engineers to come and clear a path through the minefield.

With all this we were falling behind the advance, and we also had a few air attacks, hoping to disrupt the supply lines. They were more of a nuisance than anything. They frightened us a bit, but no damage.

Did you get any warning of air attack?

When you're in the field the only warning is your own sight and hearing. When attacked from the rear you hear nothing until it happens. In the Desert you usually had an arc of some 320°, and your rear view mirror covered the other 40°. On the road it's very much a matter of chance. Depending on how quick you are to bail out and run for a hole or any type of cover. Nil in the open desert, of course; again pure chance.

In open desert we usually travelled in oblique line astern – that way we could see the whole of the convoy at all times, even though each truck was 400 yards apart. This was to make air attack diffi-cult and not worthwhile, and I think it worked very well. As I say, we only had isolated attacks, and no casualties. But this was only possible in open desert. Any defile or escarpment channelled all traffic and slowed you down. These were the points we dreaded, because they were the ones Jerry bombed and strafed.

As our lines of communication lengthened our runs became almost frantic to get food, petrol and ammo up to where it was needed. From Tobruk [the first useful port in Libya] the run was on to Benghazi [another 306 miles further west, or 681 miles from El Alamein]. The pass on the coast road at Derna was blown, so all movement was by way of the Martuba track, which bypassed Derna. This 'road' was made of lumps of rock in the soft sand, and turned out to be a nightmare for drivers. The trucks were heavily loaded, and rattled and rolled like mad. There was never any question of falling asleep at the wheel! It was all you could do to keep the truck under control, and we dreaded the return journey empty.

Once we hit the road again we speeded up. I was resting, having driven the track. Suddenly there was a bounce, a hell of a crack, and my mate tried to brake but when he hit the pedal it was too late – we had no brakes and no drive and we were freewheeling down towards the Barce Pass.

The speed was dropping off, and my co-driver said, 'Shall we bail out?' I said I'd get the chock and try to drop it under the leading wheel of the rear bogie and see if we stopped. I hooked the chain on to a side hook, lifted the chock and hung out from the side of the wagon and dropped the chock under the wheel. The initial slide of the chock under the wheel slowed us a little, then the hook holding the chain ripped off and the chock bounced away. I jumped off, ran back as the truck slowed down and dropped the chock under the wheels again. The driver ran off the road, and the sand stopped the truck 100 yards from the drop of the pass.

We inspected the damage. The connecting drive shaft between the two axles had broken, and smashed the brake air line junction box. This meant we had no drive and no brakes.

One of our wagons stopped to see if he could help. We discussed ways and means, but there was no way we could move. Then another wagon turned up, so we decided that they would give us a suspended tow. We were completely in their hands going down the pass, one towing and the other braking us. We considered we did a good job, and our truck was left on the side at the bottom of the pass whilst the other two wagons delivered their loads and promised to send a truck to offload us, plus the company break-down truck.

We were towed to our workshops, and the following morning

we were patched up and ready for the road again. At six o'clock in the evening we set off back to Tobruk for another load. At the scene of our accident we stopped to see if we could see anything that caused it. All we found was a fold in the road caused by the sun melting it. We came to the conclusion that, as our springs were 'soft', when the wheels were going over it the load flattened the springs and the transmission shaft hit the top of the drive box; the flailing shaft removed the air brake junction box. We took note of the position and resolved to be more careful the return journey.

We called at a water point on the road to Tobruk, and I filled the twenty-five 5-gallon jerricans with water. On reaching the dumps at Tobruk we started loading. The unit cook of the dump asked us if we had any clean water, as the wells at Tobruk had been salinated by the Germans, so I let them have ten cans. They put it in their water truck and gave me a good quantity of tea, sugar and evaporated milk in exchange.

That night we camped at El Adem above Tobruk, and watched an air raid develop on the port. We were glad to have got out before dark.

We set off down the Martuba track with more than a little trepidation. By midday we arrived at the water point and refilled our cans, then off to the night stop, where we camped and slept the night. The following morning we set off for Benghazi again and the fold in the road. We stopped and helped a wagon having trouble with water in the diesel. That cost us two hours. I took over the wheel and carried on.

I asked my co-driver if we were near the fold in the road and he said we should be near to it by now. Another hour and we'd still not seen it, so I decided we had passed it. After about ten minutes more I knew we hadn't, as we hit it with the front wheels. I stood on the brakes and dipped the clutch, and we skidded to a halt.

I crept underneath. I found the transmission shaft broken, but by dipping the clutch I had saved the brakes. This time we were towed to the top of the pass and came down just on the brakes. They were red hot by the time we picked the tow up at the bottom.

Once ships were into Tobruk we travelled that road far too often. It was a nightmare of a job.

We kept up the advance and left Benghazi for the 'Marble Arch' [a grandiose arch built by Mussolini on the spot marking the frontier settled in the fourth century BC between the Greek colony of Cyrenaica to the east and the Carthaginian Empire to the west] and Nofilia. We left by way of the Desert, and were to follow the track simply known as 'A' track as far as 'O' cross-track, and then on to El Agheila. My mate was at the wheel and I dozed for a while.

On waking up I looked around for the rest of our trucks and all I could see was sand and Desert. I asked if we had crossed to 'O' track yet, and he said he didn't know! I climbed out on the roof to get a look round. Nothing in sight. No tracks in the sand, nothing.

I climbed back in and told him to stop. I told him to turn round, and we would find where the wagons had turned off.

He stalled the engine, and we had no starter motor as we were waiting for a replacement.

We tried to rig a rope on the starting handle, to no avail. I told him to put a brew on while I went to the top of a sand dune to get a good look round. Nothing whatever. I stayed there for twenty minutes, and I saw a dust cloud about 5 miles away. I took my steel mirror out of my pocket and flashed away like mad – I just hoped someone would see it.

After about five minutes I saw a buggy emerge from the dust cloud and head over towards us. It took another twenty minutes before the 15-cwt came up to us. He wanted to know what had happened, but he said he couldn't tow start us with his buggy, and at first would not agree to fetching one of the bigger trucks to start us. After a lot of argument he eventually agreed to go and fetch a heavy truck to start us. We delayed him by over two hours. We were eventually started, and I thanked the officer very much for our rescue. I took over the wheel and set off back looking for the cross-track. Two hours' hard driving brought us to the sign – a piece of tin nailed to a board and stuck in a barrel of sand. I turned left into the track and after an hour driving had not caught up with our section. It was fading light by this time, and then I saw about twenty wagons ahead, but there was something odd about the disposition of them. I stopped about a quarter of a mile from them and walked over to them.

They were our wagons, but all were stuck in 'salt pan'. I talked with them and tried to find a path through. I told them where to stand as markers, and went back to our truck. I told my co-driver the situation and said I was going to make a run through. There was a chance we wouldn't make it, but at least we would all be stuck together! I turned the wagon round and went back half a mile. I lined up on the line of men, then I let her rip. As we approached the line I changed down a gear, engine flat out, and as the engine laboured I slipped the booster gear in and we ploughed through to safe sand.

We then connected all our tow ropes and hauled two more on to safe ground, then connected all the others to us, and we hauled out like a train. We camped for the night a few miles on, and in the morning set off for the 'Marble Arch'.

I reported to our officer and immediately asked to be moved from the wagon and co-driver. I was given a wagon on my own; there were no spare drivers at this stage. Two had deserted at Alamein, George Whitehead was wounded, and of course illness depleted us still further. You see, if you can't trust your co-driver you may as well not have one. One had to rely on oneself.

But you had had special training for the Desert?

No, we never had any training on surviving in the Desert; we were just expected to keep together and to support one another. That was the reason I reacted to the failure of my co-driver to keep the convoy in sight. Had I not attracted the attention of the other convoy I hate to think of the consequences. We had the 125 gallons of water, and food that could have lasted two months, but the limiting factor would have been carrying them on the walk back. Lucky for us it wasn't required.

It was really easy to get lost in the Desert. There are few landmarks, and sand dunes can blow away, and cover tracks and roads alike, so it is purely up to the individual to know what's happening at all times. We had no maps, and little knowledge of the stars. We knew of course that to the west was the front and east back to the Delta. There was no respect for anyone who let you down or put you to more risk than the normal risks of war – they were enough!

There are one or two special hazards that come to mind. One was the small tornado, or as we called it, the 'twister'; and the other the sandstorm. It was possible to see the twister develop from a spiral of sand and wind, and watch its progress from a small to a large one. You could never tell which direction it would take, and if you were unfortunate and its path crossed yours, the breath was sucked out of you and the temperature at the centre was cold as ice, even when everywhere else was at 100–120° Fahrenheit.

The sandstorm is far worse. You can't see, and to breathe is akin to choking. Every time your teeth meet there is grinding sand between them. Your eyes became sore and caked with sand. One of the most horrible things to experience. The Arabs say that five days in one is a good excuse for murder, and they're not joking.

No one could drive in one; visibility was nil, and it was far too dangerous to move.

Anyway, after this episode I managed to get a truck on my own. That meant that I alone was responsible for my own safety and that of the truck. And I made sure it had a starter motor before I took it over!

The main ports on this coast were few, and of course the Axis Army did a good job of blocking the harbour entrances, so denying us the use of the ports on a workable basis. The Royal Engineers worked desperately to extend the railway on to Tobruk from El Alamein, which took a lot of time and labour. Tobruk was only a small harbour, but it took a month's work to make it fully operational, and Benghazi took a little longer. This was the main reason for the Germans getting away so easily. Had we had a port, the Desert war would have been finished six months earlier. Monty was very pleased with our efforts over such long distances, and paid tribute to them in his papers.

Returning to Benghazi from Nofilia we were sent to Tobruk for petrol. Very little was able to be shipped to Benghazi, and the front was now at Buerat on the Gulf of Sirte. We did a five-day turn-around over the dreadful Martuba track and, although we didn't know it at the time, for us this convoy marked the end of going back to Tobruk. This was January 1943.

We kept our loads of petrol on board and were told to prepare to go up to the Buerat area. On the way back to Benghazi we passed through a small Arab settlement, and I could only recognize the village and not the Desert – it was now green and covered with flowers, and the scent was beautiful. Quite a bonus in such a landscape!

When we arrived at Buerat we were held for a day before we could unload. We were allowed to go to the sea, only a few hundred yards away, and what a surprise it was. The sand was nearly as white as snow, and when we walked into the shallows the water was too hot to bear. We decided to try a dash to the deeper water, and this proved to be all right. We learned not to linger in the shallows or stand barefoot on the sand.

One more run to Benghazi, and then off for the run to Tripoli [entered by the still advancing front-line troops on 23rd January] by way of the coast road through Misurata, Zliten and Homs and then round via Tarhuna. We camped on the outskirts of Tripoli, then took petrol and bombs for the Air Force to Zuara, where we spent some time helping the Royal Engineers make a new airstrip. Our job was fetching barrels of sea water to pour on the runway whilst the REs rolled it. They had picked a bad spot – it was salt pan, and every morning on inspection there were holes in the runway. These had to be filled, watered and rolled before any aircraft could use it.

At about this time General Leclerc of the Free French joined us, trekking from Chad across the Sahara. A nasty accident occurred with the French near Zauia, 30 miles beyond Tripoli. One of their heavy trucks ran into the back of a signals van. The petrol tank exploded and eight men in the van were burned to death. We could do nothing for them – the only things we had were shovels and sand, and we couldn't get close enough to help . . .

The enemy had now abandoned Libya to the Eighth Army, and retreated into Tunisia to make a stand on the pre-war defences of the Mareth Line.

When on convoy we rarely refuelled. We had two diesel tanks of 75-gallon capacity, which contained enough for 1500 miles. Only if diverted did we have to take on fuel, and I can only remember one such incident. This was at Mareth. The New Zealanders were sent on an outflanking op to the left of the main attack. They appeared to be in great difficulty. It was decided to pull them back, and as we had just unloaded at Mareth we were detailed to go. We topped up with diesel and set off accompanied by three armoured cars, but after about 75 miles of travel the escort halted. They told us that a radio message had come in to say that the New Zealanders had made it and joined up with the main thrust, and we should return.

Returning up the pass at Medenine I had another mishap. Turning into the last corner I found the steering failed to turn the front wheels, and my wagon went straight on for the edge of the cliff. I just managed to stop in time. I reversed a few feet back from the edge and lifted the bonnet to find out what had gone wrong. I found that the steering column had stripped out of the box. I replaced it, but knew that it wouldn't hold – it came out at the slightest turn. I was now blocking the pass, of course, so had to find a way to get to the top. After a few minutes I asked one of the spare drivers to kick the front wheels as I shunted a few feet back and a few feet forwards until I had sufficient lock on to get round. It took a good thirty minutes to get to the top, and off the road. We were told to stay there until the recovery wagon, which was two days' travel away, got to us.

The cooks' wagon had as usual gone ahead, so no food or drink was left for us. We had a sealed emergency pack, but we were told not to open that for two days. I had, however, made provision for such. I had my 125 gallons of water, a case of tomatoes, a case of peas, one of German black pudding; all from the German dump at El Daba. Also I had three dozen cans of bully, two dozen cans of peaches, a tin of hard tack biscuits, one dozen evaporated milk, tea, sugar and cocoa. So you see I was in no danger from thirst or hunger! Though we only had a few cigarettes, and they were Vs as well [a brand universally recalled with distaste].

We had no radio, and had to while away the days and nights as best we could. The spare driver, named Ray, had stayed with me. We got on quite well. It would have been awful with my previous co-drivers! I had acquired a set of periscope binoculars from an Italian dugout, so we scanned the Desert and over towards the coast. Too far to go for a swim.

We were stuck there for four nights and five days. Passing convoys stopped to see if we were OK, and the recovery wagon arrived after midday on the fifth day. We winched the front of the wagon up, put on a stabilizer bar, and were towed to some workshops at Ben Gardane. The steering was reassembled and welded to get us back on the road again. At Tripoli base there was no replacement, so two L pieces were added on to strengthen it.

By this time the toll of the miles was showing on the wagons. Tyres in particular got very short. Some had new tyres fitted only to be blown out after a few miles. Tyre specialists were flown out from Dunlop, and a policy of bleeding the tyres every hour was adopted. I didn't bleed *my* tyres – I made believe that I did for a while, and made no effort at all after a week or so, and of course I was caught out by our officer. I used to watch him through my binoculars. This particular day he watched me through his! He came back down the line of trucks, confiscated my binoculars and gave me a good roasting. I justified my behaviour by telling him to inspect my '406' – the vehicle's log-book, which recorded everything done and replaced – and he would find that my wagon was the only one in the platoon which hadn't had any new tyres. But this was no excuse for disobedience of orders.

As it turned out, the tyre deflation and inflation only increased the incidence of blow-outs to greater proportions than before and resulted in a growing number of stranded vehicles, so bleeding was stopped again. So much for 'experts'.

Did the driver have to keep the '406' up to date himself?

No, the '406' was written and signed by the workshop people, and countersigned by the driver to say that all work where possible was completed. Incidentally, if poor maintenance was the cause the driver was downgraded or removed. Every driver carried out maintenance every night and morning. The Desert was no place for mistakes. The daily essential maintenance jobs were topping up axles, gearbox, engine, and of course checking the air filter; and draining water from the fuel filters and air pressure tanks every evening when halted. It could be very cold at night, and ice was often formed on exposed water or water in containers – hence the draining.

We then went on to Wadi Akarit where quite a battle developed – we watched it from about 2 miles while we were making an advanced bomb dump for the RAF's fighter-bombers. We could see fighting but not in detail, though it was very apparent when we went through a few days later.

After that on to Sfax, Sousse, Enfidaville and Hammamet. Some of the remains we came to, like Leptis Minor [between Sfax and Sousse. Close by lies the site of Julius Caesar's victory at Thapsus in 46 BC], were very interesting, but we had little time to appreciate the history or beauty of the remains.

Following the surrender at Cap Bon, our runs to Tunisia ceased. Tripoli docks were now working, and we worked the docks to the dumps for the rest of 1943, loading the invasion craft for Pantelleria, Sicily and Italy.

7

TANKS

The Royal Armoured Corps was formed in April 1939, drawing together for the first time the Army's tank specialists, the Royal Tank Regiment, and the increasing number of Cavalry and Yeomanry regiments now joining them in the mechanized role.

From the start this was something of a shotgun marriage, especially since many of the cavalrymen had chosen to express their distaste for the whole mechanization process.

Cavalry (Regular) and Yeomanry (Territorial) 'regiments' each fielded a single battalion-sized unit, whereas the RTR was a large, multi-battalion regiment encompassing both Regulars and Territorials.

By the outbreak of war the RTR had expanded to twenty battalions (eight of Regulars, twelve of Territorials) and the balance stood at eighteen Cavalry and sixteen Yeomanry regiments armoured, to four Cavalry and seventeen Yeomanry regiments still horsed.

As the conversion programme progressed, of course, the number of horsed units continued to dwindle, until eventually all of them had been drawn into the RAC or had been retrained for other roles. The last two, the Cheshire Yeomanry and the Yorkshire Dragoons, finally relinquished their horses in February 1942.

Mel Lowry joined the Royal Tank Regiment while these events were under way, though his path to the RAC was a rather unconventional one.

> When the war began I registered as a conscientious objector. This meant I had to go before a tribunal, at which I got unconditional exemption, and so instead of the Army I joined the Friends Ambulance Unit.
>
> This had been started in the First World War, for conscientious objectors – not an official Quaker body, but it was set up by members of the Society of Friends, which gave it its name. They'd mostly worked in hospital trains and in military hospitals.

In the Second World War they did an enormous number of jobs, but just as when you join the Army everyone has to do infantry training, in the FAU everyone had to do hospital training. So I was sent to Dover Hospital for mine. I remember it took about eight hours to get to Dover from London. The reason for this was that there was an air raid on at the time, and the train kept stopping in cuttings – they could see flashes round about, and when everything seemed quiet they moved on. Eventually I arrived at Dover station very much later than I was expected, and of course there was nobody there. I eventually made my way out to the hospital, which was on the outskirts of town. Being in Dover in those days was quite hairy, because we used to get both bombed and shelled – we were just in gun range from the other side of the Channel. I remember the very first time I was in the operating theatre was to see an amputation – an arm amputation. A chap going home from work on a motor bike had a shell burst close to him, and he was badly wounded. In fact he died – he had other injuries as well as the arm.

This was a civilian?

Yes, a civilian. And I had to help lay him out. I'd never even seen a dead body at that time, of course.

We had a training camp at a place called Buckhurst Hill on the edge of Epping Forest, and we had to take our First Aid and Home Nursing Certificates there. We were also on standby for the ARP organization, so that we could be called in if need be. I remember lying in bed fully dressed while there was an air raid on, and I remember hearing a stick of bombs coming down – each one closer than the last. I thought, How many more? But we weren't actually called out, so they must have managed all right. After that, as I'd had some experience with motor vehicles, I became a mechanic in effect – because they had their own fleet of vehicles. We were moved into the students' hostel at the London Hospital, since all their medical students had been sent to the countryside somewhere for safety.

Whereabouts in London was this?

London Hospital is in Whitechapel Road; of course, the East End really got the brunt of the bombing, and we were running around most nights, putting out incendiary bombs and fires, and so on.

So how was the FAU actually organized?

We had some chaps who probably spent the whole of the war working in hospitals, just as they had in the First World War. But the FAU worked very much on the basis of seeing a need and saying, 'We can do this,' and other people giving them permission to do it. So you had these very large underground shelters, under large warehouses, in the East End of London. There was one owned by a firm of wholesale grocers with, as I say, an enormous basement, and this was one gigantic air raid shelter. So we did two things — we set up a canteen there, tea and buns; we also used to show 16 mm film. I saw most of the great Eisenstein films there. I don't know how our lot got hold of them, but I saw *Battleship Potemkin* and, oh, quite a lot of others — I remember that one in particular!

Were you directed to different jobs in the FAU?

Well, you tended to volunteer, if you thought it was the sort of thing you could do. One of the very first jobs that they did, before I joined them, was they manned ambulances in Finland. There was a war between Russia and Finland in 1939, which a lot of people have forgotten about. Our chaps just managed to get out, in fact, at more or less the last minute. We had others who were attached to the 'Hadfield Spears' [the Hadfield Spears Hospital Unit] set up by those two ladies* and attached to the Free French forces; we supplied all the men, all the chaps who drove the lorries and put up the tents, and acted as orderlies and so on. They were in the Western Desert, then they later came over to Italy. And then there was the famous China Convoy — they were very largely driving medical necessities over the Burma Road. The reason why they liked our chaps doing it was they knew they wouldn't sell the cargo on the way, and that what set out would also arrive! I volunteered for that but I got turned down. Peculiar vehicles they were driving. Petrol was restricted to the Army in China, so all these lorries ran off gas — I think it was called Producer Gas. Anyway, you'd have this contraption on the back of the lorry. We used to have them over here as well. Usually on a little trailer. And I've also seen them in French North Africa — virtually all the civil transport in French North Africa ran on this stuff, again, petrol being restricted to the military.

What did your FAU medical training consist of?

You were supposed to be able to deal with a casualty. To make him comfortable, and make him capable of being moved. So you learned about splinting and bandaging and pressure points for stopping bleeding and all that sort of thing. You took the St John's

---

* Lady Hadfield and Mrs (later Lady) Spears. The latter was better known in the 1920s and '30s as the novelist Mary Borden, which was her maiden name.

First Aid Certificate. And then you had to do Home Nursing, because that made you useful in a hospital – you even had to learn how to make beds, envelope corners and all that sort of lark. If it was an Army hospital you had to lie to attention when the Matron came round on her rounds – she was a Major.

So what was your first contact with the Army?

Ah, that was when I had to register. I was eighteen then, and of course in my case I registered as a conscientious objector, which meant that instead of being called up you had to go before this tribunal. I went before Judge Wethered. I was living in Paignton, and I had to go to Bristol, to some sort of official building – I can't remember what it was. It was a fairly informal sort of business. He wasn't in wig and gown, he was in civvies. There were about four of them, I think, sitting the other side of the table. It was a bit like an interview really. There was a very big difference in the way in which conscientious objectors were treated in the Second World War as compared with the First. They had a very rough time in the First – the whole concept wasn't recognized. Whereas the chaps who'd stuck it out, they managed to get the idea of conscientious objection recognized, so that by the time of conscription in 1939 they made provision for it.

Was the tribunal interview intimidating?

Well [laughs], you're fairly cocky when you're eighteen, you know. You're quite sure of your ground and your views; it's only when you're older you become more aware of possibilities and alternatives. I was quite prepared to go to jail if necessary. And then, of course, as time went on I gradually came to think, Well, this doesn't really make sense – you can't deal with these people any other way than by going to war with them.

What was the basis of your original objection, then?

Well, like everybody, I suppose, I was brought up as a nominal Christian, but it was rather an intellectual attitude. And still today to me it seems obvious that if you're a Christian then you should be a conscientious objector. It seems to be so laid down – the whole concept of non-violence, and not returning blow for blow, and turning the other cheek . . . the whole concept. I couldn't understand . . . I still can't understand . . . anyone taking the other view. So really my religious faith such as it was evaporated at the same time as I took up the view that it was necessary to go to war.

This was a gradual change over time?

Yes, while I was in the FAU. I don't know how many chaps left the FAU and went into the forces. I mean, I wasn't the only one. But most stayed on. Not all of them were Quakers, of course, but if you were a Quaker then you had this background going right back to the seventeenth century of refusing military service.

I was in the Peace Pledge Union, the PPU, and we had all sorts of ideas about passive resistance and so on. And I gradually realized that passive resistance against people like this is just a load of toffee. I mean, it's true it worked with Gandhi, but he was up against the British in peacetime. The Germans were quite capable of shooting people ad lib. As you know, in Occupied Europe, where there was Resistance activity – if a German soldier got killed they'd shoot ten local people who just happened to be there. You can't deal with people like this that way. You've got to fight them.

Did you discuss this with others in the FAU?

Oh, it was a great place for discussing. Quite a lot of the chaps were graduates, and it was a great place for intellectual conversations. It was almost like going to university in a way.

So how did you make the decision?

Well, I suppose it's the sort of thing . . . The decision comes up in your head, and once it's there you've got to do something about it. So I resigned.

I had to go to the local Labour Exchange, because you carried a special identity card as a conscientious objector, and I had to hand that in and get an ordinary one before I could volunteer! [Laughs.] Being sort of motor-minded, I wanted to go in the Royal Armoured Corps. I had to take an intelligence test, which I passed, and then they sent you off home.

About a month later I got a letter through the post saying report to 60th Training Regiment, Royal Armoured Corps, at Tidworth. So I did my training on Salisbury Plain.

You know, it's amazing. They had six weeks to turn you from a civilian into something that looked like a soldier. And at the end of that you passed out, with a rifle. You had to do arms drill, in a squad of about forty men. And we were like Guardsmen! We were bloody good. I'd no doubt that all the drill Sergeants had been given a real talking to – 'Now don't forget, the chaps that you're going to be dealing with aren't going to be like the chaps you've been dealing with up to now. These ones are civvies. So you've got to break them in gently.' And we had a very good drill Sergeant – Sergeant Hawkins, late of the 7th Hussars. From Bristol. 'You'n gett'n the idear,' he used to say. Of course there was one chap who *never* got the idea. He *always* turned the wrong way – when he said left turn he always turned right. He was left behind to look after the barrack room when the rest of us went for our passing out parade!

That was six weeks, and then you went off on leave. And you came back and started to do your trade training. In tank crews everyone had to have two trades, so I did a bit of gunnery as well as driving.

You did little mini-courses during the six weeks, which helped them sort people out. In fact I did so well in the sort of engineering side of it that I thought, If I'm not careful they're going to make me a vehicle fitter. So I saw my instructor as we came to the end of the course, and I said, 'Look, I don't know whether you've got the idea of me being a vehicle mechanic, because', I said, 'I don't want to be – I want to be a tank driver.' 'Oh,' he said, 'well, if you do there's plenty who don't! I'll have a word with the officer.' [Laughs.] So I got mustered as a Driver/Mech.(AFV) – Driver/Mechanic (Armoured Fighting Vehicle), which was their description of a tank driver.

Was there ever any trouble about you coming to the Army from the Friends Ambulance Unit?

Oh, I suppose some of them might have thought it was a bit odd. Because there was very much this attitude of 'don't volunteer'.

Mel's letters home to his brother and sister-in-law, which he had no idea they were keeping, are full of enthusiasm for his new profession.

It's all lies. [Reading.] 'I certify that this letter refers only to private and personal matters.' It's all full of politics and comments on the tanks!

Such as?

Hm. [Reading.] '. . . the Grant has been boosted a lot in the papers, but I have never heard any man in the RAC have a good word for it. The armour is thin and in most places presents a 90° angle to anything which is fired at it – the best angle for penetration. In addition, it is extremely high compared with British and German tanks.'

Yes, it was just the best of a bad job; I mean, it was the only thing we could get off the Americans at short notice. It had French influence – the Char B, which was a much better tank really because it had much thicker armour, and also had a very good anti-tank gun in the turret as well as the 75 mm in the hull. In fact it was a better tank than anything the Germans had. Really we shouldn't have lost in 1940! [Laughs.] I mean, the Germans had nothing that was anything like as good as the Matilda [at 26½ tons, the heaviest of the British tanks in service in 1940].

So what were you trained on?

After you finished your wheels training you went on to Carden-Loyds, which were little supply carriers, with tracks of course, and with stick steering. That's to get you used to driving a tracked vehicle. And then after you'd been on them for a bit you might get a go on a bren-gun carrier, which was different steering because it was a wheel – the first movement of the wheel bows the track and the second movement of the wheel puts a brake on one side. And then after that you went on the Vickers Light.

These actually were used in action in the Western Desert and in France in 1940. I mean, they were about the size of a large pram. [Laughs.] They had a two- or three-man crew, armament of machine guns. Meadows engine. They were fairly nippy, and quite fun to drive, really, because of that. But you see, the other side had similar sort of kit. I think it was in order to keep the cavalry units happy. There was no future for horses so they were becoming mechanized, and they gave them these things to play with. Anyway, they had to go into action with them in the early part of the war. But you see, all the countries were producing this sort of very light tank, though there were some bigger ones as well.

And then the Valentine [a contemporary of the Matilda]. You couldn't turn the Valentine sharply because of the defects of its suspension. If the ground was at all soft and you tried to turn too sharply, the soil would build up on the track and it would lift the track off the sprocket.

Once qualified he was posted to the 12th Battalion of the Royal Tank Regiment, quartered at Stobs in the Scottish borders. The 12th was equipped with Vauxhall's new 40-ton Churchill, which was destined to replace both the Matilda and the Valentine in front-line service.

We went to Stobs in about June, I think. It was absolutely pouring. I remember they met us with a 3-tonner at Hawick station and we set off into this desolate countryside. We eventually arrived outside a gateway with one miserable little tree about 12 feet high and leaning over at about 45°. That was the only tree anywhere near there! And up on the crest of the hill there was a row of Nissen huts glistening with wet. And a little further down there were a lot of scout cars, sheeted up, and the sheets were flapping in the wind. And there was a poor wretched sentry with a cape – we were issued with a groundsheet which you could turn into a cape. And that was that.

I was sent to 'A' Squadron, 3 Troop, but before we went overseas in the spring of 1943 they decided to form a reserve squadron, and I was sent to that, so I was in 'R' Squadron then.

21st Tank Brigade [to which the 12th RTR belonged] was part of the 4th British Infantry Division which went to French North Africa to join the First Army.

The First Army had been in North Africa since November the previous year, and had spent a miserable winter making little headway against the German and Italian troops cornered in Tunisia. The 4th Division was one of the units sent out to reinforce it, so that it could link up with the Desert veterans of the Eighth Army, and North Africa could finally be cleared.

The 4th was actually an experimental formation known as a mixed division – an infantry division in which one of the three infantry brigades had been replaced by a tank brigade, to give it its own integral armoured support.

We had no idea where we were going. We were given a vague idea that it was going to be hot. We landed in about March, I think – warming up, because I remember we were in shirt-sleeve order.

By train to Greenock – the train went right into the docks – and out of the train and up the gangplank.

What about the vehicles?

They went on another ship. There was a problem there, because one of them broke loose and started to smash its way through the side of the ship, so the ship had to go back – they had to tether the tank first, of course – and then they had to put a great big concrete patch where it had damaged the side of the ship.

It took ages, because we went almost to America – this was to dodge the U-boats and the bombers from the west of France. Eventually, curiously, we went through the Straits of Gibraltar in broad daylight, which I thought an odd thing, because there must have been stacks of German spies in Spain. Anyway, we did.

I remember smelling Algiers, this exotic, spicy smell, before we saw it. And then you saw it – all these glittering white buildings. We pulled in at the docks, and I saw the most ragged men I'd ever seen in my life – these were the Algerian dockers. Arabs, you see. Their clothes were not only patched, but they had patches on patches! A few months later they were all in battledress, of course. [Laughs.] A certain amount of slippage always seems to occur with Army stores, the people who handle them.

Was this your first time abroad?

First time abroad [nodding]. That was true of most people. Only the comparatively wealthy went abroad.

We landed at Algiers docks and then we went to a place called La Perouse, which was on the opposite side of the bay. I remember there was a French cadet unit there – we used to see them marching about the town. That was the first time I ever spoke French. I was amazed – I went to this shop and asked for a packet of dates in French. And to my amazement I got a packet of dates! You know, you can't really believe that it's a language, and if you speak it people will actually understand you! They used to have marvellous oranges, too. Chap used to come round on a donkey with panniers on each side.

We were in tents. Saw a couple of air raids on Algiers – that was quite spectacular, because there was a tremendous light anti-aircraft barrage, like a monumental firework display. I saw a couple of German bombers hit. We were all right over on our side.

Then the ship which had had to go back to be patched up, that arrived at Bone, which was the next port up the coast. Because Algiers was as far as the convoys went. After that it was too dangerous. Ships after that sneaked up one at a time, at night, close to the coast. So our ship got into Bone and so the drivers were sent along to help unload.

Funny feeling, down in the hold of a ship. You drove the tank underneath, and the hoist came down. And 40 tons of Churchill went up through this hole – if that thing broke away it would go straight through the bottom! We got them all out. But either on that ship or on another one, the derrick gave way before they'd unloaded it. So they sent a mobile crane up – you know, a water-borne crane; but I think before it arrived they managed to repair the derrick. Anyway, we got all the tanks off sooner or later.

And then the unit went into action. 'A' Squadron took quite a hammering. In fact its baptism of fire was the worst action it was ever in. Partly, I suppose, due to lack of experience, because all the training in the world doesn't make up for experience in warfare. And then of course they needed tanks, and they needed crews, so 'R' Squadron did its job, which was to bring up the reserve tanks. I remember going up towards 'A' Squadron along this road, with just myself and a wireless operator in the tank, and away up ahead of us we could see 25-pounder bursts, these flashes of light – this was at night, of course. And every now and again we would stop, to see how close we were. Because the last thing we wanted to do was barge into the German lines and have somebody with a coal scuttle helmet say, 'For you ze war iss ofer.' [Laughs.] So anyway, eventually somebody jumped out in the road and flashed a torch, and we had arrived. We drove the tank in.

I was then told that I was going to take the tank over as a driver – I was back in 3 Troop, 'A' Squadron. Which I stayed in right to the end of the war.

A day or two later we went into action, and after the experience a few days before I thought it was going to be my last day on earth. It was a bit of an anticlimax really, because our squadron was held in reserve. We did this advance over a bare hill – there's not much grass in French North Africa, the hillsides are covered with vegetation but it's all little sort of spiky stuff. And peppermint. The smell of peppermint always makes me think of North Africa. Because the tanks would crush it, and you'd get the smell of peppermint coming through the hatch.

And then we came to a stop. I remember there was some tall grass, and the infantry had done an attack earlier. Some of them had been hit, and there were wounded lying there in the grass. And they were waving their rifles, because they were obviously terrified they were going to get run over. It must be pretty unpleasant being unable to move and to hear the sound of tanks . . . So we avoided them, and then we were told to stop. And just behind my tank was a dead soldier. Dead British infantry soldier with no top to him. From about here [indicates shoulder height] he'd disappeared. And I'd gone over him, as well. Once we were able to dismount, because first of all of course you've got to stay in the tank, I found this chap. And some way further on I found a German 37 mm anti-tank gun. And that's what had killed this chap. He was a bren-gunner, because we found the remains of his bren-gun. The crew were dead, lying in a slit trench by the gun; two German soldiers. That was the first I'd seen of casualties, either ours or the enemy's. In fact, if you're a fighting soldier you don't see a lot of casualties, because your bit of the front is so narrow that what's going on is much more apparent to the people who come along behind. So there we stuck, and then eventually we moved on. It's difficult to remember in detail. I remember a breakthrough had been achieved, because we saw a whole infantry division, Indian infantry division, go through with all their vehicles – lorries and 25-pounders and Quads [Morris artillery tractors], and bren-gun carriers of course.

We had to go up the Cap Bon peninsula, which was the bit that stuck out near Tunis; this was where the Germans had retreated to. And of course off the coast was the British Navy, so there wasn't going to be any Dunkirk for them.

Because they wanted to keep them on the move we had to do this at night. I remember going through a village, I think it was called Soliman, and I took the corner off a building. You don't feel it, you know. You can do tremendous damage with a 40-ton Churchill without knowing a thing about it. You see, you've got an armoured box that sticks out each side, called the louvre, which covers the inlet to the radiators. I'd caught it with the louvre, and a little way down the road I happened to glance down at the temperature gauges and I saw one of them was going right up into the red. I said to the tank commander – because you've got earphones on, and a microphone – 'Can you see anything on the left-hand louvre?' I said. 'The left-hand bank of the engine's overheating.' 'Ooh lord, yes,' he said, 'it's covered with plaster and stones . . . Hang on, I'll shift it.' So that was from the building.

And so it gradually got daylight, and we kept pushing on. They wouldn't let us use the road, because that was kept for the infantry, so we went cross country. And it was *very* dusty. And then we started seeing complete German and Italian infantry battalions, with all their kit, marching in with white flags. There was just nowhere for them to go. We eventually ended up somewhere up near the end – and then we turned round and came back again. I have never been so tired in my life. I don't know how many hours we'd been driving, up and back, but I remember climbing out of the tank and just lying on the ground, absolutely on my chin strap. Which was an expression we used to use – it's bad enough being on your knees, but if you're *really* tired [laughs] you're 'on your chin strap'.

So you didn't get much of a chance to savour your victory?
No, we just had to drive back again.
Had your particular tank actually fired at anything?
No, we hadn't at that time.

Having finally triumphed in Africa the next step was to invade the island of Sicily. But this was to be handled by the Eighth Army, and the First Army's tanks found they had no role to play.

We pulled back out of Tunis and into Algeria, to about 30 miles inland from Bone. And we stuck there. And stuck there. And stuck there. We did some training, and then petrol was short so we weren't allowed to do any more. We began to think the little flag with '12th Royal Tank Regiment' on it had dropped off the map! We made ourselves more and more comfortable. We stole truckloads of steel [used by the RAF for temporary runways], which appeared in the camp, under the tents and so on. After a bit, unfortunately, the Air Force got to hear about it and we had to pull it all up and take it back. [Laughs.]

Another thing that appeared was beds. Chaps started making beds, getting all the bits of wood and making them instead of sleeping on their groundsheets on the floor. The beds gradually got better, so whenever a chap made a better bed he threw his old one out, and as I'm rather idle, I used to get the old one.

When we first went in there the place was full of scorpions, but every scorpion we saw we killed. Trouble with scorpions is they get in places . . . like your boots. You never put your boots on without banging them out. I've never found a scorpion in my boots, but it's the sort of place they would go. On the other hand, I've never unrolled a tent which had been rolled up for any length of time *without* finding a scorpion in it. So we always had to be careful. They're not fatal, but it's quite a nasty sting.

So, as I say, we stayed there for some time. And then the winter of '43 – North African winters are nasty. They're cold and wet and muddy. In fact it was so unpleasant that we actually got a rum ration, and getting a rum ration in the Army means you're practically at death's door! It's not handed out lightly. But most chaps didn't bother to go and collect it.

Then we went to Italy. Landed at Naples. I remember we landed on to the side of a ship – there was a ship lying on its side in the dock. Because we had bombed Naples docks, and the Germans had sabotaged them before they pulled out, so it was a real mess. We went to a place just outside of Naples, temporarily. And this is where we came in contact with the appalling poverty of southern Italy – especially during the war, I imagine. We used to collect our food in our mess tins, and then go into the mess tent and eat it; and if there was anything left over it used to go into a swill bin, then we washed our mess tins out. And we were getting intercepted by women and children between the mess tent and the swill bin. And chaps started cutting their rations down so as to leave more, for the people.

A lot of the chaps in my unit were from the building trade – you see, this was one of the trades which virtually disappeared during the war. I mean, there were chaps doing repairs on buildings, there were chaps doing heavy rescue – tunnelling under collapsed buildings to get people out, that sort of thing – but there were a lot of chaps from the building trade who were put in the Army. Our Troop Sergeant, Johnny Hornby – he was a plasterer from Manchester. He was a very good Troop Sergeant. And there were other chaps too, from that sort of background.

Were they all conscripts?

We were a mixed lot. Some were conscripts, some were volunteers. And some, of course, were Reservists. My tank commander, Corporal Wilby, he was an old sweat. He'd been in the 7th Hussars, he'd been in India. Come back on the Reserve and then he was called up. I suppose he'd have been round about thirty. He looked older, but that was due to dissipation. India and booze. He was all right, but he wouldn't do a *thing* unless he got a direct order. You know, he wouldn't use his initiative – he was very much a Regular soldier.

I remember one occasion when we'd crossed a canal – an armoured 'dozer had bulldozed earth into the canal so that we could cross over. And then they went out on to an embankment, and they found the embankment had been blown – so there was a whole squadron strung out along an embankment, a lovely target. And so it was panic stations, and about turn. We were the first tank back over the canal. Second tank, the Troop Officer's tank, got stuck. I heard about this, because everything is coming in through your earphones. So I said to Wilby, 'Look, we'd better go back and pull him out.' 'Hang on,' he said, 'we'll wait till we're told.' So of course next thing the Troop Officer: 'Come back and pull us out, Corp. Wilby.' By then, of course, we were under heavy fire. I remember the Troop Officer's wireless operator got out to hook up the tow rope. We always used to carry a tow rope, all connected up ready, so that we'd waste as little time as possible. And I remember the ground was shaking with the gunfire. It wouldn't come out at first, so I let the tank run forward until the rope was slack, and then went back as fast as I could – the rope came up like a bow string, and plucked him out. Got him back up, and the rest of the squadron followed.

Did you lose many vehicles through accidents and mechanical failure?

A few, Shermans in particular – because we were re-equipped with Shermans temporarily. I turned one of those completely over once.

The Sherman was a horrible tank, very joggly. So your head tends to bump on the sides of the hatch – when you're driving a Sherman not in action you drive with your head out the hatch. They were supplied with crash hats, so I used to wear one. Whereas in the Churchill I just used to drive in my beret with my earphones over the top. In the Churchill you're completely inside, looking out through a driver's hatch. The earlier ones you could open everything – you had a square about 9 inches by 6 inches – and wear goggles. Then the next stage was you could bring in a block of glass, which was about 5 inches thick, I suppose. Armour-plated glass. Then there was armour you could close over that, and you drove using two periscopes. On the Sherman, as I say, if you weren't in action you drove with your head out the top. But you had to go down, and close your hatch, if you went into action, otherwise the turret would foul the hatch when it traversed. I always went into action opened up on a Churchill, unless our gun was firing, in which case I had to close down because of muzzle blast.

In the Sherman you adjusted the height of your seat?

Yes, it was spring-loaded. You had a little catch that you released, and you slid down until you got the right height. So the sticks – you steered with sticks on a Sherman – had to be long enough so you could drive opened up. So when you were closed down they were up *here*! And then you had a biggish periscope in the hatch, when you closed it.

How did this differ from the Churchill?

The Churchill had a bar with a handgrip each side, and you turned the bar that way to go to the right and that way to go to the left. The Churchill was a much more sophisticated tank – the clutch and the steering were both air-assisted. On the Sherman nothing was assisted! It was hard work, driving a Sherman. They were a cheapo. They were reliable, I'll give them that, but there wasn't much else in their favour. Of course they were pleased to get them in the Western Desert because they were that much better than anything they'd had before. Because they had a lot of funny old kit out there, in the early days of the war, when they were fighting the Italians.

In the Sherman you had an escape hatch in the floor for the driver and co-driver, behind the co-driver's seat. As I say, I had to use that once, because I turned the tank upside down. My hatches couldn't open, though the turret crew managed to creep out through the little triangular space between the top of the turret, the hatch and the ground.

What caused the accident?

Well, we were under fire so I was closed up, and we were told to pull back. We were on a slope, and diagonally across this slope there was a path, which I couldn't see. The commander had his head in because we were being shelled, so he didn't see it either. So one track went down on to this slope, and over she went, like a hippo. Of course you have everything to hand when you're in action, like the ammunition. So all the ammunition racks emptied, and there were machine gun belts all over the place, and next minute something liquid was cascading over me, which I thought at first was petrol but turned out to be the acid from the batteries. Because they're underneath the turret floor. Next day my trousers fell to pieces! My skin stung a bit, and it was a bit pink, but battery acid isn't all that strong. I'm glad I didn't get any in my eyes, though – that would have been nasty.

This was in Italy?

Italy, yes. We were very glad to get into the action – we were feeling a bit fed up with being stuck in Algeria, so we were well pleased.

During its winter in Algeria the 21st Tank Brigade had been removed from the 4th Division, so that the latter could return to being a normal infantry division. The mixed division concept had not turned out as well as expected, largely because the lack of a third infantry brigade had been sorely felt in the kind of fighting experienced in mountainous Tunisia, and now being experienced in equally mountainous Italy.

Italy's not a place you would think of as good tank country.

No, it isn't. In fact when they captured maps they found that part of the area that we were operating in was marked as not suitable for tanks by the Germans. The Germans had far fewer tanks than we did, and the Luftwaffe hardly existed. I saw one raid on Naples – this is when we were just outside the city – and on another occasion, some time later, I saw two German fighters. And we were all lined up [laughs] collecting our food just before going into the mess tent. I thought, My God, if they see us, what a lovely target! But fortunately they didn't. And there was somebody banging away with a Bofors at them, and every round was going behind, I think; they weren't aiming off enough. Anti-aircraft gunners in Italy hardly ever saw anything to fire at!

So what was your job in Italy?

Our regular job was still infantry support, it's just that now we were attached to the 1st Canadian Infantry Division.

Did people show much interest in what division they were in?

Well, everybody wore battledress, of course, and the unit signs were something that distinguished you from other people. You ended up with quite a lot of gubbins really. You had the red and yellow flash, which meant you were Royal Armoured Corps. You had a circular badge for 21st Tank Brigade. Then when we were with the 4th British Division we had 'the Cheese' – I don't know if you know the divisional signs – it was a circle with a quarter cut out; we used to call it 'the Cheese'. Then when we were with the 1st Canadian they let us wear a quarter-sized red flash – they used to wear a big red square on their shoulder, which was their divisional sign.

But there was no distinguishing badge for the 12th RTR itself?

No, not for the battalion.

So people were quite keen on these?

Oh, you had to – you were improperly dressed otherwise. These things were issued and you had to stitch them on yourself.

So whenever the brigade moved to another division you had to unstitch the old one and put the new one on?

Yes, but we tended not to move about very much, we tended to be with the same division for a long time. The only reason we left the Canadians was because the Canadians went to Northern Europe.

Was there ever a suggestion that they should move you there too?

No, they decided to leave us there until the end of the war. I think in fact, partly as a result of the blitzkrieg in 1940, the British Army ended up with too many tanks, and too many tank units. I know towards the end of the war in Italy, some of the tank units which had been converted from infantry – we had one in our brigade, the 145th Regiment RAC, which had been a battalion of the Duke of Wellington's Regiment – were converted *back* to infantry. Because they had a shortage of infantrymen.

In fact, one of the last actions we did was with a mob who had been converted from light ack-ack. They [laughs] were not the best of infantry, at all. They were not used to people *shooting at them*, you know. It was a very different experience for them!

How much of a regimental feeling was there?

Oh, it was quite strong. You were quite proud of being in the Royal Tank Regiment. The RTR in general, and of course your particular battalion – the 12th. The Army is very good at applied psychology, you see. They start on you as soon as you get in, and it works very well. There's no doubt about that. They're very good at producing *esprit de corps*. I think it's the regimental system, which has turned out to be a good thing.

I must admit we did look down our noses a bit at the Cavalry – the donkey wallopers!

We were conscious of being in the 21st Tank Brigade, too. There were two brigades of heavy tanks in Italy – ours, the 21st, and the

25th. And then they did away with the 25th Tank Brigade because they found they had more tanks than they really needed, and the North Irish Horse, which was a Yeomanry regiment, they came in our brigade.

Another thing that people don't realize is that the Eighth Army in Italy was like the League of Nations. [Laughs.] Whereas in the Desert it had been largely Commonwealth – you know, the British, the Indians, the South Africans, the Australians and New Zealanders – in Italy you had the Free French, the Poles, the Americans, the Italians, and towards the end of the war we had a Brazilian division. You see, when it was obvious that Germany was going to lose the war, *everybody* declared war on Germany, and Brazil was one of the few countries which actually sent any troops in. I remember seeing them – they were great tall chaps with big moustaches. Their uniform was very similar to the American Army.

I saw a lot of the Poles, too. We used to see their road signs all over the place, in Polish.

You were working with the Canadians. Did you have many dealings with them?

Well, you only meet up when you're going into action, you see, so you don't have what you might call a social relationship. You get these peculiar messages . . . I always thought these messages which were supposed to be to preserve security were absolutely useless. In the first place, of course, there is *nothing* which has as many radio sets as a tank unit. So if you've got all these radio sets all coming up and chatting, you know it must be a tank unit because nothing else has got as many radio sets. And of course towards the end of the day they do an ammunition count, you see, and they ask how many 'coconuts' and 'peanuts' you want – boxes of machine gun ammunition, and 75 mm, or whatever. And the infantry are never referred to as the infantry, they are 'our friends'. 'We will rendezvous with our friends at such-and-such a place' . . . It's a bit silly, all this wireless procedure. I can't believe it deceives anybody.

Our normal ratio was we would support an infantry company, which if it was at full strength would be somewhere about 120 men, with a troop, which was three tanks. People tend to think of things as they were in the First World War, tanks trundling along and infantry behind them. Well, we worked the other way round: the infantry went in front, because the Germans had anti-tank weapons – infantry anti-tank weapons – which were quite capable of knocking our tanks out. So you usually had to have the infantry in front to flush out the bazooka and Panzerfaust men if they were there. Though I have *done* that sort of attack, like when we attacked the Santerno river bank. You see, these rivers which run down from the Apennines into the Adriatic, because they rise a lot in the spring from meltwater from snow, they have very high floodbanks. Now the Germans turned these floodbanks into forts – they used to tunnel through from the other side, you see, and you'd have machine gun slits pointing out. So the Santerno was like that. By that time the Canadians had gone to fight in the Netherlands and Belgium, and we were attached to the 8th Indian. And we did the Santerno job with the Gurkhas – they were going in at the high port, while we were trundling along, blasting away . . .

You rarely had something you could call a target – all you could do was identify likely places where the Germans would have a slit trench, and just blast it with your 75 mm and Besa [7.92 mm machine gun].

Another thing, of course, is that people tend to think that tanks spend all their time fighting other tanks. I think this is largely due to the experience of the Western Desert, which was a very funny war. Both the terrain and the general circumstances were funny in that they emphasized the tanks' role. And of course it wasn't very big. That was another thing that people forget – that it was a *very* narrow front. It was based on one supply route which ran along parallel with the coast, and inland you had this great open flank, of the Desert, which virtually had no limits. Which meant, of course, that you could always get round the end. People like the Long Range Desert Group used to exploit this, and get behind the German lines. Whereas the fighting in French North Africa, and then in Italy, was more conventional, in the sense that you had an area of conflict which ran from coast to coast, the Mediterranean to the Adriatic.

And of course with the Western Desert, practically nobody lives there.

That's right. The Italians certainly suffered very badly from the war – because the amount of physical destruction was enormous. The total railway system was destroyed. Completely. When I say destroyed I mean every single *rail*. They had a device [known as a 'Rooter'] which they used to pull behind the last train pulling out, which delivered a small charge on every rail which blew a gap about 6 inches long. So that you had to relay the whole system. And of course the Italian railway system was electrified. So they blew up every pylon, they blew up every substation. The railway which was relaid was a steam railway, because that was the quickest way to get a railway system going. But the damage was enormous.

Of course Rome wasn't damaged, Rome was an open city. And the large cities to the north didn't get a lot of bombing. But in the countryside generally there was a tremendous amount of damage.

We not only had enormous air power, total air supremacy – so much so that, as I said, you hardly saw anything at all of the Luftwaffe – we also had a tremendous amount of artillery. Cassino had the heaviest bombing, for its size, of any target in the war. I went up there after the fighting was over – we weren't in fact involved – and there were enormous bomb craters all over the place. The rubble became a sort of fort. Like a lot of Italian towns, every house had a cellar and when they were being shelled the Germans just went down in the cellar. As soon as the shelling stopped they came up with their machine guns. It was just like the Somme.

The Italian civilians used their cellars too, to get out of the way. Because the war was like an expanding bubble, if you like – the front line moved over you. If you could keep your head down until the fighting had passed you and then popped your head up you were behind another Army then.

So I was never in what you might call a tank battle. Fortunately, because we were always aware of our inferiority. I mean, we could throw anything at Tigers – they used to try *bombing* them . . . but it's a very difficult target to hit. A tank's not very big really, as a target for a bomber. And they could throw any amount of HE [high explosive] at it, and any of the AP [armour piercing] we had wouldn't penetrate the frontal armour. They would sit on the forward slope, completely invulnerable. Considering how few tanks the Germans had, a single Tiger in a good position would hold up a divisional front. Anything that moved was just picked off.

And they could do things with their tanks we couldn't do. I remember coming across a Panther which had been knocked out by a 17-pounder anti-tank gun. And just out of curiosity I walked back along the track marks. And for some distance he'd gone along – Italian country lanes have very deep ditches, for carrying away floodwater – he'd gone along with one track in the bottom of the ditch and the other one up on the field. Now, there's no British tank you could have done that with. If you tried that with a Churchill it'd slide off its tracks. But *he* did it.

I very nearly got knocked out by a bazooka once, but it was

anti-tank guns generally speaking that were the danger. And of course mines, which were always a worry.

Presumably one man with a bazooka is almost impossible to spot when you're closed up?

Oh yes, quite true. That's why you rely on your infantry, to flush them out, you see. I know one of our tanks got knocked out by a chap in a pillbox with a bazooka – he just popped out and let fly.

We fired mostly HE, which is why fairly early in Italy we got re-equipped with what was called the Bone Conversion [or, as it was known officially, the Churchill NA 75], because it was carried out at the Army workshops at Bone. Our Mk.III and Mk.IV Churchills had 6-pounders. Now, although they did produce a 6-pounder HE it wasn't much good, because the fragmentation was poor, so what they did was they sawed the front off a Sherman turret and they sawed the front off a Churchill turret and they turned the Sherman turret upside down, which they had to do to bring the gunner on the proper side – because their gunner was on the opposite side from ours – and then welded it on to the back of a Churchill turret. So you had a Churchill with a Sherman 75 mm and a Browning .30 machine gun, and of course we had a Besa in the hull, so we had to carry two lots of machine gun ammunition. Then later on they brought out the Mk.VII Churchill which had a bored-out 6-pounder which fired the same ammunition as a Sherman 75.

It seems a lot of work to go to, but I suppose the gun is worth it?

Well, you see, the trouble is you produce a tank for a certain type of warfare. Then you find that these 6-pounders aren't much cop in support of infantry because they're really an anti-tank weapon, so what's the best thing to do? You've got all these Shermans about the place – they've got a good gun for HE, so . . . The only way they could do it was to take the whole front off. You can't just take a Sherman gun and put it in a Churchill, because all the mounting's different.

Do you think there was a lot of British equipment which wasn't quite right, and which you had to fix in the field?

I think this is one of the aspects of warfare, that you're always coming across the unexpected, and you're always having to modify. Later on in the Italian campaign, because of the threat from bazookas we had extra armour put on. They did that at Ravenna. We had brigade workshops at Ravenna. We used to go up one at a time, by tank transporter, to the workshops and they'd do this job in a day.

Welding extra armour on?

On the sides, yes. We were in Bagnacavallo at the time, which was within enemy shell range. We used to get shelled now and again. So when we were brought back at night on a tank transporter, we were amazed that the crew were in a blue funk – you know, they couldn't get rid of us fast enough! And as soon as we'd unloaded they upped ramps and turned the thing around and off down the road! I thought, Good lord, what's the matter with them! [Laughs.] You get used to the front-line situation, you know. Being shelled is something you get used to.

Do you mean you stop thinking about it?

Oh, you're thinking about it all the time, because all the time you're *listening*. Because you know the difference, the different sound, between a shell going out and a shell coming in. Also a shell that's going to go over, a shell that's going to go to the side, and a shell that's going to come close to you! They all make different sounds, and you very soon learn these. And all the time you're walking around, without really thinking about it, you're looking for cover. There was one place where for a week we were in a sort of salient. We weren't in action, we were in reserve, but we were shelled night and day. By 88s. Now the 88 mm is a high velocity gun, which means you get very little warning.

The infantry used to say, Well, we can always find cover – but you blokes, you're stuck up there in those boxes, and you've just got to take whatever is fired at you. Which is true enough, though we tried always to use cover when possible. We tended to move from cover to cover. And the way tanks were used in the British Army was that the troop operated as a unit. One tank moves at a time, two tanks keeping observation. So if fire is opened on that tank, because they're stationary they're much more likely to spot where it comes from than the one that's on the move. Then once he's achieved cover, another one moves. There were some Troop Officers who always moved first. There were other Troop Officers who always sent the 'Baker' tank – which is the Corporal's tank – first. It made sense, I suppose, in a way, that if anybody's going to be a casualty it's better for the Corporal to be knocked out than the Troop Officer.

I'd say on the whole we respected our officers. Certainly *when we were in action* we respected our officers. If we were out of action for a long time we became very bolshie, and used to think wouldn't it be marvellous to throw phosphorus bombs into the officers' mess and then mow the bastards down when they ran out. You used to think of things like that. But you see when you're in the line your lives are exactly the same, whether you're an officer or a man. Everybody did an hour's guard duty when we were in the line, if we weren't actually in action. Well the Troop Officer, he does his hour with the other chaps.

So the officers were a fairly reasonable bunch?

Oh yes, mind you, you got the best of the officers in the tanks and the infantry. And I suppose in the artillery too – in other words, the fighting arms. They got the best.

So you never had any problems with somebody you thought wasn't up to the job?

Well, there was one – our Troop Officer, in fact. I told you when I joined the 12th I was put in 3 Troop, 'A' Squadron. And then I was taken from there into 'R' Squadron, and then came back. Well, 'A' Squadron went into action while I was in 'R' Squadron, and the Troop Officer got in such a blue funk that after that action he disappeared. Which is what happened in the Second World War. To the best of my knowledge no one was shot for cowardice or anything like that in the Second World War. People who couldn't take it were just found jobs somewhere behind the line. But I mean, this was rare. Most chaps stood up to it.

What about your NCOs – were most of them conscripts?

Yes, they'd come in as troopers. Johnny Hornby, he had something about him, as I say – he was a good Troop Sergeant. He was good at handling his tank, he was very good with the chaps . . . though I remember once the Troop Officer was away – I think he'd been sent on a course or something or other – and Johnny Hornby had to take over his tank, and when he came back Johnny said something about being glad to hand over his load of prima donnas! So evidently he hadn't got on quite as well with that crew as he had with his own.

Was there any recourse, if people didn't get on?

Well, there was this occasion when we'd been moving by train in heavy rain, and it had got into the intercom. Because tanks are so noisy that everybody in the crew has to wear earphones. All the time. In fact, this is one of the things you find difficult when you first start being a member of a tank crew, when you're doing your training, is getting used to having earphones on for hour upon hour upon hour. But you get used to it – it's just one of those things. Anyway, as I say, the rain had mucked up the intercom. We'd been travelling by train, and we got to our destination and had to unload – this was in Shermans. Next thing I felt was a kick on the head from the tank commander. I looked around and was ordered out of the driving seat, and the co-driver was put in. I

wondered what all this was about. We moved off, and of course
he gave an order to the co-driver and the same thing happened,
nothing came through. But he didn't have the grace to *apologize*!
So when we got to where we were going the other chaps in the
tank said, 'You're not going to let him get away with that, are
you?' I was pretty annoyed too, so I went along to the Troop
Officer and I said, 'Could I be transferred to another tank, sir, due
to temperamental differences with Sergeant Thorpe?' 'Oh,' he said,
'you'll have to go in as a co-driver,' but although I was nominally
the co-driver in this tank in fact I did most of the driving.

Driver and co-driver were interchangeable, then?

Supposed to be, yes. The co-driver was the machine gunner as
well – he had the hull machine gun. But you could hardly ever use
it, because if you had infantry in front of you you were likely to
shoot your own infantry. It was rarely used, and I don't think any
modern tanks have hull guns.

So the crew consisted of . . . ?

Driver, co-driver, and then in the turret you'd have commander,
gunner and wireless operator. In other words, five in all. Same on
both the Sherman and the Churchill. The wireless operator was
also the loader. The commander could also handle the wireless,
but the wireless operator did the tuning in. Because you always
had this business of getting 'on net', you see, when you first started
off. In other words, getting all the tanks so that they could all
speak to each other. And they got fairly good at it, wireless operators. They were supposed to 'lock up', but they never used to,
because if you lock up it drifts off and you have to unlock and
mess about. So if it started to go off they'd fiddle about and get it
back again.

Was it claustrophobic for the crew?

Well, yes. I can only remember one chap in the squadron who
suffered a bit from claustrophobia. He used to wake up screaming
under his mosquito net and frighten the guard. I suppose he could
have put in to get transferred to something else, but he didn't, he
stuck it out.

You've not got a lot of room really. Churchills aren't bad –
you've got a nice big front compartment on a Churchill. Turret's
a bit cramped. Sherman's the other way round – *huge* turret and
a little poky driving compartment with a great big gearbox in it,
because the Sherman's driven from the front sprocket and in the
Churchill the tracks are driven from the back sprocket. So in
the Sherman the transmission goes underneath the turret to the
gearbox, which used to get so hot you couldn't touch it. And it

was only about a foot away from you, in between the driver and the co-driver. So you had that blessed thing. And it always so happened that I always seemed to be driving Shermans in the summer and Churchills in the winter!

I can see why the infantry would regard them as targets on the move. It's a pretty horrific prospect getting trapped in a tank once hit.

Yes, of course quite a lot of tank crews got badly burnt, because you've got such a lot of inflammable stuff – the ammunition; people think of the fuel but I mean the fuel's at the back – the worst burns are caused by ammunition. If you got penetration, if a round comes through and hits the ammunition, and sets that off . . .

The only case I heard of . . . one tank in 4 Troop lost the whole crew, just because it was so sudden. That's the trouble. You get a flash fire. So the temperature suddenly goes whoosh through the roof, and although you might not be killed instantly you've probably got most of your skin burned off, and you die within a fairly short time.

But that was on Coriano Ridge. That was a Sherman. There was an airfield at Rimini, you see, and the Germans had at each corner a concrete emplacement under the ground, and on top they had a Panther turret. With the long-barrelled, high velocity 75 mm. And this tank was knocked out at – must have been 1500, 2000 yards, hit up the backside. And the round went right through the rather thin doors at the back of the engine, through the engine – which was an aero engine, radial aero engine – through the turret, hit the ammunition and set that off, and then almost out of velocity it hit the back of the driver's seat and the driver's neck was broken [motions whiplash effect]. We were told about this afterwards. That was the only case I know of a complete crew being knocked out by a single round. That was unusual, for *everybody* to be a casualty.

How bad were your losses?

By the standards of some of the units that fought in Northern Europe they were comparatively light. The total number of tank crews at any one time – that's officers and men – was about 300. And our casualties were fifty killed and a hundred wounded, so it came out at half. But I know some of the units which fought in North-West Europe replaced their total number of tank crews two or three times over. Though that doesn't mean to say that every individual, of course, was killed – some of them lived right through.

And of course the Eighth Army which fought in Italy wasn't the same Eighth Army as had fought in the Western Desert. Most of the British units of the old Eighth Army went to take part in the invasion of Normandy. That's why in the British Army in the Second World War some units carried really a disproportionate amount of burden of the fighting. Because once a unit has become experienced it then becomes valuable, because there is no alternative to battle experience. There's nothing like battle experience for making a good unit.

But you liked being a tank man?

Oh yes – I mean, there's something rather special about the tank. And I've always got a soft spot for tank men. *Any* tank men. You know, when the Russians went into Hungary [in 1956], these bastards chucking bottles of petrol at these tanks and brewing them up – I took a pretty dim view of that. Being another tank man myself.

In fact twice I had to go out of my way, you might say, to stay in tanks. The first was when they sent us to the wrong place. When I was training to be a Driver/Mech. we were sent off to Kettering, only to find that it was a vehicle mechanics' course. But we had a piece of enormous luck – the Colonel in charge of technical training was visiting the unit, so we asked if we could see him. We said we thought there'd been a mistake, because we were Driver/Mech.(AFV)s and now we understood we were going to be trained as vehicle mechanics. 'Oh, I'll look into that straight away.' Sure enough, in no time at all we went to the Motor Fitters' School at Aldershot. Otherwise we'd have been trained as wheeled vehicle motor mechanics.

Then, when we were in Scotland, I got taken out for a driving test by the Sergeant who was in charge of transport. And I said, 'Look, I hope this isn't to test me for driving trucks,' I said, 'because I want to stay in tanks.'

Oh, and a *third* opportunity when the sergeants' mess waiter went sick. So they shot me into the sergeants' mess, and I did such a good job they said, 'Do you want to carry on?' [Laughs.] I said, 'No, I want to get back to me tank!' This is when we were in North Africa.

Did they still maintain separate messes in the field?

Oh, not in field conditions. In field conditions the officers lived with their troops, you see. When you were in the line. But when you pulled out of the line they set up an officers' mess and a sergeants' mess, though they never had corporals' messes. You see, in the Regular Army before the war they had corporals' messes. Our Corporals always lived with the troopers.

So a troop was an officer and his crew, a Sergeant and his crew and a Corporal and his crew?

Yes. As we were in 3 Troop, on the radio the Troop Officer's tank was '3'. The Sergeant's tank was '3 Able', and the Corporal's tank was '3 Baker'. So mine was always called the Baker tank.

What did you do when you were out of the line?

You had a lot of maintenance to do. I've just found my old driver's handbook for the Churchill again. A *tremendous* amount of maintenance. The life of an engine – this sounds beyond belief – was 500 miles. After 500 miles the engines were absolutely whacked. They were burning practically as much oil as petrol. I mean, you used to pour it in from a 5-gallon drum! Of course, you didn't do enormous distances on your tracks, because if there were any big distances you went on a transporter. This is a thing that impresses me about the Russian and German tanks – they covered very big distances on their tracks. Ours were not capable of it.

They would just break down?

Yes, they would.

Crews would change tracks, or bogies. I remember changing a bogie – bearings went. We were told how to do it; basically you dig a hole, you drive the tank over it so that the track goes down like that, then you unbolt the bogie and pull it out. Then you go along to the tech. storeman and say, 'Have you got a bogie?', and he finds a bogie in his lorry and chucks it off the back, and you wheel it back and lever it in with crowbars, jack it up and there you are.

But they found out one thing in France in 1940 – that any job, whether it was on a lorry or a tank, that was going to take longer than a certain amount, it was replaced. The vehicle was replaced and the one that needed repair was taken back. Because they got caught out, you see, when the Germans came through in 1940. There were loads of tanks and lorries which were in bits, and they couldn't move them.

Oh, you get emergencies too. I had the governor go on my tank once. And it wouldn't respond to the throttle. We did an approach march, and I saw the Troop Officer and said it wasn't fit to go into action. He wasn't too happy about that. Anyway, along came one of the fitters and he took it out on a driving test. He must have agreed, because next thing that happened was a despatch rider was sent off – because a governor's not all that big – and he came back with a governor and the fitters, working in the dark, changed it. That was Churchills.

Did attacks always start at first light?

Yes. Of course, in those days we didn't have any night sights. Right at the very end of the war they produced infra-red lights and the driver had a pair of sort of enormous binoculars which were on a frame because they were too heavy for him to hold up. And he looked through those and it was like looking at daylight. So that you could drive about at night. But even then I don't think they developed night sights for the gunners. This is one of the differences between modern warfare and the Second World War – that tank warfare virtually came to a standstill when it got dark. You couldn't see out of them, and another thing of course – you were *awfully* vulnerable at night. Because you were always afraid of the Teds creeping up with a bazooka.

We always called them Teds. In Italy the Germans were 'the Teds' – the Italian word for Germans is Tedeschi.

Even in daylight, if you've got terrain which is difficult to get over and also provides a lot of cover for the enemy, your infantry have a difficult time. And it's no good you bombing on without them, because (a) you may be bazooka'd and (b) you're leaving the infantry on their own. It does make an enormous difference if an infantry attack is supported by tanks, because you can blot out anything that's firing at the infantry. I personally put our gunner on to one Spandau [German infantry machine gun].

Again this was probably the incident I mentioned earlier, where they were going to cross a canal with these canvas collapsible boats – this was the converted light anti-aircraft mob. And they had gone to ground as soon as they came under Spandau fire – I could see their officers waving their pistols at them, but the blighters wouldn't get up! I was closed down, because our gun was being used, and looking through the periscope I saw, away over the other side of the canal, two little pink faces sticking up out of a slit trench. So I got on to my microphone, I said, 'Wilby, I've spotted them!', and I tried to describe where they were, but it was rather featureless. So I said, 'Look, put a round down and I'll correct you there.' So he put a round down, and something like 100 to the left, 200 up, and then I heard the gunner say, 'I've got him.' And then he put a round over and he either landed it right in the slit trench or just on the edge of it. But anyway, they disappeared and we didn't get any more fire back from that, and then they got across in the boats.

You always feel protective towards your infantry, you know. Your job is to help them as much as possible. So the fact that you have to kill people on the other side to protect your infantry is something you accept. I mean, there was one occasion – it was when we were attacking the Santerno river bank – when Wilby had been given a bottle of whisky, by Johnny Hornby I think; junior NCOs don't normally get whisky; and he put it in the back bin. And he suddenly thought, Back bin! It's only made of thin steel, it's no protection at all. Might get a bullet through it! So he *hops out of the turret* to get his whisky out. And somewhere in the Santerno river bank there's a Ted with a Spandau. And he immediately opens fire. So Wilby hops in with bullets flying all round him, breathing fire and smoke, and saying, 'I saw that bastard, we'll get him.' So he got the gunner on to him, and he landed a round very close. And the two chaps – I didn't see this – but the two chaps jumped out of the slit trench and started to run in to give themselves up. But Wilby, he was a bit of a fire-eater, he put the gunner on to them and he dropped another round on them.

I saved one other German soldier's life, or Wilby would have done the same thing. This was near the end of the war, very flat, open ground. Very wet, I remember, and there was a single house there. We were doing an advance with infantry and we put some fire on to this house. So the Teds came out and they were coming in with their hands up. Here again, I didn't see this, but I heard the talk over the intercom, you see; apparently there was a Ted crawling down a ditch towards us. And I heard Wilby giving the gunner instructions. I said, 'Wilby,' I said, 'he's coming in to give himself up. He hasn't got a chance.' Because all our infantry were ready to pick him up. And Wilby said, 'He might have a hand grenade.' I said, 'Look, Wilby, I'll sit in this tank and you can throw hand grenades at me until your arm drops off. I'm not going to let you do this.' A Churchill, you see, had a peculiarity – it had what was called neutral steering. If you were in neutral and you operated the steering bar you could turn the tank on its own axis – one track would drive one way, and the other track would drive the other. So I just did this [turning the steering to and fro] so he couldn't aim. Eventually the bloke got closer to us and he got up then and the infantry picked him up. But I never saw him. And I've often thought, you'll never know how close you were!

If there was going to be major offensive, they always moved the tanks up at the last minute. So, there you were in camp. We used to carry sheets, tarpaulins in the bin on the back of the turret. And you would make a sort of lean-to tent up against the side of the tank with that – if you were far enough away not to be exposed to shell or mortar fire.

So your tank was quite self-contained?

Oh yes, carried all your kit and everything. You had a device for cooking which ran off petrol – a little petrol stove. And of course, you had the famous 'brew can'. Which was an invention I think in the Western Desert which carried on. You had an empty M&V tin – whereas in the First World War the Army ran on bully beef, in the Second World War it ran on Maconochie's M&V, meat and vegetable, in a tin – you filled it with earth and then poured petrol on it, and the earth acted as a wick. You set it alight and you put your dixie on it, and that's how you brewed up tea. It was quicker than getting the stove out and pumping it up and so on.

If there was going to be a major offensive, like say the Spring Offensive of '45, then the Brigadier used to come round, and you'd all be drawn up in squadrons. And he used to climb up on a scout car or something convenient, and say, 'Come on, chaps,' and you'd gather in a circle. And he'd have a big map up and he'd say, 'Right, I'll tell you what you're up against. There's the umpteenth Paras there, and up at the top are some Cossacks – I shouldn't bother about them, I don't imagine they'll be in the line . . .' This is how I found out what the Cossacks were doing, of course; the Cossacks were being used for internal security, in other words they were fighting the Partisans. And so when I heard about what a rough time the Cossacks had afterwards when they were sent back to Russia I didn't have any sympathy for them, because they had behaved extremely badly in Italy.

The Waffen SS consisted very largely of foreigners, as opposed to Germans. And every country that the Germans occupied, they made up units of the Waffen SS from volunteers. This is what you've got to remember, that not everybody was opposed to the Nazis. Certain peoples like the Flemings in Belgium were rather favourably disposed. And they volunteered in quite large numbers. Of course a lot of these chaps fought on the Eastern Front. And I've no doubt it would have happened here, if they had occupied this country there would have been people from this country who would have volunteered for the Waffen SS.

You never *know*, until a country's occupied. That's when you know who's on which side. The people in the Resistance are always going to be in a very small minority, because you've got to be a very special sort of person to go in for that sort of thing – because you know perfectly well that if you get caught you're going to have a very rough time while they try and get information out of you, and you're going to end up being shot. I don't think within the Army we really gave the Partisans the credit which was due to them, because they must have been a perpetual nuisance to the Germans. And the effect on the French railway system after D-Day – the French railway workers virtually brought the French railway system to a standstill.

Anyway, you would move off as it started to get dark. And you'd hear the clang-clang, clang-clang getting louder and louder – tank transporters. The noise was made by the ramps, which were secured, but they used to rattle up and down. And then the roar of the big Hercules diesel. And then you'd get your kit on board and you'd climb on, start up and move out on to the road and climb up. There'd be a chap standing up on the top of the towing vehicle, giving you directions, whether you were left or right.

Must have been a tricky manoeuvring job, to get the tank on to the transporter.

Oh yes. We used to do it in the pitch dark – I don't know how we used to do it! [Laughs.] Then you'd feel it beginning to go over, and you'd ease the throttle back, because if you didn't – if you went over the point of balance too fast – the 40 tons would just about push the transporter through the floor! So you took a great pride in putting it on gently. And they'd chain you up, and all the chaps would get out of the tank and they'd climb up . . . they used to have a little caboose, which they built on top of the ballast – you see, at the back of the towing unit there were I don't know how many tons of concrete, to stop the back wheels from spinning. And on top of this they used to put some bits of wood, and build a little shelter. And the tank crews used to go in that when they were on the move. So off she would go, come to the first Bailey bridge. Bailey bridges would carry 40 tons. You were more than 40 tons, because the tank weighed 40 tons. So you'd come to a standstill, and you'd hear, 'Offload, offload.' And then the crew would climb down, and they would drop the ramps, and you'd get in, start the engine up. Then ramps up, he'd go across the bridge, you'd wait till he was over, then you went over. And how on earth we used to do it, in the dark . . . We had 2 inches to spare each side on a Bailey bridge. Then you'd chase him down the road. He'd come to a stop, ramps down, you'd climb up. Same old business. And off we went again. Next river, next Bailey bridge . . . And so it went on, all night.

Then you would pull into wherever you were going. So you'd offload and then you'd be directed into the place to harbour up. Usually they'd have camouflage nets up. So the tank transporters would all push off – you'd hear them going clang-clang,

clang-clang, disappearing into the distance. And then the next thing, of course, somebody would come along and say, 'Petrol!' And along would come the half-track which carried the petrol. They always insisted on you going into action with full tanks. So you'd lug off these jerricans and climb on the back of the tank – you had a big funnel you used to stick in – and then you'd think, Well, I'll get my head down now. So you'd crawl under the tank – because you're fairly forward now, and might come under shellfire – so you grab a hold of your small pack as a pillow and put your greatcoat on; you crawl under the tank and get your head down. You would seem to have been asleep about five minutes and you'd come to with somebody kicking your boots, you see. It'd be old Wilby. You'd crawl out. Somebody would get the brew fire going, and there'd be, 'Let's have your mug, then.' Everybody had an enamel mug which you used to secure to one of the straps of your small pack. And you'd all be standing around in your greatcoats, with your hands around the mug. And behind you the sky would be flickering with shellfire – over your head 'zhoum', 'zhoum', 'zhoum'; 25-pounders going over.

Then you'd hear the cry, 'Tank commanders!' and old Wilby would wander off. When he came back – 'Righto, lads' – you'd climb aboard, put on your earphones, and you'd hear all this crackling and buzzing, which was with you for the next so many hours. There was always a lot of interference. And all the chat would start. Then you'd move off, and you'd come up to the start line. You'd spread out and take up positions. Then you'd start to see the infantry. It was just getting light – they'd all be spread out, then they'd start to move forward.

What would you be feeling?

Well, you see, Nature's marvellous really. The only time I thought, This is going to be my last day on earth, was the first time I went into action. And we never actually *went* into action, because they kept us in reserve – that was in North Africa. But Nature says, 'It won't be you – it'll be one of the other chaps.' And you always feel that. You'll survive, you'll come through. It'll be one of the other chaps. It's a sort of natural defence mechanism. I mean, if you didn't have it, if you had this awful apprehension every time you went – 'I'm going to get killed today . . .' – I don't know if blokes could stand it. But they don't feel that way.

Do you think the First World War had had an effect?

Well, there wasn't this, I suppose 'gung-ho' feeling which people obviously did have at the start of the First World War. 'It'll all be over by Christmas,' you know, and people volunteering scared out of their wits that the war would be over before they had a chance to get in. There wasn't that sort of atmosphere at all. Men were prepared to do their duty, but there was a feeling that you shouldn't volunteer for anything. If you volunteered for anything you would definitely get killed. So there was this feeling that if you were sent, well, you went. There wasn't the illusion. And of course it was a long war. I went into action long before I was in the Army, in the sense that I was in the East End under the bombing, so I was used to being exposed to danger which was deliberate and carried out by somebody else. So that in a sense was a sort of preparation. And you get a very professional attitude. I mentioned to you about how your ears get attuned to the different sounds which shells and mortar bombs and so on make. And this is part of being a fighting man, as opposed to being a soldier. All the training in the world is no substitute for this.

What did you think of the Germans?

Well, you have to remember two things. One, after the First World War it became apparent that an awful lot of lies had been told about the Germans. So people were very sceptical about things that were said. In the second place, of course, until we started overrunning places like Belsen most people really had no conception of the appalling atrocities which they carried out in the countries which they occupied. And as regards our opposite numbers on the other side we had a fellow feeling for them, simply because we were both suffering the same experiences. You would hear a barrage going over, perhaps for several hours, and you'd think, Poor sods, I wouldn't like to be on the receiving end of that lot, you know. It's rather ambivalent in a way. Although it may sound a bit priggish, I never looted German soldiers. A lot of our chaps did. Anything on them, like pens or wrist-watches, anything like that, they would take. I've seen that done myself. But apart from that, I've never seen prisoners ill-treated. And I remember one place we captured, the infantry officer was going around saying, 'Make sure all these chaps have got a blanket, because when they go back it may be several days before they get issued with one.' And that was a British infantry officer being concerned about the welfare of German prisoners of war.

The thing which I noticed was, the further from the line you got the more bloodthirsty were the remarks from the people that you came across! You know, all these base wallahs who'd never seen an angry German. We were absolutely staggered, because we didn't feel like that at all.

We had a great respect for them. They were very good soldiers.

They were always catching you out. You'd attack an objective and get on it and find there was nobody there. And then you would immediately come under heavy mortar and shellfire . . . They were extremely good at camouflage, too – you could never see them, never see their positions. And of course, although we had this enormous air power, there was usually nothing for them to bomb! Because they tried not to move during the daytime. Everything was totally quiet. All their supplies and so on were all moved at night. Of course, compared with our Army it was rather an old-fashioned Army. I mean, from the start of the war we had the most highly mechanized Army in the world in 1939. The German Army used a huge number of horses – they still had a lot of horse-drawn transport, and the artillery in their infantry divisions was all horse-drawn. Another thing. When you see films they always seem to be in their best bib and tucker. Well, the chaps I came across often wore boots and gaiters – not necessarily high boots – and ordinary field grey trousers, camouflage jackets and of course their steel helmets. But not all poshed up. The front line soldiers were scruffy. I mean, we never shaved; the officers always did, of course, they always had to look smart. But the rest of us were a scruffy lot. Same with the German Army.

And a lot of German infantry soldiers would not have been in infantry battalions in the British Army – they were too old. They were scraping the bottom of the barrel, there's no doubt about that.

Because don't forget the enormous wastage on the Eastern Front. The Eastern Front is the clue to the Second World War. If the same thing had happened there as happened in 1917, and the Germans brought all those divisions back from the Eastern Front . . . They very nearly won the war in 1918. If the Eastern front had collapsed, all those Panthers and Tigers, all those squadrons of aircraft which we never saw because they were busy on the Eastern Front . . . what a difference it would have made.

A lot of the troops we encountered in the West were odds and sods that they'd rounded up and shoved in German Army uniform with a rifle behind them. Well, I mean, they weren't very keen to get killed – they'd already escaped getting killed once. And they weren't particularly keen on fighting for the Germans, either.

I suppose the Italians felt rather that way too.

Well, they changed sides during the war. We had two Italian divisions on *our* side in Italy.

We used to have a day off every week when we were in North Africa, and they used to take us by truck into Bone. And I was having a swim in the Mediterranean, and I saw these very smart pale grey warships coming into the bay. At the time I wondered what on earth they were, but that was part of the Italian Navy surrendering.

From what I've heard, the quality of Italian units varied enormously. Their Regular units were quite good. But the Italian conscript felt that although Mussolini was a good chap who'd done a lot for Italy, he shouldn't have got them into that war. And they weren't going to fight for him. So that's why you had these huge numbers of prisoners in the Western Desert. Because once they'd taken a bit of a hammering they thought, Blow this, I'm packing this lot in. You may have seen the newsreels of the time, of these enormous columns of men walking across the Desert with one solitary British soldier escorting them.

Battles against the Germans, however, did not always go so well, as a letter to his brother from near the end of the war records:

[Reading] 'The infantry were completely pinned down. We tried to get them out under cover of smoke, but they wouldn't budge. We were ordered to pull back. We took on board through the pannier door a bren-gunner who would otherwise have been left without cover. We pulled out and gave the area the fire seemed to be coming from a terrific pasting – Besa, 75 mm and 6-pounder from six tanks. Then we turned and got on to the road. I was just getting into top when I felt a shock and heard a shell burst behind me. The commander shouted, "Speed up!" and I gave it the gas and ignited the tail smoke generator by pressing a button on my dashboard. They had another duffy at us on the way, dropping an instantaneous Phosphorus Smoke in front of us – hoping I suppose to brew us up if they got a hit.

'We pulled into the square of the village, and I heard over my headset that we were on fire aft. I looked round and saw the turret crew bailing out. I followed the infantry bren-gunner through the pannier door, snapping my microphone lead in the process. Outside I saw a complete stranger in battledress trousers and a pullover, wearing neither hat nor equipment, standing on the gearbox hatches with a pyrene. Only the lid of the back bin was left, the exhaust pipes were smashed and the right rear track cover was torn to ribbons. A healthy fire caused by the contents of the back bin – including 300-round drums of bren ammunition – was blazing on the back. I fed the stranger with pyrenes and methyl bromides from the other tanks and he got the fire out, passing out from fumes shortly after. When he came round we found that he was drunk, and was a Guardsman who'd been working with the Partisans. He was last seen striding off somewhere with a pistol "to sort out the Jerry". He did a very good job of work, as the tank had suffered no serious damage. We pulled back to the railway station.

'In the evening we crossed the canal without opposition by Ark [Churchill bridgelayer, used by engineers to span obstacles by positioning itself in the dip and allowing other vehicles to drive over it.] Further on, to the left of the town, we advanced down the bank and shot up the defended location that had been giving us the trouble. We started some lovely fires, and the infantry went in and took about seventy prisoners altogether. Three of us found two after dark sleeping in a slit trench. We had no arms with us, but they didn't make any fuss.

'I see I've left one action out. It was the first job we did on the 56th Div. front. We took a lot of prisoners, and 3 Baker had a bit chipped off its front plate by a 75 mm AP. We had a couple of nuts wiped off the exhaust by another one. A 1 Troop tank had his pannier door driver's side blown off, and other damage. A good time was had by all.

'We stayed there that night and next morning moved off with orders to reach the Po. Once again we bumped into another canal, well defended by Spandaus. The bridge was blown of course, and the infantry were not keen on making the crossing as it involved using assault boats, the canal being too deep to wade. Bren-carriers brought up two assault boats, and we pulled off to the right and started shooting up the bank and houses the other side. The infantry ran up to the bank, paused, and then went over the top and got across OK. They pushed on a bit and established a bridgehead. We pulled back and cooked some grub. The engineers tried to put an Ark in, but hadn't much success. So we had to wait for a proper Bailey. The next morning we crossed and pushed on a day behind schedule, and encountered no further opposition. Reached the Po in a largish village – I don't know the name, but it's about due south from Rovigo. Much to our annoyance we were pulled back to rest. We all champed at the bit at the thought of all the loot lying around over the river and up north, where everything was disorganized. Around and in the village, on the banks of the river, were the signs of the power of the RAF. Thousands of rusted brewed-up trucks and guns that never made the crossing. Two days later we crossed by ferry and harboured up, where we were told that our operational role in Italy had come to an end.

'We all felt very flat and browned off, particularly when we heard the 6th Armoured Div. were bombing on north after being in Army Reserve for most of the offensive. The news of the general capitulation in Italy, and the end of the war in Europe, was received with little enthusiasm. We used it as an excuse to get drunk and I woke up the next morning suffering from the symptoms that have been so often described before.'

What was a pyrene?

It's a pump thing. It's got a big body, you've got a sort of tube going down the middle, and when you pull the handle back fluid from the big body goes in there, and when you push it forwards it comes out as a jet.

Like a fly spray?

Yes, that's it. This was standard equipment. The reason why the methyl bromides, which were pressurized, were from other tanks was because the methyl bromides were mounted inside the back bin – and our back bin had been blown off!

And what was the pannier door?

Well, a Churchill is a peculiar design. You know in the First World War the tracks went over the top of the hull – well, they did on a Churchill too. But the Churchill, of course, had a turret up above. This was a problem. This restricted its development, because you couldn't make the turret wider because of the tracks. You'd have had to expand the turret ring, and there was no way you could – the tracks were in the way.

So when you're in the driving seat, up and to your right and up and to your left the tracks ran over the top of the hull. And in the side of the hull there was a door, on each side – in the Mk.IV it was square with rounded corners, and in the Mk.VII it was round. It was for use as an escape hatch actually, but you would use it also for things like if you had to take the batteries out. You'd get the batteries into the turret and then you'd traverse the turret round, and drag them through and then push them out through the side hatch. Well, this is the way we got out, so as not to expose ourselves, when the thing brewed up at the back – we didn't know how bad it was. It was about 18 inches across, round, or as I say, square on the earlier ones.

What was the rest of the space taken up with?

Bogie assemblies. And of course each side of the turret you had ammunition stowage. The dashboard was up there, offset to the right, so that in front of me I had the driving hatch. In between the driver and co-driver was the rack which carried the box of Besa ammunition, because the co-driver operated the hull gun. Driver on the right.

If only Wilby had had the sense to traverse the turret when we pulled out – we were the last tank out, you see – so that it was facing the way we'd come. Because obviously that SP [Self-propelled Gun] had been lying up for a long time, but he didn't dare open fire while there were six tanks looking his way. So he waited till we were pushing off and with, as I say, nobody looking towards him, he thought, Well, I'll have a go now . . .

There's one thing I didn't mention in the letter – of course you can't get everything in a letter. When we'd pulled back to this village and bailed out, we were invited to tea by an Italian [laughs] with two very pretty daughters, who would have been about fifteen or sixteen, I suppose. And there we were sitting just outside his house around the table while he was giving us coffee and little cakes. The wireless operator had his long lead on, because they used to have a long lead to plug in so they could be out of the tank and still keep a wireless watch, you see. It's things like that that nobody would *invent* if they were writing a novel!

The thing that is strange is how very clear your memories are of certain incidents, although as I say, when I came to read some of these letters I can see things were in a slightly different *order* from the way I thought they were. And that sort of thing. And also, you see, there are things which I've left out. I remember having tea with this chap and his two daughters – it was such a peculiar situation. We'd arrived in his village with everything on the back of the tank in flames. And he invited us to tea. It was so weird. And we must have stunk! It was springtime in Italy – it's quite hot, and boiling hot in a tank. They had no form of cooling. I can't *imagine* what the temperature was inside our tanks in Italy in the summer. I can remember once pulling out my water bottle which I'd stuck behind the dashboard for convenience, and it was almost hot enough to make tea! You could only just about drink it! [Laughs.] So that was just from the ambient temperature inside the tank.

And of course in the winter there was no form of heating. You would lose the feeling in your feet, which wasn't very pleasant. One of the worst nights I've ever had in my life was after we'd done one of these funny advances – I don't know exactly what we were doing. But we pulled into a farm, into the farmyard, which was covered in about 6 inches of freezing mud. Usually you sit in the tank for a bit, and then you're told you can switch off and dismount. The infantry with us had grabbed a lot of bundles of maize stalks, which the Italians used to use for fuel; there was a great big open fireplace and they had a good fire going there. The kitchen was absolutely crammed – there'd be something approaching a hundred men in there. So you'd gradually work your way forward until you got to this marvellous fire, and you'd thaw out. And then obviously you'd have to make room for somebody else, so you'd work your way back again, and you went across this freezing slushy farmyard, climbed into the tank and went to sleep. Until the cold woke you up again. And then you'd repeat the performance. I don't know how many times it was. It was as if that night was going to last for ever.

Soldiering in winter's not much fun. Keeping alive and keeping comfortable, that's what fighting men are good at.

If you're not alive you're no good to anybody.

8

INFANTRY

The least sought-after job in the Army was undoubtedly that of an infantryman. The infantry, called upon to spend long periods in the line, not only experienced the worst possible conditions but also consistently suffered more casualties than all the other arms of service put together.

Nineteen-year-old *Bill Scully*'s introduction to front-line soldiering was typically brutal.

When I first got to Cerasola I'd never seen anything like it in my life. That first night was a novelty – you couldn't see the bodies, not in t'dark. But in the morning you looked down and you saw the litter, and clots of congealed blood, and only a few feet from our sangar [roughly constructed individual stone fortification, used for cover when the ground was too unyielding for trenches] wall you saw a dead German. He'd been rocked over – you couldn't bury them. You see, the nearer you got to the top of the mountain the more all the soil'd been washed away. It were nearly all boulders and shingle. Old Fritz, he'd been shot. Shot in the head. You could see the bullet hole plainly. And with it being cold he were preserved. I can see him now. Young man, about twenty. Blondish. Quite good-looking. I've seen him in my sleep many a time.

I'd been on manoeuvres and that, but I'd never been in action. I'd never even climbed mountains. Ilkley Moor'd be about as high as I'd got. We'd been training in Egypt, in tents in the sand, you know. A vast difference coming from there, and then landing. We were only two days in Italy before we were in the line. One day and night in a farm that'd been half knocked down, and then straight into the line. So it were a vast shock, know what I mean. Coming from the ship, where we'd been playing cards, you know. I don't think anybody really thought that we were going to be heading for anything like that.

You see, you don't know, till you get into action. Nobody gives you any build-up. They don't say, Oh, you're going to Italy, you're going into action. Nobody tells you anything.

Did you think your training was adequate?

I'm glad you asked me that. [Pause.] I don't think we were prepared for mountain fighting, no. It was good training – use of infantry weapons, bren-gun, grenades, the lot. But no, we certainly weren't trained for mountain fighting, 'cos that's what it were. Three-quarters of the whole Italian Campaign were mountain fighting. Either mountain fighting or house-to-house fighting, and the only time we ever got trained in *that* were in Woodford, Essex, using a dummy wooden house that looked like it'd fall down by itself.

When I look back, you got your discipline, and your marching, and all that. But you weren't prepared for actual combat. You stuck a bayonet in a sandbag now and again and made a big scream, but it were nothing like that.

But we were well trained in the art of weapons, you know, the riflemen . . . when you see a rifleman, he's trained in everything. The Lee Enfield [the British Army rifle], the 2-inch mortar, the 3-inch mortar, the hand grenade, the PIAT [the spring-loaded Projector, Infantry, Anti-Tank], even smoke bombs. Same as the bren-gun. Every man was accurate with the bren-gun, in the section, even though you had a bren-gunner – I was our bren-gunner, and my No.2 was Charlie Fright, from Islington. Great name, isn't it, Fright? [Laughs.] But if we got killed, anyone could pick it up straight away and into action.

Were you happy being the bren-gunner?

I *was* happy, yes. Of course, when it got into heavy marching, mud up to your kneecaps, you'd no mates. You could have your best mate going . . . They'd lay down their life for you, but they wouldn't carry that bren-gun. The bren was 23 pounds [between two and three times the weight of the Lee Enfield], but after a 10-mile march it would feel more like 40.

A lot didn't want the bren, because they knew that. And when you was in action, you've got to remember, a section that's at full strength – which was very rare – consisted of an NCO as section leader, carrying a tommy-gun [the American Thompson submachine gun], a bren-gunner and his No. 2, and seven riflemen. Now then, when the action started, the Germans knew what the formation would be. They knew a company had three platoons, each of three sections, and a section had only one bren-gun. It wasn't like now. Now they've got light automatic weapons equivalent to a bren-gun if not better, every man. A lot more firepower than our seven rifles, one tommy-gun and one bren.

So as soon as you went into action them German Spandaus opened up, and they was after *you*. They knocked the bren-gunner out, they could wipe the floor with the riflemen. Because the Spandau ... you're talking a belt-fed machine gun that'd fire 1200 rounds *a minute*. Fantastic. You couldn't do that with the bren. We'd just thirty rounds in a magazine. Charlie Fright couldn't even put three mags on in a minute, three magazines.

So that was Charlie's job in action, then?

Yes. When you were firing, your mags were there, of course. You didn't have time to start rummaging. Could be dark, couldn't it? But the snag was you could only fire thirty rounds. Twenty-eight if the spring had gone. You see, the springs went on mags. When you went in positions like Cerasola, constant action, but static, the mob going out left their ammo. I mean, they didn't have the strength to carry it out anyway, plus it came in handy for you. When we went out we were the same. So your magazines had been used that much. They don't last, not the way we were firing 'em. Know what I mean? So they'd get slacker and slacker, and if you put thirty in, they'd jam up the gun.

The spring wouldn't have the strength to chamber the next round.

Doesn't have the power. That's right, hit the nail on the head. But that were it, you see. And that was where you had to use your loaf. Charlie and me had some real arguments about him overloading the mags. If there'd been prizes awarded for stubbornness Charlie would've walked away with 'em.

Spandau were a remarkable weapon. We had belt-fed machine guns, like the Vickers, but they were too heavy, you see. You couldn't use 'em. 'Cos you've got to move stuff, like when you're advancing. Light machine guns, that's what they're for. They're mobile. And if you had Spandaus firing tracer they'd zip. They'd come floating, you know, floating lazily, and then they'd get close and zip by. That rate of fire – you could use 'em for cutting the grass.

So you had to look at it a couple of ways, on the bren-gun. A lot of the lads didn't like the bren, but I liked it because you were king of your own cabbage patch. Like me and Charlie. We felt, you know, we had that little edge over them. You were a little bit more important than the rest! [Laughs.] I mean Jonas – Bill Jones, the section commander – he was a Lance-Corporal, but he didn't get paid extra. Lance-Corporals didn't get paid any more, but *we* got paid. We got 6d a day extra. Which was a lot of money, when you think of them days. I mean, when I joined up it were 2/- a day. So 6d was a vast amount. Once you got established as the bren-gunner in your section, it were worth it. You didn't have the bullshit.

How did you use the bren?

Well, you could set it for single shots or for bursts. I used short bursts most of the time. Five or six rounds. I think some lads used to use long bursts to give 'em a bit of confidence. You know what I mean? And if you got, you know, a Spandau having a bash at you, well, you'd do the same. Not when *he* was doing it, mind – you'd think, Right, we'll give *you* a go now. And then you'd give the long bursts. Seemed a waste of ammunition, but it weren't really.

Sounds like a duel, between the machine gunners.

I think what it is is that you've got to remember he knows your tricks and you know his. Like Stand To, at six o'clock. Now, I fought in loads of actions, and I never ever saw one at six o'clock in the morning. [Laughs.] And when you weigh it up, I mean, who'd start trouble at six o'clock on the dot?

Especially if you know the enemy has everything ready for you!

Exactly. But they used to do it. Come six o'clock the shout'd go up, 'Staaaand Toooo!' You could hear it for miles. Nobody took any notice half the time, stuck in our sangars. It came from the First World War, you know. I suppose they might have done it to keep you on your toes, sleeping dogs and all that. They were comical about things like that. I bet German were laughing his head off.

Then up would come the rum ration, and Do you want any ammo, you know. Grenades, and what have you. The NCOs were in charge of that.

I've thought many a time, I wonder what happened to 'Darkie' Roberts. He were the RSM [Regimental Sergeant-Major, the senior 'other rank' of the battalion]. You needed men like that. They called him Darkie 'cos he had a dark face – right swarthy skin. He knew you. He knew every man in the battalion, you know what I mean?

You found out people's capabilities, you know. Some blokes do a lot of shouting, but when you get in the line . . . You got it, don't think we didn't. You got NCOs that were flipping useless. And you got blokes that surprised you. Quiet bloke, who were a marvel.

But most of the time we had brilliant NCOs. Sergeant Le Fanu,

who got killed on Cerasola Ridge. He were 6 foot 4 or 5, and
when you saw him looming through the mist . . . They'd come at
first light, or just before first light, with the platoon commander.
He got killed at Cassino. You felt confident when you saw 'em,
you know. It were the NCOs that carried you really.

Same as the officers. We had good officers. And your Corporals,
your section commanders. You used to have a ten-man section,
with a Corporal in charge and a Lance-Corporal second-in-
command, a bren-gunner and his No. 2, and six riflemen. But in
our section the Corporal . . . God knows what had happened to
him, so Bill Jones the Lance Corporal was the section commander.
One rifleman was sent to work with the mule train, old Bob Evans.
And another, Harry Vine, got wounded before we even reached
our positions, so that was our section down to seven straight away.
Pretty soon your sections are down to nothing.

*I'm looking at the list you've written of your section, and of the
nine you started off with, five were killed and only four survived
the war.*

And I were wounded . . . so that's six out of nine. But that were
common. That were pretty common in Italy. *And* you've got to
remember that was our section *at the time*. They got killed in
different actions. But you have to remember replacements were
being fed in and *they* were getting killed. So it's actually even worse
than six out of nine. Our battalion had 100 per cent casualties.

*The equivalent of the entire strength of the battalion were killed
or wounded?*

That's right. And in how many months? We'll dispense with
February, because we landed about the 21st in Italy, so let's say
March to November – nine months. And then taking, say, two
months for your bits out of the line – maybe the longest a week
or a fortnight. Out of the nine months you could say maybe seven.
100 per cent casualties. And that was the quota for every infantry
battalion in Italy.

*People think, don't they, that because the overall losses for the
Second World War were less than for the First . . .*

I know what you're going to say [Nodding.]

*. . . that things must have been easier. But it's not true when
you study the statistics more closely, is it?*

You're right. I've thought about that myself. I think the difference with the Second World War from the First was that now you
had hell of a lot more tanks, and you'd all kinds of special units.
And your supply lines were longer, you know, like in the Desert
they were 1000 miles, weren't they? And Italy.

When I went to hospital I was amazed when I came back out, and went through these transit camps. And there were *thousands* of back-of-the-lines merchants, *thousands*. All kinds of mobs I'd never flipping heard of . . . transport mobs, and depots and all these.

But you still got your quota of infantrymen killed. *They* lost just as many. If you take an infantry battalion, they lost just as many in that type of fighting as what they did in the First World War. You knew eventually you'd get done. There was no way out for us apart from getting wounded or getting killed.

Because every time you come out the line, and they'd give you two days, three days to write your letters, you'd just be nicely settled when bang, the trucks would come. 'Load up!', dishing the ammo out. Then you knew. You always had that. You always had to go back in again. Even when I was wounded in hospital I still thought about it. But I couldn't do a thing.

Were you jealous of the people behind the line?

You what? 'Course we were. Without a doubt. There were a vast difference between your fighting troops and your base troops – and there was plenty of 'em. Of course civilians didn't know. If you came home on leave, people didn't know. Women especially. Men, you might get an old soldier, they'd see your red bar [the arm of service indicator on the battledress sleeve, scarlet for the infantry, dull cherry for the Royal Army Medical Corps, etc.]. You'd not a lot to denote you're infantry. But women never knew all that. So you'd get somebody who'd never fired a shot in anger, but he could still say he were in Eighth Army. Every time I came home it'd be [imitates proud female neighbour], 'My lad's in t'Eighth Army. He's in Cairo. He's been there three year. [Laughs.] I hope he's safe.' I thought, Blimey, wish I were!

So you never get any credit. Even at Cenotaph parade it's just the same. I've watched 'em on here [the TV] and really, it's heart-breaking, innit. You know, to see the proper old sweats. But you've a lot that's marching round that Cenotaph that have got more medals than Montgomery, and they were only in t' cookhouse banging two tin cans together. There was all kinds, but people don't know that. But *we* know. It rankles, but we have laughs over it too.

'Course it's best if they can laugh with you. If you can get a bloke that'll laugh with you, that's better still. I'd a mate called Noddy – dead now – he were a truck driver in t' Desert, RASC. He were a bit older than me. 'They'd have been buggered without us tekkin t' ammunition up to 'em,' he said, 'and they used to plaster us.' I said, 'You got plastered *in Cairo* all right!' [Laughs.] You could always take the mickey out of 'im. He got the Africa Star, Italy Star [laughs], *France and Germany* Star, '39–'45 and the Defence Medal. But you see the difference. Fair enough like, they can't all be in the front line. But you see, he knew. He knew in his own heart. When he'd had a few, he'd get a little bit ... His conscience, you see. I said to him, It's your conscience. 'We done our whack,' he said. I'd say, 'You did that, mate. Flogged all our flipping fags.' They did! Seven a day you were supposed to get. Big deal. And they were knocking them off. We got them V cigarettes – anybody will tell you about them! Diabolical. Made out of camel dung and brown paper, I think. If the RAF had dropped 'em over Germany the war would've been over a lot quicker. Came from India actually. When we started complaining they gave us proper fags, Senior Service. And when you came out the line they used to give you fifty, box of matches, bar of chocolate and a bottle of beer. And sometimes, if they thought you were a bit of a mug, they'd throw a stripe on top. [Laughs.]

In them days anybody with a lighter were well off. Or a watch. You didn't have a watch. Never saw watches. Nobody could afford 'em. When I were in action I were on 3/6 a day, and I were letting my sister have 10/6 a week. When I joined up I got 14/- a week – two bob a day. I let our Rosie have 10/6, as her husband had blown, and in them days there were no hand-outs like now. There was a means test. She was my favourite sister, because she'd looked after me when I came out the orphanage. Plenty of common sense. You never really needed a watch. In t' front line you never knew what time it was. You never bothered about time.

You got some boring days, you know, in action. Terribly boring. You got days that went like a week. And you just got fed up. It's a bit like being at home, you know, two or three days when nobody calls, and you think, Oh, what's happened? Is summat wrong? It were the same. Mind you, you get bored with life anyway.

It's funny to think of you getting bored face-to-face with the Germans!

Yes, but you did. You actually did. When we were up at Cassino and I got wounded, the day lasted. It seemed to drag and drag, know what I mean? It's a very funny sensation, time, when it goes really slow. You don't realize how long a day is. Nobody's moving. There's no movement, because as soon as there's movement the shells start.

When I got blown up, it were a stupid mistake. The Germans put in an attack on 'B' Company, and they brought a tank up.

Anyway, they hammered it back, did 'B' Company. The Germans opened up with machine guns and all the rest. And what happened was, they got word about this tank up at our company, where we were straddling this dirt road. 'D' Company were straddling the road, just had a few men in the ditch. What happened was, Major Charkham ['D' Company commander] must have got a message that the tanks were expected again, so they wanted a bren-gunner, and they picked on me. And they picked Vic Filby, who had the PIAT — rubbish weapon. Bloke won a VC at Cassino for knocking out a tank with one.* Ever read about that? Lancashire Fusiliers. I wouldn't like to face a Panzer with a flipping PIAT. Hell of a brave bloke. 'Course, we all knew about it, 'cos when you get the VC . . . and with a PIAT! That's what amazed us all! [Laughs.] 'Cos if you fired a PIAT it threw you back about 10 yards anyway. You wanted a VC to fire it. It's all right to see in books that it was a brilliant weapon, but these blokes that write all that, they don't fire 'em, do they?

I knew Vic, though he were in different platoon. This dirt track road, where they'd dug slit trenches, had some of our lads. And they put us further down it. Of course, the further you go down the better you could see the monastery at Cassino, overlooking you. We were 4 mile away from the monastery, and it were still overlooking you, you know. Anyway, we gets digging, and gets that far down, about up to your waist; you want to go a bit further. There were no cover. I were only a Private, and I could see that. I set the bren-gun up, Vic set up the PIAT with the bomb in it. They give us mines, so we put a mine in front of us, only a little thing. I think this would be about nine, ten o'clock – as I say, you lost all track of time. When you're in a line you're comfy. You've got your mates, you've got company. But we were stuck out on our own. Vic came from St Albans. Nice lad; quiet, you know. I think we lasted about three-quarters of an hour, feeling a bit sleepy, 'cos we'd been on our feet all night. Jonas had just paid us a flying visit, and as soon as he left, the Nebs [Nebelwerfer multi-barrelled mortars] opened up a stonk. The old 'Sobbing Sisters', you know. A high wailing moan, louder and louder. I heard Vic say, 'We've 'ad it!' Then suddenly I was seeing every light and hearing every bell in Italy. I just remember falling back to earth again. Luckily I landed off the dirt road, on the grass. Next thing, smell of cordite;

---

* 22-year-old Fusilier Francis Arthur Jefferson, of the 2nd Battalion, the Lancashire Fusiliers.

scorched smell. And Jonas was applying field dressings to me. He must have thought I'd had it. Blood everywhere. All the skin were off my right hand and arm, and I had shrapnel in both legs. He put my good arm over his shoulder, and I could just about manage to walk.

Vic were dead. His PIAT bomb had detonated in the explosion. They never found his grave. They should have done – I could have took them to where he was – but tanks come over, and churned it up.

One of our Sergeants in the battalion married his sister, Victoria. Sadly his parents got divorced after the war, and I lost contact with them. I've a photo of him somewhere, in civvies. Funny that, isn't it? He never had time to get his photograph taken in khaki. You see, they got desperate, as they got into t' war. Infantry were always short. You were always crying out for infantry, always.

In the battle where I was wounded, the 4th Battle of Cassino, our battalion lost fifteen officers and 204 other ranks. In 'D' Company you've got three platoons, three Second Lieutenants. We had two killed out of the three. We'd the Major killed, and his second-in-command, a Captain, wounded. So we lost 'em all, except for one officer. Platoon commanders had terrible losses. Most of ours were killed, one after another. You didn't get many Lieutenants in rifle companies survived, at all. And even company commanders – Major Charkham was killed, and Major Wilson, who took over his job, he got badly wounded later.

You were always short of men. It's not just the killed and wounded, you've the poorly. You didn't only just get bullets in people's guts, they were away with frostbite and all kinds of stuff. They pick up all kinds, you know. And every infantry mob that were there got the same.

A rifle company had three platoons, three platoon officers, Second Lieutenants. One Captain, second-in-command, and one Major, company commander. A company should work out about 120 men at full strength, but you never got to full strength. And you had four rifle companies in a battalion, plus you have your HQ and support companies, in which were your pioneer platoon, who lifted mines, and your bren-gun carrier platoon, and the Colonel and his hangers-on – a lot of blokes who we never knew what they were. [Laughs.] I expect they were all important in their own way, it's just that we never saw them.

You see, you never see the whole battalion except on parades. You never see your HQ for a start – they always seem to be a bit further back, or whatever. You fought more as a company. I mean,

I were in the battalion what, three and a half year; and I only knew about six or eight men from other companies – more than knowing them by sight, I mean. I was in 3 Section, 18 Platoon, 'D' Company, of the 2nd Battalion, the Bedfordshire and Hertfordshire Regiment.

Even though I come from Bradford. Of course, the idea of that were, after the 1914–18 war, with the Bradford Pals and suchlike, you wiped out a whole generation of young men in those areas. There were two Bradford Pals battalions in the Battle of the Somme, and they used to say that afterwards every family in the city had someone, or knew somebody, who'd been killed. So the idea were to stop that. Because when they got the newspaper, and they got a page of all these names . . . That's why they made sure they didn't do it again. If the Bedfords had all been from Bedford, or the surrounding area, when they got wiped out at Cassino . . . So they were spread out all over.

And I was lucky that I served my whole five year in one regiment. A lot of infantrymen didn't have that luck. When an infantry battalion got smashed up, at the back they'd have camps, reinforcements coming from England. But there were never enough. So what they'd do was they'd dispense with a couple of battalions, disband 'em, and send the survivors to the others. We got a load of Warwickshires [Royal Warwickshire Regiment] before the Cassino battle. Hell of a lot of 'em got killed. They came in at the back end of the Garigliano fighting, so they'd only been in about a month when we hit Cassino, which was a bad place to hit.

Some lads went through three or four different regiments. Know what I mean? We were lucky in that sense. We were never disbanded. I don't know why, because we certainly got plenty of casualties. But they done it a lot.

Obviously out of desperation, because it went completely against the regimental spirit they tried to foster, didn't it?

Exactly. Desperation. They were so hard up, you see, for infantry.

When we buried our lads, when anybody got killed, they'd come up, the pioneer platoon – they made the crosses, you see – and it was always called the 16th Foot. They didn't call them Beds and Herts. It were an elaborate cross, and what they had on the cross was 'Private So-and-So, 16th Foot, Beds and Herts.' But the 16th Foot were the prominent bit. And they stuck to that.

When I were in the depot, all the wagons had blazoned on them '16th Foot', all very traditional. And they called themselves that, the officers, because the 16th was quite a senior regiment, which they were proud of. You know, when regiments went on numbers. Like the 1st Foot is the Royal Scots, and you work your way down in seniority.

So when they reburied 'em all, and put 'em in the different cemeteries at Cassino, they done away with the 16th, just put the badge and 'Bedfordshire and Hertfordshire Regiment', which was not liked, at all. But it's funny, isn't it, tradition?

You had your good times, I mean they weren't *all* bad. I think when you've been through things like that, you have a spirit, don't you? Comradeship. It sounds a bit daft now, but you had it.

So where were you hospitalized, after you were wounded?

Naples, and then Syracuse, in Sicily. They had a massive hospital there, and they needed it. This was at the time of Anzio, and the wounded were streaming in.

This hospital had tank men, infantrymen, every regiment going. The bloke in the next bed was from the Duke of Cornwall's Light Infantry. We called him 'Inkspot'. He'd been splattered by a mine. Besides getting shrapnel all up and down, it'd gone in his face, fine shrapnel.

When you became walking wounded you had these silly blue trousers, white shirt and red tie. They were probably the old uniform from the Crimean War. [Laughs.] They must have had thousands left. Everybody thought we were escaped lunatics.

Venereal disease cost 'em a lot of men what should have been up at the front, or doing their job. When I were in Sicily they had a ward there full of 'em. You weren't allowed to talk to them, they had them segregated. They even had part of the canteen roped off – VD on one side, wounded on t' other. We got better food than them. Plus, the ones that dished out the food to them were men. Ours were Italian women. Not that we could do much, with our crutches 'an all. It must have been bad for them.

They had a side ward for the psychiatric patients. You could hear 'em screaming and howling . . . oh, it were terrible. I saw a couple of bomb-happy cases. You could tell if they were genuine – it were a case of they were transfixed; they couldn't move. You could've kicked 'em with hobnailed boots. It didn't happen just in the shelling and bombing. It could happen before they went into the line. They froze. Some shot themselves – I never knew it in 'D' Company, but it did happen. The medical officers were very strict. You've got a job to work anything on a British MO. One of 'em sent me back, and I wasn't really fit.

Did the people who'd been in the Desert find it difficult to adjust to Italy?

Oh yes, it were completely different, it were grinding forward all the way. It were infantry warfare. In the Desert there were thousands upon thousands of trucks – Royal Army Service Corps and that – and you only had a few infantry divisions. You know. It were tank warfare, weren't it. You didn't get the casualties they did in Italy. Because in Italy it was such close fighting; if you weren't fighting hand-to-hand you were getting shelled every inch of the way.

Did you know there was a mutiny in Italy? At Salerno? They kept it well hushed up. It happened before we landed, of course. The Salerno landing was when . . . September 1943. The Eighth Army had landed in Calabria first, but the hard fighting started at Salerno. What it was, they'd promised these Desert veterans that they were going home. But when the boats got going and they found they were going to Salerno, they caused a riot. Altogether about 300 men. Eventually the three ringleaders were put in the glasshouse, sentenced to death. They kept 'em waiting for weeks and weeks.

But nobody knew about this at the time?

No. We were there in February, and we didn't have an inkling. And yet there was so much gossip. You got a lot of tales, you know. In fact it were well kept, because a lot never knew till after the war.

Funnily enough we had two characters sent to us. Proper Desert veterans, you know – the Desert veterans had a tan, which we never got, from being two or three years in the Desert. We got a bit of a tan in Egypt, but it were gone by the time we got to Italy. [Laughs.] But old soldiers had a tan – you get an old soldier who's served in India . . . In the depot we'd NCOs who'd served in India and Palestine – 'cos they used to do five or six years out there, pre-war. That were soldiering. Believe me, they were tanned. They were like nutmegs. You could tell 'em a mile away. I mean, when we were in the depot, you got 'em, you know. Fly. They had to be, didn't they? At the depot you have your Quartermaster, then they have his mucko, the hanger-oner. Well, he was always an old soldier. And in them days we had one, I think he done about thirty years in the Army. You know, they had long service stripes, the stripes come up to his elbows! [Laughs.] He'd one [Lance-Corporal's] stripe up. They'd give him one stripe. He'd never earned it, they just give it him 'cos what could they do with him? They couldn't tell him owt, could they? He knew all the answers, you know. Long as you dropped him something, he'd get it for you, on the quiet. The regiment were proud of 'em, you know –

'He's been in the Bedfords thirty years.' Never done a day's work in his life. But you could tell 'em, you know. They were *gnarled* by the sun. They looked old. I mean, they were smart, they stood like ramrods, but they were old in the face.

And these two were the same, they'd been in the Desert. 'Cos we never knew where they came from – they just appeared in the battalion. And ever since I read about that mutiny at Salerno, I've wondered whether they two were from there. 'Cos they sent them all to other units, see. There could have been more in the other companies – you never knew what were going on in the other companies. Probably just dished a couple out, round the battalion. 'Course, they were off like the clappers. I mean, when they saw them mountains . . . they thought, We're not going to get killed with this mob. I'd put money on it. I don't remember their names. They weren't old sweats, but certainly Desert.

Did you know where you were when you were in the line?

No, when you're fighting these actions, these small actions, you don't know. Because, how can I put it, you weren't there long enough, or there's no signs – they're all smashed into t' ground, know what I mean? All the little mountain positions that I never knew the names of. Unless you got a place like Cerasola Ridge – that were famous, because there was a lot of action there. Whereas some of the other positions were quiet. If you got in a quiet position nobody ever bothered. Nobody ever mentioned it. And that's the difference.

So it's the worst places that you remember the names of, really?

That's correct. I'd put Cerasola, in the Garigliano bridgehead, as the worst, for really rough conditions. It rained constantly, it never *stopped* raining. And you'd be in the mud. Everything you'd touch was mud. You know, you'd wipe your face and it were all mud. In your biscuits, your bully beef. But you're young, you see; you don't bother, do you? When you're young you'll eat it. I mean, me and Charlie Fright could eat like horses. If there'd been dead mules we'd have eaten *them*.

Mules, in fact, provided much of the front line with its supplies. Despite the fact that they were fighting the most mechanized war yet seen, the infantry frequently found themselves in terrain which no vehicles could reach.

The mule trains would come up to t' supply dump. From then on – I think it were about a mile, maybe a bit less, from our positions

A recruit for the ATS

Horsa glider components, and the workers who made them

Cleaners prepare the *Queen Mary* for another trooping run

Armoured car firing at night in the desert

Transferring jerricans at a railhead

Churchill of the 21st Tank Brigade in Tunisia

Stretcher-bearers

Priest being replenished by its crew

25 pdr field gun, ejecting a spent cartridge case

Sappers clear a gap in a minefield so the infantry can follow through

Parachute training in the Middle East

Derby Day in Normandy, 17 June 1944. The winner was the Earl of Rosebery's *Ocean Swell*, which came in at 28-1

Led by their Bren gunner, an infantry section enters Arras

Mortar team in action in the jungle

– they had porters to bring it from the dump to the back of our positions.

Then you picked it up from there?

That's right. You'd send a party out. Different parties'd go out different nights. *Every* night, obviously. For grenades, 'cos you ran out of grenades eventually. And water were vital. Everything had to be brought up. What wells there'd been in the mountains the Germans had put mules down. And a dead Italian, when they felt like it. So all the wells were poisoned. Some of the platoons used to catch water on gas capes, you know – put the gas capes on top of the sangar, and when it rained, which it continually did, catch it.

The way the firing went up there you always wanted more ammunition. The mules were always laden down with ammunition, mortar bombs and so on – 'cos you had your mortars backing you up.

Of course, when a mule stopped it was every man to the stick, and they'd all batter the mule. 'Course, the more they battered it the more stubborn it got! They lost a lot of mules – a lot of 'em fell off. You could smell 'em. You smelled a lot of death in the mountains.

At night there was always activity somewhere. The Germans knew where all the tracks were, all the dumps. I mean, that's why the Italian campaign was so bad. When they fell back, everything was pin-pointed. They knew exactly where everything was. In daylight you could never move out of your sangar – the constant mortaring all the time, you daren't. You daren't go out. So you were sat there, trapped in your own little sangar all the time. You never saw anybody in daylight, you just sat tied to your gun. Then as soon as darkness fell you'd hear the activity, you know. People creeping about. You'd have a party going for rations, an NCO taking somebody down to the Gulley, relieving somebody. You'd have your officer coming round, know what I mean. Putting his head in, 'All right? Are you well?'

What was the Gulley?

On Cerasola the Gulley split 'D' Company positions; it were the weak spot. So we had an OP [Observation Post] there, and in front of it two strands of wire, maybe three, with tin cans on. Which seems a bit primitive today, but that's the way it was. Mixed German cans, and our cans. And Jerry were on t' other side. He was there. Then there were the bodies. Dead Germans, loads of litter. When it were windy, which were very often, all the old cans'd start clattering, and you were sat there like this [finger on the trigger]. You couldn't smoke or anything like that, know what I mean?

You had your leather jerkin on, and greatcoat, and your balaclava, and mittens – because you can't fight in gloves – and you'd have your pocket full of biscuits, and have a chew, and think of 'ome. But you always had the suspicion of the Germans creeping up on you. Always. No matter how many times you went down that Gulley. And of course you'd get flares going up – either the Germans'd have a go, or we'd have a go. If they thought the Germans were creeping over, they'd fire flares up [to illuminate no man's land]. And of course you got a lot of machine gun fire, lot of tracer. You got some lads that'd fire at owt. If they saw a shadow, they'd fire.

When you went down the Gulley you were on your own. It was only a one-man sangar, the OP, and you were stuck there for two hours, chewing your fingernails. It were really creepy. And you got the smell, of the bodies. The Germans must have tried to attack up the Gulley, and one of the battalions previous to us had done 'em, either with a Vickers or whatever.

After your two hours you were only too glad to get back to your own sangar.

The British Army was also keen on patrolling, wasn't it? It seems to have thought highly of keeping up pressure . . .

. . . on the enemy, yes. Lost a lot of men, an' all. *We* didn't think highly of it, of course. A lot of it was for information. It depends who it was – some regiments were more keen than others. It's amazing, though, what information you get from patrols. You know, you don't have to take a prisoner. I mean, you can come upon a German position and it's empty, so you know they've gone.

We used to have standing patrols. What they used to do was send you out into no man's land. Maybe the night before a German patrol might have had a go at you. So what they used to do was send like eight, nine men, heavily armed, and hope that a German patrol would come along, so you could ambush them.

I went on three along the Garigliano, and believe you me, we must have been out there two or three hours in no man's land. The icicles were growing on my ears! It's true – and I had a balaclava on! It were freezing; raw freezing. One of t' lads started weeping at end, sobbing. I thought, God, wish 'em Germans'd come and take us all prisoner! [Laughs.] We were that stiff. Because you couldn't stand up. You never stood up on patrol.

Bit hairy, them patrols. Used to send us out with clubs as well – with pickaxe handles. They'd some crazy ideas.

It were terrifying place, but I suppose Cerasola Ridge was a good thing for the battalion. It seasoned us, didn't it? Toughened us up. All that climbing, and the rigours of the sangars. There weren't many skilled veterans, because most of them had been killed in Tunisia.

You could always tell lads who were on their first time in action. And when you come out of the line, when you queued for food, all the mess tins would be rattling, because lads had the shakes. Their hands would be like this [trembling uncontrollably].

Did people recover after a few days out of it?

Yes [rather doubtfully]. From machine guns, fair enough. You got a bit of hammer then they'd stop. But sometimes, you know, you'd get constant shelling. Or mortaring. I think mortaring was the worst. When they used them they were close. You know, a mortar ain't like a gun – a 5-mile sniper. Mortars might be just 200 yards away. If the mortars opened up you knew they were on your ground, the mob facing you. Them mortars were deadly.

The Germans had big six-barrelled mortars, which we never had. 'Sobbing Sisters' we called 'em. You've never heard anything like it in your life. When they come down they screamed and howled. Terrible. 'Cos that was the German idea, wasn't it? Fear. You didn't know where to dive. When they fired a six-barrelled mortar you *knew* they knew where you were. It was as simple as that. They never wasted six bombs on probing for you . . .

They used to have some devilish ideas. You didn't know where they'd put mines. Do a river crossing and they'd put trip wires in the banks. When you come across mines, you couldn't just stop. Like when Jonas was killed, after he went to 'A' Company as a Sergeant. Forty men we lost there. Forty men. Never saw the Germans. We were going up this hill, 'A' Company leading. And no sign of anything. No sign of a German at all. No noise, no nothing. German weren't like that. He'd have caught us well further down; he'd have opened up somewhere. So it's pretty obvious when you're going up, and there's a village on the top, he's either in the village or he's gone. An Italian came down, yapping away, you know. 'Cos what they did, the Italians, when the Germans took over, they hid – got in the cellars and what have you. He said there were mines. But we had our orders; the Brigadier had told us to take the place at all costs. So of course when we gets up there, it were booby trapped that heavy that we lost a lot. But the thing is, you see, when we went up in daylight you could see the booby traps, the trip wires, all over. In daylight you wouldn't have gone near the place. It nearly took the top off the hill.

I'd never make a General. You'd have to be hard, wouldn't you?

Same as the Colonel of a battalion. Ours was Lieutenant-Colonel Whittaker. He were a good Colonel. When you get to CO of an infantry battalion you've not got your pips for nowt. You've come from, you know, Platoon Lieutenant. You'll have put bayonet charges in and gone forward wi' t' revolver . . . It must be hard on him, because he's got thirty officers in an infantry battalion, and he knows every one of them personal. It's like a family, the battalion. It's like us, in our section.

We had a lot of respect for the Germans in Italy, you know what I mean? Look at Cassino. When we finally captured that we had to use three men to their every one. Which sounds like, blimey, we should have murdered 'em. But the positions. The German positions were all up on the hills, always above you. They were brilliant tacticians, the best. They'd have the odd killing, but I never heard of prisoners getting shot, or anything like that. A lot of them weren't Germans, of course; they had Ukrainians and all kinds of stuff.

That year, 1944, they had some terrible weather conditions in Italy. 'Sunny Italy' – you what? Rain pelting down . . . Your mess tins filling up with water while you waited for grub. You know, a lot of people think that if you get bad weather, wars stop. In fact I had an idea of that myself, before going there. I never realized that you could fight in such conditions, as mud all the way, slipping all over. And then you had to attack, and you had to go forward in it. Never dawned on me – I always thought, like, come to a bit of bad weather it'd be like football. You know, cancelled.

And your sangars were open to the elements?

Most of them, yes. You couldn't have a roof on your sangars because you wouldn't be able to see what were going on. Because your Jerry used to crawl up. And they were cramped. You didn't want your sangars too big, because if they were big there was more chance that a mortar bomb would drop in . . . One of my original section, lad called Hendin, he and his mate had to be buried together in a double grave. Their sangar got a direct hit . . . the blast in that confined space . . . you can imagine the mess. So you had them so you could just squash in.

What form did your food take?

Well, when you were in the line it were tins, but when you came out the line it was dixies. We even had tinned cheese, of all things. You could roll it down the hill! I'd never seen tinned cheese before. It were solid. And corned beef. Tins of M&V stew. Eating that cold in a freezing sangar would give the toughest stomach the runs.

How did you get the tins open?

You had your knife, your clasp knife. Black. It had a tin opener, a blade. You might have a tin of jam, too, between a section – to put on your biscuits. Though we used to mash 'em up. It were all nourishing stuff. Vitamin chocolate. You had a little 'Tommy cooker' – methylated spirit block, round, and it sat on three prongs. Put the block on top – it had a rim, so that the block kept in – and you lit it with a match. The food improved when we got out of the mountains, 'cos they can't carry everything up to you.

We didn't get them tins of stew what warmed themselves, like they did in France. We got the outdated stuff. All the new tanks went to France, all the new gear. When D-Day came along, well, the Italian campaign got forgotten, didn't it? When they gave out these communiqués in the paper and that, they'd have a little bit about Italy, and the rest were all France. When *they* put an attack in they had all these fighter-bombers. When *we* got any air support they bombed *us*! [Laughs.] They got all the new weapons and the new ideas.

The same thing applied out in Burma. They called themselves the 'Forgotten Army'. Now I've been to meetings, you know, ex-service dos. The Burma lads are very bitter – 'Nobody bothered about us, we were the Forgotten Army.' But we were the same. Just the same. But nobody told them; it's like nobody told us about them. The Poles – they're very bitter too. They've got nothing good to say about the Germans. Good blokes, the Poles. They got some stick.

But we were just the 'D-Day Dodgers'. Lady Astor's supposed to have said it [although Lady Astor herself strenuously denied that the term had originated with her]. She was an MP; she was an American actually – Lord Astor married her. I've heard a couple of versions of this, but something cropped up about us in Italy dodging D-Day. Comical really, but the lads took it hard. Some of them lads had been in the Desert, then Tunisia, so they'd been fighting what, two year, or more, before the landing at D-Day. And they were on about dodging! But if you hear the actual song, it's brilliant. I don't know who wrote it, but whoever's worded it, it's brilliant. I mean, what it does is it's taking the mickey. Whenever we get to these Monte Cassino Veterans Association gatherings of ours, we always sing it. It's so simple, yet so true, you know. [Sings . . .]

We landed at Salerno – a holiday with pay.
The Germans brought the bands out, to cheer us on our way.

They showed us the sights and the beer was free.
We kissed all the girls in Napoli.
We are the D-Day Dodgers,
Still out in Italy.

The end bit, you see; that's when you get it. Because you realize . . .

Look around the mountains in the mud and rain.
Groups of scattered crosses, some that bear no name.
Heartbreak and toil and suffering done,
The boys beneath can slumber on.
They are the D-Day Dodgers,
And they'll stay in Italy.

Nobody wanted our job. Nobody. When the battalion came out of Cassino – the remnants of the battalion – they were cheered and clapped by the Gunners. I weren't there, of course, I were nicely tucked up in a little hospital bed.

It must have been really thrilling . . . you know what I mean . . . you'd never forget a thing like that. To be clapped by your Gunners.

9

GUNNERS

Artillery support was an indispensable aid to the tanks and infantry in accomplishing most tasks.

Without calling on outside assistance, a British infantry division had at its disposal no fewer than five Royal Artillery regiments – a light anti-aircraft regiment equipped with 40 mm Bofors guns, an anti-tank regiment with 6-pounder or 17-pounder anti-tank guns, and three field regiments with 25-pounder field guns. Armoured divisions, being smaller, had two 25-pounder regiments instead of three.

The same combination of tanks, infantry and guns would often fight together for lengthy periods, becoming a close-knit team.

Arthur Ward's regiment enjoyed such a relationship in North Africa.

> In the Desert we fought with an armoured brigade – the 2nd. In the 1st Armoured Division. And we each supported 'our' regiment of tanks. 'A' Battery supported the Queen's Bays, 'B' Battery the 10th Royal Hussars and 'E' Battery the 9th Queen's Royal Lancers.

Arthur's own unit was a regiment of the Royal Horse Artillery, which had a distinct identity within the Royal Artillery as a whole, and whose members regarded themselves as the cream of the profession. New technology, and particularly mechanization, had blurred the old differences in mobility between the RHA and the rest, but in a nod towards tradition RHA units tended to be concentrated in the armoured divisions.

> My regiment was the 11th (Honourable Artillery Company) Regiment, RHA. The HAC are said to be the oldest regiment in the British Army, and there have been many arguments on large parades when our regiment insisted on marching at the right of

the line. I think the Royal Scots also claim to be the oldest.* We were very pleased to wear the HAC badges, but I think most men in the Army were proud of their own unit.

The conditions in the Desert were terrible at times – the heat, in which we had to carry on as normal; the sandstorms, which at one time blew up at the same time every day and stopped everything until they blew out; the occasional electric storms, which were very frightening; the heavy rain, which allowed many Germans to escape after El Alamein whilst we were unable to receive petrol; the flies, which were everywhere, including on the food, and the desert sores which we all suffered from. I still have some scars on my arms. Then there were the nights, which were so cold. And the shortage of water, which when we had some was warm and very often had little red weevils floating in it. And the inability to 'hide' when attacked by fighters or the dreaded Stukas.

Just before El Alamein the 11th (HAC) had become the first artillery regiment in the Eighth Army to be re-equipped with self-propelled guns, and these quickly proved their value in action.

We were issued with Priests, which had an American 105 mm gun/ howitzer on a Grant tank chassis. We all had to retrain, as the dial sights and so on were calibrated differently to what we were used to.

The Priests and later the Sextons [self-propelled 25-pounders] were used as artillery and not as tank regiments. We had troops of four guns, and when in action were deployed in the same positions as 25-pounder guns would have been. We found out that we had more protection with an SP gun than with the 25-pounders, and our casualties were a lot less. The only men in the open were the ammunition numbers, who every so often had to climb out and load us up with ammo. This is when they were most at risk from enemy shelling.

I had two pals killed at El Alamein stood within 2 yards of me, when a shell from a German tank landed nearby. I was stood

---

* The Honourable Artillery Company dates from 1537, when Henry VIII granted it a Charter of Incorporation. The Royal Scots, although not raised until the following century, are the oldest Regular regiment. Within the Territorial Army, the HAC and arch rivals the Royal Monmouthshire Royal Engineers (Militia) remain locked in disagreement as to which of them is senior to the other.

behind the Priest so had some protection, but they were killed instantly.

We didn't have to worry much about the actual maintenance, as we had trained fitters and mechanics to see to them. Each Priest or Sexton had a Sergeant as No. 1. No. 2 was in charge of the breech. No. 3 was the gunlayer. No. 4 the loader. And 5 and 6 were the ammunition numbers. The Priest also had a .50 Browning machine gun in a pulpit – or gun turret – used for anti-aircraft protection.

The SP guns were much safer and I would think much quicker to get into action – and to retreat if necessary! – than the field guns. Also in the cold and wet weather in Italy we fitted shelter over them with large sheets, so that made them more comfortable. During night-time raids by enemy planes we were able to shelter under the tank chassis, so again had less casualties than the field regiments.

I think the self-propelled guns were a great improvement, and the tank regiments which we supported in the 1st Armoured Division were very often thankful that the Gunners were close behind them to give them supporting fire. The regiment's OPs had Sherman tanks, so they were able to be right forward with the leading tanks and send their orders for fire back to the Command Posts with the guns. We also had a tannoy system on board to receive our orders, which was much better than the shouted orders in the noise of battle.

Occasionally we were able to go forward and fire over open sights, but this was only as a last resort, as we were no match for a German tank in this capacity.

We travelled to Sicily in an LST [tank landing ship] which was much larger than the LCT [tank landing craft] on which we had trained. The seas were very rough, and many of the troops were seasick. I think we anchored in Valletta harbour [Malta] for a few hours and even then we still didn't know where we were due to land. When daylight arrived we were amazed to see the number of ships all around us. The large ships were firing heavy shells over our heads on to the beach – the noise was terrific!

Our Priests had been waterproofed, in other words the exhausts were extended to discharge at high level, and so forth. We drove off the LST and through about 5-feet deep water on to the beach at Pachino.

I've just come across my diary written at the time [reads]: '3.7.43 Boarded LST 361 at Sousse then moved to Sfax. In harbour for three days. Air raids . . . Set sail . . . In convoy was LST 361, with convoy commander on board, 42 LCTs, 4 minesweepers, 4 MTBs, 3 destroyers and 2 light cruisers . . . Friday 9.7.43 Sea very rough. Felt ill. Passed Valletta harbour, with battleships. Saturday 10.7.43 Zero hour 2.45 a.m. 51st (Highland) Division landed. We went ashore at 8.30 a.m. Our regiment's guns the first artillery to land in Europe!'

On our right were the 231st (Malta) Brigade, on the left the Canadians then Americans. From memory, the sun was shining, the birds were singing and not a sound of warfare as we landed. The Germans had withdrawn inland. The first day we advanced 9 miles without firing a shot. First real hold-up was at Vizzini, for two days. Later for eighteen days we continually moved from one sector of the front to another, firing barrages at night and targets during the day. We supported the Canadians, infantry of the 78th Division and 51st (Highland) Division, and tanks of the 23rd Armoured Brigade.

On 30th July I took over as No. 1 of 'C' Sub-Section. This meant that I was in charge of the Priest, doing the job of a Sergeant although I was only a Bombardier with two stripes. A lot of the men were sick with malaria – I had a slight attack, but put up with it without going to hospital. I was afraid of losing the chance of promotion! I still had attacks of malaria for several years after the war, then no more. This was despite mosquito nets – which admittedly were no use in action – and mepacrine tablets.

From the diary [reads]: '9.8.43 Near Adrano. Now on very rough stony ground . . .' We were on the foothills of Mount Etna, and when we left the road – which was mined – we had difficulty in finding a gun position, as the ground was covered with black, solid lava from the volcano. The higher we climbed the worse it was. Then [reads]: 'to a gun position near Maletto . . . On 12.8.43 came out of action to a rear area. 13.8.43 Promoted Lance-Sergeant and took charge of 'D' Sub-Section . . . 17.8.43 Moved 30 miles to a camp near Catania.' I was promoted to full Sergeant a few weeks later.

Our battery commander had captured a very old German field gun, and he planned to take it to Messina to fire across to Italy, but it didn't work out.

Sicily is a very picturesque country – narrow, winding roads, large plains, hilly parts with small villages perched on the top, but very heavily damaged by bombs and shells. And the lava-strewn slopes of Mount Etna. The smoke from the top could be seen from all over the island – ideal for an OP for the Germans.

The British Eighth Army, of which the 11th (HAC) formed a part, had landed alongside the United States Seventh Army. Both of the Army commanders, Montgomery and Patton, had wanted to be the driving force behind the conquest of the island.

Were you aware of the rivalry at the top, between Monty and Patton?

No, we didn't even notice it. All we knew at the time about the Americans was that it was said they'd chosen the 'easy' route in Sicily. But these things are usual when in battle. I expect they thought the same about us. We didn't like it at all when we were once strafed by American fighters, but I don't think rivalries would have affected our thinking at the time; we had other things on our minds.

And then you went on to the mainland. What images does Italy bring to mind?

Oh, the various types of reception from the locals. The sunny weather then the very heavy rain, which brought everything to a halt. The cold and frosty mornings in the mountains of North Italy when we slept in water-filled slit trenches and bivvies which were frozen with the frost. Then the pleasure of a week's leave in Rome, and the relief of the day in May 1945 when it was all over. We celebrated by drinking gallons of vino which made us all ill, and we set fire to a captured German office truck for our bonfire.

As soon as we got to Italy we were re-equipped with Sextons.

We fired the guns at all hours of the day and night. Very often in the night time it was 'harassing fire', just to keep the enemy alert and to keep him awake – as it did for us! Or sometimes a barrage, where the targets had all been worked out for us at the Command Post.

The shells for the Sexton were brought up in metal boxes, four to a box carried by two men. The cartridge cases were separate. The ammo lorries would stack them near to the guns, and the ammo numbers would load them on to the SP guns as required.

You may be interested to know that I have partial deafness which has now been put down to war service, and after several years of trying I have just been awarded a pension for it. Not bad, as I was demobbed in December 1945! Both the 105 mm howitzer on the Priest and the 25-pounder on the Sexton had very loud 'bangs' when firing. I can't remember how many times we fired, except that the last gun I had in the last six months or so in Italy I shouted 'Fire!' over 8000 times. No wonder many artillerymen are deaf.

We couldn't wear ear-plugs as we had to listen for orders from the command posts, either shouted or on the tannoy system.

Most artillery units, however, continued to rely on towed guns. *John Wise* was in a field regiment.

In late 1942 I was home on leave, having married in March. My wife'd had our fortunes told. 'You will not be going abroad,' my wife said.

December 1942 I was home again on embarkation leave. 'Top secret. Tell no one,' we were told. Had a word with my next-door neighbour. 'Hello,' he said. 'Embarkation leave? North Africa?'

No one told us where we were going, but he was dead right. On Christmas Day we left Liverpool on a troopship, and landed in Algiers about a fortnight later. We were moved up from Algiers, reunited with our transport and sent off to go to Tunisia. I think it took about four days.

The gun-towing vehicles were named Quads. They were four wheel drive, had three forward normal gears with a very low extra gear, and a forward and reverse to operate a winch drum under the rear of the vehicle. The Quad could be described as looking like a large beetle on wheels. There were seats for six men, two doors and a hatch which was on the front nearside. The seats were just thin cushions on a metal platform, with no backrest. There were two seats at the front, one for the driver, the other for the No. 1. The 6th Gunner travelled in the ammo truck.

The Atlas Mountains divide Tunisia and Algeria, and they're a hell of a climb. We set off going up this bloody great mountain, all hairpin bends, sheer drops at the side, and tunnels cut into the outcrops. We were up, round, up, round for a whole day and never got out of first gear. My driver and I took turns at the wheel. Pulling that wheel round about every 200 yards was hard work.

But going up was a piece of cake compared to the following day, when we spent half a day going down the other side.

With a crash gearbox – no synchromesh – when you start going down a steep hill with a load you have to stop at the top, put it in low gear and never take it out of gear. If you do, the thing gathers speed and it's impossible to get the gear back, and you run away. It means the engine is going flat out in first gear and you have one foot on the dashboard, the other on the footbrake, and getting to a corner you're pulling up the handbrake with leverage from your leg. Hair-raising stuff.

When we were first issued with Quads you could get all the

ammo and stores required for six men in, but they had no room for our equipment – packs, blankets, and so on. So our mechanics fitted all the Quads with roof racks, and we were piled up with all sorts of junk. The officers didn't like it but we got away with it. I even had a portable latrine, for use of my sub-section only, which was much admired.

As I said, the Quads were pigs to handle. It was essential to have a driver who knew the ropes and worked with the gun Sergeant. On the road it was a heavy load, prone to front wheel wobble and gun snaking – no brakes on the gun. The guns were usually taken into position at night, with no lights and no shouting. Sound travels at night. A system of hand signals with a masked torch was devised, and was very successful. The Gunners too had to be taught how to use the winch – woe betide anyone if the rope snarled on the drum.

My first driver was Scottish, a good bloke, but after our first experience in action he went bomb happy, and was returned to base. His replacement was killed the second time in action with me; 10 yards behind my gun a shell burst, and he was cut in two. The third one was a budding Stirling Moss. Once when we approached a Bailey bridge some of our infantry were crossing, but he just barged on, the poor devils running and jumping over the sides. I got rid of him pretty quick. Being shelled was bad enough without a maniac driver. The one after that was a good driver, but he too went bomb happy. After the war I met him, and sadly he was still bomb happy. He was in trouble with the police due to his behaviour. However, my next driver was perfect in every way. Good driving ability, no flapping – very quiet and dependable man.

The biggest nightmare I had was when the Eighth Army and the First Army joined up for the final battle for Tunis. The British units of the First Army were in the north, around the Beja area. The Yanks and Free French in the south, next to the Eighth Army. It was decided to change the force around so the British would be closer together, so we all packed up on the same day and when it became dark we moved south, the Yanks moving north. What a nightmare. The Tunisian roads were only narrow, deep ditched on either side, and they had funny bridges which halved the road width. In the dark they were difficult to see. How we got to our destination in one piece I have no idea. The Yanks were as mad as hatters. Another difficulty – Quads were normal British steering for driving on the left; Tunisia was the right-hand side of the road.

The role of the field artillery was primarily to support our infantry. Our division, the 46th, was a North Midland division, and the divisional sign was an oak tree. The formations of a division were broadly in threes – three infantry brigades to an infantry division, three battalions of infantry to a brigade, and three field regiments, RA. Field regiments [each of which had an establishment of twenty-four guns] were made up of three batteries, and batteries of four-gun troops. I was in Charlie Troop, 279 Battery, 70th Field Regiment. The troop in turn was divided into two sections, Left Section and Right Section. My gun and crew were always 'A' Sub-Section, the others 'B', 'C' and 'D'. I was No. 1 of 'A' Sub, the leading gun in the order of march, and the first gun on the right when we occupied our gun positions. Everyone was RA – signals, drivers, and so on.

Did you find that most people got on together?

I think anyone who hasn't had Army life in wartime can grasp what it's like by selecting a lonely field cut off from civilization and living there with the same faces, not for days on end, but months and years. No comforts at all, no fires, lights, radio, TV. Monotonous food. Having to eat stood up. Dirty clothes and blankets, not having a proper bath or bed for *years*. Pure drinking water just a memory. Hard, dangerous work; never a full night's sleep. I could go on. But the point I'm making is that you ask about pals and people mixing. In those conditions I've described you *have* to be pals with everyone. Minor hiccups have to be forgotten.

By the way, we used to have hot water in our gun pit. We saved the unused cordite bags. Split open, they contained a propellant which when ignited sent the shell on its way. Our junk we carried around had a filthy old gallon biscuit tin. We had a wire handle, and made a small fire between stones. Putting the can full of water on top of the fire, standing at a safe distance, we threw the cordite, which resembled macaroni, on to the fire. After a minute of whooshes of cordite our water was hot. The bloke who lit it had first wash and shave. But when the sixth bloke came up I'm afraid it was rather 'pea-soupy'. 'How many has been in here?' was the cry. It didn't matter how many – there was no more water.

The worst water we had was in Tunisia. We were in action in front of Djebel Kournine, a hill we called 'The Twin Tits', for obvious reasons. Between The Twin Tits and us was salt lakes. That was our water supply. Try a spoon of salt in your tea some time, or a lovely warm drink of chlorinated salt lake water instead of your usual pint. We got this every day, all day, for over a week.

What did you think about your equipment?

Our 18-pounders from the First World War were made into so-called 18/25-pounders, and then we eventually got the 25-pounder Mk. II. The 25-pounder was the workhorse of the infantry division. Very accurate, and a rapid rate of fire. We had HE, anti-tank and smoke shells with a time fuse. It could be put into very convenient positions and was quick to come into action. A shoe was fitted over its spade, so the gun didn't dig in and was easy to traverse when making big switches. The old 18-pounder had a sharp pointed spade, and when the gun recoiled after firing this dug into the ground. The gun crew was constantly having to man-handle the gun back into position.

All the HE shells were fitted with a fixed contact fuse. They came four to a box, and had a safety cap at the point of the fuse. This was simply unscrewed and put back into the empty shell box. Two standard fuses were used – the No. 117 and the No. 119. The only difference was the 119 had a slight delay. Armour-piercing shells – AP – were lighter, 20 pounds, and had no fuse fitted.

Smoke shells had a time fuse. The GPO [Gun Position Officer] worked out the fuse setting, say 9.2 seconds, from his data. The Gunners had a spanner-like key which fitted on to a ring and set the number required on the fuse. The shell exploded in mid-air over the target, blowing the end of the shell off and allowing the ignited smoke canisters to fall to the ground.

The ranges we actually fired in action in North Africa and Italy were from 3500 yards – a bit hairy, that – up to about 13,000 yards. If my memory serves me right that was by using Super Charge. We hated that; my ears have never been the same.

Usually we mostly used Charge 2. There were three bags in the brass cartridge case. A small one at the bottom, Charge 1. Firing the gun with this charge was normal up to 4000 yards. Charge 2 was Charge 1 plus a second bag marked '2'. This was used for 4000–8000 range. All three bags in the case were for 8000–12,000. The base of the case contained the primer, which exploded when the firing pin was released by the gunlayer.

The empty cartridge cases were packed back into their boxes and were piled up ready for removal, hopefully. I can remember after a hectic week in one gun position we were firing at 3000 yards range, which in artillery is eyeball-to-eyeball stuff. We were getting mortared, which was unusual, for mortars didn't have a long range. We had to leave in a hurry and retreat. As we'd been firing for hours without respite – we were putting a wall of HE

between the infantry and the advancing German Army – there was
no clearing up there!

When the gun fired the piece recoiled and then ran back, the
No. 2 man caught the breech handle, the block fell and ejected the
cartridge case. The breech remained open, and could be loaded
within seconds if required.

To give you an idea of the speed. In action in Tunisia we were
firing ranging rounds on a small wood occupied by Italian troops.
The ranging rounds were fired by my gun, observed by our battery
commander. When he had the range he gave orders for five rounds
per gun. Eight guns times five rounds each equals forty 25-pounder
shells landing in less than a minute. The Italians, when the first
rounds arrived, ran out of the wood with their hands up. The OP
sent down 'Stop Firing!', but in that short space of time the rounds
were on their way. When you are being shelled you get down and
stay down. Running about is fatal.

German ranging was different to ours. Instead of rounds on the
ground to observe the fall of shot, they used airburst shells. If a
shell burst over your position, you were in for it.

The 25-pounder had a crew of six. A Sergeant No. 1, a Bombardier No. 3, and 2, 4, 5 and 6 were Gunners. No. 2 operated the
breech opening and closing, No. 4 put the shell and cartridge in
the gun. The driver of the gun-towing vehicle wasn't on the gun
position, but moved down to the wagon lines to the rear.

I was the No. 1, a full Sergeant, in charge of the gun. I gave all
the fire orders and made checks on the ammo for correct charges,
fuses, and so on. I was responsible for getting the gun into action,
ensuring gun pits and slit trenches were dug, and things like that.
The No. 3 was the gunlayer, and when he put settings on the dial
sight I had to check it was correct before firing.

The training was pretty hard for the No. 1 position. I had to go
down to Larkhill several times for weeks, and a month once, for
gunnery courses. The RA School of Artillery was there on Salisbury
Plain, and it was very hard going.

The Gunners were just ordinary lads; they had to be strong and
fit. Humping a box of 25-pounder shells which weighed 1 cwt,
digging a gun pit, and having to manhandle a gun wasn't easy. A
lot had to be sent back to base before we could get the blokes who
were any good.

Apart from the physical side, the mental make-up was just as
important. Some of the chaps when we were under shellfire
couldn't cope. I had two men in my sub who I had to send back
for that reason. Also when soldiers who'd been wounded came

back into action, they weren't the same. You see, you were in fear all the time. Unlike the infantry, we had to stay in the line even if we were in a silent role. The winters in Italy in the mountains were very harsh. We would be weeks in the open getting little sleep. In a battle zone there's always noise and movement. No fires or lights allowed.

Washing clothes was an impossible task, and we smelt awful. But the main thing was fear of the unknown, and to me the fear of being wounded in a bad way. I got slightly wounded once in Italy – I was in a house and a shell exploded just outside and I was cut by flying glass. But some of the chaps in hospital with stomach wounds or amputations were grim. I was very lucky – I had a bomb from a Focke Wulf Fw. 190 fighter-bomber explode 30 yards from me, and two huge shells from a railway gun, killing five men and wounding two, and all I got was shrapnel on my tin hat. My gun was hit and had holes through the trail; four men were killed yards behind my gun in Africa; the gun position was strafed by cannon fire and machine guns missing me by inches – a bullet pierced a pickaxe handle beside me – and several more instances. I had my whole kit destroyed by shellfire twice. The QM wasn't pleased about that!

And yet we got replacements from base, and within days they would be dead. I always thought it would be my turn next. However, you got used to it in the end.

Were there any disadvantages to being the No. 1 on the gun?

Well, one thing I didn't like was when we were driving in convoy. The trouble for me being the No. 1 was I had to stand on my seat and face the rear, with the top half of my body through the hatch. The convoy could only travel at the speed of the slowest vehicle, so each vehicle watched the one behind and slowed down to keep the regulation distance between vehicles. A good idea, but tiring and bloody cold and wet in winter.

The system failed for me once in Italy. We were moving up to occupy a new position. I was the first gun following the troop leader, a Second Lieutenant. It was a winding country lane and we passed the usual wartime scene – ruined houses, beat-up trucks, and a couple of 25-pounder gun positions. Then rounding a corner there was no truck in front. I went on, no one in front, no one in rear. Another 100 yards, and everything was deserted. Round the corner was a British Army truck on fire with a dead British soldier next to it. The road was narrow and had ditches either side. There was no way we could turn a Quad, limber and gun round there. We had to go on. Round the next corner we came to an Italian cemetery with a British soldier up a tree fixing signal wire. I asked him if there was a gun position here. He said, 'This is an infantry position!' We were in the front line! The next corner I was never as scared as I was then; 10 yards in front with its 75 mm gun pointing at us was a tank – a German Panther. It was dead, a hole in the turret.

Just then a bren opened up. You knew the difference between it and the German machine guns – the bren went rat-tat-tat, the German ones brrrrr. I have never seen gun, limber and Quad turned round as quickly. We hot-footed it back down the lane until we came across a Gunner we knew at a turning. We went up this road, and I got to the officer who had turned off without waiting for me. I risked a court martial, I'm afraid to say; I was so mad I gave him a right mouthful. I told him he was lucky to see us again, we could easily have been blown off the road.

Some of the officers were a dead loss, but we had a high turnover. We had four battery commanders killed – one by an armoured car which nearly reached our position; another one, a mortar landed on his tank and nearly removed his head.

The Quads were a good vehicle for towing. Using the winch we could get the gun into very awkward places. But they were pigs to drive. The gearbox was a crash box, the brakes weren't up to much, and they were hard work. No power steering then.

But the really hard work was in action. During the final push up to Tunis we had massed 500-plus gun bombardments. These were sheer hell for two hours. The night starts still and quiet, just the odd bang and flash in the distance. We're all prepared, loaded, ammo in separate piles for different targets. When zero hour arrives we're waiting, and when the order comes through – 'Fire!' – we all open up. The noise is ear-splitting. Flashes blinding us. Smoke soon covers the gun position. We'd work to a timetable – when we'd fired Target 1 we'd switch to Target 2, and so on.

As the guns were all off the road and the ammo was dumped at the roadside we had to carry it sometimes over 100 yards to the gun. A 1 cwt box on your shoulders in the dark, over uneven ground, is no picnic, and everyone took turns; no hiding behind a stripe.

One particular night, whilst we were firing, there was the most terrific explosion in front about 2 miles away. We thought bloody hell, what was *that*? When we moved up a day or so after, we passed the cause of the explosion. The Royal Engineers had cleared German Teller mines – the big anti-tank ones – and piled them in a big pile at a road junction. One of the advancing Churchill tanks had driven into them in the dark . . . There was a crater as big as a house.

Our next gun position when we moved again was a former target. What a shambles. It was a farm with cows – dead ones – all on their backs, legs sticking in the air. I think we were there about two days. Talk about a smell. We passed many such things. The villages which had been shelled stank of death, and it's an awful smell. We used to bury Germans if they were on our position when we got there, but burying a cow or two was a bit much.

We had a very tough foe. I remember the very first action we were involved in. Our infantry were the 5th Battalion, the Sherwood Foresters. We watched their bren-carriers go up the hill in front of us, and heard the sound of battle. We were firing in support. But in no time at all the German artillery started on us. Fortunately for us our OP was overrun and silenced – the OP officer was taken prisoner – so we had to cease firing. The troop in front of us were able to carry on for a while, but the Germans hit the gun position and their ammo caught fire and exploded. They had two gun Sergeants killed and several Gunners wounded.

The attack failed and the Sherwoods had to retreat with heavy losses. We had to retreat too, to new gun positions 2 miles or so down the road.

Actions similar to this took place over months, and we found ourselves supporting other units. Once an infantry battalion was mauled they were taken out and it was a while before they were back in the line.

In comparison we didn't suffer the same losses as they did; any casualties were replaced and the battery was kept in action.

10

SAPPERS

The Royal Engineers, or 'Sappers' as they were nicknamed, were responsible for an extraordinary diversity of tasks. Their list of tradesmen included such jobs as Blacksmith, Quarryman, Tool-maker, Fitter (Steam Locomotive), Riveter, Bricklayer, Driver (Road Roller), Electrician, Printer Compositor, Postal Worker, Draughtsman (Architectural) and Mason.

Around 80 per cent of Sappers belonged to a particular trade, but they were not employed full-time on their own specialization, and a lot of their work was of a more general nature, like water supply, road construction and demolitions.

Alfred Sheppard was a Mason.

> My eventual enlistment in the Royal Engineers was influenced from the time I started my apprenticeship to a stonemason in 1932, at the age of fourteen.
>
> After my indentures had been signed I was a bound apprentice for four years, with set weekly wages of 12/- for the first year, 15/- for the second, £1 for the third and half the prevailing skilled rate for the fourth, which was 1/4d per hour in 1936.
>
> From the start I was put with a highly skilled mason called Bill Dyke, who'd been appointed to instruct me in his craft for the four years. In those days masons instructing apprentices were expected to do as much finished stonework as anyone else, and the employer also wanted a good profit from the apprentice. In my last year I was producing as much, if not more than some of the masons. At one time there was over forty, so there was always lots going on around you.
>
> Bill had enlisted in the Royal Engineers at the outbreak of the First World War, and had risen to the rank of Sergeant, so when there was conversation between him and me other than about work, much of it was about the REs. I soon learnt that they had

mostly tradesmen, for which there was trade pay. There was a recognized trade of Mason. From some of the things told to me by Bill I became drawn to the REs more than any other unit.

During the 1930s, up to the outbreak of the Second World War, men joined the Army through being unemployed, and it's likely that I would have applied to join the REs had I not had regular employment after I finished my contract as an apprentice.

Towards the end of 1937 I had the chance of a regular job in Somerset, about 50 miles from home. There was no assistance to get there, but there were good prospects; by the time I was twenty in 1938 I had been appointed a deputy foreman. The small amount of extra money was a good help towards my 'digs', which were 25/- a week. At home I paid £1. The general foreman, to whom I was a great help, would work me in a couple of hours' extra by way of 'under the counter' bonus.

Then the war clouds began to appear.

Immediately after the outbreak of war the King made a proclamation that all men born between two given dates must register for National Service under a new Act just brought in. This was my age group, so I went to the nearest labour exchange at Martock, Somerset and signed on the dotted line on 21st October 1939, the date laid down. I was instructed to present myself before the Medical Board at the Police Sports Ground, Taunton on 10th November, and I was pleased to pass A1. An Army officer who interviewed me asked if I preferred any particular regiment, to which I said that I was keen to enlist in the REs.

Eventually I was notified that I was to join my unit, No. 1 Training Battalion, RE, at Napier Barracks, Shorncliffe, Kent on 15th January 1940. A railway warrant and, I think, a small amount for contingency expenses were enclosed. All I had to do was get there, by catching the earliest train to Paddington and then the Tube to London Bridge to catch a train to Folkestone. It was a great relief to find that the train was crowded with other people on the same mission! Shorncliffe was a vast military area and the nearest railway station was Cheriton, which is where instructions were given to alight.

The sixteen weeks' training in No. 1 TBRE included the usual square-bashing, saluting at the halt and on the march, firing on the range at Hythe, and PT outside and in the gym, because in the Royal Engineers first of all you're a soldier. Soldier first, tradesman second. Then there were the Sapper field works, which could be done on the area allocated for the purpose. Most bridges at this early stage of the war were built with the use of pontoons and their accessories, and pontoon training was done at a place called Wouldham, on the River Medway. We went by train to Rochester and marched the several miles to the camp in full 'marching order'. During the two weeks we were there we also marched to Chatham to do demolition training. We used explosives to 'blow' hulks and tree trunks, and so on.

Some time in March 1940 I was put 'on draft', but wasn't sent to France or Norway as some were. At the end of the training, which was longer in the REs, I was transferred to the depot company and was sent on detachment to a brickyard on the outskirts of Folkestone. This was to make room for more recruits in the Regular Army quarters. From there we had to construct machine gun posts all along the coast as far as Dymchurch. This entailed mostly excavating and sandbagging. In several cases we manned the posts with Lewis guns until they were taken over by the infantry.

It was then that the evacuation of Dunkirk took place, and we were able to give a hand to some of the men who were coming back. We thought that *we* were roughing it, but those men had had a rotten time. I remember feeling guilty that I hadn't been over there. The next day we were put on patrol on the Folkestone road, where we had to stop and search any vehicles, including military. I remember going on the buses and checking the identity cards of the passengers. We had to look out for a man and a woman who had been acting suspiciously in the area. All this happened within a week or so of the evacuation of Dunkirk, and then we were recalled to Shorncliffe to be issued with tropical gear – Mussolini had just declared war on the Allies.

Most of us thought we would embark at Liverpool, but that was not to be, and we went to Gourock, on the Clyde. Whilst on the train I was able to write a letter to my mother, in pencil, standing up, to tell her what I thought was about to happen and not to worry. On the docks at Gourock I gave the letter to one of the dockers, who said he would be glad to post it.

We set sail during the night, and there were no bands or crowds to see us off. Over nine weeks later, having sailed around the African continent and via Trincomalee, Colombo and Bombay, we finally disembarked at Port Taufiq. On arrival at Abbassia Barracks near Cairo we were told that the overseas period for troops was set at five years. The unit I was posted to in the Desert was the 2nd (Cheshire) Field Squadron, RE, and except for a spell in hospital with jaundice, and being wounded at El Alamein, I was with them until I was repatriated under the 'Python' scheme after four and a half years.

Did you know you would be going to the 2nd Field Squadron before you got to Egypt?

No, there were a number of Sapper units in the Middle East, and it was just pot luck which one you were posted to.

Actually, being posted to the 2nd Field Squadron was quite funny, because although they were in the 7th Armoured Division when I joined them, they had originally gone out to the Middle East in January 1940, to Palestine, with the 1st Cavalry Division. They were actually the 1st Cav. Div. REs. And when I went in the Army, that day at Cheriton, on the platform, it was 'REs over there. Cavalry over here.' Because right next to us was the 6th Cavalry Training Regiment. We saw them training, galloping across fields. So those blokes who went in the Army the same day as me, probably a lot of them were posted to the Middle East with the Cavalry Division.

'Course, they all became mechanized eventually.

Anyhow, we went on the train from Cairo, Abbassia Barracks – there was sidings there, and a big troop area – on the track which goes all up towards Alexandria, then curves round and starts going west through El Alamein, and Fuka, till we got to Mersa Matruh. Well, in 1940 the railway only went as far as Mersa Matruh. And when we got there – I think it took about two days – there was these wagons there to take us on across the Desert.

When we got to our unit, there was a Sergeant-Major shouting in the dark, 'Get down where you are – the enemy's only just there.' And they were. The Eyeties were about 200 yards away. So soon as I joined it, my field squadron withdrew, about 4 miles. What was happening was that we were making what they call 'a strategic withdrawal'. That was because they were reducing our numbers, and we'd been heavily outnumbered even at the start.

Anyhow, we came back, and then back some more, and eventually I was back to the east of Mersa Matruh.

What did you make of ending up further east than where you'd got off the train?

Oh, I thought we were in serious trouble. We had all these different fronts in the Middle East; all different places where we had to try and hold things with our small Army. The Western Desert was only one of them. But as the year went on we were able to push the Italians right back through the Libyan frontier at Fort Capuzzo.

On Christmas Day 1940 the 25-pounders were shelling Bardia,

which is just inside of Libya. And we were there, waiting to go in. We had jobs to do in there, demolition and that. I didn't feel well. I hadn't been feeling well for two or three days. But I was afraid to tell anybody, because I thought they might think I was trying to get out of it. And our Old Man, a Captain – formerly a Sergeant-Major; good bloke – he came round. It was Christmas Day, and he was dishing out rum. I felt *terrible*. And the shelling was going on. 'There ain't much I can give you,' he said, 'Christmas Day. All I can do is give you extra issue of rum.' His Sergeant was pouring the rum out of a jar, you see. He poured about that much in my cup, which was all filthy dirty. I took a couple of swigs, and was immediately sick. And one of the Corporals come along and said, 'Christ, Shep, you're not well. Why didn't you say?' And I was evacuated.

Jaundice. That's what I had. So I went right back – it took three days – to Hilmiya, near Cairo. Then I was transferred to another hospital, to make room for wounded coming in, and then to a convalescent depot. That was at El Arish, on the shores of the Med, half-way between Egypt and Palestine.

Soon after I got back to the 2nd Field Squadron we were withdrawn – you know, you get pulled out every so often – because the unit itself had done a long time at the front. We were withdrawn, and brought back to a place called Mena, right by the Pyramids. And in early 1941 we got sent to Palestine, to do all these fortifications on the road between Nazareth and Tiberias, the Sea of Galilee. This was another one of the fronts in the Middle East. At the time the Turks were neutral, and the story went that we were doing these fortifications because we didn't know whether they were going to let the Germans come through. Because if they got through Syria, where the Vichy French were, then we'd have to face them there, at Tiberias.

Anyhow, we did a lot of work there. We did a lot of galleries under the road, to blow the road. What we were doing was we were making a gallery up and under the road, lined with pre-cast slabs. So that you could go in, and if the Germans got through you could blow the road. Didn't go all the way through the road, just into the middle.

When we got down to the southern end of the Sea of Galilee we were doing anti-tank obstacles, made of concrete, and pillboxes. And anti-tank ditches. We did all that, and then all of a sudden, after we'd spent all that money, we went and attacked the bloody Vichy French. It [the Syrian campaign] only lasted just over a month. And what I remember of it, we didn't have a lot of casualties. Not what we were used to. Then we were brought back to Palestine, training. Lot of training.

Meanwhile Rommel had arrived. And we were sent back to the Desert again, against Rommel.

More often, however, the Sappers found themselves called in to deal with the enemy's defences rather than to construct their own.

Before El Alamein, for example, the lavish German minefields had to have corridors cleared through them to allow the tanks and infantry to press home their attacks.

John Jefferis was one of the first to step into the mined area.

Our three platoons were ordered to open three gaps in the enemy minefields, so as when completed it would allow the armour through. My job was to walk into the minefield on foot laying white tape all the way, to mark the edge of the gap.

We'd been ordered to move to our positions at night, so what a fright I got when suddenly a thousand guns of all kinds unleashed a barrage – which at that time was our biggest of the war. I didn't know they were in that position, and it scared me more than entering the minefield! I'd never heard so many express trains passing overhead.

It must have been quite a test of nerve, deliberately walking into a minefield.

Well, it wasn't a case of having nerves of steel or anything. It was just doing a job you were trained to do. It was just a case of trusting to luck, and as you can see my luck held, thank God.

You never knew what type of mines were laid by the enemy. The German Teller mine was an anti-tank mine. It had a cast metal case, and was shaped like a dinner plate. Their anti-personnel mines were filled with ¼-inch ball bearings at the start of the war, and later on filled with any old scrap iron. If stepped on, they would jump about 3 feet in the air, and then explode, spraying the whole area with shrapnel.

When our 500-yard tapes ran out we had to get back to our starting points as fast as possible, to stand by to replace the casualties in the detection and clearance parties following on behind.

The detection parties' job was to find the mines, either with detectors or by prodding with bayonets, and then mark them for the clearance parties. The clearance parties lifted the mines. You had to be careful, as Teller mines often had booby traps fastened either to the side, or to the bottom. So you had to feel all the way round to make sure.

What fun – I don't think.

As the fighting moved on into Sicily and Italy, the additional hazards of river crossings were added. *Henry Hodgson* found out the hard way that these assignments too could never be taken lightly.

We had already crossed two rivers, the Biferno and the Trigno, and both of these were very heavy going because the Germans had the advantage of being in defensive positions on the banks. We knew that the Sangro would be much harder. The Germans had command of all the main heights, and the river itself was much wider and also had a much stronger and faster current.

Four Sappers, myself – I was then a Sergeant – and our officer Lieutenant Hosie tried to get across and make fast in an old Italian cutter. On our bank, more Sappers were holding on to a length of cordage fastened to the boat. But the river was running too fast, and instead of drifting across, the cordage tightened up and the boat capsized in mid-stream. We narrowly escaped death by grabbing at overhanging trees, but all the equipment was lost.

Further up the river the water was calmer, and men and equipment were able to get across, but even there we suffered the dislocation of one Bailey bridge, which was swept away by the force of the river, together with quite a number of men.

On 22nd November 1943 we were at a place called Casalbordino, and in the afternoon about 16.00 hours we received orders to collect six of our best Sappers as a working party to clear mines from very treacherous territory which we knew to be honeycombed with them. There were not many men left to choose from; out of sixty-two we only had eighteen left. Most of them had been on similar missions before many times. Every man knew what to expect, and although he smoked and chatted with his friends on the reverse slopes [the sides of the hill or ridge out of sight of the enemy] he knew that once over the ridge the going would be hard.

We weren't told when the next attack was to take place for the reason that if we were caught we should have no times, dates or information of any kind for the enemy, but we were all old campaigners and had a good idea through our past experiences of what was to happen. Everything was being got ready, and the Sangro valley was alive with activity under cover of darkness, when the Germans couldn't see what was happening. Each night for about a week the trucks loaded with supplies and ammunition had poured out of Casalbordino until the reverse slopes were chock-a-block with trucks nose to tail.

We had every reason to believe that the attack was scheduled to take place early morning of the 23rd, because of the particular task assigned to us for the 22nd. Lieutenant Hosie had been to the Buffs headquarters [the HQ of the 5th Battalion, the Royal East Kent Regiment, one of the infantry battalions of the division] and arranged for us to have an infantry fighting patrol to cover for us whilst we were completing our operation of mine lifting. Frankly, I think if anything the infantry were more nervous than us, because they were responsible for our safety, whilst we on the other hand had a job to do.

We moved off from Casalbordino at 17.30 hours, just as night was falling, taking four hours over the 10-mile journey due to the amassed transport *en route*. We took the risk of taking the White scout car [a four-wheeled, lightly armoured vehicle issued to RE units to aid mobility. White was the name of the American manufacturer] over the hill into the valley to give us more time for the job. We held our breath going down the main road, and left the car with the wireless operator and driver – lucky men – in a well-covered area, and set off on foot. The night was now an inky blackness, as we plodded on and crossed the Bailey bridge over the Sangro which was well on the way to being completed by another RE company of our division, the 78th Div.

Once over the bridge we fell in with our infantry patrol, who were grumbling about having to escort us, and who took up their positions behind us for our cover. The number of men in a patrol was normally about six, with an officer or Sergeant in charge, and they were armed with bren- and tommy-guns. We were also armed, the Sappers with tommy-guns and myself and Lieutenant Hosie with .455 revolvers, besides our mine detectors, cables, grappling-irons, tape and probing rods. The number of men on these missions was always limited because speed and silence are essential factors, and they attract less attention from the enemy.

We walked up the gradient by route of an old worn track to the coastal road, where we began operating. First we decided to clear the long length of roadway that was to our left, towards the main crossroads junction going north. We took it fairly steady, our main job being to clear the road and the verges. We reached the crossroads at 24.00 hours and we then retraced our steps to the little junction where we first began operations. We stayed there about fifteen minutes chatting to another infantry patrol, at what was eventually to be the main route for the attack. On leaving them we said our usual commonplace remarks, 'We'll be seeing you,' 'T.T.F.N.' and so on, and moved off to the right of the junction.

On this sector we took even more care, because we had seen the photographs taken by our reconnaissance planes, and they showed that the surface of the road had been disturbed in a number of places. This was proved as we came across a belt of Italian box mines, which had been booby trapped. I decided to stay and lift these mines myself, and Lieutenant Hosie said he would go on with Lance-Corporal Dixon and four Sappers to see if there were any further mines ahead, as we had not yet reached our map reference point and time was getting short.

About half an hour had elapsed when a Sapper came running back to tell me that they had located another belt of Italian box mines similar to that which I was disarming. By now it was 02.00 hours and pouring with rain, so rather than try to defuse them under these conditions we decided to 'draw' them out.

Lieutenant Hosie went a little way back down the road to locate a suitable place to provide us with cover from blast in case the mine exploded whilst we were drawing it from its position. I made fast the cordage to one of the mines, paying it out along the road and into the little cul-de-sac amongst the rocks which he had selected for our cover.

We had just got settled in this position when I side-stepped to my right to see that the cable wasn't obstructed in any way before the command was given to withdraw the mine. Lieutenant Hosie must have had the same thing in mind, for he too side-stepped to the right. He was no more than 3 feet away from me when he stepped on a German anti-personnel mine, the same type as I was wounded by in the Sicilian campaign. For a split second I saw a red ball of fire, and felt a terrific burning in parts of my body. I think I got the shrapnel that came through Lieutenant Hosie.

After that I was pushed up, put on a bren-carrier and taken back over the Sangro to an Advanced Dressing Station with a number of swinging oil lamps. And then further back still. Had an operation to remove shrapnel – that was in Brindisi. Some Americans were brought into the hospital and treated for mustard gas. Their ship had been bombed.*

---

* Although as it turned out neither side chose to initiate chemical warfare, both the Allies and the Axis powers were fully prepared for it. On 2nd December 1943 an American merchantman, the SS *John Harvey*, carrying chemical munitions, was bombed at Bari and her cargo of mustard gas released into the harbour. Thousands of servicemen and civilians were killed or injured, although the authorities did their best to conceal the truth for fear that the Germans might begin using gas for real.

Then home via Algiers. Nine operations at a hospital in Whalley, Lancashire, and then to a convalescent depot in Blackburn.

That was where Colonel Hosie contacted me and asked if I would go down to see him in Middlesex, where he was in charge of a REME [Royal Electrical and Mechanical Engineers] depot. He arranged for a travel warrant and accommodation, and I travelled down to see him. He asked me to explain exactly what happened to his only son. His adjutant wrote down for him everything I said. He wanted me to take a post down there with him, but I told him I'd like to go home and think it over. I thought, Every time he sees me he'll see his son. And I didn't want him to be constantly reminded. Then he asked me to please go and visit his wife.

She was very upset, and it was quite an ordeal for both of us.

At the outbreak of war the Royal Engineers had possessed no armoured vehicles for crossing ground swept by enemy fire, but by the time of the Italian and North-West Europe Campaigns certain specialized units had at last begun to receive them.

Mervyn Thomas was a tank man transferred to one of the new units.

I'd never heard of an assault regiment until I was posted to one – the 1st Assault Regiment, RE. I joined them in the San Marino–Rimini area, and was immediately told to stand by a deserted, broken-down Churchill until the fitters or recovery vehicle arrived. I assumed that the unit were in action somewhere. The vehicle and myself were eventually recovered, and I joined up with the rest of the squadron, where I managed to gain a rough idea of what the regiment did.

I gathered it consisted of a squadron of Sherman bulldozers and two mixed squadrons of Churchill AVRE engineer vehicles and Arks. I received no training in my duties, and picked them up as I went along. No officer or senior NCO ever put me in the picture, and I had the feeling that Royal Armoured Corps personnel were not particularly welcome. It was always difficult to join another corps, and an additional problem was that there were so few RAC people in the regiment – just the AFV drivers and fitters. The only RAC officer was the Technical Adjutant. Certainly after I was wounded on 8th November 1944, when a mine exploded under my AVRE while I was trying to fill an anti-tank ditch in front of Forli airfield, I never had any contact with the assault regiment. No visits or letters.

Was dealing with anti-tank ditches your principal task?

Yes. We had the facilities for mine clearing and demolition of obstacles, but these alternatives weren't used while I was driving. I got an AVRE of my own immediately, and from then until I was wounded we were almost continually in action. The hours we used to spend without rest were quite long. We used to spend the days making fascines [cylindrical bundles of chestnut paling and brushwood, bound with wire rope]. Then the vehicles had to be maintained.

We usually planned on dropping our fascines [into the anti-tank ditch or other obstacle] at dawn, and this would require a long night march without lights, which could prove very tiring for drivers. But things seldom went to plan. Often we would plan to drop a fascine at dawn and finally do it at eleven o'clock, which meant sitting for about five hours with the engine idling. I don't want to appear immodest, but the driver needed some skill to ensure that the fascine dropped smoothly. It was necessary to get the AVRE on its point of balance to be sure of success. Driving a Churchill with a fascine on board was quite an adventure; it was big, awkward, and could always find things to foul on – posts, walls, wires, and so on. You name it, a fascine would find it.

After dropping a fascine we got back out of the way as quickly as possible, for armoured bulldozers to work to form inclines and to continue to fill the ditch. We would withdraw to reload, or to make more fascines.

How did you actually make them?

The site had to be fairly level and free from obstructions. Two wire cables were then placed parallel, roughly the width of an AVRE [10 feet 8 inches] apart. Faggots were then placed transversely across the cables. When enough had been stacked, the cables would be looped around and attached to the towing shackles of two AVREs which would be facing each other – they both faced the fascine in order to see signals. The AVREs then reversed, tightening the cables and compressing the fascine. When sufficient compression was reached, the cables were secured on top by clamps and the vehicles released.

When you were dropping the fascine in action, the additional cables holding it to the AVRE could be severed by exploding a slab of gun cotton attached to a blow-plate, which could be detonated from inside the vehicle. Unfortunately the gun cotton sometimes dispersed like a dandelion puff. Then the argument used to start to find the lucky hero who was going to cut it with a hack-saw.

The AVREs we were using in Italy weren't particularly reliable. I think that they were probably tanks which had been recovered and brought back into service, and were consequently not as strong as they might have been. The crew consisted of Sappers except for myself, and we were armed with two 7.92 mm Besa machine guns, one in the turret and one in the co-driver's position. I believe the purpose-built AVREs in North-West Europe were fitted with a spigot mortar [for demolishing concrete obstacles and pillboxes], but I never encountered these.

The vehicle I was driving had had its 6-pounder gun removed and a drain pipe substituted, and when we were travelling with the turret traversed the dummy gun fouled things. I'm 5 feet 3 inches tall, and the Italians used to be quite surprised to see a midget climb out of the driver's hatch of a 40-ton tank. But the day the said midget, in the square in Cesena, climbed out and cut 12 inches off the end of the gun convinced them it was a mad world!

Sapper units at home also had dangerous duties to perform, most notably in the field of bomb disposal.

No pre-war organization for dealing with unexploded bombs, or UXBs, had existed, but by the middle of 1940 the Royal Engineers had built up 120 Bomb Disposal Sections, each with one officer and fifteen other ranks. Under the intensive bombing of that summer and autumn, however, these proved to be inadequate, and so both the number and size of the sections were doubled. The additional manpower was found by disbanding seven General Construction and four Quarrying Companies, RE.

One of the Sappers who found himself transferred was *Francis Brown*.

The forming of the bomb disposal unit which I became a member of happened whilst we were under canvas in Cornwall, and after we separated from the 853rd Quarrying Company, RE. We started to gather around us such things as two-man pumps, digging tools, ropes, tripod legs, block and tackle, stakes and timber, and we spent two or three weeks learning how to probe suspected bomb entry holes and finding out which direction the bomb had travelled. This then gave us an idea of where to start our excavation. Also we learned how to erect a tripod complete with tackle, to harness the bomb and remove it from the excavation.

We were based, in sections of about thirty men, at various points around the south-western part of the country. Eventually our section formed part of the 7th Bomb Disposal Company, RE. The reward for being in bomb disposal was an extra shilling per day on top of normal pay. We were identified by a bomb motif worn on the lower left sleeve of the battledress.

Our first encounter with bombs was at Bristol. We seemed to learn all about German bombs and mines as we encountered them, such as the sizes, which were 50 kg, 250 kg, 500 kg, both armour-piercing and general purpose; also larger bombs with names like 'Hermann', named after Goering [head of the Luftwaffe], and 'Satan', which I presume was named after that devil Hitler [the 'Hermann' was a 1000 kg bomb, the 'Satan' a 1800 kg one].

Fuses were numbered, with one or two fuses to each bomb, small bombs having one, the larger having two. The numbers of these fuses were, as I remember, the 15, 35, 50 and 17 – the 50 and 17 being anti-withdrawal and clockwork time fuses respectively. It seemed that Jerry would incorporate the 50 and 17 together, for the simple reason that if the clock fuse was stopped, for example when we imposed a large magnet which we called a 'clock stopper' on top of it, no one would be able to withdraw it. Around the fuses were picric rings [picric acid – 2,4,6 trinitrophenol], which also surrounded the most volatile part of the fuse called the 'gaine', which was made up of fulminate of mercury – a very high explosive.

Most bombs lost their fins when they hit the ground; it was very seldom that we found many bombs complete with fins. If a bomb was fitted with an anti-tampering device we could, if it was filled with a powdered explosive, remove the base plate and empty the bomb case, leaving the anti-tampering device intact. Then we would remove the bomb to either a bomb 'cemetery' or to a place of safety, place a slab of gun cotton over the fuse, prime and detonate, to make the bomb safe.

If the bombs were filled with solidified TNT we would if necessary steam the explosive out. This was done by taking off the base plate and placing a small crucible filled with magnesium on the bomb's outer steelwork. This crucible had short legs and had about a 1-inch hole in the bottom, over which we placed a steel disc held in position by string terminating around the top of the crucible. We would then insert a detonator into the crucible and fire the magnesium. The string would part, the disc would drop off and magnesium would burn a hole through the steel casing to the TNT. This operation would be covered by a manned hose pipe ready to douse the TNT when it fired, for as you may know TNT can burn away if ignition takes place. After putting out the ignition a steam jet was introduced to the hole, eventually melting the solid TNT, which then with some help would run out of the base of the bomb. The explosive could then be gathered up after resolidifying and burnt off in a place of safety.

I participated in removing bombs from Bristol, Exeter, Plymouth, Avonmouth, Penzance, Bath and many outlying districts of the south-west. I can recall a 500 kg bomb which landed in the garden of a doctor's house at Shirehampton near Bristol. The locking ring which held the fuse in position had been distorted on impact, so I tried to release it with a hammer and punch – which you may guess is against all the rules – but I was unsuccessful, so steaming was the only way out. The Fire Service obliged us with a hose jet and water supply, and the job was done with no problems.

But in Bristol the officer in charge of my section was killed by a bomb whilst he was dealing with it. This happened in the dockside area in the central part of Bristol. It was the responsibility of the senior NCO or officer to defuse, but in the early days we all took part one way or another. Some fuses were removed by remote control – this usually took place when the bombs had fallen in an area where if they exploded people and industry weren't in danger. Should bombs fall and fail to explode on impact in factories, railway areas, hospitals or anywhere which would impede the war effort, then these bombs would have an 'A' classification which meant that, whether fitted with clock or anti-withdrawal fuses or not, they would have to be removed immediately.

I'd say there are bombs in the Avonmouth area that will never be recovered, because the ground make-up is of blue clay. Some holes we probed seemed bottomless; also the bombs would shoot off in all directions. I was also involved in the Plymouth and Devonport blitzes, and the ground situation here was completely different to the Bristol area. Being sandy, bomb penetration on average was only about 4 feet, so digging out was much quicker. We also experienced phosphorus bombs in this area, which were difficult to deal with as they would split on impact and spread their contents, which would burn anything that came in contact with it. Mines were also experienced, and were dealt with by the Royal Navy's disposal team, though we assisted at different times. This was generally at night because of their light-sensitive traps, which when the covers were removed would automatically trigger the mine.

Our billets in the Plymouth area were on the edge of Dartmoor, and our bomb 'cemetery' was also situated on the moor. This witnessed an explosion whilst ARP and other Civil Defence personnel were going through a bomb recognition exercise. We also lost men whilst clearing bombs in the Plymouth area.

We were summoned to Exeter after their first blitz, and were accommodated at Higher Barracks. The second blitz happened whilst we were in operation – I myself was working on a bomb in the middle of the main railway line and was about 10 feet down when the raid started, but work had to continue.

While we were billeted at Bodmin we travelled to Zennor and Land's End and other isolated places where bombs had been hurriedly dropped by German aircraft. Bombs were also recovered from a school in Penzance – luckily no one was injured at the time.

Whilst in Bodmin we took over the old Bodmin Prison for storage and garaging; the prison reception area building was still in good condition, but the cells and main prison were derelict.

By this time bombs were beginning to get few and far between, so we set up a battle course in the grounds of the prison and practised battle tactics using the old prison cells, and so on. This battle course was set up by a young and ambitious officer, who very soon afterwards left bomb disposal to join the 1st Parachute Squadron, RE of the new 1st Airborne Division.

11

AIRBORNE

In the late 1930s the British had watched, with only casual interest, the development of a new trend on the Continent. One by one, the Italians, the Germans, the Poles and the French had followed the lead of the Russians in deciding to invest in airborne units.

Equipping and training such units required a considerable commitment, and the under-resourced British Army had made no moves to join the airborne 'club'.

Not until June 1940 was it decided that work should start on raising a force of parachute troops as a matter of urgency.

The RAF was asked to assume responsibility for parachute training, and an instructional staff was built up from scratch at Ringway, Manchester's new civil airport. But unlike Germany, where parachute troops actually belonged to the Luftwaffe, the new para battalions were to remain firmly under Army control.

Alf Card was one of the RAF men recruited to the Ringway staff as the school expanded.

> All the trainees were volunteers from different units, and on arrival at Ringway were placed in 'sticks' of ten with a Sergeant Parachute Jumping Instructor, or PJI. He was responsible for all instruction, and usually despatched them when making their descents. All the instructors were parachutists, but little more than trainees themselves. For example, I completed my instructor's course and was promoted Sergeant, and the next day I was given my first section to train. I was also one of the youngest on the staff, being a few months short of my twenty-first birthday, but I had to present myself as an experienced jumper who knew everything there was about parachuting.
>
> There was another problem. The Army and RAF were not exactly bosom buddies, as a lot of the trainees were ex-Dunkirk veterans who used to bemoan the absence of the RAF at Dunkirk

and did not think highly of the 'Brylcreem Boys', as we were called. However, it says much for the RAF Parachute Jumping Instructors that they were able to win the confidence of their trainees and develop an amazing rapport with their sections. In discussions with many ex-paras I have yet to meet one who did not have 'the best instructor at the school'. The RAF instructors adopted a friendly, kid-glove approach, one of persuasion – not do as I say but do as I do. All the instructors jumped, and they treated all their trainees the same irrespective of their rank.

The instructional staff at Ringway in its early days was made up of Army and RAF personnel, but very little was known of how to parachute from an aircraft. The first RAF instructors were parachute packers and pre-war parachutists like Harry Ward, who used to perform with Sir Alan Cobham's Flying Circus. The training was very basic, consisting of instruction in jumping from an aircraft, very elementary flight technique, practising a gymnastic forward roll on landing and lectures on how to fit a parachute. Sometimes trainees arrived, were given a few hours to practise on the ground and then if the weather was suitable they were taken up in aircraft and dropped. There were instances where trainees arrived at the school and on reporting their presence were told, 'You're in luck, there's an aircraft ready for jumping. Get a parachute and come with me.' The instructor then led his pupils to the waiting aircraft, climbed aboard and a few minutes later all were drifting down on to Tatton Park. Not surprisingly accidents were plentiful.

Even the parachute had to be designed in a rush, as it was realized that dropping from the low altitude required made the use of a manually operated parachute undesirable. So a statically operated one was designed by the British parachute firm of Gregory Quilter, or GQ as they were known. There were no suitable aircraft available, and, if the truth were known, certain people in the higher echelons of the RAF were not too enamoured of the idea of dropping paratroops from RAF aeroplanes.

The school was, in fact, given six obsolescent Whitley bombers by a grudging Air Ministry.

This had a gun turret under the belly, and when removed it left an aperture enabling a 'stick' of ten parachutists to jump from it. Some of the early jumps were made from a Whitley using a platform at the rear of the plane made by removing the *rear* gun turret. The parachutist stood on this platform facing forward and holding

196

the ripcord of his 'chute with one hand and a bar on the aircraft with the other. On an order from the instructor crouched inside the plane, the parachutist pulled the ripcord and was subsequently dragged off the platform as the 'chute developed – a practice known as 'pull-offs'.

By the time I arrived at Ringway in mid-1942 the training had become more organized, with a set training programme established. The first two jumps were now made from a tethered barrage balloon. Five more were made from the Whitley using the aperture, and after making all seven jumps the paratrooper was given his wings. After completing an assault course at Hardwick Hall near Chesterfield he was then posted to his unit, where he made his eighth jump – a night drop from a balloon. Later this was changed and all eight jumps were made at the school.

The Chief Instructor from 1942 until 1945 was a brilliant man by the name of Flight Lieutenant John Kilkenny, known by everyone as 'J.C.K.'. A schoolteacher in civilian life, he ran the Para School as an educational establishment.

The instructional staff were a mixture of Regular and wartime Airmen and officers. In civvy street they were teachers, sportsmen – the Parachute School could boast an international rugby XV who once arrived at a fixture by parachute! – circus performers and tradesmen of all types. But all had the ability to convince their trainees that parachuting was a normal, safe means of transport, despite the fact that sadly on occasion one of their number would plummet to the ground with a badly developed parachute.

Unfortunately in those early days this was not a rare occurrence. Some of these were caused by what was known as a 'Roman Candle', so called because the canopy, instead of developing into the familiar mushroom shape, assumed the shape of an inverted pear with the rigging lines twisted round like the grooves on a candle. It was also known as a 'Whistler' owing to the fact that the air rushing through the canopy made a slight whistling noise. No one really knew why and how they happened, though the early design did have faults that were not apparent. As I say, very little was known and it was all a somewhat 'off the cuff' affair. We learned as we went along.

As I mentioned, all the men were volunteers but perhaps some were *encouraged* to volunteer. By that I mean that some of my first trainees were men of the 5th and 6th Parachute Battalions, which had been normal infantry. They were simply paraded and advised that they were to become parachute battalions – anyone who did not wish to parachute would be transferred to other units.

In the event most of them volunteered to stay, and both battalions saw service in North Africa, Italy and Southern France.

Prior to making any parachute descents all trainees were given a five-day period of ground instruction called simply 'Synthetic Training'. The aim was for each pupil to be taught and to practise every phase of a parachute descent. The motto of the Parachute School was 'Knowledge dispels Fear', and this was the aim – give the pupil the knowledge and you cut down his fear. The more he practises a given routine the more proficient he becomes; the more confident he becomes the less likelihood of him refusing or having an accident.

It was the aim of every instructor to have 100 per cent courses every time, though of course accidents did happen and men did refuse to jump. Any refusal or accident was looked upon as a fault in instructional technique that had to be eradicated, so all such refusals and accidents were thoroughly examined by the Chief Instructor. Obviously such things as parachute failure could not be blamed on any one person, but in all the years of parachuting to my knowledge only one accident was rumoured to have been caused by a packing error. Perhaps the following story best describes what I mean about instructional error. At one of our regular weekly meetings of the instructional staff presided over by John Kilkenny he made the following illustration. If a trainee caught his foot in a rabbit hole whilst making a descent, spraining his ankle or breaking a leg as a result, that was the fault of the instructional staff, because they should have seen the hole and caught the rabbit, so preventing the accident! What he meant was that if we allowed a trainee to jump before he was quite ready and he injured himself, that was our fault. If a man refused then we should examine our instructional technique to see if we had made an error in instruction, creating doubt in the trainee's mind.

On the subject of refusals, while under training no action was taken against any refusal; he was considered to have more sense than the rest of us and merely RTU'd – returned to [his previous] unit. No disciplinary action was taken and nothing was recorded against him. I knew several men who refused who had taken part in some of the severest fighting of the war, earning decorations such as the DCM and MM; it was just one of those things. Should a *trained paratrooper* refuse that was a different matter. They were charged, not with refusing to jump but with refusing to obey an order. Before every jump a trained man was told that the red and green lights constituted an order to jump, and any refusal to obey that order would be a court martial offence. Very few men refused.

I only ever had one case personally in twenty years of instruction.

At the school at Ringway in the early stages – by which I mean prior to 1942 – all the jumps were made from aircraft. However, once training began to develop a cage was attached to a barrage balloon, and the first two jumps were made from that.

The reason for this was that a balloon could only be flown in light winds, which meant that the trainee would be making his first two jumps in such conditions. More control could be exercised over him in the initial stage of the jumping phase and individual instruction given as he drifted down. There being no slipstream, the parachutist could practise his exit with no fear of somersaulting or making a bad exit and fouling his parachute as it developed. Also, the balloon could be used when aircraft could not fly due to bad visibility. With a total flying time of about five minutes for each lift of four men there was very little time spent in waiting one's turn to jump. If asked, most paratroops will say that they preferred the aircraft to the balloon. This is understandable for a number of reasons:

One, it was their first jump, a daunting event in anyone's life, so they were very nervous, despite their training and the efforts of their instructor to cheer them up as the balloon car ascended to its dropping height.

Two, there was no noise as the balloon car rose, except a slight hum of the winch as it paid out the cable to allow the balloon to rise, and sometimes a very light wind in the rigging of the balloon. The men were usually very silent, with only the despatcher giving last-minute instructions.

Three, the drop itself prior to the parachute developing. Actually this was no longer than that when jumping from an aircraft. From the aircraft the parachutist fell in an arc, appearing to go backwards but actually travelling forward with the plane until he lost his forward speed, by which time the parachute would be developing. From the balloon he dropped straight down roughly about 150–200 feet. For about 74 feet of this he would be still attached to the strong point in the balloon or aircraft via the various ties in the parachute.

Originally the height for jumping was 500 feet; later this was raised to 800 feet. The exit from the cage of the balloon was made through a hole in the floor of the cage, similar to the hole in the floor of the aircraft. A normal load was four men plus an instructor as despatcher, the jumpers leaving one at a time, their exit being in a position of attention.

The third jump was from a Whitley aircraft in what were called

'slow pairs'. The aircraft carried ten men with their instructor —
hence the reference to a 'stick' as of a stick of bombs. The men
sat in the aircraft five forward of the hole and five aft. When
they jumped the pattern was two men jumped, one from forward
followed by one from aft; the aircraft then circled the DZ [Drop-
ping Zone] and dropped two more, carrying on until all had
jumped.

The fourth jump was again in pairs but this time the period of
time between each man was less, in other words 'quick pairs'. The
fifth and sixth jumps were in sticks of five, with the sixth jump
being again a little faster. Finally the seventh and last jump was
as a full stick of ten.

Up to the end of 1943 the only item of equipment a paratrooper
carried with him whilst jumping was a sten-gun; all other equipment such as rifle or machine gun was dropped in a container.
This was synchronized to leave the aircraft between Nos. 5 and
6 in the centre of a stick of ten, so the system of jumping was the
first five jumped, then there was a slight pause to allow the containers to fall away, activated by a switch on the strop of No. 5,
No. 6 pausing and calling out, 'Container, Container' before jumping, followed by the remainder of the stick. Later kitbags were
introduced, and the men were trained to jump with a large kitbag
attached to their leg by quick release gear. This meant that men
could jump with such things as wireless sets, mortars, bombs,
rations and all kinds of loads. A rifle valise was also introduced,
enabling a man to jump and have his weapon immediately available
without having to run to collect weapons and gear from the container.

The trainees were in syndicates, with an officer instructor and a
Flight Sergeant, plus a Sergeant instructor for each stick. The size
of the syndicate varied with the number of pupils; a syndicate
could have had ten instructors each with ten pupils, and there may
have been five syndicates on a course. The Sergeant was responsible
for teaching his stick all aspects of the parachute jump, lectures
being given by the officer in charge of the syndicate. The School
Warrant-Officer organized all the arrangements for aircraft dropping. The stick instructor despatched his own stick where possible,
though this he was not always able to do, owing to other duties.

The lectures given by the syndicate officer or his Flight Sergeant
covered such subjects as exit, flight and landing, though there was
one lecture at Ringway always given by the Warrant-Officer in
charge of the Packing Section. This was understandably all about
the parachute used for jumping, known as the X Type. The interest-

ing thing about this lecture was that they were told very little about the parachute, and we always liked to leave this lecture until the day before they jumped.

The lecture was given by Joe Sunderland, who apparently joined the RAF when Pontius was a Pilot and left the junior ones of us in no doubt about it! He was a character whose like we will probably never see again. He had made many parachute descents himself, and although not an instructor was one of the first at Ringway. He kept a jealous eye on all his girls who packed the parachutes, making sure that lesser mortals such as instructors or trainees did not sully their reputation. None of us was allowed in the packing room without his permission, which was rarely given. At his lectures the only instructors present were trainee instructors there under sufferance.

His approach was always the same. The troops were sat in the lecture room to await his arrival; before entering the room he would ensure that the troops were not smoking. Once all the instructors had left he would enter the room, introduce himself then say in a shocked voice, 'What? No one smoking? Good heavens, those instructors . . . You may smoke, gentlemen.' Then he would launch into his talk, mentioning that parachutes were made of silk and nylon but could not be used to make ladies' undergarments. He would bring in the subject of the local ladies, warn them about his packers with dire threats as to what would happen if he caught any of them as much as looking at them. He would then throw in a brief reference to the parachute, very brief, then comment on the local beer, a little more about the parachute – how well made it was, well packed, they always opened. Someone always asked what happened if the parachute didn't open. His answer was always the same, 'Bring it back and I'll give you another one.' His lecture wasn't designed to tell anyone about the parachute, a subject he knew inside and out as they say, but the result was that all the troops came out of that lecture room raring to jump, he instilled so much confidence in them.

A favourite story about him is one he was fond of telling himself. During his lecture he would mention the size of the parachute canopy was 28 feet. He explained there were larger ones, and that he used a 30-foot canopy parachute of which there were a few kept for those who were over the weight limit of 13 stone – the limits were a height of 6 feet and a weight of 13 stone; however these limits could be exceeded, usually in the case of officers such as Colonels who were to take command of a parachute battalion. Although everyone was a volunteer, officers designated to command a battalion of paratroops were usually given an option; if promotion was their due and the vacancy was a paratroop unit then they either took it or lost their place in the promotion stakes.

Joe was always in evidence when parachutes were being issued for jumping, and on one occasion a Colonel who had made one jump and had a rather heavy landing was collecting a parachute for his second jump. Seeing Joe he approached him and asked if there was any chance he could use one of the 30-foot canopies Joe had mentioned. Joe thought that OK and told the Airman issuing the 'chutes to collect one for the Colonel. But back came the Airman to tell Joe that there were none available. So Joe went to the rear of the racks, pulled out a piece of chalk and scribbled '30 feet' on the side. Carrying it round he gave it to the Colonel with instructions to bring it back to him personally. Later that morning a smiling Colonel came back to Joe and, handing him the used parachute, said, 'That was great, Mr Sunderland. It's amazing what a difference it makes to the landing!' For the rest of the Colonel's course Joe made sure that he was given a parachute with the magic '30' written on it.

For the record, the X Type – designed by the GQ Parachute Company of Woking, Surrey – was a 28-foot diameter parachute with a flying diameter of 17 feet 6 inches. The normal aircrew type manually operated parachute was a 24-foot diameter parachute, though I'm not sure of the flying diameter – the flying diameter is when the 'chute is inflated as the man descends. The X Type was larger because of the need to give a paratrooper a lighter landing, whereas the main concern of the aircrew type was as a means of saving life and, of course, weight in the aircraft.

Were there any other differences, other than size?

Well, as it suggests, the manually operated parachute was operated by the wearer. The parachute consisted of a harness connected to rigging lines connected to a canopy, first made of silk but later and nowadays made of nylon. Fixed to the top or apex of the canopy was a small spring-loaded parachute. Attached to the harness by means of press studs and loops was a container somewhat in the style of an envelope. The four flaps of the envelope had holes or 'beckets', one on the top flap, one on the bottom; one side of the side flaps had two beckets and the other two cones. On the harness was a pocket for the stowage of the ripcord handle, the metal cord running through a tube for protection.

To pack the parachute it was laid flat on a long table, the canopy folded so that it looked like an elongated pyramid with the rigging lines neat and straight in the centre. The harness was laid on the table with the envelope uppermost, the rigging lines were stowed and then the canopy neatly piled on top; the flaps of the container were then drawn together and the cones on the outside of one flap passed through the beckets on the other flaps, with the pins on the ripcord pushed through holes in the cones to hold everything neatly in place. The extractor 'chute was pushed into the pack under the cones then the elastic bands on the side of the container were hooked on to enable the flaps to spring back when operated.

To use, the wearer jumped out of the aircraft; when clear he pulled the ripcord handle. This pulled the pins out of the cones, the elastic bands pulled back the flaps, the extractor parachute sprang out, filling with air and dragging out the canopy and in turn the rigging lines, and the canopy filled with air, bringing the man down safely. With this type of opening there is a considerable amount of shock as the parachute opens, the severity of which depends on the position of the body in its fall. If head-down when it develops it snatches the falling body upright, and if you're at terminal velocity this is very severe, I assure you!

It is not advised to use a manually operated parachute at low altitudes. Obviously at the low heights paratroopers were expected to jump from – a height of 300 feet was contemplated but I don't think ever used, though I and several others made one from that height during the war; I think the actual dropping height was nearer 800 feet operationally – this made the need for a static parachute imperative. Also, at such a low height a reserve 'chute was superfluous, as there wouldn't be time to use it. So all British troops and Allies trained by us only ever jumped with one parachute.

With the static parachute the canopy and rigging lines were laid and folded in the same manner as the manual parachute, but there was no extractor parachute. Instead there were *two* containers, one on the harness something similar to the manual parachute, and a bag with a static line and 'D' ring attached. This static line was about 12 feet long.

To operate, the 'D' ring of the static line was secured to a hook inside the balloon or aircraft. When the man jumped, he pulled out the strop and static line as he fell; arriving at the end of the strop and static line and still falling, his weight broke the first tie holding the bag on his back. This lifted the bag above the head. Continuing his fall the two ties holding the liftwebs and rigging lines broke, allowing the flap to unroll and the lines to pay out. When all the lines were at their full extent the next tie – the centre base tie holding the canopy in the bag – broke, allowing the canopy to be pulled out of the bag. The final tie broke, the empty bag stayed with the aircraft and the parachute inflated, bringing the man down safely. It was simple, smooth and efficient; there was no opening shock because of the way the parachute was deployed and controlled in its opening. Initially there were problems and the design altered to eliminate them, but the method is still in use today.

A typical daily programme would be: 08.00–08.45 Exit training; 08.45–09.45 Lecture on flight; 09.45–10.15 Break; 10.15–11.00 Flight training; 11.00–11.45 Landing training; 11.45–12.30 Practice fitting parachutes; 12.30–13.30 Lunch; 13.30–14.15 Dragging practice; 14.15–15.00 Landing training; 15.00–15.15 Break; 15.15–17.00 Air experience.

Dragging practice. Was that what it sounds like?

Yes, we'd take them in a field with an old parachute, fit them in it, lie them on the ground and let the wind drag them along, so that they had to get out of the harness quickly the way they were shown. That was the only time we used to like a bit of a breeze.

The lectures helped to break up the physical activity. Not all the courses could do landing practice, or whatever, at the same time, so the programmes were arranged so as to give variety and full use of available equipment. Air experience was given because in those days many men had never flown or been anywhere near an aircraft, so this was fitted in usually just before they made their first jump. Many people such as myself made two parachute descents before ever having flown in an aircraft!

In the UK all ground training was done indoors, except for dragging practice, or on a fine day practice in fitting parachutes might be done outdoors. The training hangar at Ringway was full of equipment designed by members of the staff; there were swings, chutes or slides, and aircraft fuselages. This soon became known as 'Kilkenny's Circus'.

With landing practice, initially the instructor would demonstrate the fall on a mat, then describe it, then they would practise it. The first type of landing fall was the shoulder roll or forward roll, done by most students in the gym. One put the forearm on the floor, tucked in the head and rolled across the shoulder and back. But this was liable to cause fractures, so was discontinued and a far better method developed. Some say it came about by accident, but I believe the staff had several circus performers who knew all there was to know about falling, and introduced it. It's quite simple; basically the fall is made along the side of the leg and across the back. To fall the man aims the side of the knees towards the ground, turning slightly so the fall is transmitted up the side of the legs to the thighs; the hips are turned so the fall travels diagonally across the back. With the whole body rolled like a ball, with the chin being forced to the chest, there is no strain as the whole thing is relaxed – much as a drunk or unconscious person would fall. The fall was practised from a standing position with help; a fellow pupil held the hands of the one falling. To fall forward to the right, the feet are turned slightly to the left to enable the side of the leg to contact the ground, called a forward right landing. To fall to the left, feet to the right and fall. If you imagine you are standing in the centre of a circle divided into three sections in front and three behind, the section immediately in front is taboo; you must not fall straight forward. And straight back is also out of bounds.

Of course when jumping there is no guarantee as to which way one is going to come down, but practising on the ground tries to cover all eventualities. Having mastered the art of falling from a modest height, say the height of a kitchen chair, the pupil progressed to running along a low bench, jumping off and practising his landing. As the pupil improved he moved on to a slightly higher ramp, so that he had a faster landing. There was a piece of equipment called 'the Block and Tackle', which was a parachute harness attached to two strong cables that went over a pulley on the roof. The pupil fitted on the harness and was lifted off the ground by two of his mates pulling on the block and tackle; the swing was set in motion by two men pushing him, the instructor then took hold of the rope and at a given moment he let go. Another piece of apparatus was just like a kiddies' slide or chute with the bottom half cut off, so when the pupil slid off the end he had a drop of a few feet before hitting the mats to make a landing. Initially there were several shoulder injuries using the slide, so a modification was made so that the men slid down holding on to a hand grip to support the shoulders.

There is no way a real parachute landing can be accurately copied – it can be simulated, but it's not the same. Some say it's the same as jumping off a 6-foot high wall. It's not. Such a jump can give you a much heavier landing, as you are coming down with no sideways motion. And no two parachute landings are the same. I have seen two men land a few yards from each other, one hitting the ground so lightly he could have stood up and not fallen over, the other coming in like an express train and hitting the ground with an almighty crash. As the natural tendency is to part the feet on landing, it was practise, practise all the time until 'Feet and knees together' was second nature.

Originally there was very little flight technique required, mainly because we didn't know any. We learnt as we went along. Initially the pupil was only taught to make a turn in his parachute harness if he found himself drifting backwards. This was done by reaching up to the left liftwebs of the parachute with the right hand, then bringing the left hand across inside the right to grasp the right liftwebs. When pulled together then apart the parachutist turned round in his harness; the parachute did not move, only the parachutist. Later with experience a system of cutting out the swinging motion of the parachute was developed. The parachute was redesigned so that the liftwebs were split, making a V shape on each shoulder. By grasping the front two liftwebs and pulling down, the canopy was distorted, cutting or decreasing the amount of swing. Unfortunately if the parachutist was drifting forward at the time it tended to increase the forward drift speed, so the technique was, if going backwards, pull on the forward liftwebs – this tended to decrease the drift; going forwards back liftwebs were used. Sideways drift, back liftwebs, letting up on the side to which one was drifting, so if going left let up on the left-hand ones.

All this was practised on a giant swing, much the same as a child's swing, but with a parachute harness instead of a seat. The man had to climb up to a platform some 10 feet off the ground. The harness was swung to him, and once safely in the harness he swung off and practised his drill.

Also practised was the technique for landing in trees.

Which was?

Bring the feet and knees up to the stomach, arms in front of the face, and crash into the tree . . . It works!

Landing in water was also practised, mainly because the man had to get out of the harness for the next man and practising the drill for a water descent was as good as any. The man sat back in his harness, opened his quick release box [the fastening on his chest where the various straps came together], held on to his liftwebs and let go of his harness as his feet touched water.

Exit technique was practised firstly on an aperture built on a platform some 5 or 6 feet above mats on the ground. They started off practising single exits, gradually working up to stick jumps. When the door became the normal method of exit so the exit training changed.

There was one other piece of equipment introduced when I arrived at the school, and my course were the first to try it out. This was a device called 'the Air Brake', or more simply 'the Fan'. It consisted of a strong cable some 20–25 feet in length, one end attached to a grooved drum about 3 inches in diameter and the other to a simple harness that fitted on rather like a waistcoat, fastening at the front with a hook and 'D' ring. On one end of the drum was a handle; on the other two curved fan blades. The drum and blades were attached to a framework 20 feet up in the hangar roof, over a hole in the floor built on the girders. The pupil climbed up a ladder fixed to the wall of the hangar. Once there the harness was fitted to him and he sat down in the aperture as though he were in the mock-up apertures on the ground. The cable of course had been wound up by the instructor so it was now round the drum. On the command 'Action Stations' the pupil sat on the edge of the hole, on 'Go!' he made his exit. His body dropping to the floor pulled out the cable, causing the fan blades to revolve thus slowing his fall, the landing being quite gentle on mats below.

This was quite a daunting prospect for the trainee and it was designed to fulfil two functions. Firstly it was thought that it would sort out the men from the boys. If anyone was going to refuse, this was their first test. Secondly it was an excellent exit trainer. Jumping from low platforms did not give pupils much time to attain a good exit position, as they hit the mats too soon. With the fan they had time to get a good position. In fact there were very few refusals from the fan; the hardest part was climbing the ladder fixed to the wall. Once up there it was much easier to go down the quick way rather than climb down the ladder. When they had been off the fan a couple of times there was no stopping them, and they all looked forward to that period.

The first aircraft used for parachute training, and some of the first raids, such as Bruneval and the raid on the Tragino Aqueduct in Italy, was the Armstrong Whitworth Whitley. As I said, initially the rear turret was removed, leaving a small platform, and the parachutist made his descent using a manually operated 'chute employing the 'Pull-off'. Not a good method for dropping large numbers of men.

Eventually the under-belly gun turret, called 'the Dustbin', was removed, leaving an aperture some 3 feet in diameter and about 2 feet deep with just enough clearance for a man and parachute to drop through in a position of attention. Of the stick of ten men, Nos. 1, 5 and 9 sat forward of the aperture on the starboard side, with Nos. 3 and 7 on the port side facing them. Aft of the aperture on the starboard side sat Nos. 4 and 8, with Nos. 2, 6 and 10 on the port side. The despatcher stood aft of the aperture, above which were two small lights. The red stood for Action Stations. On this command being given by the despatcher the first to jump swung his feet into the aperture and sat on the edge with feet and knees together, hands resting on the edge, with the head up. When the light changed to green and the despatcher called out, 'Go!' the parachutist lifted his body, arched his back and dropped through the hole. In stick jumping he would be followed in sequence by Nos. 2, 3 and 4 and so on, each shuffling along the aircraft until reaching the hole, then swinging into the exit position and dropping through.

Inside the aircraft and aft of the aperture on either side were strong points to which were attached ten strops, five on either side. On each strop was a hook and safety pin, and when everyone was sitting down in the aircraft the despatcher fastened the 'D' ring on the parachute static line of each man to his hook and inserted the safety pin to make sure that the flange of the hook didn't come open. When the man jumped his strop followed him through the hole, and as he fell his static line was pulled out, operating the parachute.

The main problem with this type of jumping was that it required a certain amount of gymnastic ability to perform the exit with some degree of speed and correctness. The dropping speed of the Whitley was about 60–70 knots, quite slow compared to other aircraft used then, but even so a slow stick would be spread quite a distance on the ground – creating problems when the troops landed, especially on a small DZ.

The Dakota was an American aircraft whose normal load for British paratroop training was twenty with three instructors as despatchers. It came into use at Ringway in 1943. The exit was made from a door near the tail on the port side. To make his exit the paratrooper stood in the door with his left hand on the aft side and his left foot on the edge. His static line was attached to a strop by a hook and safety pin; the other end of the strop ran freely along a cable running the whole length of the cabin on the starboard side.

To drop in a stick the men sat ten either side of the aircraft, all odd numbers on the port side, even numbers starboard side. Once airborne they fastened their static lines to the hook on the strop. On the command 'Prepare for Action' they stood up in single file, holding on to the static line of the man in front. This was to prevent fouling of the lines by them sliding between the gaps in the seats. On one occasion this happened – the strop stayed wedged between two seats, resulting in the static line not reaching the door. The parachute developed too close to the plane and was caught on the tail wheel. Despite the efforts of the pilot the unfortunate man couldn't be saved, but as I said, such things were rare. Any nasty protruding bits on the plane were also masked with tape to try to prevent any paratroops catching them as they left the aircraft. As an example the Dakota had two large hinges aft of the jumping door. These were covered with masking tape.

The last man carried his own strop as well. The red and green lights were above the door, and quite large. On 'Action Stations' No. 1 stood in the door of the aircraft, dropping his strop. On 'Go!' the man jumped, followed in quick succession by the rest of the stick. As each parachute left the bag, the bags were left flapping in the slipstream to be pulled back in by the despatchers. The dropping speed was similar to the Whitley, but although the actual exit falling through the slipstream was the same, in other words at 'Attention', it required less gymnastic skill. With the introduction of kitbags, rifle valises and other weapons being carried by the jumper it was *much* easier from a doorway than from an aperture. Also the Whitley was rather gloomy inside, there being only very tiny windows which were blacked out anyway. The Dakota by contrast was light, airy and much more comfortable. I still think it was one of the best aircraft ever to parachute from.

When I was posted to the Parachute Training School at Kabrit, on the shore of the Bitter Lakes in Egypt, they were using a third type of aircraft – the Lockheed Hudson. With this the dropping speed was about 110 knots, described by many as 'the fastest Left Turn in the Army'! The exit was again made through the small door on the port side at the rear. The man grasped the door with both hands, sat back on his haunches with his left foot on the door sill, and on the command 'Go!' launched himself into the slipstream in a position of attention. The strops were fastened to a very strong-looking bar on the starboard side at the rear. Later this bar was removed and replaced by a strong cable similar to the one in the Dakota, allowing ten men to be carried instead of eight. It was very difficult to jump from the doorway with equipment, owing to the small door.

Parachute training had been originated in the Middle East by David Stirling, founder of the SAS. Some of the original Army instructors from Ringway had been posted to the Middle East to set up the school, and when I arrived in company with about a dozen Ringway-trained PJIs I found several RAF and Army instructors on the staff under the command of an RAF Flight Lieutenant called Phil Murphy, who had been the officer in charge of my initial instructor's course.

With the war in North Africa in its closing stages the Parachute School moved from Egypt to Ramat David near Haifa in Palestine.

Our trainees were a hotch-potch of nationalities, some destined for work in Italy, Greece and Yugoslavia with the Resistance forces, others from the SAS, the SBS, the Raiding Support Regiment – mainly Gunners – and the Long Range Desert Group. The work of the latter had been mainly mapping out routes across the Desert and sending information back about German troop movements. Naturally there was great rivalry between the different units. As one LRDG chap remarked to me, 'All the SAS do is blow things up and then get lost, so that we have to find them and bring them home!'

We also had two para battalions [now officially battalions of the Parachute Regiment, created on 1st August 1942] – the 10th, formed from men who had seen action in the Western Desert, and the 156th, which had been formed in India. The 156th had been ordered home, but had disembarked in Egypt to be given a conversion course on jumping from the Hudson. Subsequently another battalion was raised, the 11th Battalion.

Another consequence of the move was that our fellow Army instructors left to join the battalions, so that the staff, like Ringway and the other new school at Chaklala in India, were all RAF. Some of our Army colleagues joined an organization called MO4, the secret group working with the Resistance. I heard an interesting story some time later, the truth of which I cannot vouch for, but as you probably know there were two groups in Yugoslavia, the Partisans under Tito and the Chetniks under Mihailovic. At the time the Allies supported both organizations despite the fact that both groups hated each other and appeared to spend more time fighting each other than fighting the Germans. On one occasion one of our ex-Sergeant instructors was with a group of Partisans that surprised a group of Chetniks, and a fire-fight ensued. During a lull in the fighting our friend, let's call him Ginger, was about to draw a bead on a Chetnik when he thought there was something familiar about him; realization dawned – it was another former instructor, his mate from the school! Needless to say neither took much interest in the rest of the engagement and as far as I know both survived the war.

During the summer of 1943 the 10th and 156th Battalions were posted back to England, though I think they both took part in an action in Italy first. The 11th Battalion stayed in Palestine to be brought up to strength. An interesting personal coincidence happened to me on one of the courses – one day we had just received a new batch of trainees, and when we finished our day's work I noticed a lone soldier standing on a slight rise. As I approached he greeted me with a broad grin, and I recognized an old mate of mine who used to work with me at Battersby's in Stockport before I joined the RAF in 1939. We had discussed joining up before the war, and despite much persuasion on my part he decided not to join the RAF with me as he didn't fancy the idea of flying; instead he joined the local TA unit, was called up when war was declared, sent to Malta and after the siege decided to volunteer for the paratroops!

In late 1943 the 11th were in action when a company were dropped in Cos in the Dodecanese Islands. I was working with a stick of Long Range Desert Group troops at the time; they were all ready for their first jump when they were whisked away to invade the islands by boat. Unfortunately when the islands were retaken by German forces a few weeks later, most of them were taken prisoner. One of my trainees was captured and placed aboard a train in Greece for transmission to a POW camp, but managed to escape. About a year after the operation he arrived back at the school, which was by then in Italy at Gioia del Colle, and it was there he told me how he escaped. Evidently he and some of his section were put aboard the train and when it slowed to negotiate a steep climb they all, in his words, 'bailed out' and evaded their captors. He remarked, 'Your training came in handy!' Having escaped they holed up in a cave living off rations stolen from a German depot, and eventually made their way through Greece to Italy, where he decided to complete his parachute training.

Another group in action were the Greek Sacred Heart Squadron [later Regiment] – Greek SAS, all para-trained by us. A true story about this unit concerns the man who committed suicide, or did he?

To explain: the Hudson carried ten jumpers and an instructor despatcher. This chap, nicknamed for some reason Little George, met an untimely end when they were making their final day jump in a stick of ten. Each man had his parachute static line hooked up by the despatcher; this was done by means of a 'D' ring attached to the parachute static line being fixed into a snap hook. To make sure the hook couldn't come free a safety pin was put through the flange on the hook, in effect putting a bar across so that it couldn't depress. When Little George reached the door for some reason he sat down on its raised edge, then fell out of the Hudson. And when the despatcher pulled in the static bags left flapping in the slipstream to his horror he counted only nine bags not ten. Those of us watching on the ground saw what seemed to be a helmet dropping in the distance but of course it was the unfortunate jumper, whose parachute had not been pulled out of its bag so could not develop.

There were several theories as to what happened, and various tests made. It was proved that the despatcher had positively secured the 'D' ring and snap hook and secured the safety pin, so what went wrong? One theory was that the jumper had decided against jumping and unhooked himself. This would have been noticed by those sitting near him, and bearing in mind that his unit was what one might term a 'Death or Glory' outfit – their badge was a sword and shield symbolizing the Greek warrior of mythology going to war and carrying home his sword and shield or being carried home on his shield having died in battle – having unhooked himself his mates sitting near may have accused him of dishonouring the group so that when they stood up to jump he reconnected his hook and 'D' ring but failed to insert the safety pin. Sitting down at the door the flange caught the edge and opened, allowing the 'D' ring to come out. This was tested and found to work, so it could have happened. The other theory was that seeing his group standing up to jump and not wishing to be thought a coward he merely held his hook and 'D' ring in his hand. Being last in the stick the despatcher, by the door, would be unable to see the rear of the jumper until it was too late – we only had one despatcher per aircraft at the time. The subsequent Board of Enquiry exonerated the despatcher completely.

Sadly this was not the only death during training which Alf was to witness.

One name that will always be with me is a young soldier trainee of mine who I saw meet his end.

Our Dropping Zone near Ramat David was a very large field, bordered by fields of crops. The farmers had huge carts to carry their implements and produce, but were well away from our range of operations except for one day. My section were the last to jump, and I was on the DZ watching them. The aircraft flew in and dropped its stick of four men then made a circuit of the field. Meanwhile the men were drifting down and landed safely, but for some reason one parachute did not collapse. It stayed inflated, and to our surprise the man was taken off the ground and into the air about 100 feet or so. We could see that he had started to release himself from his harness but on feeling himself being taken up into the air he had reconnected part of his quick release box and was dangling like a puppet. He slowly descended but was dragged back in the air again, each time being carried a little further away from the DZ and closer to the carts whose occupants were watching events. The man landed again only to be borne aloft once more, this time not so high; but to our horror we could see that as he came in to land this time he would be on or near the cart. It was too late to move it, and his body struck the huge boss of the wheel, caving in his chest.

I had heard of a 'sand devil' and evidently this is what it was — a small whirlpool of air crossing the DZ and lifting anything in its path. Only this time it was an unfortunate young soldier.

Shortly after the first parachute battalions were established, work began on forming glider-borne units to support them. It was felt that normal infantry battalions could fill this role with only a little retraining, but the pilots for the gliders were a different matter.

One of the volunteers for the new Glider Pilot Regiment, eager to try his hand, was *Eddie Raspison.*

I was twenty when World War Two started, and was then employed in a clerical capacity with an aircraft manufacturing company, the nearest I could get to flying. At that time the company in association with the Air Ministry took on the responsibility of outfitting and training pilots and navigational crew members for the Air Force. Knowing that my call-up was imminent I nurtured the hope that I would become one of these trainees, but alas it was not to be so.

My destiny one month after the outbreak of war was to become an infantry soldier in a Scottish regiment, which I accepted with good grace whilst resolving to take advantage of transfer to the RAF should any opportunity present itself in the future. I completed my infantry training and embarked with my battalion to France as part of the British Expeditionary Force. We were in action until Dunkirk, the encirclement of which we fortunately avoided, and we returned to this country from Le Havre.

In the reorganization which ensued due to our casualties I was asked on account of my civil occupation to take on the role of Company Clerk, a move I was pleased to make as this to my relief would not only excuse me from many of the arduous duties of a Fusilier but also gain me my first 'stripe'. The added incentive was, of course, that in such a position I would have access to Army Council Instructions, where possible transfer to the RAF would be promulgated!

Successful clerical trade tests followed, resulting in eventual transfer to Divisional Headquarters and promotion to Corporal in the Administrative and Quartering Section, with a small staff under my jurisdiction. One member of this staff responsible for filing Army Council Instructions was warned by me of the retribution which would follow should he fail to notify me of any future opportunities of transfer to the RAF, and this paid dividends some five months later. My attention was drawn to an ACI which called for volunteers to train under Air Force instructors as Army glider pilots, with those below the rank of Corporal automatically attaining that rank. It indicated that the War Office requirement was such that no tradesmen below the rank of Warrant-Officer were to be barred from applying. An attempt to bar my entry on trade grounds was eventually abandoned and my application was subsequently processed with an endorsement which I felt sure would at least warrant my appearance before an Aircrew Selection Board.

My first hurdle was over when in a matter of weeks I was sent on two days' detachment to Padgate near Warrington, where I successfully completed the Board's rigorous selection and medical assessments. Thankfully I was shortly afterwards transferred to the Glider Pilot Regiment Depot at Tilshead, on Salisbury Plain.

I had thought infantry training arduous, but didn't know the meaning of the word! Training and discipline under Brigade of Guards Warrant-Officers – themselves pilot volunteers – were harsh and rigid, though fair, and those of officer rank suffered equally in this strict regime. Those falling foul of Tilshead's rigorous routine and endless run/march exercises in full equipment during the six-week period there were not welcome, and were returned to their former units. It was felt that those accepted should be not only complete soldiers and airmen but be fit, strict disciplinarians, proficient in the handling and firing of all airborne weapons and the driving of all vehicles, *and* capable of acting as infantrymen or gunners, taking their place alongside the troops they carried into battle!

Our flying course was formed, and we were sent to No. 3 Elementary Flying Training School at Shellingford near Oxford, where the big hurdle loomed. Flying commenced in August 1942, and we were acquainted with the fact that not only had we to be sufficiently proficient to fly solo in Tiger Moth aircraft within 12 hours' flying time, but we also had to obtain pass marks in ground subjects consisting of theory of flight, air navigation – including the use of course and speed calculator – map reading, flying regulations and procedures, aircraft recognition, meteorology and Link

214

Trainer flying simulator. Solo night flying was also on the syllabus, and was to be accomplished in a specified time. Our numbers were further depleted by those failing in flying ability or being unable in the restricted time to assimilate ground subjects to the required standard. Flying continued on Tiger Moths on more advanced exercises – aerobatics, cross country, landing at other aerodromes, formation and instrument flying and so on, and at this stage conversion was effected to Miles Magister aircraft. The day dawned when we were considered proficient in flying and all associated activities.

Barring unforeseen circumstances we were to all intents and purposes pilots, though whilst the Air Force trainees with us on the course were at this stage awarded the coveted 'Wings', we had to await the successful completion of a further course at Glider School. After 54 hours' dual instruction and 44 hours' solo I moved with the rest of my Army course to No. 5 Glider Training School at Shobdon near Hereford.

Instruction at our new school consisted mainly of conversion to motorless flight in the Hotspur glider, with the occasional flying of powered aircraft as a 'refresher'. The towing was done by Miles Magister and Westland Lysander tugs, and glider flights consisted of normal take-off and landing both by day and night with light gliders, heavy load and live load, remote releases, dive approaches, cross country, formation, slipstream flying and flying in both the high and low tow positions. Good judgement now had to be brought into play more than with powered aircraft, and awareness of this was sharpened by the lack of motive power in free flight, though under- and overshoots were not infrequent both on dive approaches and remote releases.

On 20th April 1943 I was instructed to fly a cross country exercise in a Miles Magister, taking another trainee pilot as navigator, on a triangular course at a height of 2000 feet. When the first leg was completed I became bored, and told my navigator we would go down to ground level, where we alternately took the controls for twenty minutes. We were not to know that there were high tension cables in the area, which for aesthetic reasons had been run along a valley; nor were we to know that because of lack of background they would not be visible at low level. We crashed into the cables, cutting off the power to some of the inhabitants of Ludlow and completely writing off the aircraft. How we survived the accident I'll never know. I was concussed and had a cut in my upper lip, but my navigator wasn't even rendered unconscious!

I came to whilst being carried to an Auxiliary Fire Service vehicle, though the aircraft miraculously had not gone on fire. We were taken to Ludlow Castle which contained an emergency medical wing, my co-pilot being allowed back to base whilst I was detained for two days for treatment, and questioned about the event. My main worry at this time was that my own indiscipline would hazard my future as a pilot, and when I was taken back to Shobdon under close arrest I realized that that worry might become a reality.

At Shobdon I was charged with low flying, with an alternative charge of negligence as a pilot. My answer to the charges that I could remember nothing of the occurrence resulted in my being remanded in custody whilst a summary of evidence was taken, pending the convening of a court martial. The summary resulted in a Pilot Officer – someone completely unknown to me – being detailed to defend me at my trial. From my period in administrative duties I had become fairly well acquainted with some of the contents of King's Regulations, and was well aware that 'subject to the exigencies of the service' I had the right to nominate my own defending officer. I duly exercised this right.

Who better could I nominate than my instructor at EFTS, whose endless patience had enabled me to learn to fly and whose experience as a solicitor in civilian life would, I was sure, help in my defence? He agreed to represent me, and his own Commanding Officer at Shellingford gave him immediate permission to fly over to Shobdon in a Tiger Moth and glean all the facts necessary for my defence. I told him of my 'loss of memory', but on admitting my guilt and telling him exactly what happened he shook me by the hand warmly and said that as I had taken him completely into my confidence he would do his damnedest to get me off the main charge.

He put forward the defence that the Magister had a built-in problem in that during a steep turn there was a shielding effect by the rudder on the elevators causing the nose to drop alarmingly and unexpectedly, and this was supported by technical engineering evidence. This fact, he said, coupled with slow reaction from me due to my having been on intensive flying during the previous days and having as a consequence not partaken of regular or substantial meals – in itself an act of negligence – resulted in the aircraft dropping rapidly to ground level and causing the accident. I was found not guilty of the first charge but guilty of the second, and was reduced to the rank of Private and awarded fifty-six days' military detention.

My incarceration for two months was in a disused converted cotton mill at Stakehill near Rochdale, where my military imprisonment gave me an abundance of experiences I shall never forget. The prison Commandant, whilst averring that my offence was not of a criminal nature and expressing the opinion that I should never have been sent to his jail, said nevertheless that my treatment whilst there would be such as to ensure that I would never return. How right he was!

One outgoing letter per week was allowed, and I sacrificed one of my weekly letters home to write hopefully to my Regimental Commanding Officer both expressing remorse and requesting to be reinstated on flying duties when released. I could only now in prison jargon 'keep my nose clean', await discharge, and hope for the best.

On eventual return to the regiment I was taken before my CO, was given a stern lecturing for my misdeed and told that he had more flying hours than me yet he could not safely low fly. With tongue in cheek I politely said that I had not been found guilty of low flying, whereupon he said that the whole matter was best forgotten and asked if I had any questions. I naturally asked if I could be allowed to remain on the flying strength of the regiment, and was told that I was to be sent on leave for seven days and that within this period I would be recalled as soon as it was decided on which course I could complete my training. I was delighted at the outcome, went on leave and after three days at home I eagerly returned to flying, this time at No. 3 Glider Training School, Stoke Orchard near Cheltenham. It was here on 12th August 1943 that I was awarded the Army Flying Badge and promoted to the rank of Sergeant. I'd really made it!

You mentioned your CO. Did all your officers fly gliders like the men?

All our officers were qualified pilots, yes. Senior Airborne officers were normally flown in by officer pilots.

That same month, August 1943, our course members were moved to the Operational Training Unit at Stoney Cross, Southampton, where conversion to the renowned Horsa glider was commenced. The Horsa, a glider with a wingspan of 88 feet, capable of carrying twenty-five fully armed troops or a commensurate load, became invaluable to the Airborne forces. A wonderful aircraft which handled impeccably both on tow and in free flight, heavy or light, high or low tow and in all conditions. The Airspeed Company must have been justly proud of its design and build. Its added ability to 'hang on its flaps', which were extra large and when fully lowered allowed an angle of glide of 45° from the horizontal, was an invaluable aid to spot landings and gave great confidence to its pilots. And since it could glide approximately 2½ miles for every 1000 feet of height, a totally silent approach could be made to an objective without the noise of aircraft engines alerting the enemy – known as a remote release.

The five months of intensive flying by day and night at OTU solely on the one type equipped us well for our next move, to the Operational Unit at Brize Norton. Spot landings and strip landings were the order of the day, and were managed with such precision as to give us as much confidence in our ability as in the aircraft we were flying. This was to stand us in good stead on future operations.

How did spot landings and strip landings differ?

With spot landings the gliders involved were required to land with pin-point accuracy next to their objectives – to give such an element of surprise that the enemy had little or no time to react.

Strip landings have to be made so that the gliders finish up nose to tail – coming in at ten-second intervals – in a limited pre-prepared area. Mine was one of seventeen Horsas involved in such a task on D-Day.

On the spot landing ops the pilots went into the attack with the troops they carried. On the strip landing the pilots formed a perimeter defence party.

On 1st June 1944 everyone was confined to the aerodrome at Brize Norton. All entrances were sealed under armed guards, and we were warned that anyone breaking bounds would face a court martial. We were virtually isolated and it was obvious that an airborne operation was imminent, and when our briefing started the purpose of our specialized landing techniques began to unfold. Six Horsas from our squadron were to form *coup de main* parties and were to land as close as possible to the bridges over the River Orne and Caen Canal, carrying infantry and Royal Engineer airborne troops. Capture of these bridges intact was a vital operation, and was carried out with such precision in complete darkness that it was later described by Air Chief Marshal Sir Trafford Leigh-Mallory [C-in-C, Allied Expeditionary Air Force] as 'one of the most outstanding flying achievements of the war'.

I had a more mundane task as one of seventeen gliders scheduled to land nose to tail in an area near Caen at night some three hours after the *coup de main* assault. The enemy had 'planted' the landing area with poles to prevent landings such as ours, but paratroops were dropped in advance of our arrival, their task being to detonate explosive charges at the base of these poles, removing them. They would then place an illuminated green 'T' at the beginning of the cleared strip and a flashing white light at the top end. Our seventeen aircraft all bore airborne Royal Engineers, with the necessary equipment to clear the remainder of the area in preparation for the main landing.

The flight from base was uneventful until in the half-light just after passing over our coast, and after our Albemarle tug had in accordance with briefing switched off his navigation lights, we narrowly avoided a collision with an aircraft, possibly returning from a bombing run, which had omitted to switch *on* his lights. At the same time there was an awe-inspiring sight below us of the hundreds of boats comprising the seaborne assault force. We were not alone!

As we approached the French coast intense flak fire was concentrated on us and our tug was hit, its port engine going on fire. My offer to cast off to give the tug a chance to survive was met by a gutsy 'Hang on – I'll get you there' from its New Zealand skipper, Mike Brott. Indeed he did so and with his engine still burning we cast off at 3.20 a.m. when the green direction indicator came into view, only for us to realize to our consternation that the flashing white light on which to align was not in position. We later learned that the paratroop officer carrying it had been severely injured in landing. There was no alternative other than to attempt to steer a straight course after touchdown, but when passing over the green indicator at a height of about 150 feet another glider was seen in the half-light, directly below us, but going in to land in the completely opposite direction! An immediate turn was made several degrees to starboard, chancing collision with undemolished poles which we fortunately avoided, and we landed and came to rest with the port wing up against a haystack in a small field. Our load of four Royal Engineers, with their jeep, trailer and ammunition, was successfully unloaded without difficulty – the troops very thankfully. They hated being transported in our wooden contraption as opposed to parachuting in, despite my attempt to convince them when embarking that they were far safer with us, a fact which I certainly believed. We flew with parachutes when we were training on powered aircraft, but once we started to fly gliders we had no such insurance. We knew from the word go that we would have no emergency escape, nor did the air-landing troops we carried. This fact was what caused the apprehension of the RE paratroops; it could have been the only time they had flown without 'chutes! I understood from them that they were with us due to a shortage of RE glider-borne personnel skilled in the job of shearing poles at ground level.

We left them to their task, as we had to rendezvous on the perimeter of the allotted main landing area, taking up defensive positions and awaiting the arrival of the main force. A little enemy action ensued, but our casualties were comparatively light and after the main force landed – another awe-inspiring sight – we made our way to the coast on foot, it being necessary that we return to the UK rapidly in case another airlift was needed in support of the ground troops. All glider pilots had an endorsement in their AB64 [Army Pay Book] which read, 'No ... Rank ... Name ... of the Glider Pilot Regiment is hereby ordered by the Commander, Airborne Troops to return to the UK as soon as possible after completing his duties'.

Our return across the Channel was made by seaborne assault craft on their journey back to the UK.

Back at base we were intensely relieved to find that our tug crew had survived without injury, having just made landfall on one engine and crash landed some 2 miles in from our own coast. I still have two photographs of their 'F' for Freddie before take-off and after the crash.

Did you always fly with the same tug crew?

No. Throughout the training prior to D-Day glider pilots got to know tug pilots through the many hours of flying done together, but there was no specific flying with a particular tug. On later ops, due to losses in both tug and glider crews it was impossible to engender the same relationship between the two.

Communications with the towing aircraft took place through cables interwoven in the tow rope, though the elasticity of the latter in a bad tow often caused a break in the intercom cable.

At debriefing I elicited the fact that despite worries to the contrary we had in fact landed in the proper direction, though I never did discover who didn't do so, nor what happened to them as a consequence.

Revisionary flying in Tiger Moths was now interspersed by ferrying in Horsas to replace those lost on D-Day and in preparation for future operations. Mass landing exercises in the Horsas were now more in evidence than strip landings, and this fact gave us an insight into the planning of future ops. Operation Market Garden – Arnhem – was then upon us in mid-September.

The landing for us was an uneventful one in daylight on 18th September 1944, the second day of the overall operation. Of those landing on the first day some had come to grief through enemy action and others had turned over on their backs due to the undercarriages digging into the soft ground. The sight of this was a warning to our 'lift', but the enemy action in the area had been neutralized before we touched down in a field of turnips. Our Horsa load consisted of two soldiers of the Polish Parachute Brigade who accompanied their jeep, motor cycle and 6-pounder anti-tank gun. My co-pilot and I manned the gun with them on the western perimeter at Oosterbeek, where eventually they both became the targets of a sniper in a nearby church tower.

I was indeed one of the fortunates, coming through the action unscathed and being ferried back over the Rhine under intense fire in one of the Royal Engineers' assault boats. On the south bank of the river we were given a tot of rum and a blanket for warmth, these being supplied by the land force from the south who had reached there in only small numbers in a very narrow corridor. We made our way to Nijmegen, where our forces were more in command and where they were ably assisted by the Dutch civilians in providing the means for us to bathe, after first supplying the first substantial meal since we had landed some eight days previously. Clean, shaved and fortified again we were transported to the airfield at Eindhoven to be ferried back to our home bases, this for me now being at Earl's Colne in Essex.

I lost many good comrades at Arnhem, including the one who was closest to me, and despaired at so many young lives being sacrificed in what was an unsuccessful operation. The losses in glider pilots were proportionately greater than in any other regiment that took part in the action, and this became evident on returning to base and seeing the sparsely occupied Nissen huts . . .

Reorganization was given the utmost priority. Newly trained pilots from Glider Training Schools were transferred straight to us so that we could convert them on to Horsas, and the next weeks were spent in bringing the regiment back to strength in readiness for any other airborne assaults.

On 24th March 1945 we took part in what was the largest single-lift airborne operation of the war. We were to be part of a mass landing near the German town of Hamminkeln [to support a renewed attempt on the Rhine].

At briefing we learned that our load would be Royal Artillery troops, and that the officer and four other ranks in it constituted an Observation Post and would be accompanied by a jeep and trailer carrying their radio equipment and spare ammunition. In their role they required to be spot landed in an area some 1½ miles in advance of the main force. This constituted no problem in a daylight landing, other than that being isolated from the main landing we might be subjected to concentrated anti-aircraft fire from guns known to be in the area.

This time we were towed by a Halifax on our 3 hour 20 minute flight. We had a good and uneventful tow in our Mk. II Horsa, which not only had the advantage of a single tow-line attachment as opposed to the yoke tow of the Mk. I, but was easier to load and unload directly from the front of the fuselage – the cockpit and nose swinging aside on hinges for this purpose. Shortly after take-off the Royal Artillery officer came forward into the cockpit and proffered an uncorked full bottle of whisky, and during the next hour the bottle was emptied between pilots and gunners fortifying themselves for what lay ahead!

Gliders started to cast off and tugs turn for home above a smoke haze, the result of bombing raids in advance of our landing. The smoke partly obscured ground detail, but also hampered the enemy anti-aircraft gunners. We remained on tow alone for a time then said farewell to the tug crew and cast off, flying straight ahead and trying to make out the ground feature of a small, distinctively shaped wood which I would recognize from the sand-table model back at base. This came into view through a gap in the haze, and necessitated a turn of 180° to bring us into wind as I lost height. Our isolation brought anti-aircraft guns to bear on us and we felt two hits, despite which the controls responded normally. I applied full flap and made as normal an approach as possible, though in landing we dug a deep furrow in the earth and our landing run was as a consequence short. After coming to a halt and freeing myself from my seat harness I realized that my co-pilot Sergeant Edwards was not moving and appeared to be injured.

On opening the door from the cockpit I saw that a hole had been blasted in the port side of the fuselage at floor level near the entrance door, far bigger than the door itself. Together with the Royal Artillery driver I managed to get the wounded out through the fuselage hole and move them into the shelter of the furrow the landing had caused. A quick assessment of the injuries sustained by five out of our complement of seven showed that though badly wounded none were losing blood to an extent that we need give immediate first aid. We managed to drive the jeep and trailer out of the fuselage without undue difficulty, assisting the injured on to the transport and trailer. I instructed the driver to take them as gently as possible in the direction of the main force where medical attention would be available, as it was obviously impossible that the Observation Post could function.

I made my way back to the main force on foot and returned

with surviving fellow pilots to another new base, at Keevil, Wiltshire. Here I learned eventually that though Sergeant Edwards had sustained shrapnel wounds down the whole of his left side which prevented his move back to the UK for some three weeks, he did make a reasonable recovery. I heard nothing further of the artillerymen, and never had any opportunity of expressing regret to anyone for their misfortunes!

During the war there were four major airborne operations and other smaller ones of a specialized and *coup de main* nature. I had taken part in three of the majors, and had come through them completely unscathed. Few managed the three and were as fortunate as I had been.

I was discharged in March 1946, and whilst I knew that I would miss flying I could hardly wait to distance myself from everything military, being greatly saddened at having lost so many good comrades in action.

I put behind me the events of the previous six and a half years, thankful that I had achieved my ambition to fly, and returned to my civil occupation.

It wasn't until late 1990 that by sheer accident contact was regained with our Regimental Association. They were organizing a three-day reunion and celebration dinner for 1992 to mark the fiftieth anniversary of our short-lived regiment. It was at this unforgettable celebration that I again met some of my former comrades whom I had not seen for forty-five years; the best men anyone could ever have flown and soldiered with.

12

ALLIES

Soldiers of many nations fought alongside the British Army during the war. One of the largest foreign contingents was that of the Free Polish Forces, the bulk of whose troops had already been 'through the mill' by the time they arrived in Britain.

Some had evaded capture during the collapse of Poland only to face an identical situation in France. Others, pulling back ahead of the advancing Germans, found they had escaped one odious regime only to fall into the hands of another, when the Soviet Union joined in the dismemberment of their homeland.

Michael Wartalski was eighteen when the war came.

The German advance on all fronts was rapid. For the Poles there was disbelief, panic and chaos. Within days of the German invasion my brother Stas and I became a part of my father's Police Reserve Platoon, trekking eastward in horse-driven carts. At the time I had no idea where we were heading for, nor did I really understand the whole situation. All I heard was that we were aiming at the city of Lvov. We could hardly move forward on completely congested roads. We were perpetually attacked by Stukas; their diving sirens were terrorizing us all, and we would run away from the road whilst they machine gunned until they ran out of ammunition. From time to time small units of cavalrymen would appear. I remember when I asked them where were the Germans, 'Everywhere,' was the reply.

After a few days of trekking we reached a small village. It was dark and I could hear my father negotiating the hiring of a cart with a peasant. Stas and I loaded our few belongings and a case with Father's possessions. Our father stood in darkness, crying as I had never seen him before. He wept and wept, embraced us both, then turned to me and said, 'Look after my children, my son.' These were his last words to me. As we moved into the darkness, deeply upset and in tears, we saw him standing and waving. We parted for ever, and we have never discovered what happened to him, except that he was killed by Ukrainian nationalists. The Ukrainian insurgents were induced by German propaganda calling on them to rise against the Poles, and promising them a free Ukrainian state. I remember picking up leaflets to that effect as we moved eastwards.

The driver hardly said a word to us, but mentioned that he was instructed to take us to our grandfather's holding in the village of Stare-Siolo, my mother's birthplace – my mother had died in 1935 – and her family's home for generations. We arrived at dawn at Stare-Siolo, a village with so many happy memories from my previous years, as almost all my school vacations I had spent with my grandparents.

We soon settled down to somewhat overcrowded conditions, but were pleased to be together. Next day, early in the morning, a small group of Polish officers arrived at the door. They looked tired and frightened. From the conversation I overheard, they were retreating from Lvov and asked my grandfather to offer them provisions for their journey, as they were making for Romania. Grandpa Philip gave them quite a substantial supply.

Within days a German patrol arrived on motor cycles with machine guns mounted on the sidecars. They looked very impressive, and moved fast across the village and stopped at the gate of the old, partly ruined castle built by the Polish kings against the Mongol and Tartar invaders. Eager-looking, their eyes moved fiercely around, assessing the situation. The three motor cycles, with gunners holding their fingers on the triggers, meant business. After a while some of the patrolmen relaxed, and sat on the grass with a group of young people. We gradually came closer and closer to them. For no reason, one soldier spoke to me – I had learned German at school, and tested it for the first time on a German. He said they were Tyroleans. He asked me if there were any Jewish shops in the village. There was one, and he could see it, but didn't know it was Jewish. I did not want to reply to the question, but he told me to go to the shop and bring some chocolate. With a laugh he said, 'Tell the Jews that the Germans are here.'

But within two days the motor cyclists disappeared. The village remained very quiet, like a lull, and in our minds fear grew. What next?

The news spread that the Russians were coming in order to help Poland, but it soon became obvious that the Red Army had invaded us for the sole reason of establishing Soviet rule by annexation of the eastern parts of the country. Peace was certainly restored, but at a dreadful price to the Poles.

Stare-Siolo was only 25 kilometres from Lvov, so I ventured to have a look at the city.

With curiosity and horror I saw the destruction around the main railway station, but the platforms were in order. Gradually more and more trains were in operation. The air was somewhat stenchy, a combination of burnt debris and the Russians using open spaces for toilet purposes as proper toilets were destroyed. The city itself was not heavily bombed, but had been fortified against tanks with deep ditches and walls of paving stones removed from the pavements. The character of the city was changing rapidly. Apart from the Red Army, Soviet administration moved in swiftly. In the very centre a huge monument was erected with Stalin on the plinth and masses of red flags. Loudspeakers were perpetually issuing instructions or playing Russian music. Tanks, very impressive, moved freely around the city. Troops marched briskly, always singing. More and more Ukrainians were moving in. Cinemas showed Russian films, stores were slowly filled with Russian goods. Roubles were gradually replacing the Polish currency – zlotys. Soon the time came when Polish currency was completely abolished.

After a couple of visits I secured a place at a teaching college, which was reopened with a somewhat modified curriculum. The idea of seeking some place in education offered me free transport to and from Stare-Siolo, and tramcar facilities in the city. It also gave me the status of a student, some sense of security, and an identity. I had to avoid the stigma of being the son of a policeman. Gradually new subjects were being introduced, like 'The Bolshevik Revolution' and 'History of the USSR'. Most painful, especially for the girls, were lectures given on the denunciation of religion. Many girls at first cried quite openly. They just could not swallow it, particularly the denunciation of the Resurrection of Christ and the Immaculate Conception.

There was also the additional benefit of having a free lunch in the college dining-room. Daily commuting to Lvov became a routine. Early morning trains were packed with village women taking all sorts of agricultural produce to the city for sale. Live birds and small pigs added to an overcrowded list of passengers.

Lvov was pronounced the capital of Western Ukraine. More pictures and statues of Engels, Marx, Lenin and Stalin appeared everywhere, particularly on official buildings. Notices calling on inhabitants to surrender any firearms or dangerous weapons were numerous. Punishment was by death. Red flags with the hammer and sickle fluttered everywhere. At my college even the Polish language was gradually replaced by Russian. The Soviet educational system was eradicating all things Polish.

Christmas Eve, the greatest event in the Polish calendar, created rather a sad atmosphere. The traditional breaking and sharing of a wafer with embossed Nativity scenes and a brief prayer by my Grandpa Philip filled us, the children, with grief. Now, for the first time, we had no parents, and a struggle for survival lay ahead. But there was still a Christmas tree. There was beetroot soup with mushroom dumplings, home-baked bread, fried carp, pastry and prune compote. We then sang carols. At midnight the horse-driven sledges took us to the village church, ploughing through the thick snow, with little bells ringing on the horses' necks. We were passing small houses with their roofs covered in snow and in the windows Christmas trees were lit with candles. I still remember the Reverend's name – it was Father Blicharski – who opened the Midnight Mass with a roaring sound of the organ, 'God is born, all might trembles . . .' The congregation followed with an unusual force, as if it were the last opportunity to display the old tradition against the unknown future.

On return from the church Grandpa Philip performed his ritual of surveying his holding and thanking God for all His mercies.

New Year 1940 was not greeted or celebrated, but accepted. The spring arrived, with the rumours of deportations of all Poles engaged in state administration during the inter-war period. The idea apparently was to cleanse Western Ukraine of Polish elements.

In war, rumours are part of psychological operations, but this one proved to be a fact.

In September 1940, while the Battle of Britain was raging far away to the west, the younger members of Michael's family found they were on a list for forcible deportation to the Soviet Union. This was a fate which befell roughly 1,500,000 of their countrymen during the Soviet occupation.

The entire station was surrounded by the Red Army, and there were four trains at different platforms, being loaded. Outside the cordon crowds watched in silence, and occasionally a tin of food was thrown over the heads of the soldiers. As we were sitting in our carriage the order came to collect water, and, escorted by a soldier with his rifle and bayonet on the ready, we marched across the railway tracks to the basement of a nearby building where water was on tap. My escort left me alone in the basement.

Glancing around, I noticed some windows open. A thought of escape ran through my head, but deserting my family immediately eradicated such an idea. Though I sensed, perhaps wrongly, that the soldier wanted me to run away, I rejoined my company and they were glad to see me back.

Soon the doors were slammed and slowly the train moved forward to the unknown. Night fell by Nature's pattern, and the rhythmic sound of the wheels lulled all emotions to gradual tiredness and sleep. Each to its own curled up. Occasionally a cry or a whimper of a child interrupted the silence.

We shared food brought with us initially. No supply except water was given to us by the guards. And so we reached, as someone discovered, the Polish border. We entered the Soviet Ukraine, with its vastness of land. One could see endless fields with sparse habitations. It all looked rather monotonous. After two days the train stopped in a wilderness. When the sliding doors opened, the freshness of the air and brightness of the daylight were extraordinary. Soon the guards announced that food would be given. We all stood with empty buckets, one person per carriage. The guard quite generously filled my bucket with maize-like gruel, topped up with some vegetable oil.

No joy greeted the arrival of this bucket. However, it was food.

It is extraordinary how there was always someone in our carriage who, in spite of limitations, could follow the route destined for us and acquaint us with our whereabouts.

So we passed Kiev, Kharkov, Voronezh, Saratov, Orenburg, Aktyubinsk, and eventually stopped at a small station called Dzhurun, on the railway line to Tashkent. We were in the Soviet Republic of Kazakhstan, one of fifteen republics, where rigorous Siberia and sultry Central Asia meet.

Slowly disembarkation began. Around us, strange faces of Kazakhs, Mongolian tribesmen, looked with curiosity at the new arrivals. Around, the vast steppes, covered with a kind of small shrub, stretched into the horizon. No trees were visible.

Michael's immediate circle included his sister and two younger brothers, a girl he knew from Stare-Siolo called Nela, and a number of others. All were forced to work on the local collective farm, where they found that they were not the first to have been brought to the region against their will.

Half of the inhabitants were a mixture of Russians and Ukrainians, apparently once 'Kulaks' who were deported to this area after the

Bolshevik Revolution. Once they were the enemies of the state, now pioneers transforming this virgin land.

Our first contingent of Poles, consisting mainly of women, girls and boys including myself, gradually settled down in various hovels and were employed in all sorts of jobs on this collective farm. A second contingent of Poles from Lithuania arrived, this time with some men and quite a selection of attractive young ladies.

Some Polish girls had affairs with the Russians, often for the exchange of favours or food.

One episode still remains in my memory, when one night I was woken up by one of our ladies who held a little bundle in her arms. She sobbed and quietly whispered to me, 'My daughter has just had a stillborn baby. I wrapped it in this piece of old cloth. Please, please could you bury it for me, somewhere in the cemetery.' In darkness, holding this bundle, I crept to the cemetery over-looking the village. With the spade supplied for my work on the Kolchoz [collective farm], I quietly dug a hole – rather a shallow one, as the soil was hard – and said a short prayer. I am sure that a wolf, a dog, or a snake made a meal of it sooner or later.

Most of the harvest had to go to the state, only a certain percentage was allocated per full-time worker. If the harvest was bad the State was very reluctant to assist, and this caused starvation. In the first year, the Poles were allowed to earn half of the allocated share per full-time Soviet worker. We survived the first winter, and entered 1941.

Then, one day, Nela's brother disappeared. No sign, no trace and for no specific reason. His mother was very distressed.

The following day a car full of officers from the NKVD, the secret police, arrived.

Nela, two of my friends called Holynski, and I were promptly recalled from work and appeared before the officers, who rather aggressively accused us of knowing the whereabouts of Nela's brother, also of plotting against the Soviet Union and encouraging Nela's brother to escape back to Poland. We were accused of plan-ning his escape, but only dead silence on our part was offered in response. We were threatened with punishment for engaging in counter-revolution. Then they disappeared again.

A few weeks passed uneventfully. Our group was always engaged on similar jobs and within a short distance of one another. On this occasion we were engaged in gathering hay. It was warm, and the only tools we had were forks. The steppes looked so green and no other life was visible in the vastness. On the horizon, one of our group spotted a truck with a trail of dust, speeding towards us. It was a military truck, and it stopped suddenly. Four NKVD soldiers jumped out and roared orders: 'Drop your forks and get in the back of the truck!' They placed us in four corners facing outwards, forbidding us to talk. Four soldiers with rifles sat in the middle, watching us and looking for any sign of communication. Speedily we rolled across the steppes on a beaten track. It was a long journey, and it was dark when we reached a big town – as we all learned later, the regional capital, Aktyubinsk. The two Holynski brothers, Zygmunt and Zdzich, Nela and myself managed to exchange a last glance at each other before we were separated and led to our cells in what appeared to be a huge NKVD establishment. The door of a cell was opened, and like a well-trained domestic animal I went in. A spy hole with a shutter on the outside of the door, a small barred window high on the wall and beyond one's reach. Wooden floor with no single other object. My padded tunic was my pillow when I tried to rest and sleep.

But soon the door was quietly opened. A soldier with a bent finger made a sign, which meant, 'Come to the door.' He asked my name, then nodded, confirming that I was not the one he wanted. A few minutes later he suddenly opened the door, whispered, 'Follow me,' and led me across corridors, then a yard, to another building, an office block, and finally into a darkened office room. Behind a big desk was comfortably seated one of the NKVD officers from the car. With a grin on his face he told me to sit down on a wooden chair with my feet on the seat and my knees touching my chin. He started reading the accusations, such as, that I was secretly engaged in publishing an underground counter-revolutionary magazine, circulating it among the Poles, agitating them against the Soviet Union, criticizing their system and organizing escapes back to Poland. When he had finished this litany of accusation he concluded by saying that if I confessed and signed, no harm would come to me and I would be spared further interrogation.

My whole mental system rebelled, living in such conditions after a forceful deportation because our father was in the police force. I boiled in silence but didn't respond, though he kept repeating the same things. Sitting in that position grew painful, but eventually I was led back to my cell and told that from 6 a.m. onwards I was not to be allowed to sleep, because it was daytime.

The same routine was repeated every night, and soon the pattern became clear. Interrogation started at midnight and lasted until the early hours of the morning, then no sleep. The guards regularly watched one through the spy hole. It was so quiet. About 7 a.m. I was given a mug of boiled water and a chunk of bread. In the evening another mug of boiled water was repeated. All sorts of tricks were practised with the sole purpose of breaking me down. Solitude and perfect stillness proved to be a powerful factor in grinding you progressively.

'Admit. Admit and sign,' were the most repeated words. Then an interrogator would quietly disappear and leave me alone, but I was not allowed to change my sitting position. Then after a while, suddenly with roaring and noisy behaviour, a group of NKVD officers would roll into the room, pointing their fingers at me, telling the interrogator that I should be shot, and *will* be shot unless I confess and sign. After this performance they would disappear and dead silence would return. On two occasions I fainted, but cannot recall how I regained consciousness. On another occasion, two soldiers led me in darkness back to my cell. I could hardly walk, when unexpectedly one of them pushed me against a wall and told me to put my hands up. 'We are going to shoot you, don't move.' They aimed at me with two rifles, but did not fire. Tiredness didn't allow me to even think. Then they led me back to my cell.

An additional small raw onion was added to my morning diet of bread and boiled water. The tricks never ended. On one occasion I was led to a room with a magnificent display of various foods on a huge table. The aroma was overpowering. My interrogator repeated the same sentence: 'Admit and sign, and you can help yourself to this lovely food.' No response came from me, so back I went to my cell. It may be strange, but I was never physically assaulted.

Visits, only once per day, to an indoor latrine were strictly timed by the guard, and on no occasion I met another inmate there. This in and out routine from your cell was intended to confuse you, and gradually your body began to deteriorate. Eventually I reached a state of mental and physical exhaustion. At times I wanted to die, hoping that would bring a relief.

After about six weeks of this ordeal I signed the paper in complete resignation, not caring any more what the consequences might be.

My interrogations stopped after my signing, and the guards offered me on one or two occasions their unfinished cigarette ends.

Shortly afterwards Michael and the others were transferred to prison in Aktyubinsk to await trial.

While we were in Aktyubinsk, history was carving great events. On 22nd June 1941 Germany attacked the Soviet Union. A new alliance and diplomatic relations were established with the Polish government in exile in London, and Stalin agreed to release all Poles from labour camps and prisons, and to form a Polish Army on Soviet soil, in order to liberate Poland.

But for us, the course of Soviet justice was not yet subject to any alterations. My sister Anna brought some bread to me in Aktyubinsk jail, and whispered to me about the changes taking place and the formation of a Polish Army.

On 2nd October 1941 we were led from the cells to the court-room, and it was reassuring to see Nela keeping her chin up. To our amazement, the courtroom was packed with our families and friends from the collective farm. On our appearance loud cries were heard, as we did look, except Nela, like skeletons. All stood up on the arrival of the judge, who took up his prominent seat. The prosecutor read the charge which applied to all of us, that we had attempted to overthrow the Soviet government. Zygmunt Holynski was accused of being the editor of an underground Polish magazine. I was accused of being a co-editor, and the others of being involved in the distribution of this magazine. We had criticized the Soviet government and particularly the collective farm system; we were spies and had secret connections with a Polish underground movement in Romania; our fathers were members of the defunct Polish police, and we were counter-revolutionaries.

All our letters addressed to our families in Poland were presented to the judge with translations in Russian. When the charges were finished, the judge, a young man in an ordinary suit, asked the defending advocate to address the court. This advocate was an appointee of the state. All he said was that in view of our relatively young ages, inexperience and confessions, he begged the court to consider leniency. The judge asked if we had anything to say. My companions looked at me for a response.

I denied all the accusations and asked the judge why we were being tried against the background of the changes taking place between the Soviet Union and the Polish government. I mentioned the formation of a Polish Army and expressed our eagerness to fight the Germans.

When I sat down, the judge read the sentences: Zygmunt Holynski, ten years' imprisonment; myself, seven years'; the others, five years'. Gasps and cries received the pronouncement. The judge mentioned that he had no knowledge of the Polish Army, nor any directives in that respect. He allowed us half an hour for meeting our families, which was just enough for embraces and tears.

We were taken by an NKVD truck to Temir prison, only about 25 kilometres from Dzhurun. There we were placed in a long cell where on the floor were mattresses filled with straw or hay. There was more room to stretch your arms, and more light. It was a square type prison with a courtyard and surrounding high walls. At each corner was a tower with a soldier and a machine gun. All along the interior walls dogs ran around, fixed to an upper railing.

Boredom prompted us to invent things. One fellow managed to remove a small piece of metal from the iron stove. It took him weeks to sharpen it on the bottom of an earthen mug. He established a hairdresser's salon for shaving hair on the head. Time didn't matter – progress was very slow, and an inmate looked very funny with a small shaven patch. It took weeks before the job was completed.

An idea of producing playing cards was born. Some sheets of paper were glued together with moistened bread squeezed through a piece of material. When dry and stiffened, the hairdresser came along with his sharp piece of metal to cut the squares. The hearts and clubs, and so on, were drawn on the squares. Someone managed to obtain, no doubt by some devious methods, a candle and some rubber which looked like a piece from a rubber sole. Burning the rubber, we produced black paint which was quickly used for covering the figures of the already drawn cards. The whole process was almost completed when, unexpectedly, prompted no doubt by the peculiar smell of burning rubber, the guards invaded the cell and found the cards hidden by me in my territory. They led me into a cell for punishment. It was a very small cell like a box, where you had to stand in a foot of water and the four walls were infested with masses of cockroaches. For two days and one night I stood up, killing cockroaches, until I was exhausted. When released, just about conscious, the guards carried me back to my cell where friends offered me bits of bread for a couple of days.

Then, one day, we were called into the governor's office. The governor displayed unusual politeness and read an order of release.

We didn't react straight away, for we couldn't believe this was true. Our first reaction was that this was another trick. But the address went further, into a display of the greatness of Soviet justice and its gesture in releasing us after committing such serious crimes. He stressed the importance for us, after release, of always remaining loyal to the Bolshevik Revolution. We were led to the main gate, which was opened for our release and shut immediately after.

We stood for a while, bewildered, looking around in disbelief, holding our little possessions returned to us by the guards. Nobody met us, no one told us where to go, and we were lost for a moment with this granting of freedom. It was 8th November 1941.

Slowly we made our way to the settlement of Temir. Some roubles confiscated on arrest had been returned to us. We found an eating place, a sort of canteen, and I have never forgotten the splendour of our first meal. It was a camel meat stew, the best meal I had had since entering the Soviet Union. We asked for directions to Dzhurun, and duly started to trek and talk. After a few kilometres a column of Red Army horse-driven carts appeared, heading for Dzhurun, so we asked for a lift, which was offered without any hesitation. Conversing with the soldiers I answered their questions as to who we were, why we were here, and what had happened to us. They listened without interrupting and when acquainted with our lot, a barrage of abuse started against Stalin, the Soviet Union, the system, and so on. I was not prepared to join in this criticism. My first thought was that they might have been planted on us. We thanked them for the lift. Only afterward did I believe that the outburst on their part was genuine.

At last we were reunited with our families. What joy, what tears. The next day even the manager of our collective farm greeted us with enthusiasm, mentioning how he had looked forward to our return, particularly now when all young men on the farm had been called up to the Red Army and the labour force was grossly depleted. He offered us now the full pay and rewards on par with a Soviet worker.

We survived the severity of another winter, and this time due to a good harvest we enjoyed extra food. But in my mind was the constant desire to join the Polish Army. My sister Anna was twenty-two, Stas sixteen and Bolus nine. It was very difficult and painful for me to decide to leave my family. Rightly or wrongly in the circumstances I felt that it would be better to leave them as they were, because of the war and the unpredictability of the outcome. The Germans were galloping across the Soviet Union at that time, and I felt that they might survive better than dragging them with me into the unknown. I begged Stas to stay behind to look after Anna and Bolus, but he proved to be very stubborn and insisted on coming with me.

We set off by train towards Tashkent and the mountains, to a small place called Chok-Pak, where a Polish infantry division was being formed. On arrival we looked at the snow-clad mountains with tents on the slopes. After a medical we were ordered to join the other recruits in a tent. It was bitterly cold and damp. Stas passed his medical, though he lied about his age. In the middle of our tent we had a stove which offered some comfort, especially at night when the ground was freezing. The establishment was not like anything resembling a military camp. It was really a quarantine unit catering for survivors of terrible ordeals, particularly those who had survived the labour camps in remote parts of Siberia. The biggest barrack was the hospital, where people were dying like flies and medicine was almost non-existent.

To my horror, my first two weeks of so-called military service was spent digging graves for the dead from typhoid, which was rampant. I doubt if anybody who landed in that hospital ever survived.

After a few days Stas began to cough like a horse. He looked terrible, so I went to the commandant, reported his state of health and my family circumstances. I begged him to release my brother from this camp and allow him to go back to the farm, where my sister and my youngest brother were. The commandant called Stas in and without much hesitation ordered him to return to the rest of my family. Equipped with a supply of bread, he didn't quite appreciate the decision. We embraced heartily, and my last words were, 'It's enough for one of us to die for Poland.'

After two weeks of grave-digging, those who survived marched to a deserted coal mine about 10 kilometres from Chok-Pak. My original boots were worn out. How I did it I don't know, but I marched across the snowy land having only rags around my feet. After a few hours' rest we were shaven, then plastered with some concoctions of smelly ointments and disinfectants, followed by a hot shower. To our astonishment we were then given a complete British Army outfit. We looked at each other in amazement and burst out laughing.

The original agreement was based on the formation of Polish armed forces on Soviet soil, since the Russians wanted as quickly as possible to raise front-line formations in order to fight from Soviet territory. But the Soviet command was preoccupied with problems galore, therefore they were unable to offer proper equipment or facilities for training. So the Polish government had initiated the idea of removing as many units as possible and placing them under British command in the Middle East. To this Stalin had reluctantly agreed.

After a few days allowed for recuperation, now wearing British Army boots, we marched in thick snow back to Chok-Pak railway station. Beside our columns, horse-driven sledges followed to pick up those who were too tired to march. Trust my luck, I happened to be one of them, as something happened to me, and I simply collapsed. On arrival at the station my friend Adam and another friend supported me to the waiting train. Red Army officers stood at each door, checking if anyone was unfit for the journey. This was another turning point in my fortunes. An officer stopped us at the entrance door to the carriage and loudly asked, 'What's the matter with him, is he ill?' Adam replied, 'No,' emphatically, 'he is drunk.' The Russian officer swore and said, 'Get him in.' Otherwise I would have landed in that hospital . . .

Many years later, when I was living in England, the telephone rang. 'Am I speaking to Michael Wartalski?' a strange voice said with a strong American accent. It was a Chicago radio station, which every year before Christmas organized a special show for its listeners and contacted a person anywhere in the world who could provide a story from his or her life. 'Here in our studio is Mr Adam Swierz. Tell us, Michael: how did Adam save your life in Russia in 1942? Go ahead, please, it's live now.'

A pleasant letter of thanks, a tin of candies and a blue sweater and cap from the Chicago Bears American Football team later arrived.

Adam, with the help of another friend, carried me inside the carriage. I felt semi-conscious. Gradually as the train speeded, to my great relief, I began to regain my strength. Adam nursed me all the way to Tashkent. As he told me later, he had fed me and kept giving me in small doses diluted vodka, which he suggested would disinfect my stomach. Whatever Adam did, he saved my life.

In Tashkent, we marched to some military establishment of the Red Army. The civilians gazed at us with utmost curiosity. All smartly dressed, all in new British Army uniforms. In a huge hall, to our astonishment, decorated with numerous red flags and white and red Polish ones, a meal was served. A Red Army band played Polish and Russian tunes. Speeches were made proclaiming Soviet-Polish friendship. The Polish and Soviet national anthems were then played. I could hardly believe it.

From Tashkent via Samarkand our train took us to the Caspian Sea port of Krasnovodsk, and then by ship we surged through the heavy sea, many of us seasick and suffering from diarrhoea, braving the journey to a new world. In the strong wind, human excrement from bad toilets was spraying my rubberized Army cape, under which I sheltered.

The Iranian port of Pahlevi looked like heaven; bright colours everywhere. New hope and new purpose. We were now an Army, though I did not, as yet, quite understand discipline.

It was sad to see so many more dead bodies within our first week in Pahlevi. Those unfortunates from labour camps in remote parts of Siberia just didn't make it. After starvation, perhaps greedily eating rich meals consisting of rice, mutton and dates played havoc with their systems. But we, the younger ones, soon adjusted and recovered. Playing football in the sands of Pahlevi introduced the first spark of pleasure.

It was April 1942 when we moved by British Army trucks to Teheran, an impressive capital surrounded by high mountains with white snow-covered peaks, yet quite warm on the low levels. We were placed in a disused factory. To my surprise, some Russian officers were present in the city; we established later on that the country was under Soviet-British control.

We soon realized how lucky we were to survive and depart from the Soviet Union. Here in Teheran I said goodbye to many of my friends who were destined for Iraq. My friends the Holynski brothers went that way, to join what later became General Anders' famous Second Polish Corps. My, smaller, group headed for the Persian Gulf to a settlement called Ahwaz. A desolate place, more like a desert; an unbearably hot climate, with occasional sand-storms. We were given tropical Army issue and sat mostly in tents with towels round our heads, sweating it out from about 10 a.m. to 5 p.m.. During this period everyone felt lethargic, but with the approach of evening one forcefully accepted a meal. Jackals and hyenas howled at night.

Young Iranian boys were running around selling cool water; as we later discovered, the water was from a nearby pond where dead bodies were washed before the burial ceremony.

On one occasion, with a group of my friends, I decided to explore that pond. It confirmed the rumour that the bodies of dead people were washed there, and which we saw from the other end of the pond. In playful mood, my friends grabbed me and for fun threw me, dressed in my tropical outfit, into the pond. The water was quite warm, but later the results of the fun turned into something which proved serious for the rest of my life.

How glad I was when after a day or two we were embarked on a ship called SS *Lancashire* at Bandar Shahpur. We were in the Persian Gulf. It was 5th May 1942. The ship started smoothly, as the water was like a mill pond, but the heat was still unbearable. In spite of wearing shorts I was perpetually sweating. Maybe this unusual sweating was a prelude to what happened to me within two days of embarkation. It was due to that pond. I was covered in the most peculiar spots all over my body. My temperature was high, and swiftly I was placed in a cabin, isolated from everyone else, where the MO kept an eye on me. I felt restless and kept looking through the porthole facing the sun and bright light. On my release from the cabin I was told we had passed through the Strait of Hormuz and had entered the Arabian Sea.

Since my departure from the Soviet Union I had befriended a very nice fellow, Henryk Zakotti. From then on we developed our friendship, which lasted until his death in 1993. It was Henryk who greeted me on the top deck of SS *Lancashire*. He was glad to see me, though I was pale and weak. With curiosity we were watching all that was happening around us. Henryk was pointing out to me some ships not too far distant, but I found I couldn't see them – I had become short-sighted *and* colour blind.

Somehow I managed to conquer this disability, always using other people's vision on long distances and avoiding any conversation where colours were involved. From then on the 'mother of invention' never abandoned me.

On 16th May we landed in Suez, and from there were transported to a transit camp on Egyptian soil. A huge camp, full of tents of all sizes. There was a NAAFI canteen, too. It was our first opportunity to indulge in some monetary transactions, after receiving our first pay. You had to buy your own soap, boot polish and toothpaste, but I had enough to purchase a bar of chocolate and a can of beer. This beer and chocolate played havoc with me. I had to lie down on the sand, being violently sick and suffering dreadful pains in my stomach. On top of this the Military Policemen came along telling me off and accusing me of being drunk. They wanted to arrest me, but eventually left me alone. I dragged my feet back to the camp, swearing that never again would I mix canned beer with chocolate.

From this camp to another tented camp, in Palestine. Here proper Army drill began. Not a moment was wasted. The climate was splendid, and the smell of the orange orchards captivating. We were given rifles and ammunition, and for the first time in my life I was doing guard duties, protecting military equipment. This standing for four hours at night, leaning on my rifle and perpetually fighting the natural desire to sleep, was to me quite imposing. On one occasion I almost fell asleep standing with my rifle, when an NCO on inspection discovered it and gave me quite a severe reprimand.

Back to Suez, and on 5th June 1942 we started embarking over

10,000 troops in the famous *Mauretania*, converted from a luxury liner to a troop carrier. There was a feeling of security, boarding such a splendid ship, though instead of luxury one felt like a sardine in a tin. The daily routine of coping with so many souls was most impressive. It all worked like a clock after just being wound up. Many orders and instructions were given, which Henryk and I never obeyed. No one could find anyone in this congestion, so Henryk and I roamed the upper decks, exploring the ship, admiring the climate. It was sad to see boys being seasick, as it never affected me. I stayed close to my other friend Hubert at meal times, for the sole purpose of consuming his meals, which he couldn't stomach.

On 12th June we crossed the Equator on this vast Indian Ocean, then passed Madagascar, and on the 16th we arrived at Durban, the Union of South Africa. More orders and instructions were given. No visits to blacks' villages, no fraternization. We were warned about VD and the dangers of having intercourse with black women, but in spite of all these warnings some of our boys managed to break the rules, and some paid the price.

Due to my reasonable voice, apparently a tenor, I was asked to join the choir attached to the Divisional HQ. Our conductor was an ex-teacher, extremely able, persuasive and hard-working. Henryk and Hubert also joined the choir as tenors. We were quite privileged and exempt from square-bashing, but practising every day for at least six hours. A brass band was also formed, and our conductor was perpetually at loggerheads with them for practising too near us. They felt that we were yelling our heads off too near to *them*, but soon a distance was enforced by an officer.

The time arrived for appearing in public. Our first performance was for the schools of Pietermaritzburg, at the Town Hall. It went extremely well, particularly our final pieces with combined choir and band. Some we sang in English, learning the pronunciations by using Polish phonetics. It was emphasized that the concert was given in appreciation of the many kindnesses extended to us by the citizens of Pietermaritzburg. The next concert was given in the local studio for the BBC in London. Two more followed, one in Johannesburg and one in Cape Town.

Back to Durban, and on 4th September we embarked on an old Australian ship, the *Rangitiki*, which took us to Cape Town. We stayed there three days, and late afternoon on the third day we sailed and waved goodbye to South Africa. Out of the harbour we joined a huge convoy. My vision wasn't good enough to see it all properly, but Henryk was always giving me the description of distant objects. I slept like a log with an unusual feeling of reassurance, admiring our escort. In the morning to our shock we discovered that *Rangitiki* was on her own, sailing in a zigzag fashion. As we learned later, that was the tactic in the dangerous waters of the Atlantic. We stopped for a few hours at Freetown, Sierra Leone to replenish supplies, then turned sharply westward as if crossing the Atlantic.

On 15th October we entered Cardiff to grey waters and drizzle. It was our first experience of dull weather with a slight fog. We rejoiced at our arrival, glad that we had survived the ocean voyage. WVS ladies offered us the traditional cup of tea. They were very friendly. We then were off on a long journey, and a very tiring one too, to a distribution camp in Scotland. Back again in tents, and it rained and rained.

The camp was like a market where groups of officers and NCOs were mobilizing us into their units. Henryk and I begged to be allocated to the Polish Air Force – 'Spitfires, please.' But we were categorically told that there were no further requirements for fighter pilots. Of course on arrival we all had medicals, and I was frightened about my eyes. Fortunately I managed to learn by heart the bottom two or three lines on the board, and passed.

We were almost coerced to join the Parachute Brigade. The Navy was quite persuasive too, but like little boys, after being rejected by the Air Force we decided to join the Anti-Aircraft Regiment of the 1st Polish Armoured Division as a reaction to being let down.

Soon we reported to our regiment, stationed at Gullane, north-east of Edinburgh; a seaside holiday resort where we occupied most of the hotels. Time wasn't wasted – square-bashing, lectures, learning the English language, and basic military training. Within three months Henryk and I entered our Anti-Aircraft Cadet Officers' School – about thirty of us young and eager men.

My first pass, when I met my first Scottish lass, she asked me what my name was. I said Mietek, so she immediately suggested it was Michael, and from then on I have been known as Michael, though my proper Christian name in Polish is Mieczyslaw. I eventually adopted this name, and it appears now in my British passport.

My first visit to a dance had rather a tragic finale. On this occasion I danced with quite an attractive young lady. I wanted to see her again, but my English was in its infancy, so I approached one of my friends supposedly advanced in English studies. I repeated the sentence several times and chose an appropriate moment to whisper into her ear when dancing almost cheek to cheek. Before I finished the sentence she slapped my face and disappeared from the dance hall. Not surprising, when I had whispered, 'May I brush your chimney?' That friend ceased to be my friend! After that I was determined never to ask again, and to my utmost pleasure, later *I* used to write letters for *him* in English.

In the summer of 1943 we had a visit of General Sikorski with high-ranking British and Polish officers, and afterwards we took part in the 1st Polish Armoured Division manoeuvres. To see the whole division in action, particularly the armour moving fast and displaying such an enormous firepower, boosted our morale. We also met for the first time a contingent of the Czechoslovakian Army. The Czechs were not too happy, and in conversation one could detect their bitterness over the way Mr Chamberlain conducted his handing over to the Germans of the Sudetenland.

The date still remains in my mind, 4th July 1943, when the tragic news of General Sikorski's Gibraltar air crash swept across the Poles in Great Britain. He was our C-in-C, and Prime Minister of the Polish government in exile in London. This unfortunate episode has remained mysterious ever since. The official report only concluded mechanical failure. It was a difficult period in politics within the Alliance, weighing the importance of the Soviet contribution to the war effort against the Katyn massacre of Polish officers, which the Soviet Union blamed on the Germans. Everybody knew it was the NKVD that executed it. The Soviet government had just broken off diplomatic relations with the Polish government on account of Katyn [or rather, on account of Sikorski's repeated calls for an investigation by the International Red Cross].

I was delighted to finish my Cadet Officers' School successfully by the end of October 1943; glad also that Henryk and many others – altogether twenty-six – took part in a 'marching out' parade. Henryk and I, as Corporal Cadet Officers, went back to our regiment and were given our own 40 mm Bofors gun and crew to take charge of until we became officers. In the Polish Army, after finishing the Cadet Officers' School, a Cadet would get a rank of Lance-Corporal Cadet, or Corporal Cadet, and would be sent back to his regiment. He might even go on being promoted to Sergeant Cadet Officer, and never be commissioned. It was up to the regimental CO, who had to *recommend* him for a commission. But once one became an officer the rank was irreversible, unless subject to misdemeanour.

At the end of February 1944 the 1st Polish Armoured Division, without its equipment, gathered somewhere near Lanark to welcome General Bernard Montgomery who, surrounded by his staff officers, inspected us. I remember his piercing eyes looking at us.

Afterwards he stood up on his jeep and addressed us. I can recall some of his words: 'We are going to kill the Germans, and the more Germans you kill the better soldiers you are. Good luck to each one of you.' He was C-in-C of the Twenty-First Army Group, consisting of the Second British and the First Canadian Armies. We were part of the First Canadian Army.

In May the entire division was concentrated in and around Scarborough. Our troop occupied two hotels along the long promenade, facing the sea. A steep slope with flowers and shrubs, well cultivated, made the scenery very picturesque. Every morning we had PT on the slopes. Every night Henryk and I visited the Royal Hotel, which was always packed with troops and girls. It was infuriating for me because I couldn't dance. On many occasions I managed to meet a nice girl and buy her a drink, then another fellow would simply say, 'Excuse me, may I have a dance?' and that was the end of her as far as I was concerned. One night I decided to prompt my courage with a decent dose of alcohol, and asked a lady to dance. I led her to the dancing floor, which was always overcrowded. It happened to be a quickstep, which only resulted in quicker stepping on her feet. She must have suffered agonies, but I blamed overcrowding.

On 5th June all our radio communications were silenced. The day had come – D-Day – though our division was not to go in straight away. Our role came later; first the beachheads had to be secured. But soon, slowly, we started moving south. My 1st Anti-Aircraft Regiment had fifty-four Bofors guns, 307 vehicles altogether. Just think of the number of men and vehicles of the whole 1st Polish Armoured Division, which consisted of HQ, four tank regiments, four artillery regiments, four battalions of infantry and a string of supporting units.

Then south we moved to Ewshot – Aldershot. Somehow the whole atmosphere had changed, and everybody looked more serious from the top to the lowest ranks. Between friends we exchanged our home addresses in Poland, 'just in case'. We were joking but not as much as before. We were not allowed to leave the camp. Then, one evening at dusk, we started rolling across some suburbs of London to Tilbury Docks. There was no need for orders. MPs [Military Policemen] waving hands with white leather gloves controlled the entire movement of vehicles. What surprised us was the noise of V1 rockets flying quite low over us towards London.

In daylight I could hardly believe the number of ships covering the Channel – it was like two unbroken lines of ships moving in both directions, to Normandy and back to England. Then one could see the shores of Normandy, closer and closer. The landing craft came along, then loaded to full capacity. Slowly we moved towards the beaches. The sound of artillery greeted us, and we soon realized we were in business. It was 2nd August 1944.

Our first offensive began with a glorious sight of probably a thousand four-engined bombers appearing on the horizon. With such joy we watched them opening the hatches, and bombs like confetti coming down, but alas some, to our horror, on us. My regiment suffered, the Canadians suffered, and only later it was mentioned that casualties on our side were quite substantial. My CO, Colonel Eminowicz, was severely wounded, with a group of HQ officers and other ranks. Some of our equipment was also destroyed, and that was only within our regiment. Major Berendt took over command of the regiment immediately.

But the bulk of the bombs fell on the Germans, and as a result the entire front was paralysed for a while, when the bombers said goodbye. When the dust settled down, all the Allied artilleries opened fire in an incredible barrage which created a duel with the German artillery. Shells were exploding in front of us, and over. This artillery duel was fascinating, particularly as it progressed, and fewer and fewer German guns were responding. Again a short pause, and then the turn of the tanks came. Eventually the German lines were broken and Henryk and I followed our boys through the utter devastation. At one point the bulldozers had to clear the debris for us to get through.

My first encounter with the Germans was rather curious. A bunch of them, waving white handkerchiefs, came out from a small wood. They had no weapons. To my surprise when one of them came closer to me and noticed 'Poland' on my arm, he threw himself at my feet, begging me not to shoot him. I told him to get up, as he was crying. In my school German I told him how cruel they were to my countrymen, but I had no intention of killing him or his friends. Before they were escorted to a truck to take them to the POW point, I turned to a boy who, before we went to Normandy, had displayed such heroics and was going to kill them left, right and centre. I said to him, 'You can kill them – there is your chance.' But I knew he couldn't do it.

The news spread that Warsaw had risen against the Germans, and it was perturbing.

Henryk and I were very lucky because we always followed some unit; we weren't in the front line. The greatest respect I had was for the infantrymen. On many occasions I watched them sitting on the tanks before an attack, and often I wondered what their thoughts were. Then slowly the tanks moved, and they followed on foot with bayonets on their rifles.

The worst sight of destruction I saw was after the so-called Falaise Gap was closed on the retreating German Panzer divisions. It was my division that succeeded in holding the trapped Germans in the Falaise–Chambois pocket. The battle at Mont Ormel became a symbol of the Battle of Normandy. Narrow roads around Mont Ormel were literally covered with dead soldiers, massive armoured equipment, horses and vehicles of all sorts.

After the Falaise–Chambois battle all sorts of news, views and rumours circulated around, as we moved pretty fast across France in the chase. We moved on through St Omer, Ypres, on to Roulers, then Thielt. I can't remember all the names. The Luftwaffe was hardly seen, and our engagements were rarer and rarer, as far as aircraft were concerned.

In Belgium there were crowds of people, shouting *vive* this and *vive* that; flowers, even fresh fruit were thrown at us. Henryk was hit on his forehead with a pear and didn't appreciate it. For the first time we felt like liberators.

Holland was a complete contrast to Belgium. No triumphant entry. The Dutch looked bewildered, subjugated by starvation. It was the children that we pitied most, standing beside our guns, often in silence, and just gazing. I don't remember a single meal which we all ate without sharing it with the children, and it was a joy to extract from them a faint smile.

As their own supply problems slowed the Allies' advance and the German resistance stiffened, however, another Polish unit – Major-General Stanislaw Sosabowski's 1st Polish Parachute Brigade – was thrown into the fight.

Felix Relidzinski was Sosabowski's signals officer.

By August 1944 the German armies which four years before had overrun so swiftly the Low Countries and France were retreating towards the borders of their own country. The Allied armies which had driven forward from the congested beachheads in Normandy were sweeping in a fury towards Germany.

While these battles were being fought, the Polish Brigade were waiting impatiently in England. The waiting time seemed so long, for between 6th June and 17th September no less than sixteen operations were planned, and all of them came to naught.

The last operation, 'Market Garden', was based on a plan

to form a corridor along the Eindhoven–Veghel–Grave–Nijmegen–Arnhem road. The bridges over the canals and rivers along the road were to be seized by the American 101st Airborne and 82nd Airborne Divisions, and the British 1st Airborne Division and Polish Brigade [at the very end of the corridor] had to seize the road bridge at Arnhem. If successful the operation would ensure a straight and swift advance right to the threshold of Germany.

Because there were insufficient transport planes to carry everyone, the units involved would be delivered to their drop zones over the course of three days – 17th, 18th and 19th September 1944.

At Arnhem the British, plus the Polish gliders, would land on the far bank of the river; then the Polish paratroopers would land on the near bank.

As soon as the battle began, however, it became apparent that German strength in the Arnhem area had been badly underestimated. In fact the British and Poles found themselves facing two SS Panzer divisions equipped with precisely the kind of tanks and heavy weapons they themselves lacked. Only a single British battalion – the 2nd Battalion, the Parachute Regiment – reached the bridge before the Germans sealed it off. To compound the 1st Airborne's problems, the weather closed in.

Having spent the 19th (the day they were originally scheduled to jump) waiting at Saltby and Spanhoe for orders which never came, the Poles emplaned on the 20th and had actually reached the runways, understandably keyed up for the flight to come, before the operation was again cancelled.

On 21st September, in the quarters occupied by the Polish paras at Stamford, in the early hours of the raising day, the paratroopers were making the last preparations for the upcoming action. The weather was a factor as in previous days. The heavy concentration of shifting dark clouds threatened to bring the rain, or at best uncertain conditions. The delays and the continuous gnawing thoughts about the unknown future ahead of us were adding to the ever-growing tension and frustration of the men.

We worried about the location of our landings during the operation. Was it going to be in water; in trees; or worse, in high tension wires? Would the pilots drop us right on to targets? Were we going to be lucky enough to reach the landing zones safely? What would happen if our plane was hit by enemy anti-aircraft fire? All these and more doubts and fears ran through our thoughts.

We watched a row of Army trucks lining up in front of the barracks for the loading of the paratroopers and their equipment.

The place, until now quiet and peaceful, became a bustle of activity. Loud commands and orders calling on soldiers to take their seats in the assigned trucks rang through the air.

Throughout the ride to the airfields we were silent. There was not much to talk about. The news coming from the fighting going on at Arnhem bridge was short, and inadequate enough to cause excitement; the radio kept broadcasting over-optimistic war communiqués. At some point the convoy passed a small group of ATS girls, walking lazily and slowly, most likely after spending late hours of the last night at some dancing hall or similar entertainment. We greeted them with shouts of appreciation.

We were approaching the airfield at Saltby from which we would take off to our unknown destiny. The airfield spread across the green space of an empty land used in peacetime as farmlands. The cement-covered runways, grey in colour, contrasted sharply with the short clipped grass looking clean after night rains; they ran in straight lines, in asymmetrical order to accommodate planes landing from all directions and in changing winds.

The place looked familiar to us with its scattered aircraft – mostly Americans with their insignia painted on the wings and the bodies. Thankfully the sun started playing peek-a-boo with us, bringing smiles and relief to the faces of the men. The weather was clearly improving; patches of the bright blue skies were visible on the horizon. But from time to time the milky fog covered the sun so as to remind us that after all we were dealing with English weather.

We unloaded the equipment from the trucks, said our goodbyes to the drivers, and started the march towards the row of Dakotas which would take us into the battle.

The crew of the plane we were assigned to entered the aircraft and occupied their places. In addition to the crew, eighteen paratroopers in full gear were assigned to each plane. The pilot was in charge of operating and flying the aircraft to the dropping zone. The responsibility for the paratroopers belonged to the jumpmaster – as a rule one of us, regardless of rank, who took charge of the loading and acted as liaison with the crew, responsible for jump time when the pilot gave the signal to empty the aircraft as it flew over the target.

As jumpmaster I made the usual inspection of the men to be satisfied that everyone was ready for the flight. I approached the American pilot and after introducing myself according to the military etiquette, I started asking questions. Since we were trained to follow British procedure the first question, which really bothered me, was what the pilot would like us to do if we were hit by enemy fire.

'Brother,' he said to me, 'if and when we are in trouble, the crew will be the first to jump out of the plane. You just follow us!'

Captain Middleton then suggested that from now on we should be on first-name basis. Meanwhile, messengers delivered orders to the officers scattered all over the airfield with their units. Due to the improving weather, aerial transport with escorting fighters was considered safe, and further delays or postponement of the operation were not anticipated. The time for the Para Brigade to take off was set for two o'clock in the afternoon. The day was 21st September 1944.

Captain Middleton put the paratroopers on alert for boarding the plane. One by one, using stepladders, the soldiers boarded the Dakota and took their seats on both sides of the aisle. Coming from the daylight into the hull, it took a while to get used to the place in which we would spend the next few hours. Looking over the drab interior we noticed a long metal rod affixed to the upper part of the hull, running in the middle and whole length of it. On this rod we would hook up our parachutes before jumping out of the aircraft.

One of the crew members entered our section and said, 'We are just about ready, and it won't be long before we are off. From the captain and the crew, I wish you good luck and God bless . . .' The guy was visibly moved, and disappeared quickly behind the door of the cabin.

On given radio signals the pilot started the engines. The ground personnel gathered on the grass, watching the last movements of planes waiting in threes on the runways for the signal to take off.

The first three aircraft with engines working at full power and perfectly synchronized gradually increased their speed, lifted their bodies above the runway and began climbing. At the point where the horizon and the land merged they took a sharp half-circle turn, heading towards the sea and beyond. They were followed by a series of threes, at one-minute intervals, performing the same manoeuvre. The armada was joined over the marshalling points by escort fighters, and was on its way to Arnhem. It would be impossible not to get excited being part of these fateful events.

We flew at 11,000 feet over the waters of the North Sea. The temperature inside the aircraft was dropping; the occasional clouds laden with moist droplets added wetness to the air in the cabin, making us shivery and uncomfortable. Realizing that it wouldn't take long before we reached the target, we became alive and began the preparation for the jump. Those who liked to travel light had removed the parachutes from their backs at the beginning of the flight. Now was the time to put them on. After some commotion and shifting position from sitting to standing, the men calmed down, and peace and quiet reigned. The Dakota began its descent, causing the change of air pressure in the cabin and producing a feeling of temporary deafness in our ears.

We were now flying over the northern parts of Belgium, which were already under the control of the Allied forces. The unsettled weather conditions of the morning hours gave way to clear and bright skies. We could watch the movements of the trucks on the roads. Here and there burned houses indicated the fighting in this area. We received the message from the pilots' cabin that within the next couple of minutes we would reach the dropping zone.

The red light flashed its bright colour. I shouted the command, 'Action Stations!' The rays of the setting sun over the horizon brightened up the green light bulb and confused me for a moment, then the clear green light flashed. I yelled at the top of my voice, 'Go!'

I barely put my foot outside the door when a powerful stream of air pulled me out of the plane into the endless expanse. My body was twisted from upright to a backward position, face up and floating weightlessly. For the longest few seconds in my life I managed to catch a view of the tail of the Dakota, the falling body of another paratrooper, waiting and waiting for my parachute to open.

With a sudden jerk which was an indication of the parachute filling with air, I promptly started preparations for the landing. There was not much swinging of the parachute, which in addition to the weight of my body had to support something like 100 kg of ammunition and other equipment going down with me. I landed on slightly elevated ground with huge Dutch cows grazing, sharing the pasture with the horses. The roar of the planes, strange objects falling from the skies and multiple colours of the parachutes caused the animals to panic. One of the big containers full of weapons and ammunition hit a running horse, scoring our first and instant kill. From the elevated railroad came heavy machine gun fire. I looked at my watch – it was eight minutes past five in the afternoon.

From the distance we could see and hear the planes heading towards the borders of Germany.

The landing field was about 2 kilometres in width and 3 kilometres in depth; the small village of Driel protected it from the west; railroad and high tension wires formed the eastern defences; the tall dike alongside the River Rhine defended it from the north. The road in the south served as an observation point.

The area was criss-crossed by draining ditches, some of them up to 5 metres wide and filled with muddy water. Men were struggling with heavy equipment on the wet ground. Motor cycles turned out to be especially difficult and awkward to handle in these unforeseen conditions. Tired and discouraged, the men abandoned their futile efforts and laid the motor cycles in the water of the canals as improvised bridges.

Wave after wave of paratroopers landed in the orchards, in the yards of the farmers' houses, on the roads, near the buildings of the now abandoned and deserted farms. Some of them landed in trees, or on the high tension wires. Fortunately the power houses had been knocked out by the heavy bombardment of the Allied Air Forces.

There was a short skirmish with the German defenders before they withdrew from the barns and houses. From preliminary interviews with the first German prisoners captured in the fighting, there was no indication of a larger concentration of the enemy in the area.

The first reports and the estimations of casualties indicated that from approximately 1600 paratroopers who left England that afternoon, less than 1000 could be accounted for. There was no radio answer from the 1st Battalion; only a mortar platoon landed. Almost half of the 3rd Battalion was missing. The 2nd Battalion, Engineers, Signals and other services reported full contingents. Altogether, at the time of landing, 803 paratroopers were under the command of General Sosabowski.

The dining-room in a farmhouse, because of its size and its ample amount of chairs, was selected as a temporary command post. On the basis of the information received shortly before the brigade took off from England, the General's first decision after landing in Driel was to despatch a patrol to check conditions for the brigade to cross the river and join the 1st Airborne Division. Since the efforts to establish radio contact with the Divisional HQ came to naught there was nothing else to do but wait for the return of the patrol. Meanwhile, a young woman from the Dutch underground, by the name of Cora Baltussen, brought the news that the ferry across the river had been sunk and that the Germans were in control of the area. Soon after this information was confirmed by the returning patrol.

The General issued the order to all units to proceed to the region of De Nevel, a short distance from the Rhine, where, according to the promises made by the British, we were going to find boats and rafts.

We began the march at about ten o'clock in the evening. It was pitch dark and we were laden with heavy equipment. Fences presented additional problems of finding the right way and getting through with the equipment. We stopped behind a huge dike separating us from the river. It acted as a shield against the wind. The silence of the men and the peace and quiet of the surroundings were interrupted from time to time by the crack of rifle fire. It seemed distant, and the unknown direction created a surrealistic air of uneasiness.

We had an unexpected visitor, Captain Ludwig Zwolanski, whose position was that of Polish liaison officer to the Divisional HQ. He had had to swim across the river from the northern side to deliver a message from the commander of the 1st Airborne Division to General Sosabowski. Captain Zwolanski reported that the 2nd Battalion, the Parachute Regiment, under the command of Lieutenant-Colonel John Frost, was no longer in control of the bridge at Arnhem and that the situation of the rest of the division, concentrated in the Oosterbeek area [to the west of Arnhem], was very difficult as well. The loss of the ferry complicated things even more. Sosabowski was asked to provide immediate help to improve the defences of the perimeter. After midnight, at about one o'clock on the 22nd, a British liaison officer contacted Sosabowski to repeat the request. He promised the arrival of the boats in a very short time.

Meanwhile the Germans began a cannonade of artillery from the northern hills of Arnhem. Several farms were on fire, throwing light on our positions and brightening the peacefully flowing waters of the Rhine. The late hour of the night, the position of the brigade – open to attacks and unsafe from the defence point of view – and finally the fact that the promised boats did not arrive on time forced Sosabowski to call off the crossing of the river. After carefully evaluating the situation, the General decided to withdraw the brigade to new positions at Driel. He elaborated the situation, as he saw it, to the small group of officers, listening attentively. 'The brigade will form a defensive core opposite the Oosterbeek perimeter, resisting the Germans' attacks and keeping the access to the river free and open. This kind of warfare can be compared to the tactics of the porcupine, when surrounded and attacked from many directions by enemies. Tomorrow we will again try to ford the river.'

We started the retreat to Driel. This time it was not only a repetition of the night's hard struggle with the unknown terrain; some new elements of discomfort were added – feelings of exhaustion, lack of sleep and empty stomachs. Some of the narrow roads and passages were temporarily clogged up by the slow-moving traffic. To compound the situation, some of the units lost their cohesiveness and short tempers flared up. One of my signallers, loaded with the heavy radio set on his back and two batteries in both hands, inadvertently bumped into the General, who in an infuriated tone of voice said to him, 'Go away, you are following me too closely! Can I have some room to do my thinking?' The Private, realizing the jam he'd got himself into, jumped to attention and said promptly, 'Sir, it is my duty to protect the Commanding Officer.'

I had no way to know how effectively he mollified the General, but a couple of hours later that same General bumped into me. He gave me a sound dressing down together with a reprimand for the poor discipline among my men. I obediently assured the General that I had every intention to take care of the situation.

We reached Driel at dawn on 22nd September, digging in in a hurry. The signal patrols went out to set up the telephone communication between the Brigade HQ and the battalions occupying the forward positions. It did not take long before we learnt that the wires were in a shambles because of enemy artillery fire. The patrols had to go out again to do the repair job. The first messages reported enemy penetrations of our defence lines, especially in the area where we had landed the day before.

Our sudden and unexpected appearance in Driel caused much joy and enthusiasm among the inhabitants. It seemed that the long years of German occupation had come to an end, and it was time to celebrate the liberation. Little did they know that the real ordeal for them was just starting.

The failure to establish contact with the Polish radio station attached to Divisional HQ worried us for many reasons. The distance between the stations was no more than 6 miles, but the area was flat and covered in some sections with trees and other, man-made, objects interfering with good reception. Corporal Pajak, in charge of the station, belonged to the top class of radio operators we had in our company, yet we failed to get through, very much like the rest of the division. The mystery was never fully explained or understood.

Finally, in the early hours of the morning, Corporal Pajak's station answered our call. We were simply elated.

Pajak lost two men belonging to the regular crew operating the station with him when they left the relative security of the Hartenstein Hotel [site of the Divisional HQ in Oosterbeek] in search of some lost batteries and were killed by German snipers. Pajak found a replacement by co-opting the well-known war correspondent Marek Swiecicki, and the partnership worked well throughout the division's stay in the Oosterbeek perimeter. In the exchange Marek obviously risked losing the status of non-combatant member of the division.

Just before noon a reconnaissance unit [from the 2nd Household Cavalry Regiment] appeared from the direction of the western sector of the brigade defences. They spearheaded the moving columns of the Second Army, and by going round the German positions at Elst had managed to join the brigade in Driel. It was an uplifting feeling to see them here sitting in the small square, not far from the command post. A small group surrounded them, engaging the crews in conversation about the general situation of the front line, so close to us. Soon after we were joined by General Sosabowski, who had left the command post some while before with the intention to reconnoitre the defences manned by various units. The General had dispensed with the usual entourage of protective personnel and with two bicycles, idling in the basement, now serving as a means of transportation was, together with his Adjutant, on his way to find out for himself the state of his brigade. With maps under their arms, a little bit shaky in handling the unruly bicycles on the wet, slippery road, they looked more like two gentlemen taking the Saturday ride in the English countryside.

A platoon from the Supply Company tried to recover the containers with ammunition and food left uncollected from the dropping zone after the landing of the brigade. The paratroopers met very heavy enemy fire, and a number of men were killed and wounded. On the way back from the unsuccessful mission they found two glider pilots and the entire crew of one of the shot-down planes, hiding in the tall grass of the marshes.

In the latter hours of the afternoon we watched the supply planes dropping food and ammunition destined for the division in the perimeter. The heavy transport planes kept bravely on course, dropping the supplies attached to their multi-coloured parachutes. The crew from one of the Dakotas on fire continued dropping supplies till the moment when the fire reached the tail. Then with the damaged steering the plane lost its balance and hit the ground, exploding like a ball of flame.

The other planes, after dropping the containers, turned to the west and disappeared. The irony of it all was the fact that most of the supplies were dropped on the old dropping zones which were by now under German control.

The transport crews were unaware of the problems with the drop zones because of the lack of a reliable radio link with the paratroopers. Aircrews were expressly forbidden to follow unsubstantiated signals from the ground.

In the early evening of the 22nd, in the quarters of the command post building, some wanted and expected and also some unwanted and unexpected visitors filled the rooms. One of the visitors, Lieutenant-Colonel Mackenzie, Chief of Staff of the 1st Airborne Division [who had crossed the river in a rubber boat], described the very critical position of the paratroopers in the Oosterbeek perimeter and asked for immediate help. The point at issue was how to get the Polish paratroopers across the Rhine in the shortest possible time to replace the defenders of the perimeter.

Both British and Polish commanders could not muster a sufficient number of boats for this kind of operation. A search for them among the Dutch people had not produced the anticipated results. Improvised rafts could not be considered seriously because of their inherent difficulties in being controlled in the swiftly moving waters of the river. Besides, no more than 300–400 metres of the northern shore were in British hands. The only available means of transportation were the rubber dinghies used by the Polish Sappers, and these were used during the coming night's crossings as decided at the meeting.

That night altogether about fifty Polish paratroopers crossed the river, reinforcing the British defences. They were assigned to close the Oosterbeek–Heveadorp road and to protect the perimeter from the south-west.

23rd September began with good news. The British 43rd (Wessex) Division, after a well-executed assault on the German positions at Elst, opened up a safe passage to Driel, thus doing away with our isolation.

In the early hours of the morning arrived a liaison officer from the HQ of General Browning, commander of airborne forces engaged in Operation Market Garden. He reported that the 1st Battalion of the Polish Brigade, and some units of the 3rd, recalled back to England from the flight on the 21st because of bad weather over the Channel, were preparing to drop in the region of Grave that very afternoon.

From my room, just above the General's quarters, I could follow the conversation between the two officers. General Sosabowski was quite open in criticizing the progress and conduct of the operation. He was very adamant in demanding the fulfilment of his conditions before the next crossing of the river could be considered. His paratroopers had been engaged in continuous fighting for the last three days without rest or food. They were tired.

Food and ammunition, in addition to providing the boats, were the first priority on the list of supplies. The liaison officer promised to meet those requirements at the end of the day. Shortly after this conversation, the Chief of Staff of the brigade [Major Malaszkiewicz] left for the HQ of the 43rd Division to talk about the crossings and boats. Meanwhile the German artillery operating from the north of Arnhem scored a direct hit on the school building in which the field hospital was located. The new wounded and killed were added to the ever-increasing number of casualties.

The supplies, as promised, arrived at about nine o'clock in the evening. The distribution of the canned food and the ammunition went on in the light of the brightly burning farmhouses. Then we began our march of ghosts, following the same road remembered so well from the first night after landing. This time we knew exactly what the dark night had in store for us.

The organization of the crossing was in the hands of the brigade Sappers. In the two previous days they had investigated thoroughly the terrain, ditches, dikes, configuration of both banks, and entries and exits before and after the crossing.

The road and the free space before the dike filled up with the paratroopers. We inspected with interest the twenty-nine boats provided by the 43rd Division, which were different from the ones promised in the conference. They differed in size, which required changes in assignment of the men and improvisation at a time when the increased enemy fire caused enough confusion. In some cases they were missing the paddles. Meanwhile the night hours so important for our safety in the critical time of the crossing of the river were becoming shorter and shorter . . .

The chilly air mixed with the occasional rain brought the odour from the direction of the Rhine. In the excitement and confusion of the moment I got in the mood of having no cares in the world, except one, which was the number of the boat I was assigned to – boat No. 3. I lay down on the wet grass and fell fast asleep. The Germans knew the area well, and sporadic fire and phosphorus flares indicated their interest in what was going on.

Along the tall dike, from the river side, the low-lying land was utilized for orchards. The cider factory in this area was on fire, together with a farmhouse, producing billowy and colourful smoke and shooting flames into the air.

The surface of the dike was used as a road; at the bottom, the flat grassland stretched out 200 metres towards the lower dike, protecting the area from lesser floods. Between the lower dike and the bank of the river was a distance of approximately 60 metres.

I woke up to the shouts, 'Boat No. 3, get ready for the crossing!' We gathered quickly round Second Lieutenant Mieczyslaw Gruenbaum from the Sapper Company. He was assigned to lead our group. There were altogether ten of us, including four Sappers to man the boat – five on each side. The boat was ungainly and rested uncomfortably on our shoulders.

'Once we get to the top of the dike,' warned the Lieutenant, 'we'll face a heavy concentration of machine gun fire. The Germans are waiting for us.'

Trying to co-ordinate our movements and to harmonize the steps, we pushed strenuously up the steep slope. The wet and slippery grass gave little support to our feet. One of the soldiers lost his balance and tripped over, pulling with him the others. 'Get up! Get up!' shouted Gruenbaum. 'And let's try again!'

This time we reached the top, to be immediately overwhelmed by the intensity of the flares hanging over our heads, the detonation of projectiles and the profusion of ricocheting bullets. We unintentionally dropped the boat, and finding safety behind it we pushed it down the slope to the bottom of the dike.

Dazed and disorientated, we lifted it again and kept marching. A machine gun from the right side was giving us a hard time. This was a most vulnerable place to be, and soon the first casualties came from that machine gun. Some of the men panicked in the situation and ran to the other side of the boat. Lieutenant Gruenbaum ordered two of the Sappers to move to the right side.

We were approaching the lower dike with two more wounded men. They were moaning, obviously in great pain. Here we met other boats with paratroopers, happy that they had got so far alive. From behind the dike one could smell and feel the silently flowing waters of the Lower Rhine. The cold night made us shiver, apprehensive and tense. Safe from the enemy fire we listened to the last instructions from Gruenbaum.

The last 60 metres before reaching the river, with the boat carried by fewer men trudging in the muddy marshlands, under increasing artillery fire, became slow and painful torture to our tired bodies.

When we got to what we thought was deep enough water, we dropped the boat and all of us jumped into it.

The water was too shallow to support the boat, and it stuck in the mud.

After much heaving, rocking and pushing we finally began moving on, fighting the stream. In the middle we ran into a violent current which carried the boat downriver. We paddled frantically to avoid the change of course. Meanwhile the boat started moving in a circle, colliding with another one and bowing very heavily. In the darkness we noticed that we were in the company of many more boats heading towards the shore. Someone, impatient to put his feet on firm ground, jumped into the water. He was followed immediately by others. Boat after boat was brought to a sudden halt on the sandbanks. We quickly waded into the water and rushed to the security of the higher northern bank. The men from other boats gathered, relieved that the ordeal was left behind.

We shook hands with Lieutenant Gruenbaum and expressed our gratitude for getting us safely across the river. We also wished him good luck, since he had to go back with wounded oarsmen to join the brigade on the other side of the Rhine.

On his way back, as he ran over the high dike, Lieutenant Gruenbaum was hit by a rifle bullet in the head and lost the seeing in one eye.

Altogether, approximately 250 Polish paratroopers crossed the river and joined the defences of the Oosterbeek perimeter that night. Not all men and boats were lucky. Some of them, in the darkness of the night, lost their direction and landed in German positions. Some of the boats were sunk and the men went down with them. Out of a total of twenty-nine boats, thirteen were sunk as a result of enemy fire.

Now on the far bank of the river, the Poles settled into the routine of the besieged Oosterbeek perimeter. The Germans were content to crush the enclave at their own pace, letting their artillery do much of the work.

At six o'clock in the morning the place would look ominously quiet. We still had another hour or so before the Germans began the merciless pounding of our positions. It gave us a little time to prepare a meagre breakfast, consisting of dehydrated rations recovered from air-dropped supplies that had luckily landed in the region outside the enemy's hands.

Paratroopers in singles or in small groups kept emerging from barns and half-destroyed houses where they had spent the night. Temporarily abandoned shell holes and trenches were reoccupied in preparation for the imminent attacks.

As expected the enemy began the daily, one-sided dialogue with us by shelling our positions with a savage intensity. The air was filled with the penetrating noise of shells, followed by frightening explosions. Mortar fragments kept falling on the trenches, now covered with branches of the trees but giving little protection against the hot metal. We did not have enough ammunition, mortars or guns to answer the assault.

Cringing in the deep and narrow fox holes we counted each second, fearing most of all being buried alive in the constantly moving and trembling earth. In the horror of the moment we just prayed, repeating long forgotten words we were taught in our youth.

The casualties were mounting rapidly. The Sergeant in the trench next to mine reported the death of an officer commanding the mortar platoon. Despite the danger I ran to see him. Due to a severe wound below the neck he lay there grotesquely with his tongue hanging out. The Sergeant covered the dead man's face with the grey beret hanging on the tree next to his fox hole; so was the demise of Lieutenant Kutrzeba. Soon after, I heard the moaning of somebody in distress. A young soldier was crying hysterically, and complained that he had lost his hearing. Suspecting battle shock I gently offered the advice that as soon as the Germans would stop shelling our positions, he would recover his hearing.

On the way back to my fox hole I met another soldier who asked me to dress his wound. He had been hit in the forearm. The blood was flowing from the ruptured veins in an uneven rhythm, forming irregular patterns. When dressing the wound I used my emergency kit with bandages. The soldier protested vehemently: 'Use mine, sir, you might need them.'

In the early hours of the afternoon an ear-splitting noise shattered the air in the Oosterbeek perimeter. Instantly the heads of the paratroopers popped up from fox holes, scanning the terrain anxiously. Through the small opening in the cover of my trench I tried to see what was going on. The silhouette of a dreaded Tiger manoeuvred skilfully on the narrow road, moving slowly and inexorably towards our positions. The size of the tank gave the impression of a monster threatening destruction of everything in its path. A massive attack with the intention to overrun our defences appeared a likely possibility. Someone jumped out of his trench with a flame-thrower and directed the stream of fire against the intruder. Others kept shooting their light machine guns and rifles. Detonating grenades raised a cloud of dust. All of a sudden the mighty Tiger turned back, and we sent the monster off with derisive shouting and heavy swearing.

Word of mouth reminded everybody that the enemy's snipers would be moving on us soon. In the falling darkness of the approaching evening, behind the camouflage of their nests in the trees, the Germans looked for targets.

The day was coming slowly to an end. It was time to start thinking of supper and a safe place to spend yet another night.

When it came to eating I survived the Arnhem affair on a diet of nothing else but Yorkshire pudding washed down with water. Since I am neither Chinese nor English I did not care much for tea.

My problem was too much water in the fox hole, brought on by the steady rain all day long. Before we took off from England, preparing for the action, my good landlady had added to those things I couldn't go without a pair of brand-new pyjamas. She bought them as a gift for me at a time when we were ready and anxiously anticipating landing in France, near Paris. That operation like many others was postponed then cancelled. Instead we landed at Arnhem and here I was, having to learn how to swim in ankle-deep water. What was worse, my pyjamas were wet and absolutely useless.

While musing about these things I heard someone call my name. I looked out from my hole and I noticed Captain Zwolanski, so I promptly asked what was new.

He replied with the startling news that we were to leave Arnhem that evening [25th September]. The orders were simply to get the men ready and bury the dead in marked burial places. His final comment was, 'We shall meet again in Driel tomorrow morning, God willing.'

We were left with no more than three hours before the start of the evacuation and the march towards the river. The word about our leaving the perimeter got around quickly. My first task was to take care of my dead. We had six of them and they were kept in the barn, with the hope that after the main forces had joined us in the perimeter, the Para Brigade would make arrangements for the disposition of their earthly remains.

Without sentimentality I took a last look at my fox hole. It was 2 metres long and about 3 metres deep. I asked one of the boys for help and told him to bring out our dead comrades. I decided that my fox hole and the one next to it would act as graves.

We laid the first body alongside the trench and then together holding shoulders and feet laid him to rest. We repeated the operation with two more, and all fell upon each other. We covered the grave with wet earth mixed up with autumnal leaves. In similar fashion we proceeded with the fourth body, now resting at the edge of the open hole. This time one of the boys, obviously upset and nervous, let go of the head too soon and the dead soldier landed at the bottom of the hole head first with feet sticking out. Realizing his responsibility for the mishap, the young boy jumped into the hole, stepping on the chest of the dead man. At this moment what sounded like a weak groan hit our ears. The petrified soldier shouted from below, 'Sir, we are burying this man alive!'

'Continue to straighten out the body,' I ordered, knowing full well we could not make such a mistake. Fighting the doubts which momentarily came to mind, we pulled the shivering boy out. After burying the dead men we marked their graves with crosses. In the darkness of the night we could hear the cracking noise of falling tree branches and the cry of a child coming from a nearby farm. The wind increased in velocity, bringing with it the occasional bout of heavy rain and chilling the night air.

We stood over the graves silently, paying our last respects to our fallen comrades in arms. No flowers or other honours for them. May the Fatherland remember their supreme sacrifice of the broken life, the early youth and the unfulfilled dreams. We dispersed quietly and started preparation for the crossing of the river.

At exactly nine o'clock the massed artillery from the Second Army began pounding German positions located on the elevated ground of the city. Meanwhile twenty motorized boats idled under the protective northern bank of the Rhine, waiting to ferry the paratroopers to safety.

The first group of paratroopers, following the white tape marking the direction towards the river, passed by our positions. We blended into the marching column, moving quickly and silently. Soon the trouble started. The tapes which were used to mark our way to safety were dirtied under the boots of the soldiers and torn into disjointed ends. Some men lost direction, others engaged in arguments or wandered aimlessly in the bushes and trees. The enemy surveyed the area with their powerful searchlights, trying to pin-point our movements. Whenever we got too close to the Germans we slowed down or stood still and waited in silence, ready to resume the march to safety. Some individuals and small groups got involved in exchanges with the enemy; sporadic fire and shouting kept interrupting our movements.

With the backdrop of artillery fire illuminating the river, we could see through the trees the silhouettes of houses at the southern end of Oosterbeek Park, indicating that the Rhine was close.

We stopped in front of a big building and were told to wait for new orders. I entered the dimly lit building and realized that it was one of the emergency stations tending the ever-increasing number of casualties. The wounded lay on the cement floor. Doctors, both Army and civilian, nurses, mostly Dutch women, and orderlies moved around distributing medication to the wounded paratroopers. Despite the hectic activity the huge hall looked orderly and quiet.

I stood close to the entrance leaning against a column supporting the ceiling. A youthful-looking doctor walked up to me and asked whether I needed attention. When told that I was on my way to the river he politely enquired whether I wished to see some wounded Polish paratroopers. I followed him to the far corner of the hall where the Polish soldiers were being tended. I bent over one soldier and, holding his hand in mine, I asked the question, 'Do you feel much pain?'

'Not really,' answered the wounded man. 'The doctors give us morphine which kills the pain; however, I do feel tired . . .'

Moved and having nothing else appropriate to say, I left him with the words, 'Be of good hope, everything will be fine. These are the last moments of our sufferings.'

The word got around that we were just about ready to resume our march. I ran outside in the intensifying rain and joined the marching paratroopers. The marching column of four abreast moved slowly. It was already two o'clock in the morning and some soldiers started growing more impatient with every passing minute. 'What's going on?' they grumbled. 'What slows us down?'

Uninterrupted rain soaked and softened up the ground under our feet. From the direction of the river we could hear the muted sound of boats ferrying those ahead of us to the safety of the southern bank.

The ferrying across the Rhine was in full swing. The beachmasters worked hard and packed men into the boats as fast as they could. The lights of flares above our heads betrayed the ferrying operation, and soon the enemy started shelling, wounding many paratroopers. The evacuation fleet of boats was reduced by half in less than one hour as a result of being hit or flooded. The ones still operating shuffled between the two banks, hurriedly unloading their human cargo on the southern side.

In the bright light of the phosphorus flares one could see men wading out to them. Some of the boats had capsized, blocking the traffic with flotsam and jetsam. Men struggling in the water screamed for help, clinging to the wreckage or trying to swim.

Meanwhile as dawn was approaching the men became increasingly restless under the mortar fire and demanded openly that something had to be done to speed up the evacuation. They huddled in the rain, fearful that they would have no chance to get ferried across. The order was issued that everybody should find shelter behind the elevated northern bank. Confusion took place in the crowded lines and men started pushing forward. In no time they covered the distance of a couple of hundred yards and gathered along the bank of the river. In the breaking daylight only a handful of boats were still ferrying. From the direction of Oosterbeek Park we could hear the noise of German tanks. They stopped at the edge of no man's land, three of them, barrels directed at us, and waited in silence.

The feelings of resignation and hopelessness fell heavily upon our hearts. The voices of the crowd subsided to the level of whispers. A man, sitting on a pile of rocks, worked intensely, preparing a white flag. The rain stopped for a while, and the new day was slowly dawning. More and more men decided to swim across in a last-ditch effort to avoid capture by the enemy.

I fixed my life belt around my waist and waded into the cold water. It did not take long before I started losing ground under my feet, and I started paddling vigorously, making some progress towards the southern bank.

Half-way through my tortuous efforts I heard the motor of an approaching boat. It caught up quickly with me and at this moment an unseen pair of hands lifted me from the water and threw me in the boat like a potato sack. Dazed by this sudden and unexpected turn in my fortune I went through the gamut of feelings from the joy of being alive to believing – almost – in a miracle.

As the boat got close to the flat bank we jumped into the shallow water and ran at full speed to the low dyke, 60 metres ahead of us. From the dike ran ditches which were perpendicular to the river; they were wide enough to accommodate a man. I jumped into one of them and started crawling with the speed of a turtle, slowed down by soaked battledress and boots full of water. Some German from my left side took a good aim at me and as if to say goodbye sent a series of short bursts from a machine gun. The bullets flew over my head and, hitting the ground, ricocheted with a strange sound. I made short leaps forward till I reached the main dike. I jumped over it and, sliding down, I lost my tormentor.

We were safe and free at last! The small bunch of us could hardly believe our good fortune. We were euphoric. The realization that we had survived this fatal night was overwhelming. Exhausted but spiritually reborn we marched westward to the point where the Rhine bends slightly *en route* toward the North Sea. A solitary farm stood there, aloof and far from the centre of human madness, deaths and war. We paused inside for a while, then continued walking to Driel.

13

KICKING IN THE
FRONT DOOR

By the beginning of summer 1944 the time had finally come to recross
the Channel, in the longest-awaited and most meticulously prepared of
all the British Army's wartime operations.

For the bulk of the troops involved this would be their first time in
action, but three veteran divisions had been brought back from the
Mediterranean to add some experience. *Tom Ridley* was sent to join
one of them as an NCO.

> When I was posted to the 50th (Northumbrian) Division I was
> very nervous indeed at the prospect, as they and the other Eighth
> Army divisions – the 7th Armoured and 51st (Highland) – were
> what General Montgomery referred to as his 'battle-hardened' or
> 'seasoned' troops. I on the other hand had not seen any action at
> all, except with an ATS girl.
>
> Afterwards when I finally did get to the sharp end in Normandy
> I discovered I needn't have worried too much about it, because
> operating in the Normandy bocage was entirely different from the
> Desert. For instance one of the lads in my section had earned the
> Military Medal for getting past German sentries in the dark, blow-
> ing up a tank and getting back to base safely. In Normandy that
> kind of thing was just not on. In this kind of country the veterans
> knew no more than the new boy.
>
> By then I had arrived at the conclusion that in varying degrees
> of quantity we each have our quota of 'bottle', or whatever you
> wish to call it, and when that is used up there is no guarantee
> when the man will become 'normal' again. Which is one of the
> reasons I'm not convinced that the Generals, when they say battle-
> hardened troops are the best, are right. No one remains the best
> for ever.

The 50th (Northumbrian) was one of the two British divisions detailed to land by sea in the first wave, and had been given the Gold Sector beaches to assault.

Marching through the streets of Southampton was a very subdued affair. The best-kept secret of the war was no secret to the people who turned out to see us off. Some of them of course were women who had sons or boyfriends or husbands somewhere in the UK moving towards the start point exactly as we were, and there were a few tears here and there. They knew as well as we did this one was no exercise.

On board the *Empire Rapier* we got sorted out, in my case fairly quickly since my party consisted of only six Sappers and myself. I also had been given a detailed instruction sheet before we boarded, such as time of landing H + 45 minutes, beach King Green (Gold), and with 7th Battalion, the Green Howards.

The day we embarked was 4th June. D-Day was to be 5th June. Oddly and unexpectedly no one talked about what might happen next morning; the subject seemed to be taboo. I suppose the lads in my party didn't need to talk about it, they had done it all before in Sicily; and in the event nothing happened next morning because an announcement came over the tannoy from Admiral Ramsay* telling us that sailing was postponed for twenty-four hours since conditions were too rough.

Next day all we could do was wait and read and play cards and enjoy the great food they were giving us, but the good food seemed uncomfortably like the condemned man's hearty breakfast. In the afternoon another message came over the tannoy. It announced weather conditions were no better, but we would go anyway.

So I went up on deck, took a long look at the white cliffs, and having decided in my opinion the chances of survival when we landed would be about even, I said goodbye to my parents and sister, and since there was no one else there, I said it out loud. I then decided if I was going to die I might as well die clean, so I looked for and found the ship's showers. Not one of my better ideas. Apparently salt water requires salt water soap. Michael Caine would have known that, but I did not.

Sometime in the small hours of the morning of 6th June the tannoy came to life again, ordering NCOs in charge to get parties

---

* Admiral Sir Bertram Ramsay, who had organized the evacuation of the BEF in 1940, and was now the Naval C-in-C for the invasion.

and equipment ready to get aboard their respective LCAs [Landing Craft, Assault]. Getting on board the LCA was all right, but after we were lowered without mishap into that damned sea in the dark, that was when all the trouble started. Because it was very, very rough indeed, and *mal de mer* struck almost immediately and continued for the rest of that miserable trip. As far as I can remember, when it became light enough to see there were perhaps only three or four men not sick, and I was one of them. In fact a Green Howards Corporal near me looked so ill I thought he was dying. He was so bad I managed to move over to his officer and told him just that. He turned to me slowly and carefully and said, 'Me too, Corporal, me too.' When I got back to the Corporal he informed me in a desperately anguished voice that he had to get to a toilet very urgently indeed. He didn't put it quite in those words, but I understood that time was of the essence. By this time it was light enough to see that the back of the boat had a flat area with two small cleats about 3 feet apart that might just do to hang on to, so somehow I managed to get him there and without going into detail got the job done and got him back inboard.

By now the obstacles ahead could be clearly seen, and we weren't alone, we had company. Away to our left there was a barge-type craft firing rockets. And better still and very close to us a warship firing her big guns. In my quiet pre-war life I never in my wildest dreams imagined I would see a British man-of-war in almost spitting distance flying a battle ensign and firing broadsides in anger in support of the infantry. But I did see it, and felt a lot better.

At this point the business in hand was becoming very close, and no matter how impressive the big guns were, land battles could only be won by the infantry, tanks and artillery, and only after they got ashore.

We immediately got into trouble, because when trying to get through the gap made by the frogmen we swung broadside on to the wooden hedgehog-type obstacles festooned with mines and what looked like mortar bombs, which we guessed correctly didn't need to be hit with a hammer to detonate. Fortunately the mines and bombs were above the height of the LCA's gunwale, so we manhandled the craft safely through the gap, the ramp went down and we scrambled off into waist-high water and headed for the beach.

I tried to close my mind to the very unpleasant things that could happen to me any second now, and just put one foot in front of the other, hoping to get to that beach without stepping into a hole, which was not advisable when carrying about 40 pounds of gear.

The only thing to do, since there was no choice, was to accept that this was the ultimate game of Russian roulette. If a sniper or machine gunner didn't have you in his sights, or a mortar bomb didn't drop near you, then you got lucky.

When we did get to dry land the first dead man I saw was one of the brave frogmen who'd cleared the obstacles under water. Actually he was lying on his back at the water's edge and not a mark on him. I hoped he was only concussed. As we made our way quickly across the beach the only dead man I recognized was a Lance-Corporal from our platoon I'd visited Winchester with on our last day of freedom.

For some odd reason it crossed my mind as I looked at him that it was almost like a film set. The difference was on the film set when the cameraman stopped shooting, the film extra got up and walked away. But this wasn't Hollywood, the shooting was different, and the Lance-Corporal wasn't going to get up again.

Then with the luck still holding we got to the sand dunes, which was a relatively safe place to be. I use the term loosely. As soon as we got there four or five Germans came over the dunes to the beach, urged on at bayonet point by a very small infantryman.

So far so good, but the next thing to do was to get to where we were supposed to be, which turned out to be about 200 yards to the east of where we were. But being undecided since there were no recognizable landmarks, I asked the Green Howards officer whether we should go left or right. 'Left, Corporal,' he said, 'unless you want to join the Americans.'

So left we went, and before going very far came to two of our lads who were wounded but sitting up and taking notice. One of them was Corporal Billy Hall, and the other was Sapper Davies. I very quickly lit and gave each of them a cigarette, then we had to leave them and go on our way.

Before long and without trouble we found our platoon getting organized and ready to move inland and head for Bayeux.

But the thing that pleased me most was to find my supernumerary Lance-Corporal Ron Davis alive and well. He had volunteered with Sapper Mills to land with the first troops ashore, to sweep and mark with white tape a clear lane for vehicles. But as soon as they hit the beach Sapper Mills was shot in the leg by a sniper, and shot again in the shoulder as Ron dragged him to a shell hole. Ron carried on to finish the job, was awarded the Military Medal, and survived to take it home.

Also struggling ashore that morning was *Anthony Silver*, who landed with the 5th Beach Group. A Beach Group was a specially organized unit built around an infantry battalion, and tasked with securing its assigned beach and then keeping it open and unobstructed.

The pictures here'll show you the kind of thing I landed on, on D-Day morning. Off one of them. An LCI(L) – Landing Craft, Infantry (Large). They had gangplanks down each side of the front. With that type of craft the front doesn't drop down; when it butts into the beach it stays there, and you run down the planks.

I didn't land on one of these – the front drops down on one of them, and you flow forward. They're called Assaults; Landing Craft, Assault [shows me another photograph]. There they are going in there. After dodging through the mincs [on the beach obstacles] – everything there's mined. You touch one of them, up she goes.

What you were looking for was the deepest hole you could find, quite frankly. [Laughs.] All you were thinking about was your own bloody safety. Ah [another photo], now that's quite a good one. Our plank fell, our side; we were going to come down this right-hand side, but that went, so we all had to funnel down the other one. See, there's the planks. They've lost theirs this side, so they're all going in off that side. And that's how deep the water was, at the bottom.

Up to your chest.

Or *over* your chest. You were about up to your neck sometimes. I was holding up a little feller in front of me, who seemed to be only about 4 foot 3. [Laughs.] And I had to hold his head above water. Scots Lance-Corporal, he was, from the Royal Army Medical Corps. He couldn't get his head up, 'cos we had all this gear on, so I held it up for him and we managed to get ashore. Once you got your feet on the beach and realized you were still in one piece, you went like mad. Best 100 yards dash I've ever done. We looked for the nearest hole and found one.

The only good thing about it was some of the Germans weren't Germans. They were conscripted Poles, Russians, anything you like; and they didn't want to fight anybody. So it was out with the white handkerchiefs. Adolf didn't mean a thing to *them*. They didn't want to know.

For the first couple of days we were assisting the medics with stretcher-bearing. Carrying the bodies off the beach, to wherever they wanted them taken. And when they'd get to the doctors, they'd stand in front and go – that way if they were going to live

– that way you're not going to live. Just like that. And they had to make that decision in a split second. If they were going to live they went straight in with them and got cracking. If they weren't going to live they just put them by the burying area.

They had big holes dug by the bulldozers, to bury the bodies as they were picked up. But that was only for the first couple of days. Once that was over, and you knew no more dead bodies would be washed ashore, you were all right then.

Meanwhile troops continued to pour into the beachheads. *Ronnie Masterton* was in the 2nd Battalion, the Glasgow Highlanders.

The weather had deteriorated, and as we prepared to disembark we all had our special sickness to contend with. The gangway was under water, with a rope above it as a guide and for us to hold on to, with Royal Navy Seamen spaced out at intervals along it. We couldn't have done it without them, as a number of our lads were already swimming in the water with their packs and rifles and were all doomed to go to the bottom if they hadn't been grabbed by the Seamen.

As I was Company Runner I had a pushbike, which was promptly tossed into the drink as it was impossible to push it against the heavy waves. This was done by the first Seaman I met, who must have thought I was going ashore on a cycling picnic. We all had our problems, and if there were a few mortar bombs raining down, we had enough troubles of our own to bother about them.

We got to our allocated piece of ground, and prepared for a big attack the following dawn. Firstly, though, that afternoon my company commander, Major White, having found out about my 'lost' bike, could hardly put the sailor on a charge, but not to be outdone, sent me back to the Beach Officer-in-Charge to see if it had been recovered. I got chased for my life with a few choice words from him, saying that they had tanks and about everything else underwater, and I was worrying him about a mere bike!

One radical idea intended to make the landing of vehicles and supplies less of a problem was the construction of two prefabricated harbours codenamed 'Mulberries' – one for the American landing area, and one for the British. *Mick Crossley* found himself assigned to crew part of the British Mulberry during its crossing to France.

We'd been taken out from Folkestone harbour in commandeered fishing boats, a detachment to each boat, and introduced to the large 6000-ton concrete 'Phoenix' caissons, which were to form the outer wall of the Mulberry harbour to be assembled at Arromanches in the coming June, after each section had been floated and towed across the Channel by seagoing tugs – though we didn't know this at the time.

On the way we noted that the caissons, each over 204 feet long and 30 feet high from the water level, were dotted along the coastline, about a quarter of a mile offshore. Each had a Bofors gun mounted on a central tower. We climbed from the fishing boat on to a lower ledge of the caisson, and then had to climb the 30 feet up a vertical iron-runged ladder to reach the top and deck. I remember that there were one or two members who were too scared to make the climb, which was understandable, and they had to be roped up.

Once on the top we found that the caisson was hollow, divided into compartments, and each compartment was filled with water to the level of the tide at the time. When it had been positioned there the sea cocks would have been opened, allowing the sea to flow in, thereby allowing the caisson to sink on to the sea bed. We found a small deck at each end with a catwalk leading down the middle of the caisson to the gun tower.

We were to live on these monsters for a week at a time to get used to them. The designers had made a small concrete room at one end with a small window for any gun crew to shelter in. We found that sleeping was impossible there and we all had claustrophobia, preferring to bunk down underneath the gun tower. Equipment on the caisson was found to consist of ropes, a generator for pumping out the water when the time came to 'float', several lifebuoys, and signalling lamps.

This practice of going to Folkestone by lorry, by boat to the caisson, staying aboard for a week, and returning to Littlestone carried on for a long time. Rations were delivered to us by boat, with everything having to be roped up from the lower platform. Only parts of the end decks were railed, and there was the continual fear that one day a man would fall from the top of the caisson to the lower platform and instant death.

During the middle of May 1944 our whole unit – 416 Battery, 127th Light Anti-Aircraft Regiment, RA – moved down the coast to Selsey Bill near Portsmouth, and we realized then that our battery had been selected to travel across to Normandy on these particular sections of the Mulberry harbour and there defend the harbour with our Bofors. After a few days in a sealed camp, we were put aboard caisson A54. The south coast at this time was packed with troops and equipment of the Allied forces. There was tight security, all leave had been cancelled, and everyone was aware that it was all ready to happen.

As darkness fell on the eve of 6th June the dark clouded sky was blackened further with gliders and aircraft bearing the 6th Airborne Division and others towards Normandy, and we also watched from our vantage point the thousands of craft of the invasion force assembling in the Solent and heading out into the Channel.

We had already received our copies of the personal messages and good wishes from General Eisenhower, the Supreme Commander of the Allied Forces, and from General Montgomery, Commander of the Allied Armies. Throughout the day of 6th June we were made aware that all the landings on the French coast had been successful.

On the caisson we waited for our turn to come. There was no more leave, and we were on those boxed rations. Each box contained a day's ration for so many men, and included a supply of biscuits, chocolate, cigarettes and even toilet roll. The boxes had different letters on, so that you could vary your menu throughout a week. It was to be a long time before we had fresh meat and vegetables again.

Eventually our big day arrived. First, two Royal Engineers Sappers and two Royal Navy ratings came aboard to accompany us across the Channel, the Engineers to man the generator and 'pump out', and the Naval men to assist in the positioning of our caisson at Arromanches. Also to join us were three men from our Battery Headquarters, again just for the crossing.

A blue US ocean-going tug came alongside, which was to tow our 6000-ton concrete caisson over to France. The sea cocks had been closed and the generator was working flat out, pumping the water out of the caisson's interior chambers. After what seemed like hours of pumping and watching the level of the water fall, suddenly we were floating.

Another long wait until as little water as possible remained in the caisson, and then the crew of the tug attached two steel hawsers to one end of the caisson for the tow.

We were off, but it was to be a long and very slow journey. I remember seeing ahead another of our detachments on a similar caisson making about the same knots, and the tug towing it was dwarfed by the concrete bulk behind her. At this time there was little roll, on account of our weight, and the journey seemed quite smooth. The weather was deteriorating, though, and that night we huddled in blankets under the gun tower with hardly any sleep.

The next morning there was bad luck for us when one of the steel hawsers between the tug and the caisson snapped, so we were being towed with one line at a slightly off-straight angle, and the weather was getting rougher. We estimated that we were midway over the Channel. The worst thing was that we were taking in water because of the high seas and the angle of our course. We signalled by Morse lamp to the tug's crew, and we had the reply that 'she looked OK'.

The tug was perhaps 60–70 yards ahead and rolling heavily, and even from our high position on the caisson we sometimes almost lost view of her. Our other detachment's caisson had forged ahead and out of sight.

After a worrying day, darkness fell and we were taking in more water. The caisson now had a list to starboard, and I remember that we moved everything of weight to the port side and even bedded down to that side, though it made no difference. Credit to the Sergeant and the Corporal who had been signalling all night at intervals to the tug towing us, and to any other ship that came in sight.

The next day a Royal Navy frigate, obviously in answer to our SOS calls, came as near to us as she dared. I'll never forget our cheers and joy to see her. I'm sure that each one of us expected a miracle and to find ourselves magically winched into the safe and warm quarters of the frigate, but it wasn't to be. The crew of the frigate fired lines by rocket towards us but they failed to land a line near enough for us to catch, owing to the high seas. The frigate was rolling and heaving in the swell, more than we were, and moving with us about 60 yards to starboard. I remember that they made about six attempts on this dark, cloudy, rainy day without success, and then they gave up. Sailing in our sight for an hour, and continually exchanging signals with the American tug, the frigate was eventually to sail away.

Reaching the Normandy coast, still listing badly, we saw through the rain and mist a mass of vessels at the half-assembled harbour. Still in contact with the American tug by lamp, we were made to understand from the captain that it was not possible to land us owing to the weather and seas, and that we were a danger to other shipping. We were to spend another night at sea, and were towed up and down the coast well away from any other craft.

Morale was low, and everyone was getting frightened at this stage because of darkness falling. Tempers were frayed at the assumed attitude of the American tug crew, who seemed to have no interest in our plight. The water in the caisson's chambers was deeper at one end than the other, so the list was getting worse. There was nobody to communicate with, and the tug crew were now ignoring us.

We had all worn our life-jackets for the last 48 hours. Two of the lads were too scared to speak even, and just sat huddled up in blankets. I was scared myself, and most of us realized the strong possibility of the caisson going down during the night. There was a feeling of helplessness. Some of us took it in turns, in pairs, to walk the catwalk to the far end and check the water level by torch. It was always reported higher. By three o'clock in the morning I remember agreeing with Jack Crabtree that we jump together, as we were certain now that the caisson was doomed. Most of us thought that it was best to go down to the lower platform that ran the full length of the caisson and which was only a few feet above normal sea level. So we climbed down the iron-runged ladder in turn, and positioned ourselves on the highest corner. I remember that some of them must have been too scared to climb down such a ladder in those circumstances, because I only remember being aware of about eight of us on the lower ledge.

According to a letter that I wrote to my mother a few days hence, the caisson actually went down at three thirty. At that particular time on the caisson I remember seeing in the distance the far end of our lower platform go under water, at the same time aware that our end was getting higher. It was obvious that the thing was going under, so I jumped.

I seemed to go a long way down in the water for a long time, and when I surfaced I remember thanking God for a large wooden beam that had appeared from nowhere. I slung my arm over it and called out to two bobbing heads nearby. It was Jack Crabtree and Alf Holmes the cook, and they joined me. I saw nothing of any caisson and no other heads in the water, though there was still a heavy swell.

As the hours passed Jack's condition got worse. He was an older man and had swallowed too much water. I was determined to survive, and trod the water continually to keep my blood circulating and to avoid any cramp.

At dawn a fishing trawler suddenly appeared and spotted us. She had been engaged in laying smoke screens off the beaches, and was returning to her home port in England. I remember being pulled in by a boat hook and lifted aboard by the crew, and then nothing except drinking rum and being put into a bunk with warm blankets below decks.

The first thing that I noted on waking up was a mess table top covered with our personal possessions that had been dried. The vessel was rolling and pitching, but I couldn't have cared less. I was alive and safe. We had been picked up about six o'clock according to the crew, and were heading for Portland Bill and Weymouth harbour. The captain and crew were super and gave us all fifty cigarettes.

In dried clothes, with a meal inside me, and in the calm waters of Weymouth Bay, I went on deck to find the covered bodies of Jack Crabtree and three others. I had survived the ordeal with only a very stiff shoulder and bruising.

We were landed, examined by a doctor in a room at the quayside, and then transported to a holding camp, 103 Reinforcement Group, at Aldershot. Holding camps were where any soldiers lost or strayed were sent to until they were redrafted or returned to their regiments.

At Aldershot we luckily saw on the first day a truck from our battery – it was our rear party, ready to leave for Normandy. Wishing to be reunited with our own unit we saw the CO and quickly found ourselves at Tilbury docks, joining a small party from our Battery Headquarters aboard an American-manned LST bound for Arromanches.

It felt strange that within seven days of leaving Selsey Bill on that piece of the Mulberry harbour I was to arrive at Arromanches once more, but this time on an LST crammed with vehicles, equipment and follow-up troops.

The round-the-clock flow of follow-up units to the Continent was a considerable feat of organization, although not everything ran to plan, as *Ian Munro* found out to his cost.

Some time before the invasion we'd been told that the Twenty-First Army Group, of which we then formed part, were going to invade Europe 'by the front door'. During the first month casualties were expected to be heavy.

It was also made clear that the invasion *must* succeed, as otherwise the war might drag on for years before sufficient force could again be gathered to warrant another attempt.

The regiment in which I was a Lieutenant – the 112th Heavy Anti-Aircraft Regiment, RA – was moved down to the south coast of England early in May to enable us to prepare our guns and equipment. The loading of the vehicles was a real headache which constantly broke out again just when apparently finally settled.

Each man was only allowed to take what he could carry on his back.

The battery was divided into two groups – the fighting group and the administration group. We had to get all the fighting equipment and stores, with the appropriate men, into the fighting vehicles. For a long time the problem seemed impossible even with gross overloading, but by squeezing and repacking we eventually got everything stowed away. Motor cycles, which couldn't easily be waterproofed, were slung on the outside of gun tractor tailboards, while the guns themselves were festooned with ammunition and stores. Despite my protests we were ordered to take four boxes of wooden [practice] ammunition!

When fully loaded the gun tractors all weighed over 14 tons, an appalling weight for a 7½-ton vehicle with a carrying capacity of 3–5 tons. It seemed impossible for them to mount the Normandy beaches in this state, but that problem could only be dealt with when we landed.

A week before D-Day we moved into a wired-in camp which was then sealed to prevent any leakage of information. The security side was first class, for even the officers had no idea when or where they were going. We were issued with two 24-hour ration packs per man, a tin of emergency rations, a life belt like a rubber sausage which could be inflated and tied under the arms, some chocolate and biscuits, a small 'Tommy cooker' with methylated spirit fuel, and two seasickness pills.

Forms had to be filled in giving nominal rolls of the men so that in the event of a ship being sunk it would be known at the port of embarkation what men would require to be replaced. We had already given full vehicle-loading details, and when a vehicle with our sister battery refused to start the Royal Army Ordnance Corps replaced it complete with stores within, I believe, 24 hours. The nominal roll problem was sorted out eventually, and things settled down. Then came the day when we were paid in French currency.

Even then it wasn't clear whether we were bound for France or not. On the following day all officers in the camp were briefed and issued with maps which we were ordered not to open until we were aboard. Luckily I decided to do a Nelson to this order and, posting an officer at the door of our hut, opened them and briefed the other officers before collecting the maps again. The officers then had knowledge of the site picked for our battery.

The organization was very impressive and encouraging. Every building had been allocated in advance. Details were given of the positions of the Casualty Clearing Station, and even where and when the dentist and paymaster would be in action. One realized what a magnificent job the RAF had done in getting complete aerial photographs of the whole area.

At the briefing we were told to expect 75 per cent casualties on landing. It was quite a thought to realize that if the briefing was correct one had only a 25 per cent chance of being alive in 24 hours! Some silly ass had leaked this to the troops, which in my view did nothing to raise morale. I got the padre, called a parade and told him he would never have a better opportunity of getting his message over. Alas in my view he made a dismal mess of his chance.

Next day we were ordered to send the guns and equipment to the docks for loading. The information was that only the No. 1 of each gun team was needed to superintend the loading, and that they would be back with us the same night. The following morning we would all embark on the same vessel as our equipment. A red light warned me of trouble, so I sent an officer with the guns, and to my alarm the party was kept on board and did not return.

Worse was to follow, for that night I was awakened by a Movement Control Officer who told me that all the remaining personnel must travel on a different vessel. Needless to say I protested violently, saying that we had not enough personnel with the equipment and guns to unload them on landing, and that divorcing artillery personnel from their guns was fantastic. This plea fell on stony ground, and eventually I was ordered to prepare new lists. It was promised that we would unload at the same time as our guns and equipment, and at the same quay. Cursing I got out of bed, and as we had no clerks with us I broke into a hut where I could see a typewriter and, with the help of one of the other officers, hammered out new lists. During the day we had heard over the wireless that the invasion had gone in and apparently was going well.

Next morning at the docks I was greeted by a very agitated officer – the one I had sent with the guns. He raised the same points that I had raised with Movement Control, and since there was now no one to order us about we tackled the Embarkation Officer and bullied him into allowing the gun teams to travel with the guns.

This meant a *further* change to the embarkation lists, and a shifting of other units from the equipment vessel on to our one. All this time the two ships' captains were breathing fire and saying that they would sail without us if necessary. Grumbling like blazes the lads forced themselves into holds and found a few spare inches of room. With everyone's personal kit lying about, the chaos can be imagined. At last we were all aboard, and when I went up the gangplank it was raised almost under my feet and we sailed at once.

On the morning of D + 3, which was our official landing day, we saw the French coast for the first time. Cliffs lined most of it, but they were low and between them were good, sandy beaches. The sea was dotted as far as the eye could see with hundreds of vessels of all sizes and descriptions. Wreckage and litter were thick on the surface of the water.

Late in the afternoon we moved inshore and anchored about a mile out. Hours passed with no sign of unloading, and tempers began to fray.

Night fell with us still on board and no news of our landing. We began to wonder whether the invasion was going ahead all right. As soon as darkness fell the Germans became more active, sending planes over to have a go at the anchorage. The whole sky was patterned by red tracer curling up in all directions. Our troops were sent below during alerts, which made it worse for them as they had little idea of what was going on but could feel the ship tremble when she opened up with everything she had, or when a bomb landed nearby. A perfect hail of small pieces of metal made the deck unsafe, while at intervals the whine of a Heavy AA fuse cap coming down sent us all flat on our faces.

As the anchorage was so vast we didn't see continuous action, but we had enough to be going on with. One bomb struck a vessel close by; she went on fire and lit up the whole area. My first thoughts were what a perfect target *we* must make, and not how unpleasant it must be on the vessel that had been hit. We were glad to see the dawn.

Next day, D + 4, we still lay at anchor fretting, with nothing happening except for occasional shells falling and mines blowing up ashore and an odd Fw.190 strafing the lads landing on the beach. During the day I was able to fix our position on the map as being just off Le Hamel, and was thus able to plan a route to our gunsite in the event of the organization ashore breaking down. Late in the day an LCT tied up alongside. The OC Troops [the Army officer attached to the ship's crew to oversee his service's side of the operation] refused to disembark us that night but expressed willingness to do so in the morning, so once again we had the firework display and general unpleasantness. During the day we discovered that the vessel that had been hit close to us was the one carrying our Battery Headquarters. Thanks to some heroic firefighting she was still afloat, but she looked very scarred and was flying her ensign at half-mast. About dusk she raised her anchor and disappeared out to sea. We assumed that she had returned to England, but discovered later that she had gone out into deep water to bury her dead, and she soon returned to her usual place.

Next morning as promised we were first for the shore. This was not a very easy matter, as it meant getting all the lads down two rope ladders in a fair swell. We had some difficulty with one lad, who had to be blindfolded before he could face the climb. I was glad to see the last man down without an accident. The LCT skipper, an excellent American who was smoking a cigar and whose craft showed the bullet holes of previous trips to the beaches, was only too pleased to help us if he could.

When we had a full load we set out for the shore, but another hitch then occurred. The beach personnel flagged our LCT out again, and for over an hour we hung about, half a mile offshore. I expect that there was a good reason for this, but it was exasperating for us. Our turn came at last, and we touched down on firm sand in about 2 feet of water. The bow ramp was lowered and we stumbled ashore in France. I tripped over something in the sea and found it to be a rifle, which I added to my kit.

A good deal of cleaning up had already been done, but there was still the musty smell of war hanging about. Occasional graves with rough driftwood crosses told their own story, while the beach was littered with personal equipment no longer, alas, needed by its owners. Many of the German anti-landing defences still stuck up drunkenly out of the sea, and barbed wire and minefields seemed everywhere. The going was heavy in the loose sand, and we were glad to reach the end of the beach and turn up a rough road leading inland.

I started my bird list from the moment of landing, where there were Swifts and a Sedge Warbler singing in a minefield. There was a splendid Black Redstart on one of the damaged houses.

My interest in ornithology I suppose really started through my uncle, and by the time I joined the Army in 1938 at the time of Munich I'd been birdwatching for about eighteen years or so. I had decided early on that I would follow the example of Philip Gosse in 1914–18: the author of A Naturalist goes to War!

The dusty untarred road was crowded with troops, all marching in single file along the verges.

I had sent an officer on ahead to our Report Centre, which was some way off our chosen unofficial route, to find out whether it was essential for us to pass through the Centre and then to the assembly area before proceeding to our gunsite. He soon returned saying that no one at the Report Centre seemed to be the least worried as to *where* we went. This suited us excellently, so we struck off the official route and set out to cover the last 3 miles. These proved hilly, but with the early prospect of getting the weight off our shoulders before us we made good progress.

We occasionally met groups of French civilians returning to their shattered homes. It came as rather a shock to realize that some of the urchins one saw had German fathers. Four years is a long time!

At last we reached the point where the road to our site was marked on the map as leaving the main road. We found that in fact this road was only a rough track which was probably mined, so it was necessary to continue further on the main road and approach the site from the rear. Before nightfall we were complete and in action. That evening a sniper made one section of the site uncomfortable, but he was liquidated next day.

Later in the week we had an example of our air power. A game of cricket was in progress when the angry crack of AA broke the silence. Suddenly a Messerschmitt Bf.109 hurtled vertically down out of a cloud, hotly pursued by a Spitfire. When it seemed that both must crash into the ground the Hun flattened out and shot away at full speed for the German lines, weaving and dodging in an attempt to throw off his pursuer, which proved fruitless. The Spit went aloft and, disregarding the Hun flak, rolled proclaiming victory before setting course for home. Later in the day another sudden and intense outburst of AA so low that it appeared to be skimming the ground made it necessary to lie flat and hope for the best. Equally as suddenly an Fw.190 appeared very low over us leaving a trail of smoke and obviously hard hit. Everything that could fire was hitting him time and time again. The pilot jettisoned the cockpit cover and, waving his arms in a futile endeavour to stop the hail of metal, threw himself out wildly. The plane hurtled on, hit the ground and burst into flames while the airman, either too low for his parachute to open or hit by bullets, became a human bomb and disappeared from sight turning over and over in the sky. Even then he might have struck a soft field or trees and escaped with his life, but it was not to be. His body struck a water pipe in a farmyard, and one more Hun had paid in full for some of the atrocities committed by the Reich.

One afternoon I walked over to see Jock Richardson in a sister battery not far away from our position, who had found a hawk on the beach in an exhausted condition. This proved to be an adult male Peregrine, so exhausted and emaciated it could hardly stand. After a bit of forcible coaxing it ate a little stewed meat, so we sallied forth and shot a young rabbit.

The next time I saw the Peregrine it was much stronger. It put up with human interest and interference with regal tolerance, but any familiarity was met by beak or talon. On food being offered, the Peri shuffled along the ground in its wire netting enclosure and grabbed the rabbit or pigeon greedily. It then retired to a corner, stood over the kill and tore it up with evident enjoyment. After the meal it would tolerate being picked up and sat quietly on one's wrist. Any attempt to scratch its neck was met by its hooked beak, which was sharp! It appeared to have little grip in its left leg, but otherwise showed no signs of injury.

We were able to release it after about three weeks, and it flew off strongly.

Despite Allied air superiority, however, attempts to expand the increasingly crowded beachhead met with ferocious resistance.

Eddy Edwards was a tank crewman in the 4th County of London Yeomanry, part of the veteran 7th Armoured Division.

The bocage area we had to operate in had high hedgerows and few good roads, which were well covered by anti-tank guns and mines. The infantry often showed a dislike for us, as very often with our inferior armour we were unable to protect them from the more powerful guns of the Tigers and Panthers. In dry weather we would create a vast cloud of grey dust which gave the opposition ample warning of our approach. And when it rained it all turned into a sticky, gluey mess.

The bad weather in the Channel was causing some delay in supplies. Being unable to capture Caen in the very early stages caused serious concern, and there were heavy losses when several attempts failed.

The 7th Armoured were, however, to attempt to occupy some high ground beyond a small town called Villers Bocage. All went well until the regiment was half-way through the town, when out of concealment appeared some Tigers. The regiment was caught nose-to-tail in the main street, and proved to be sitting targets.

The squadron I belonged to, 'C' Squadron, were in the rear that day, so we were able to escape that devastating trap, but we knew that HQ and 'A' Squadrons had been decimated, and our role for the day became to hold and explore an escape route. This we managed to do until last light, when our guns laid on a tremendous stonk which I suppose discouraged the enemy from pursuing us. That night we withdrew again to the starting point.

The losses to the regiment were grievous. Our CO Lord Cranley and the whole of RHQ had been killed or captured, and 'A' Squadron destroyed. I had been in Lord Cranley's tank for long periods in the Desert – he was a true leader, and had the confidence and trust of the regiment.

I remember one story about him. On one occasion in the Desert we captured an elaborate Italian dugout, and among the splendid fittings and furnishings we found a camp bed – a very ornate one. I thought that Lord Cranley, my tank commander, might fancy it, but he refused it, saying that having captured this underground mini palace I was to enjoy the comfort that I deserved, anyway he enjoyed sleeping on sand. All went well until one pre-dawn morning at Reveille. I was awakened nice and gently by the sentry. Lord Cranley was next on the sand asleep. He was unfortunately rather roughly reminded that it was time to get up by a heavy boot in the ribs, and in the explosion that followed the sentry was told in no uncertain manner that smashing people's ribs was better left to the Germans – their jackboots were much better suited for the task. A few days later when Lord Cranley was finally persuaded to take over the camp bed the same sentry came to perform his pre-dawn duty, no doubt thinking that the Corporal in the camp bed was due for a rude awakening, but to his horror it was Lord Cranley who he was once more guilty of mishandling, causing explosion number two. I don't know what happened to this unfortunate individual, but I think that the bed finished up with the Cairo Red Cross.

Villers Bocage was the last action that the 4th CLY were to be engaged in, for we were told that we were to be amalgamated with the 3rd [the 3rd County of London Yeomanry, the sister regiment from which the 4th CLY had been created during the doubling of the TA] as the 3rd/4th CLY.

As a result of this reorganization I was made a Lance-Sergeant – unpaid, of course – and took over a new Firefly, which was a Sherman rearmed with a British 17-pounder, a gun that could at last compete with the German 88 mm. I was told of my promotion by Major MacColl, who was then CO of 'C' Squadron. I took over a tank which had been commanded by Sergeant Bert Harris – in the reshuffle he was made Squadron Sergeant-Major.

The fighting in Normandy was now the British Army's major contribution to the war effort, and had first call on all available reinforcements. So as units like the 4th CLY burned out, fresh ones were fed in to take their place.

The 28th Armoured Brigade, which had not yet left for the Continent, was broken up and its component units parcelled out among the divisions already in action. One of its regiments, the 5th Royal Inniskilling Dragoon Guards, went to the 7th Armoured Division to take the place of the 4th CLY. Another, the 15th/19th the King's Royal Hussars, went to fill a gap which had opened up in the 11th Armoured Division. *Ernie Hamilton* went with it.

When the invasion was announced on 6th June we were up in Kirkcudbright, Scotland, firing at targets on a battle range. But we soon found that we were gradually moving south, down the east coast. It was a huge operation – as troops moved from the south coast ports across the Channel, waves of regiments moved south in stages of a few miles. We moved to Scarborough, Bridlington, Bury St Edmunds, spending a few days at each, till eventually we got to Portsmouth and then it was 'Jerry look out.'

We were to take over from the 2nd Northamptonshire Yeomanry as the Armoured Reconnaissance Regiment to the 11th Armoured Division. They had very heavy casualties, and were being disbanded.

We received brand-new – and full of grease – Cromwell Tanks. After a time cleaning and storing all the ammo, we were able to help close the Falaise Gap – our first and very successful initiation into war.

I was gunner to our Troop Sergeant, so my first weeks were a through-the-telescope, highly magnified view of death and destruction. Dead horses, cows, sheep, but worst of all people – sometimes so badly burned they just blended into charred surroundings. The many different attitudes of the dead held one hypnotized for a few days, but later nothing affected one; it was just another corpse. In some cases troops became so hardened to events that some would go and search corpses for rings or other valuables. Any story one may hear of the atrocities of war by both sides are very likely true. Sanity no longer applies; you may be dead the same day yourself. The German would booby trap the bodies of his own dead which fell into our hands while advancing, so sometimes one had to use great care.

When we met stiff resistance in a day battle, losing some of our tanks, at the end of the day we had to withdraw, because a tank then was a sitting duck – not being able to fire the guns, as there weren't any night sights. Next day our mechanics would venture to recover the dead and the tanks; the Germans had then retreated, but would have booby trapped anything we tried to recover. One clever ruse by German engineers – they knew we would advance in the tracks left by some previous tank, thinking if a tank had passed this way it was mine-free. But they used to dig out the pattern of the track, lay sometimes as many as six Teller mines on top of each other, then place the track pattern back . . . Every day new lessons were learned.

The Sherman crews were the real heroes. The armour was too thin, size too high. They had few mechanical luxuries inside, which didn't add to their capabilities. The success they received was due to the sheer numbers the Americans turned out. They could afford to lose them. I always thought that a special medal should have been struck for the Sherman crews. We were very glad we didn't have to fight in one. The British tank men called it the Ronson, because like the cigarette lighter of the day, it always lit first time. There were many charred Sherman hulks in our trek across Europe.

The nearer we advanced to the Fatherland the stiffer the resistance – he had less ground to defend, we had more. And our supply lines grew longer. The petrol used by each tank on most average days would be around 60 gallons. Heavy going over rough or soft earth I believe the Rolls-Royce Meteor engine did 8 gallons to the mile. We never bothered to check.

A day that summer and autumn would never be less than twelve hours of sitting in cramped positions in the turret. If we'd done a lot of firing of the Besa machine gun the cordite fumes in the turret really choked, as the extractor fan was never capable of clearing them. The bodily functions had to be taken care of as best as possible; empty 75 mm shell cases were used as urinals. Bowel movements had to be taken care of either before sleep or before breakfast, and there was much cursing if someone broke wind in the tank.

The ration for a tank crew – five men – was a wooden case with the words '15 man pack 1 day' on. This was meant to last our crew three days. A pack also had the year of manufacture and, most important to us, a letter of the alphabet. 'A' meant it was very good, with canned peaches and so on, but the higher the letter the poorer the goodies. Each time the provision lorry came up a man from each tank had to queue for our entitlement, so with some sixty men in single file past the tail board of the lorry it was the luck of the draw. When your man came back with this pack on his shoulder, if the letter was high he was a man without mother or father according to the rest of the crew.

Whilst on the subject of meals, each man had a job. One would prime the cooker for heating food and brewing the tea, which at that time was in the shape of three Oxo cubes but consisted of tea, sugar and dried milk, and was really horrible to taste. Another man would open tins.

The driver and front gunner/co-driver were to fill the two fuel tanks [combined capacity 116 gallons] with petrol each day. The radio operator sometimes sat in the turret with headset on at night. When darkness fell the tank, which would be in leaguer, had to have guards, so after a very tiring day one might have to do a tour of duty two on four off patrolling the leaguer.

Eight weeks into the campaign I became tank commander with the lofty rank of Lance-Corporal. Each evening after the day's warfare we had to attend an 'O' Group, receiving our orders for the direction of the war the following day, the town or village which was to receive the attention of our shells and machine gun fire. Now someone always had to be the first tank leading the whole Army. This was hated duty, as usually the lead tank would receive the attention of an 88 mm gun or maybe the projectile from someone hiding with his Panzerfaust in the verges of the country lanes.

The progress of our unit's battle could be followed through the headphones each crewman wore. Radio traffic was very busy during action. You heard the code names of each tank, and if one received a hit, the faces of the crew would flash through the mind.

As we approached the Dutch border we crossed the Meuse–Escaut Canal and took over the defence of a small bridgehead there, which as we now know was a very important part of history – it would be the jumping-off point for what became known as 'a bridge too far'.

My troop – 2 Troop, 'C' Squadron – were in the van [lead], astride the road. All was quiet till next morning, 14th September 1944, when we fought a tank battle – four German tanks against four of ours. The action didn't last long. My tank was hit twice, my wireless operator was killed and I spent four months in hospital.

At the time of this misfortune my thoughts were, 'This bloody rotten American ammo!' We found that the projectile separated from the 75 mm casing if you had to withdraw the round because it hadn't seated itself in the breech. At this moment this occurred, leaving the projectile in the breech, so for those moments we were unable to fire the 75 mm gun. At that precise minute we were hit twice from different directions. I ordered the driver to reverse into a small copse behind me so we could free the round, not realizing the damage to our tank. It took some time before I realized we were no longer an asset to the British Army. Then the next I knew was a ten-hour journey by ambulance back to Brussels, and then being flown home in a Dakota loaded with racks on either side to hold stretchers. All these thousands of British soldiers, all strangers, all silently wondering what life now held for them, many saying how they couldn't wait to see the wife. But mostly the relief and sudden realization of no more shells, mortars, snipers or mines. On landing, the lovely motherly ladies of the WVS, who were so eager to help and write off the official cards to our next of kin to inform them we had been wounded – you ticked off either 'lightly' or 'seriously'. Many of the lads really appreciated this service, as to be wounded on their writing hand side made them realize they were to experience many obstacles in future.

I was sent by train to Derby Royal Infirmary as walking wounded. It was very late in the evening when we arrived, and the stretcher cases were dealt with first. I was so dirty and unshaven; this was my second full day without a wash, and I was just as I had left my disabled tank. I was instructed to follow a nurse to my bed in a ward on the second floor. It was very dim lighting here, probably due to fear of air raids. The ward was quiet except for the snores of some unidentifiable persons. I was embarrassed getting into a lovely clean bed in my condition, but I slept so heavily that night.

I woke to stirrings in the ward. It turned out that I, a lowly unpaid Lance-Corporal, was here among a ward full of officers. A Major who was fortyish, suffering from an arthritic shoulder, had a map on the ward wall and the inevitable pins stuck in it. He wanted to know where I was wounded, meaning in Belgium, as he was following the war at home. He and the other people in the ward thought I must be an officer; of course I let them think so. That night I was in the operating theatre; it was 17th September, and Operation Market Garden had begun.

I was then taken with a few others to the Chesterfield Royal Infirmary Annexe to get well. At the Annexe there were about eighty wounded, and the senior was a Sergeant-Major with thick pebble glasses from the Army Physical Training Corps. Can you imagine legless men versus arm and leg wounded playing soccer? It was awfully dirty football, plaster casts being swung at crutches, and the like. The spirit of these men was so high. The nurses had to steer clear of some legless Errol Flynns.

I then volunteered to return to the fighting just to get back with my old pals – the ones still left.

I was finally discharged on 14th September 1946, but unknown to myself was transferred to Reserve Liability until 30th June 1959. I was at a loss to understand why each year after my discharge I received from the War Office a short questionnaire checking did I still live at the same address, and so on. I simply consigned them to my dustbin each year, and probably missed being called up for Malaya, Korea, Suez and so forth. Enough is enough of seeing your comrades massacred.

As a member of the 1st Airborne Division, *Alfred Frampton* also had cause to remember 17th September 1944.

At that particular time my wife was expecting our child in a few months, and although she wasn't allowed to leave her employment until much nearer the event I decided she should have some time in Lincolnshire with me. The management said she would be reported for leaving early, but we heard nothing further about it.

After she'd been in Horncastle for several weeks, there were sudden rumours of an exercise leading to an action, obviously on the Continent. All those who had their wives in the area were advised to let them go home at once. Our unit – the 181st Airlanding Field Ambulance, RAMC – was divided into three groups; the airborne lift was the largest, with two smaller first and second sealifts. I was on the airlift, which was to leave for the airfields the next day, so I asked the Commanding Officer if I could have a few hours to take my wife to London to see her safely on the train to Weymouth at Waterloo, because the Germans were dropping the V2s and doodle bugs on London. He said, 'I can't let you take her as far as London, but you can see her over the first change at Peterborough, then return to camp.' When I returned some hours later, I found the camp at Martin Manor was almost deserted. The airlift had moved to the airfields earlier than expected, and the first 'seatail' had also left for another rendezvous. When I asked who had gone in my place they said Lance-Corporal Dadswell, and that I was now on the second seatail.

Fate certainly plays a strange part in our lives, because David Dadswell was killed in the first few days of the Arnhem operation. I've attended the Arnhem Pilgrimages several times, and with bowed head have stood by David's grave and thought, There but for the grace of God go I.

The second seatail from the division was given various tasks for the next few days. My job was to take a Medical Officer from Divisional HQ, a Sergeant from 181 and a Staff Sergeant from the

133rd Parachute Field Ambulance to the various airfields to check that the panniers with equipment and supplies were ready to be airlifted and dropped in the correct rotation at Arnhem.

After a few days we joined the convoy of the remainder of the division to Tilbury docks and embarked for the Continent, a journey of only a few hours if everything had gone to plan. But we all know too well it didn't, and after some delay in the Channel came news that we were returning to Tilbury, only to find the headlines of the newspapers quoting 'the hell of Arnhem'. We lost the larger part of the division. Of the 10,000 men who landed by parachute or glider, only 2000 managed to get back across the fast-flowing River Rhine. The remainder were either killed or taken prisoner of war. The Medical Officers and Royal Army Medical Corps personnel had decided not to try to escape but to stay and care for the wounded.

We returned to the same billets in the Lincolnshire area to find only one member of the airlift from the 181, an RASC man, had returned. The first seatail had followed behind the Second Army and never crossed the Rhine, but rescued those who got back across the river to safety. They returned to England within a few days.

There was fourteen days' immediate leave for what was left of the unit, comprising the first and second seatails plus a few who were left behind because of illness when the operation started.

I was in charge of a few Royal Army Service Corps chaps; it was our job to help with the billets and to clean and check the vehicles, and to clear out all the rubbish accumulated on the journey back through Belgium. Most of the vehicles had ammunition boxes packed with grapes. After all, it was September and in Belgium the grapes were at their best. But what to do with them, that was the problem. Had we kept them until the chaps returned from leave they would have had to be thrown away, so we sent some home – remember they hadn't seen grapes in England all through the war – and the rest we took to the village pub, The Green Man, at Scamblesby where we persuaded the landlord and his wife to auction them to raise money for the Red Cross. So with a nice bunch of grapes displayed on a plate, with the help of an attractive doily cut from an old roll of wallpaper, we were in business.

Fourteen days soon went by, and the men returned from leave. The first morning on parade our Transport Officer told us he thought we did a good job, the billets were clean and the vehicles immaculate. He asked what had happened to the grapes left in the vehicles. I told him we threw them away because they were going bad. He seemed satisfied, and asked me to report to his office when the parade was dismissed. When I went to his office and saluted, he said, 'Sit down, Corporal,' and gave me a letter to read. Imagine my horror when I saw it was from the Red Cross thanking the unit for the sum raised from the sale of grapes at The Green Man! As I looked up he was smiling and said, 'That's all I wanted to see you about, Corporal. You may go.' I whipped up a smart salute and said, 'Thank you, sir!'

When I returned from leave I had to endure a lot of leg-pulling. Our Transport Officer was never far behind with a whimsical quip either.

Our daughter, Hilary, was born on 18th November 1944, just two months after the Battle of Arnhem.

But heavy losses were not confined to the Airborne. In the bloody fighting to break out from Normandy the British Army had been losing infantrymen far faster than they could be replaced, with the result that whole divisions soon had to be disbanded in an effort to keep the remainder up to strength. First to go was the 59th (Staffordshire) Division, selected simply because it was the most junior of the eight British infantry divisions in France.

Gordon Hornsby had landed on the Continent as a water truck driver. Now he greeted the news of a compulsory transfer to the infantry with remarkable equanimity.

After the breakout from Falaise our division, the 59th (Staffordshire), was broken up to provide infantry reinforcements, as the infantry had suffered heavy losses in the bocage of Normandy. I was sent, with thirty others, to the 1st Battalion, the East Lancashire Regiment.

The original intention was that as we were all tradesmen – cooks, drivers, medical orderlies, Military Policemen, and so on – we were to take these positions in the battalion to release trained infantrymen. Instead we were put in Rifle Companies as infantrymen ourselves. But I couldn't blame the CO for not wanting to disrupt his organization at a critical time.

What was the mood among your party of thirty?

I would say apprehension. We all knew the number of casualties experienced by the infantry, where life was very different to that of a driver in the RASC. The infantry weren't told what was going on, as we had been used to being told. On reflection I can see the sense of this, as if captured you couldn't tell much, but after being used to being briefed as to what was happening and what it was hoped to achieve, I found just having to do what you were told very unsettling. My sympathy went to people like the cooks and Military Police, who had an even greater culture shock in store for them than myself.

The battalion received us with a very good spirit, as more numbers made things easier for them, and we were each placed with a skilled infantryman who looked after us and taught us the tricks of the trade. Care was taken with whom we were placed – George Gee, who I was placed with, was thirty-three, old for the infantry. I felt very inadequate, as being in action from the start we had no time to have any training. I've often wondered if George might have been still alive if he'd had an experienced man with him. He was a great help to me, and could not have been kinder.

I feel the NCOs thought we'd had a raw deal in being sent to them without training. I think later on this policy was discontinued, and when units were disbanded the men were sent on conversion courses. We didn't have time to be taught traditions and history of the regiment. Survival was the most important thing on everyone's mind. You lived hour by hour and day by day.

What was it like, going into action as an infantryman for the first time?

Again, I think it was the fact that we didn't know *what* to expect through lack of training. And the thought that we might let our comrades down. They were much more experienced in what's called 'fieldcraft' – they could look at ground in front of them and spot the danger points.

Fear was a very personal matter. It stuck out like a sore thumb in the infantry that if someone was wounded or killed this fact was never mentioned, just as though there was some unwritten rule.

Not many people showed signs of fear. Perhaps they didn't want to appear to be the weak link.

Sometimes the weak links were not the men but the machines.

Ron Perry was in a Light Aid Detachment of the Royal Electrical and Mechanical Engineers, responsible for maintaining the Churchills of the 147th Regiment, RAC. All tank regiments had such an LAD attached to them, though the lengthier servicing and repair jobs had to be passed on to brigade workshops.

One of our tanks came back with a hydraulic leak in the driver's compartment. Captain Burke had a look and told the Sergeant tank commander it would take longer than our allotted hours to repair, so he would have to collect another one. Tank crews were a very superstitious species – lose their tank, lose their luck; he was horrified. I knew him as of days gone by, so I had a look to see what the problem was. In front of the driving compartment were all the hydraulic services, bolted up above the knees of the driver and co-driver/machine gunner. This is where the leak was.

I said to the Sergeant that I could fix it with the help of his driver, then went to Captain Burke and persuaded him to let me do it. I won't go into detail what the job was, but we had to use two hydraulic jacks; unbolt the [hydraulic fluid] reservoir and lower the jacks – this is where the driver was needed and we had to be very careful, because if it had tipped and fallen off the jacks I'd have been in trouble. I cut a new gasket, reassembled everything and finished about nine o'clock at night. The Sergeant said, 'How did you know you could do it in the time?' I didn't, but when it was apart the tank was immobile, so I had to carry on and finish it. This was a very rewarding job, just to see that Sergeant's happy face! You had to be totally committed, working as a team.

We got a lot of tanks that had bogies and tracks damaged due to running over mines. This was heavy work, and the welder was very busy. During the campaign our welder was replaced. He had a medical grade of B5, not fit for overseas duty, but he'd been overlooked. The new one, being from Glasgow, had worked in the shipyards and was a good electric welder, which was required on tanks.

I also had jobs like a new radiator to fit on a Humber scout car for the Captain of the Intercommunications Troop. It was amazing how shrapnel got through the armoured slats of the air intake.

And there were a lot of cooking stoves for repair; these were twin-burner portable stoves used by the tank crews, fuelled by petrol. One of the fitters was given the job to repair them. Before the war he was an insurance agent; he'd never have made a good fitter, but he was OK at fixing cookers!

Mail filtered through. The last had been a long time before, back in England. One of our Staff Sergeants was sat, elbows on knees, head in hands weeping after reading his mail. I sat down on the grass beside him. 'What's the matter, Staff?' He said, 'My wife's been killed in an air raid at home . . .'

Our war out there didn't seem to exist at that moment.

We moved position as the regiment moved forward, sleeping in our vehicles. We fitters had an American White scout car, lightly armoured with a canvas removable roof. Our kit was carried in one of the 3-ton Bedford trucks, but we each had with us our small pack, eating utensils, gas cape, gas mask, rifle and ammunition. As time went by we scrounged a tank crew tent.

When my old pal Bill Titford, now a recovery tank commander, came back to the LAD to collect some spares he said his fitter had been killed and he was waiting for a replacement. I went to Captain Burke and said that I wanted to volunteer, but he wouldn't let me go.

Later on Bill's tank broke down, the final drive being the culprit. He was several kilometres away, so I had to go with Stan Gibson in his 15-cwt to see him. When out on a job like this you always took your bed roll, small pack, and so on, as you never knew when or where you were going to meet up with your unit again. We found that Bill had had the luck to break down in a farmyard, and had already arranged with the farmer to use the barn to sleep in. It not being too urgent and the weather horrid, I went up the few wooden steps and made my way into the far corner, only to disappear through the rotted floor! They found me among barrels of wine, in the dark; we went back next morning to sample it. Filthy stuff – no wonder there was plenty of it. But I was lucky not to have been injured.

The final drive on a Churchill was similar to a half-shaft on a car, but much shorter and with a larger diameter. To remove the inner portion might take quite a time, depending how badly it had been chewed up; the place and conditions also had to be taken into account. While I was repairing and fitting the new drive shaft Bill was missing, and on his return he was in possession of a Luftwaffe officer's dress sword. He'd been chatting up the farmer – Bill spoke French – and the farmer was so relieved to be liberated he gave Bill the sword.

The wireless operator contacted the Intercommunications Troop officer, who came and gave us directions to our unit, his being the same scout car I had fitted the radiator to in Normandy. We had a meal with Bill and his crew, then Stan and I checked the map and found our way to the new location of the LAD.

There followed a rest period for the 147th, during which we were extra busy, as tanks require a lot of work when out of use. We also had the first shower bath since being over on the Continent, in a mobile unit with a large marquee tent and portable showers heated by burners similar to the type the cooks used. It was a mucky affair, being in a field; there were duckboards to stand on, but after bathing your feet were muddy so you had to wipe them in your towel. You handed in your underwear for exchange for clean. If you were lucky the replacement clothing fitted! Anyway, it was a welcome bath. These were few and far between.

Winter was now upon us. A few days before Christmas we had to make a quick move to the Ardennes [where the Germans were launching a sharp counterattack against the Americans]. The tanks had to go by road. I can't remember if this was by transporter or on their tracks. I *do* know it was the worst journey I have ever had, travelling in our White scout car through frost and snow. Being all-steel with a canvas roof it was like being in a fridge. We stopped on the roadside to have our Christmas dinner, and at night stayed in an empty *estaminet*, which never gave us much comfort as that too had no heating. There was one consolation and that was our unit's food was as good as it could be with the tinned rations, due to the cook we had allotted to us.

One incident I remember at this Christmas time was when Tom Tucker was cleaning his rifle. After cleaning you closed the bolt. We always had five rounds in the magazine; when pushing the bolt forward the top round had to be pushed down with the left thumb to prevent it being loaded for firing, after which the trigger was pulled then the safety catch applied, always pointing the muzzle in the air. This Tom omitted to do. There was one big bang, and the bullet lodged itself in the wall after passing through the paper being held by Jock Witherspoon, another of our drivers. He was laying flat on his bed holding the paper up reading it; if he'd been sat up he'd have been shot. The noise in the room was deafening; everyone was shocked then relieved. Tom thought he had pushed the round back into the magazine ... He had a telling off from Captain Burke. Just shows how complacent you can get.

On our way through the snow and ice, when we stopped for a hot drink and a bite I was so cold after being in our tin can of a vehicle I thought I was walking on my ankles. I was glad when we arrived in Dinant and our billet, where there was a large stove on the ground floor which we soon got working to thaw ourselves out. It was a large rambling building, more than enough for our requirements. Dinant reminded me of Bath, with the river running through and a bridge like the Old Bath Bridge was. The River Meuse which flowed through the town was frozen in places. Our vehicles were parked on a cobbled area alongside the river; opposite were large houses and a hotel. The hotel was occupied by an American anti-aircraft gun crew, a quick-firing gun of small calibre. We had a small empty shop for our guardroom. Because of the weather guard duty was cut from a two-hour patrol to one hour through the night. Your breath froze the woollen balaclava helmet to your mouth.

The American gun was manned at all times by one crew member, and at the side of the gun was a small stove, enclosed so as not to be visible in the dark. We spent a lot of time warming our feet by it, as it was in the same area as our vehicles. One night I was stood there warming my feet when we heard an aircraft, miles away. The gunner started firing, with spent shell cases flying everywhere; the rest of the crew came running out, but by the time they arrived the firing had stopped – 'You're too late, I've shot him down. Chalk another one up on the wall.' He didn't see or know where his target was when he was firing, just fired indiscriminately.

The tanks were in battle in the Rochefort area south-east of Dinant, still in the snow and frost. Captain Burke said he had a good job for me, an engine change. A tank had broken down in the middle of a field with the snow nearly a foot deep in places. We went to the site in Old Faithful, the White scout car fridge, together with a Scammell breakdown tractor. There were three of us fitters and my pal 'Happy' Dixon with his Scammell. To remove á Churchill engine in a workshop must be a piece of cake compared with the conditions we had to work in, with the temperature sub-zero. First things first, we had to have some warmth. We had two petrol cans with the tops removed and three-quarters filled with earth saturated with petrol; this was our only heat, but very welcome to the fingers. One of the most useful articles of clothing we had when working under these conditions was the leather jerkin, which could be worn over the overalls leaving the arms free.

The twin exhaust system which was mounted on the top deck had to be removed. Next the top deck or armoured engine cover had to be removed; there were four flaps which gave access for servicing – these were part of the deck and were removed in one unit using the extended jib of the Scammell and then stood against the side of the tank. This revealed the engine, gearbox and final drive. Next move was to remove the foam fire-fighting bottles, operated from inside the turret to extinguish a fire in the engine compartment, so as to gain access to the front bolts holding down the engine. After a day's work we covered over the engine with a sheet and left it for the next day. The tank crew were not far away in a tumbledown old shack, so kept guard overnight as there was plenty of ammunition on board.

We eventually fitted the new engine – a job we'd never been allowed to do before due to the time limit – and did the final adjustments with the top deck off. After a few seconds of the engine turning over it spat back through the four carburettors, and the top of the engine was on fire. The fire-fighting equipment wasn't yet reinstalled, so we had to move *very quickly*! There were two foam extinguishers on the side of the turret and two pyrenes in the driving compartment. The foam ones put the fire out – being only a surface fire, the foam smothered it. What a mess to clean up.

Why did this happen, I thought. Ah yes, carb flooding. They were Solex carbs. Removed the float chambers to find the floats inoperative – back in the factory when assembling they'd greased the pivot pin, and due to the cold the grease had solidified, preventing the float from working. I told Captain Burke about the problem and he said he'd reported it to the CREME [Commander, REME] at Brigade HQ so they could put a memo out to guard against a recurrence.

The German counterattack having been contained, the regiment returned north to take part in the battle for the Reichswald Forest.

The snow was now gone and it was into February 1945. Rain and more rain. The forest was part of the so-called Siegfried Line, and was about 8 miles long and 3–5 miles deep. The tanks of the 147th Regiment together with the 9th Battalion, the Royal Tank Regiment and the infantry were to fight their way through it. We, the LAD, were very involved. Fitters were required only, but due to a signals misunderstanding the complete LAD moved into the forest with the fighting units.

The forest before the war must have been lonely and peaceful, with the birds singing and bluebells in the spring, but now it had been turned into hell on earth. We dug in, as it wasn't safe to be above ground. It was dank and cold. We used a corrugated iron sheet to try and stave off the rain.

Night was never dark; you could see quite well due to 'Monty's Moonlight', this being made by shining searchlights on to the clouds to reflect the light. As the battle moved on it became a little quieter, but you could distinguish the sound of a Spandau in the not too far distance.

I can't remember if I was going to or returning from a job when I witnessed the burial of some infantrymen. A shallow grave had been dug. Four of their comrades lifted them into the grave and folded the blanket over them, and the padre held a brief service in the rain.

Captain Burke detailed me together with a Sergeant from the 147th, one of our fitters and a driver to seek out a tank that'd been immobilized. The only way of finding it was by a map reference – this is where the Sergeant's services were required, being a good map reader. We set off in the truck, but had to abandon it and leave it with the driver while we went on foot to find this tank. How the Sergeant found it I'll never know, as it was in a thicket. It had been hit in the idler sprocket mounting by a 75-mm self-propelled gun, thus bending it so the track ran off the sprocket when driven. The kit we'd carried for about a mile was of no use, but using the spanners they used to adjust the tracks, we adjusted the idler to put it in line. Everyone happy, we made our way back to the truck, now in the near-dark. The Sergeant was reading the map and compass with a torch, when 'Halt! Who goes there?' Out of a fox hole jumped an officer with drawn revolver, then an infantryman with a sten-gun. We had to give up our AB64s and were then interrogated. Once satisfied, the officer asked us if we knew where we were. We told him of our mission. He said they were forward infantry, and had thought we were a German patrol, so if we hadn't stopped they would have fired on us.

We eventually found the truck, where the driver was worried because we'd been so long away. We trundled our way back to the unit and reported to Captain Burke. I was so tired I slept through the gunfire.

The battle for the Reichswald Forest lasted for nine days. We then served as a line-holding reserve before being withdrawn back into Holland. On 3rd April we moved forward again, over the Rhine, to keep order and to guard lines of communication and dangerous stores the Germans had left behind. We continued with these duties, pushing deeper into Germany to Burgsteinfurt and then south-east to Münster. We were in the Münster area when VE Day came.

We moved back to a small town called Ochtrup to be with HQ Squadron, and had a small garage for our workshop. We were billeted in empty houses. On the outskirts of the town was a super outdoor swimming pool, part of a Hitler Youth training camp. They certainly fitted them out well with every facility, and now we had the use of the pool.

Kit had to be blancoed, and boots polished, to create an impression. There was a twelve-man guard with two NCOs, and when guard mounting there were thirteen men – the best turned out man being relieved from duty.

Not all aspects of occupation duty were conducted quite so punctiliously, however.

We were working in the garage when a Lieutenant arrived driving a jeep and asking a favour. He and his pal had had a night out, probably in Münster, and on returning to where they had parked their jeep they were astonished to find it had been stolen. To solve their problem they stole one to replace it! What he wanted was the numbers that were stencilled on the sides of the bonnet changed to the number of the one belonging to our unit. This we did, so there were two jeeps running around the area with the same number.

Then the Colonel wanted to fire a twenty-one gun Victory salute at the railway siding, and wanted blank rounds made from live AP shells. I don't know how many tanks were involved, but I do know we had to prepare a hundred or so blanks from these 75 mm shells. This was done by clamping the round in a vice and by means of levering the case by hand the shell was loosened and then removed. The propellant inside was like ¼-inch long pieces of macaroni of different colours. The case was cut at the opening by tin-snips. After some of the propellant had been removed a topping of cotton wool and cardboard was put in, then the segments were bent inwards to seal it. A tank was brought into the yard which ran along the side of the garage to check that the blank would enter the breech. It wouldn't, due to the segments not having been bent to the shape of the circumference, so we had to file every one to make it fit, testing each one. The garage floor was covered with the propellant that came out when the shell was removed, so it was strictly 'No smoking'. The Corporal Electrician decided filing was too slow, so used the grindstone, knowing that brass wouldn't produce sparks. Unfortunately it got red hot, burnt his finger and he dropped it on the floor, catching the propellant alight. We thought the garage would blow up when it reached the live shells stacked nearby, but nothing happened, so we crept back to find it had burnt itself out before reaching them!

The CO decided they had to test one to hear the result of our work. When the gunner fired the bang was terrific, the garage and the house on the other side of the tank had their windows shattered, and there was the tinkle of glass falling to the ground. Fraus came out shaking their fists and shouting abuse. This was the first time they'd had any damage done in their town during the whole war. We had to reduce the amount of propellant, and the next test was OK.

Not all towns had escaped retribution from the bombers. *Stan Squires* was able to see at first hand the devastation wrought in Berlin, as the Allies took over the administration of the city.

Our whole unit – the 241st Provost Company, CMP – was ordered to proceed to Berlin. While travelling through the Russian Zone we almost had a dust-up with a Russian unit, who I think came from the Mongolian border. They wanted to take all the stuff off our trucks to inspect them. This was at the border, at Helmstedt.

Motoring down the Autobahn to Berlin I was most impressed, as I'd never seen such a road as this before. Every few kilometres the Russians had erected large red banners on the centre grass strip, and at every junction or bridge was a Russian soldier on guard.

On our arrival in Berlin we were billeted in a bombed building which was one of the few with a roof. This was in a side turning just off the Kurfurstendamm.

When walking down this main street I thought of Mr Churchill's words about every bomb they dropped on us being paid back many times over. We did just that all right. Quite a battle had taken place in the Berlin Zoo, and there were bullet and shrapnel holes in all the buildings.

I was walking down a street, I think it was called the Kantstrasse, late one night. It was very dark, no one about – they were all then living more or less under the rubble – when I heard footsteps behind me. I thought I was going to be attacked, and as the footsteps got louder I undid the button on my holster, at the same time flicking my cigarette butt up on to the rubble. The footsteps suddenly ran up the rubble to get the cig butt. He was following me until I had finished the cigarette . . .

We British patrolled Berlin with the American MPs and the Russian MPs, mostly in American jeeps. I always remember how smart-looking the Russian girl soldier was with her red epaulettes, standing on a wooden box directing the traffic by the Brandenburg Gate.

Actually on one occasion I had to go through the Brandenburg Gate to the Russian Sector, to arrest one of our soldiers who had no right to be there. He said that he had wandered into the sector to see his girlfriend, and that he never thought that he'd be so pleased to see a British Military Policeman!

14

FORGOTTEN ARMY

With the end of the fighting in Europe, the Far East belatedly became the principal theatre.

Like the war in the West, the war against the Japanese had involved a long and difficult recovery from initial disasters, and a large part in this success had been played by the massively expanded Indian Army.

Ever since the Indian Mutiny of 1857, following which the private forces of the British East India Company had been taken over by the Crown, the British and Indian Regular Armies had been closely linked.

The officers in Indian and Gurkha units were largely British, and although the proportion of British officers dropped significantly during the Indian Army's wartime expansion, large numbers of them still had to be found. As at home, many were obtained by promoting suitable candidates from the ranks.

Anthony Lamb was one of those who attended an interview.

I don't remember much about it, nor what questions were asked, nor who was with me; and I duly returned to duties and forgot all about it.

We radar operators were excused such mundane duties as cook-house fatigues and guards, but we had our own chores to do. And on one particular hot, muggy afternoon I was down on my knees with bucket, soap and coarse brush scrubbing the floor of the transmitter. Somebody shouted, 'Hey, Gunner Lamb, you're wanted at the battery office straight away'. I was wearing gym shorts and a pair of plimsolls, and was sweating as I ran along the paddy ridges to BHQ office. Somebody, probably a clerk, said, 'You've to pack up all your personal belongings, *now* – and a truck will be laid on to take you to Regimental HQ. No, I don't know what it's for. Get a move on.'

Already at RHQ was a small knot of Sergeants I didn't know, and a Bombardier, and my own Section Sergeant, grinning. 'We're off to the Officer Training School at Mhow!' And so it was. The following day we were given third-class travel warrants, transported to a railway station, and found the third-class carriage allotted to us for the journey to Calcutta, where we had been booked in at Brown's Hotel. We were received somewhat askance, as this was an officers-only hotel, and we were a scruffy-looking lot.

The following day saw us on board another third-class compartment – bare wooden benches along both sides, back-to-back benches down the centre, a hole-in-the-floor, look-you-can-see-the-ground lavatory, and doors which opened inwards so that you could sit on the threshold for a bit of a breeze. Uncomfortable, hard, dirty, riddled with cockroaches and offering no defence against mosquitoes. It took the best part of two nights and two days, so that eventually we arrived at Mhow station dirty, sweaty, smelly and scruffy.

I suppose it's contrasts which add interest to life. At the school we were met by a cheerful young Lieutenant who told us to dump our kit and come and have some tea. A large, airy room, long polished tables, one of which was set with china cups and saucers and plates, with trays of thin bread and butter, sandwiches, and little iced cakes. Smartly dressed, barefoot Indian waiters poured tea. We were told that dinner was at seven thirty, and that when we heard the gong at seven we were to make our way to the ante-room, where drinks would be available. Then we were shown our rooms, and bearers were allotted to take charge of our kit and prepare our beds – clean sheets, pillows and pillow cases.

The morning following our arrival at the school we were taken along to the officers' shop and compulsorily purchased – from a very reasonable allowance – smart bush shirt, shorts, slacks, brown shoes and a malacca cane with silver pommel and knob all polished beautifully. And my own special purchase of purple pyjamas and a brown dressing-gown. As a Gunner I just wore underpants at night, although I had acquired from a hospital stay a voluminous pair of thick cotton pyjama trousers. A dressing-gown was, of course, total luxury.

Mhow was an Infantry Training School for basic officer training; an eight-week course, to be followed by a longer course in whatever arm we were destined for – in our case artillery training. It was a very different world indeed from the jungle and plains of Assam, the bamboo bashas in which we lived, the enamel mugs and plates.

But we had to work hard. Classes in Urdu, map reading, animal management – mules! – theory of the internal combustion engine, Morse code, driving Army vehicles, square-bashing, even bicycle drill. And the assault course. Parts of it I could manage, even the three rigid platforms sticking out from the wall of a building at heights of 8, 10 and 12 feet, reached with the aid of a rope, footing it up the wall. We were assured that the choice was our own and no marks would be deducted for jumping from the lowest platform. But we all wore our personal school numbers, and not many risked marking-down. I didn't. I used to clamber up to the 12-foot platform and look down at the tiny sandpit below from my own 6-foot height and feel terrified; but I used to jump. Nearly funked it when carrying a pack and rifle, but managed. I could spreadeagle over triple concertina wiring as a bridge for the others, and crawling through the claustrophobic tunnel of oil drums was no problem. But I couldn't run along the narrow ridge, and had to straddle along it. And I couldn't clear the second of two concrete pits. You swung across the first holding a rope, and were supposed to leap the second. I don't think I even tried, but just leapt into the pit and scrambled out. There was one chap, who'd already been commissioned in the field for outstanding conduct, who caught the concrete edge of the far side of the pit with his face and made a horrible mess. My old Radar Section Sergeant broke his ankle on the 12-foot drop and finished the training course in plaster.

We were taken out in closed lorries and dumped in the hills and told to find our way back by compass. And we had a 17-mile forced march on a pitch-black night, literally holding on to the man in front so as not to get lost. I had to carry an awkward lump of metal and wood representing a bren-gun for the last few miles, getting a lacerated shoulder in the process. Most of us were shattered at the end.

We worked hard – always the nightmare of RTU to spur us on. Mentally and physically it wasn't easy. But we were addressed as 'gentlemen', we wore smart uniforms, we fed well, and on returning from an arduous outing we simply kicked everything off and left it to our bearers to clear up, clean up and put out fresh clothing. Our counterparts in the UK had all that to do themselves.

The barracks were a wonderful example of nineteenth-century Army architecture – two or three storeys high, immensely thick walls, whitewashed, open balconies, always cool and airy.

Unless on night manoeuvres we were usually free to go out in the evenings, but I can't remember that Mhow was in the least bit entertaining – a few shops and restaurants. Neighbouring Indore was said to be more interesting – it must have been, because it was out of bounds!

I had thought that the rank of Gunner was low enough, but

Officer Cadet was sort of nothing – despised by all other ranks, a joke to the officers. We could only speak to each other; support each other. And in view of the fact that we had all come from a variety of ranks – one, two and three stripes, Company and Battery Sergeant-Majors, Regimental Sergeant-Majors – all rank was forgotten and we got on remarkably well. We had to.

After eight weeks we then went away for further training – signals, artillery, engineers – or, if infantry, stayed on at Mhow. We artillerymen went south to Deolali, to the School of Artillery. Deolali itself was a God-forsaken place. The largest military post was the transit camp, a sort of sorting base; a collecting and distributing centre for personnel of all kinds. There was a bazaar of shops of all kinds, a Chinese restaurant, a cinema . . . all set in the plains leading to the Western Ghats, 100 miles or so from Bombay.

The School of Artillery catered for all types of gunnery instruction – field guns, howitzers, anti-tank, ack-ack both heavy and light – and we had to have a smattering of them all. But my section was mainly tied to Heavy AA. Looking through my carefully written and illustrated book of notes, I think it could be fairly said that our teaching was to university standard. In fact I'm astonished at the knowledge I must have had to learn! Much of it was based on trigonometrical theory, using quite a bit of the Greek alphabet for our equations. The study of gunnery is a complicated process, but the art of bringing a shell to burst at a target thousands of feet up made it even more so. I was able at that time to take any of the six positions on the Predictor, that most ingenious computer, or the three on the Heightfinder, or the five on the Radar – which incidentally wasn't a term in common use; to us it was 'GL', standing for 'Gun Laying' – but I knew nothing of *how* the instruments worked, or how they were evolved. And this we had to learn. And, of course, the complicated workings of the 3.7-inch heavy AA gun.

I suppose there were about twenty of us sleeping in a dormitory hut, beds down the sides, long table and benches down the centre. Our bearers brought hot water and we washed and shaved at the table. I remember there were three or four Sikhs among us, some of the finest-featured men I'd ever seen. The Sikhs had never shaved nor cut their hair, which was waist-length, thick and glossy with coconut oil, as were their beards. In a way the vainest of men, because they would sit for minutes on end brushing and combing hair and beards, preening in their mirrors. They got a little gentle leg-pulling, too, but one had to be extremely careful for they could get touchy, since the ordering of their hair is to do with their religion. The hair was coiled into a tight 'bun' on top, bound with a white cloth, the beard divided down the middle and the two ends brought up and tied in with the head hair, and then yards of puggree formed into a turban.

Ablutions done, we would wander over to the dining-hall for breakfast; after which it was full military discipline, marching down to the gun park and lecture rooms. The Sergeant-Major in charge knew his stuff but was somewhat contemptuous of cadets – though he had become one himself before I left! He could put us through it pretty drastically, and was a stickler for correct procedures. It could be very hot around midday, yet he had six of us lifting the Predictor out of its box and on to the stand three times in quick succession. I don't know if we could have done it a fourth time without someone collapsing.

Lunchtime would come at last and we would march back to barracks – good lunches, as I remember. Appetizing curries with all the trimmings, iced limeade, delightful Indian sweets. I have no idea how many people were on the various gun courses, but quite a few were Hindus, Muslims and Sikhs, so their dietary habits had to be catered for as well. Though the big majority of us were British.

The afternoons were taken up with lectures until about four o'clock, when we were free. Free to return to our quarters, bathe, change and get down to writing up our notes, that is. Dinner, with perhaps a drink or two before, provided welcome relief. Even so, as often as not it was back to swotting for a while before finally turning in.

I think it was the mental part which was my downfall. No athlete, no gamesman, I was nevertheless able to take all the physical stuff, coming in near the last if it was running, near the front if climbing – or, at Mhow, swimming – and average or a bit below at most things. But the final straw was I could *not* understand breech mechanisms. I couldn't remember the various 'screws, retaining', the names of the bits and pieces. I could put up with making a fool of myself in front of fellow cadets – I wouldn't be the only one – but I had visions of myself commissioned and on a gunsite and unable to explain or demonstrate the mechanism to those for whom I was responsible. Everything else was within my capabilities, but not the guns, which were after all the central and most important part of our training.

All this time, only four or five weeks from the end of the six-month course, people had been weeded out. Those too good for RTU but not good enough for artillery were commissioned and sent to various duties. Administration work up at the transit camp was one. Somebody else was sent to Intelligence. I was so bothered about my own difficulties that I got to wondering if I could make a change. Foolishly, without telling anyone else, I requested an interview with the Commandant of the school, which was duly granted, and I explained my position. While I was the only one to *volunteer* suicide, there were four or five others who were in a similar position, and we sort of clubbed together and made our own little clique.

After perhaps two or three weeks we received orders to attend a War Office Selection Board – WOSB, or 'Wozby'. This was a blow indeed, and showed that our futures were by no means assured.

The WOSB was in Jubbulpore in Central India, and we were allocated second-class sleeping compartments for the journey. The course lasted about three days and was a curious mixture, with I suppose twenty or thirty 'selectees' of all ranks plus we cadets of no rank. It started on the evening of our arrival with a series of psychological tests, of which we were all terrified in case they revealed all our sex secrets. There was a series of slides, all of them vague and somehow indefinable; the lights went out and a slide was shown, a man climbing down a castle wall on a rope. We viewed this for a minute, the lights went up, and we had two minutes in which to write a story about the slide, a story which must have 'a beginning, a middle and an end'. Lights off, a minute's showing of three men staring intently, one of them with a cello. Lights, and two minutes to write a story. There must have been half a dozen or more of these virtually meaningless scenes – then lights out and the last, a blank screen for a minute, and then two minutes in which to write a story with 'a beginning, a middle and an end'. If nothing else, it was mentally quite exhausting. My supposition was that the examiners would ignore the lot except the last, most difficult blank screen one, written with an exhausted brain.

Then word cards were held up, with just a few seconds in which to write down any ideas they might convey. Words like Bread, Chum, Cage, Mother, Howl. We played along because we had to – much seemed to depend on it all.

The daytime tests were of a practical nature, mostly with an odd assortment of equipment like planks, a piece of rope, an empty oil drum, and so on. We were split into groups of seven or eight, and given problems – a high wire fence said to be electrified, which had to be got over by the entire group, a crocodile-infested river, and others. The examiners watched carefully and made notes. Each problem was obviously set to bring out bright ideas, and also to bring out the 'natural leader'. This was so obvious that we all clamoured our ideas, many of which failed, but you just had to be in on the scene. There were two tests which had to be done solo – one a croc-infested stream where the bridge was said to be broken, leaving a V-shaped remnant on the near side and a bit jutting out on the far side. The equipment was a short plank and a long plank, too short to span the two bits of remains, and a piece of rope. A kind friend who had been through it managed to whisper the solution to me, but I went in and played a mystified part, scratching my head, picking up the rope – tie the planks together? Then suddenly seeing the solution – short plank across the arms of the V, long plank then just fitting from the centre to the far side. I would have earned good marks for quick perception on that!

The other solo test took place in a small wood where the path had been marked out with red and blue patches of paint. The difficulty was that you had to go through every pair of paint patches *always* with the red on your left and blue on your right. The devil of a test of agility when you followed the paint marks up into the branches of a large tree. But a passable test.

For me, the worst test was the lecturette, all of us together. We drew subjects on a slip of paper drawn from a hat. Mine was: 'You are taking your company into a town where the previous troops have made themselves very unpopular with the local inhabitants. What advice will you give your men?'

I left the room, passing the next lecturer going in. The lecture lasted, I think, three minutes, so I had that time in which to sort myself out. The subject was reasonable and a few ideas came to mind, and eventually I was called in. I had decided on a 'no nonsense' attitude, gave my audience some imaginary instances of what the previous troops had been up to, and then began to harangue my men pretty severely on what action I would take if there was any such behaviour on their part. I thought I was doing quite well, until the audience tittered a bit, and there were a few smiles. I carried on, ending up pretty peeved.

The examiner thanked me, and then went on to explain that accidentally two pieces of paper with the same subject on had got into the hat. It was sheer coincidence that the speaker before me had drawn 'my' talk and had treated the matter entirely differently, facetiously and a bit offhand, and the examiner apologized for any embarrassment caused to myself.

The dismissal procedure came after breakfast on the last morning. The entire examining staff were ranged at tables along two sides of a marquee, with the Commandant of the WOSB and some senior assistants at a 'head' table at the far end. One by one we each had to march in, up to the Commandant, who said exactly the same thing to each of us: 'Good morning. I hope you enjoyed the course. Thank you for coming. Goodbye.' One saluted, about turned and marched out – and that was it. Smart turn-out, smart deportment, easy enough for us cadets. And so back to Deolali and the good life at the School of Artillery.

A week or so later things began to happen. One of our bridge four was called to the office. He came back with the worst of all news – RTU. Which gave me immediate depression because he was so much better a man than I was – popular, public schoolboy, good rugger player, a thoroughly nice bloke. We managed to live on, and a few days later I was summoned by a clerk and followed him to the office, neither of us speaking. I can't remember if there was anybody of any particular rank present, but I was informed, as a matter of no importance – which it wasn't – that my commission had come through and that I was gazetted Second Lieutenant in the Indian Army, attached for administrative purposes to the 12th Frontier Force Regiment. I was to take up transport duties under the Rail Transport Officer at Jubbulpore. A first-class railway warrant and a movement order were handed to me, and that was that.

Back to my friends, much congratulation, and just time to catch the officers' shop before it closed to purchase a bedding valise, a folding camp bed, a canvas wash-basin, and those two blessed pips, one for each shoulder.

My train was at eleven thirty, and the evening was spent awash in beer, culminating in a three or four-a-side rugby match on a concrete slab floor, with a brass ashtray as a ball – which I managed to catch in the face, losing an obvious portion of one front tooth. But it didn't matter; nothing could matter. Goodbyes all round, my worldly goods loaded up, three or four friends with me and away to the railway station. And when the train came in, there was my compartment for my sole use. Final goodbyes and I was alone; and to this day, more than fifty years later, I remember how I banged my fists on the berth and swore and swore, using every word and expression I could think of – not in anger, but in sheer joy and relief.

Finding the manpower for additional British units was also a problem, putting pressure on the depots back in the UK to send out men ill-suited to the known rigours of climate and disease. *Sydney Oliver* had just returned from hospital when he learned he was to be posted overseas.

At that time at Woolwich, 90 per cent was like me – you know, there'd been something wrong with them. But when you'd been there a couple of days you was A1, no matter what you were; they classed you A1. Well, our draft that went out to India – although we didn't know we was going to end up there – I should say that most of 'em should have been discharged.

Now your records never went on the same ship. So from when I got called up, until leaving Greenock, all them was on another ship. That ship got sunk, so they had no records of me. We didn't know that until they called a special parade, and wanted to know when we'd joined up, this, that and the other, you know. So I said I'd had typhoid fever, and they said, 'Well, what the hell are you doing here then?' You know, coming out to India. But you were classed A1 if you could walk. I went down well below 9 stone, in Burma. But luckily I had just two small doses of malaria, and nothing else.

It took from 10th January to the early part of March to get to India, by boat. And we only stopped at Sierra Leone and Durban, where 'The Lady in White' sang for us.* We stayed in Durban four days; we had a good time there. When we left we sailed up past Madagascar, but we'd only been out a few hours from Durban when they said the pocket battleship *Admiral Scheer* was about. Our ship was from the First World War and she could only do about 17 knots flat out, so we put in somewhere else, stayed two or three days, and then legged it across to Bombay.

Same ship all the way from the UK to India?

Yes, stayed on the same ship. Unless you jumped ship – which one of our Gunners did at Durban.

Once in India Sydney found himself posted to a new British unit, the 158th Field Regiment, RA. The low priority accorded to the Far East as regards equipment and supplies made an immediate and powerful impression on him.

The Regular Army, the Indian Regular Army, had still got First World War guns, rifles, everything. It was so backward. We'd been trained in modern methods, and we got out there and it was like

* Perla Gibson, who stood on the quayside to sing patriotic songs for arriving troopships and warships. Her son Second Lieutenant Roy Gibson was killed in March 1944 in Italy with the 6th Battalion, the Black Watch.

going back in time. It took quite a while before the 25-pounders came, and all modern equipment, the jeeps and everything.

We moved about a lot. From Meerut near Delhi up into the hills to Dehra Dun, and then from Dehra Dun to Campbellpore and Nowshera on the North-West Frontier with Afghanistan. While we were at Nowshera we travelled down to Lahore for a special job – there was a big do, and we had to fire a salute. Then we moved across to Ranchi, where we did some more training.

At Ranchi his regiment joined an Indian division which was in the process of being formed.

We became part of the 23rd Indian Division – there it is, look [indicates the divisional sign displayed on his wall]. Our insignia was a cockerel, and they called us 'The Fighting Cocks'. Although they were Indian divisions, you'd got a lot of British in them.

The rapid advance of the Japanese had opened up a threat to India's North-East Frontier, and the 23rd Indian was earmarked to fill one of the many gaps in this new front. The terrain was largely trackless, jungle-clad mountain ranges, and even getting to the assigned positions proved difficult.

When you got to the Brahmaputra river you had to go on a ferry. Not straight across; it went up from one railhead, and the ferry chugged miles upriver against the current. Took hours. And then we went on the train with the 25-pounders to Dimapur. That was as far as you could go on the railway. And from there to Kohima and on down to Imphal, you drove on the only dirt jeep track there was. It kept disappearing, the road, and they were constantly having to build it up. It was absolutely sheeting down with rain, and about 5 feet deep in sludge – it was coming into the monsoon season. A day later there was only three of us left – everybody else went in the hospital at Imphal. Something they'd picked up, and everybody seemed to get it at the same time, except me!

Then we got settled in, and took over a village. Our batteries in the regiment did a month up on 'The Saddle' at Shenam [in the hills south-east of Imphal, looking into Japanese-occupied Burma], and then came back again.

Imphal itself was on a plain, flat as a pancake, with a big lake in the south, Lake Logtak. They grew everything on the plain, the villagers. But all around you had the hills and mountains there.

And from the hills and mountains you have ridges, very narrow strips coming down to meet the plain.

While we were there they turned us from the ordinary 158th Field Regiment, RA into the 158th Jungle Field Regiment, RA. They took the 25-pounders off our battery and gave us eight 3-inch mortars instead. The other batteries kept their guns. I was sent on a mortars course, and when I came back I was supposed to know everything about them, so I had to train the rest of them.

Now at first we tried jeeps to move the mortars around. They was all right. They could go up tracks. But they couldn't go *off* the tracks, so that meant leaving them where they'd likely be captured.

Then we tried what they called 'Everest' packs. They split the mortar up into three. Our 3-inch mortars, the base plate was reinforced to take a heavier charge. Principally we were supposed to fire them about a couple of mile. But we never did. The most we fired them at was about 500 yards. [Laughs.] So that didn't work, because after you'd been carrying them . . . I mean, I'd got to carry a side pack as well . . . This is what you had to carry, all day – you'd got the essentials, a day's food, in your side pack, and just a bare change of clothing. Then on your back you had either the base plate, or the tripod or the barrel. And two 10-pound bombs. Your rifle, fifty rounds of ammunition. We started off with steel helmets, but changed to bush hats, like the Australians wore; they were a lot better.

Well, when you'd had that lot on your back for two or three hours your arms went numb. And you just couldn't do anything. You couldn't do anything much because you was too exhausted. So after three or four weeks of that, they gave us mules. We had eight Argentine mules, which was big ones, to carry the mortar stuff; and then half of the rest was for fodder for themselves, and the remainder carried all the ammunition, and everything that you wanted.

We moved around everywhere round Imphal. Every blooming where. We knew it like the back of us hand. We was up there for nearly two years, before the Japs finally attacked.

How did you spend your time, when you weren't in the field?

When we was on the Imphal Plain, before the fighting started, we used to go out and catch snakes. With a forked stick, you know. Get it in the back of the neck. They were only a few feet in length. Though we did once see a big one, about 20 feet long, up a tree at Dimapur. I shot it. So we used to catch these snakes, and take a razor blade – they're soft down the inside – slit it from head to tail, peel the skin off and pin the skin out on a board. And in about ten minutes the sun was that hot that it dried it. You rubbed salt on it, rolled it up and tied it, and put it in a box. And whenever anyone went on leave, down to Calcutta or wherever, they used to take them and sell 'em on the street where they made shoes, ladies' shoes. It made us quite a lot of money.

And for pastimes we used dung beetles. Big beetles, that used to get manure, or soil, into a round ball and push it. So we used to flatten out a patch, put a dung beetle this side, and a dung beetle that side, and a ball in front, and see who got there first. You used to bet on that.

Mind you, a lot of the creepy-crawlies weren't so much fun. Like the blooming leeches. If you didn't smoke, you did out there. You were issued Vs, and it was the only way you could get a leech off you. If you just knocked 'em off otherwise, you left the head in, and that went septic. There were red ants and black ants – the red ones were small, the black ones much bigger. And white ants. White ants was the worst. You had to keep everything off the ground; put anything on the ground, like a kitbag, and when you woke up the next morning and picked it up, they'd have eaten all the bottom out.

On the subject of eating, what were the rations like at the end of that tenuous supply line from Dimapur?

Bully beef and hard biscuits *every* day. The hard biscuits you turned into whatever you could. You made porridge of it; did everything imaginable with corned beef. You didn't get much else – dried potatoes, occasionally.

Actually the Indians in the division fed much better than what we did, because for some of 'em it all had to be on foot. Alive. And they'd kill a goat every day, or whatever, and have it with rice, and other things.

How much leave did you get at a time?

You were lucky if you got a fortnight. Of course, to go from Imphal to Calcutta *took* two weeks. You went up the jeep track, staying in transit camps for one night, two nights, until there was something to take you on to the next one, until you got to Dimapur.

When you got to your destination you went to the Redcaps' place and signed a chit with the time you got there. And your fourteen days started from then. After twelve days, or thirteen days, you went back to the railway station to see if there was a train going your way. And if there wasn't, well, you had another day.

I got my first leave in two years just before the Japs attacked in March 1944. I went on leave, came back, and found the battery had moved up to Ukhrul [in the Naga Hills, north-east of Imphal]. In anticipation of the trouble that was building up, you see.

When the long-awaited attack finally came, its audacity caught everyone by surprise. The Japanese in effect gambled everything on one throw of the dice, plunging across country to sever the single supply road connecting the 23rd Indian Division to the outside world, and hoping to encircle and destroy it and the two other Indian divisions protecting the Imphal Plain. If they failed, and were unable to capture the vital supply dumps, they would themselves face complete destruction.

I'd only been back a few hours when the Japs broke through. We got took by surprise again, you see. Some was ready for it and others weren't. Messages was coming through from various places, but they was confused. The first time we knew the Japs was almost on us was when a 15-cwt wireless truck with wounded came past – 'The Japs is coming!'
Straight away we had a big bonfire and burnt all the surplus kit. And then jogged off up the road. Met a small party of Japs coming up this road, singing away. And we just managed to get off the road and fire a few bombs at them. And then we scooted off again, 'cos there was too many. We had to keep moving quick, else we'd have been cut off. We almost had to run, marching ever so fast, back to a Naga village called Sangshak, where the 50th Indian Parachute Brigade and some of our own [23rd Indian Division] infantry were digging in.

The combined force was ordered to stand fast and fight at Sangshak, to slow the headlong Japanese advance on Kohima.

We was the last to get in. We just made it by about two minutes, before the Japs encircled it. Within a few minutes we got the mortars set up, and the word came down to get plenty of bombs ready.
There was sniping all day. Captain Hutton, with me at the side of my mortar, he got missed by a bullet. And about half an hour later a Jap in a bush at the top of the hill hit the shiny part of my mortar and the bullet went psssst [past his head by a fraction of an inch]. For quite some time my ear was ringing like mad. It must've been that close. And that went on all day like that, sniping.
And as soon as it started to get dark, the Japs came . . .
You didn't know what was happening most of the time. No orders came down as such. Now, they'd always said Japanese were small. But most of this first lot we encountered were great big

blokes. We got one or two of 'em wounded, and they were 6 foot.

You didn't get many prisoners, though, because they killed themselves. If they were wounded and they knew they were going to be taken prisoner. Their life didn't count a candle to them.

How did you feel, knowing you were surrounded by an enemy like that?

Anyone that says they weren't petrified are bloody liars. There's very few people can say they're not scared. When you're close up with it. We were artillery. We'd not been used to being up with the infantry like that. But anyone who says they're not affected by what's going on around them, I don't believe them. There was an officer there, he'd lost his mind. And he was just wandering around, day after day. Others got shot at and killed, but they never bothered with him – I suppose they could see. We had to take off all our ranks; officers had to take their pips off. And you never carried paper, or anything that shone. You was important if you'd got a bit of paper, and you became a target. So therefore you got killed.

Did you always feel you were going to get out?

No [matter of factly], oh no. I thought many a time I'd had my chips. Many a time. I got shot at directly, and missed every time. You got used to it after a bit. You had to.

So after 24 hours we had to retreat back to another position. That were vulnerable. The Japs soon found a way and got a gun, out of range of our mortars, on a slope and just started to fire. And they came down and down and down, until one of our mortars suffered a direct hit. It hit a phosphorus bomb, and burned 'em all to death. They just got buried where they were.

That was just before six o'clock. And it gets dark so sudden, you know. And they started again. The Japs broke through into the village, sixty of 'em. There was an Indian Mountain Battery there – they got overrun, 'cos they couldn't fire the guns at those ranges anyway. We had to winkle 'em out, those that'd broke in. Our Major, Major Smith, went charging in. He says, 'Follow me!', you know. Down to where these Japs were, and they just cut him up. Nearly sliced him in half.

We had to retreat the mortars again because they were too close to fire. You couldn't fire them at 100 yards. You didn't get any sleep, it was impossible. If you got five minutes' snooze that was it, and then you were firing again.

So the fiercest fighting was always at night.

Yes, in the daytime it was sniping and shelling. Stand To was always at two or three o'clock in the morning. That's when they did most of the fighting. Breaking in in little groups; kill or be killed. But we held us own.

Then the next day – I think this was about the fourth day – the Japs brought another gun up to where we were, and started firing solid shot. Point-blank range. The shot'd come smashing through the trees – we was in amongst trees now – and we were so confined it was very difficult to get the alignment of the mortar to fire back, but we destroyed it. Within two or three rounds. So that put paid to that.

In the meantime the Air Force had dropped supplies to us. The RAF were bloody good at it, you know; they flew in so low . . . but even so, the Japs got most of it.

So with little food and no water there was nothing else to do but to break out.

About eight o'clock the following night [26th March, the fifth day of the siege] they just gave us a bearing to fire on, and we had to fire all the remaining ammunition, everywhere. So the Japs was confused – they didn't know what was happening. We was just firing and firing, but that gave us a breathing space. And about quarter to nine I and my mortar crew slipped off, across the track.

All that we was told was that we would have a tin of condensed milk and a packet of biscuits, and that we were to march due south till six o'clock in the morning, then march due west. And that's what we did.

It took about five days, over all the rugged mountains; up and down, up and down. Occasionally we came across one or two others. Met some officers at one point, sloshing down this river that was only that deep. They told us the right direction to go. And the next morning we reached a hill with a Naga village at the top. All the locals came out and guided us up this huge hill, and we stayed there. They couldn't give us much food, but they provided us with a guide, a fourteen-year-old. He took us for two days, staying in each village that we came to. We just got a tiny bit of rice, and some water. And then on the third day we came across three Gurkhas, who were eating these big flowers off the trees. They took the stamen out, the centre, and ate the rest. There was no leaves on the tree, just these great big trumpet-like flowers. They said, 'Take the centre out, 'cos that's poisonous.'

So that and green bananas got us through. Then this lad, on the fourth day . . . I *think* it was the fourth day . . . said, 'Keep going now and you'll get on the plain – you can see it.' And he went back then. I gave him a silk handkerchief. Wouldn't take money. Wouldn't take any money whatsoever.

So the people in these remote villages were quite friendly to the British?

Not *all* of them, no. But the Nagas were. And the Manipuris. There was all different tribes, you see. The Nagas used to fight another lot. All their villages was fortified, with trenches and stockades.

When we got down on to the Imphal Plain we got picked up then.

I don't know what happened to all the wounded. I still don't know for sure, what happened to all the wounded at Sangshak. Because I can tell you this, all the wounded had to be left behind that couldn't walk. Next morning the Japs were so confused they didn't attack. They waited. And then they found they could just walk in, eventually.

Some say they killed a lot of our wounded, and others say they didn't. But to this day I don't know myself what happened. No one talks about that.

The stand at Sangshak allowed the Fourteenth Army to hastily move more units into position, and the Japanese found they were simply not strong enough to take Kohima and Imphal. For a time they clung on to their untenable positions, but in June, almost unnoticed at home amongst all the press coverage for Normandy, the back of their offensive was broken. The scale of the battles can be judged from the fact that the Fourteenth Army inflicted 53,500 casualties and suffered 16,700 of its own.

Then, after the big battles, they was withdrawing. We was on top of 'em then. And they was coming through starved to death. They was just dropping dead, from no food. And our role was mopping up, then. So you was knocking them off one ridge, and they'd retreat to another, and you'd follow up. For some time it was like that, chasing the Japs from one ridge to another.

Further north, the British 36th Division began to fight its way down the length of Burma. *Cecil Daniels* was in one of its infantry battalions – the 2nd Battalion, the Buffs (Royal East Kent Regiment).

We weren't in the Fourteenth Army, who were down south. We came under what was called the Northern Combat Area Command, in other words, under the Americans. Which was quite fortunate really, because it meant we got supplied by the Americans with their K rations, which were much nicer than the British ones.

They had all sorts of things in them; my personal favourites were the fruit bars.

The men of the battalion were veterans of El Alamein, but the conditions in the Far East were vastly different from the Desert, and they were first sent on the training courses laid on for new arrivals.

We arrived in Bombay having enjoyed a spell of garrison duty in the Middle East, and having provided security for the Teheran Conference [between Churchill, Roosevelt and Stalin] in November 1943. My job during the conference had been as driver to the RAF officer in charge of the catering for the VIPs.

From Bombay we moved down into Southern India by stages, and ended up at Bangalore. Did our initial training there, getting used to camouflage, and getting all our jungle green stuff. Dyed our equipment green as well; they had a big drum, and you dipped your webbing in to dye it. And then final training, you know, actually in the jungle, at a place called Balehonnur. We had to build our own basha out of bamboo, and that.

And learn about mules. That was quite interesting, learning how to load a mule up. You had to do it in a certain way — both panniers had to go on, each side, at the same time. You couldn't load one side up and then go round and do the other, because it wouldn't stand for it. So you had to make it balanced, and make sure it wasn't rubbing. Pernickety sort of animal. And of course if they didn't want to go, they wouldn't go. [Laughs.] They'd do a rodeo on you.

We started suppressive treatment for malaria in Bangalore, taking mepacrine. And we had a sort of insect-repellent cream, though of course that went by the board up in the jungle. And we'd been given injections for typhus and cholera, and all that sort of thing.

Just before Christmas 1944 we were sent to Northern Burma to join the 36th Division. The battalion flew in, but I went in overland. Took some jeeps in.

And then we started pushing south, looking for the Japs. I remember the first time we 'bumped' them when we was advancing.

By 'bumped', you mean ran into them?

Encountered them, yes. They opened fire on us in fact. We couldn't get forward; every time somebody got up to go forward they were immediately shot, you know. We were pinned down. So we called for an air strike, and we prepared to put in a bayonet charge. Fixed bayonets and dropped our packs, you know, our small packs. Then as soon as the planes had done the old bombing run, we was up and away. Yowl and scream, like you're taught.

But there was nothing there – they'd scarpered. Which was a bit of luck really, that we didn't come to any close quarter stuff. I wasn't too sorry, to tell the truth.

So we pushed on. There weren't any roads as such, they were just tracks. But the Yanks used to come along behind us with a bulldozer and make 'em wider for, you know, transport.

The Japs were very good at ambushes. Like every clearing you came to, you had to be very careful because it could be a trap. Because they'd let you in, but not out again.

The worst time they caught us was crossing the River Shweli, beside Myitson. The Shweli was a good 300 yards wide, and flowed into the Irrawaddy, but it was supposed to have been a piece of cake. We'd advanced down through the jungle, and we'd had one or two skirmishes. And lost one or two, not too bad. And we got to the river, which was the next major obstacle. We sent a patrol across, who came back and said, 'It's all clear – there's trenches there, but no sign of any occupation.'

So next day – because we had to wait for more boats to come up – at twelve noon we set off for the other bank. The Gunners laid a smoke barrage. We got about half-way across and all hell was let loose. We was fired on from the side, because upriver there was an island, you know, so we got sort of a crossfire. But we were fortunate where we were, because we went across in two places; we went a bit higher up. So we caught the enfilade stuff coming down from the island, but the ones lower down caught it from the front as well. Because they was opposite the village, which was only a matter of a couple of shacks, you know. So there were splashes all round us.

Anyway, we got across the other side and we dug in, on the river bank. Meanwhile the others were trying to get across, but they was getting shot up. Then 'B' Company tried to get across, and they copped it pretty bad as well. So in the end it was given up, and we were left marooned.

It got dark, you know, and during the night the Japs broke into our position. And our Platoon Sergeant told us to get out of it, it was every man for himself.

I managed to make it back across the river. They must've chased us right to the water's edge, because there were shots fired after us and bullets zipped into the water.

Of course the worst thing about it next day was, you know,

'Have you seen so-and-so . . . ?' Because I lost a good mate of mine there. Londoner. I'd sort of taken him under my wing. I used to write home for him, because he was one of those who'd never write, you know. I used to write to his family, because he'd lost his father in the blitz, and there was only his mum and two sisters. So I had the unenviable job of writing to tell them that he'd been killed. He had rather a lingering end really, because apparently he had a bullet through the neck and gradually bled to death . . .

Did he get back to the British side?

No. He was posted as missing, initially. But we recovered a lot of our dead because the Japs just threw the bodies in the river. They weren't like us – we would have buried them and marked the grave, or something like that. It was different from the European war. The Japs were pretty unpleasant. They killed the Burmese, and their own too. We found one one day, we felt he was one of theirs trying to get away. He'd been shot, just laying in the middle of the track, he was.

So we were sort of licking our wounds, and burying the dead. And then we went across again further downstream. That was on the 1st [1st February 1945] when it happened, when we first went across.

Our Company was left quite under strength, you know. There were three platoons in a company; we could muster about two platoons. Matter of fact at one time we had a Private, an old soldier, who was doing Company Sergeant-Major, because our CSM was killed on that crossing. And until we got sorted out, he did the job. Being an old soldier he knew the ropes, so he took over the Company Sergeant-Major's role for a while.

So how did the second attempt go?

Oh, it wasn't any bother, the second crossing. Only when we got back to Myitson, where we originally were going. Because we went across the river well downstream and then came back up the Jap side. We had to wade across another chaung, which wasn't as wide as the river, and then the Indians was in the van then. They took the village. And then we took over from them. We relieved them. We got to the village and we consolidated there, and then it was decided we had to advance to enlarge the bridgehead. Just as we were setting off we had a creeping barrage to support us, you know. And one of those fell short and fell on Battalion HQ.

But that was quite a rare occurrence, to fall that badly short. Apparently, I learned afterwards – because I correspond with a Battery Sergeant-Major, who was supporting us up the jungle – apparently they'd retrieved a gun from an earlier episode, and they'd put it into the line because they was getting short, you know, they were wearing out, and they hadn't zeroed it in or anything. And this was the one that did the damage.

But normally a creeping barrage was very useful for the infantry. It kept their heads down while you got forward. You'd advance so many yards and then stop, while they lifted it, and then go forward again, and so on. Step by step.

So that river crossing was quite a sticky job. And of course it wasn't over then.

We advanced up the track to a new position, and we had quite a ding-dong battle up there, 'cos we had a dropping zone there for food, and there was no way they could drop supplies to us without the Japs seeing. So that was quite nasty too.

Another mate of mine was wounded there, and he was laying on his stretcher as I went past. He said, 'Oh well, I'm out of it now.' But next I heard, he'd been killed. Going back across the river. Shell got him. Just when you thought you were comparatively safe, you know . . .

We established ourselves on this track, and lost quite a few more from sniping. I had a grenade discharge cup which you fitted on your rifle, to fire grenades. You had a 7-second and a 4-second fuse, and I found that the 4-second one was ideal, 'cos it burst sort of tree height, you know. So anybody up trees, which they was very fond of doing, it shifted 'em. They liked putting their snipers up trees, to pick us off.

And they attacked the flanks one day – the Indians caught that. That was in rear of us. Then we done a couple of attacks on a hill.

When they eventually retreated, we went up this hill we'd tried to take, and the defences . . . You'd never have taken it. Because they were dug in. They had thick tree trunks overhead, and bunkers. The only way to do it would've been to lob grenades in there, but you'd have had to get up close to them to do that.

The Japs were good in the jungle. They'd come up through Malaya, and they'd done it all. So well camouflaged.

That chap I told you about, who took over the role of CSM, he *stood* on one once. Actually put his foot on him, and he moved. The Jap had dug a hole, and had got a dirty old piece of rag over his head, you know. So of course he jumped back and opened up.

They'd rush your positions by night. They'd try and rush into your positions with a hand grenade, or something like that. One time a chap chucked a phosphorus grenade and actually hit this Jap. Couldn't see him, it was just a lucky throw, but he hit him and set him alight. And we could hear this Jap screaming all night. Broke the attack up, though.

As you got further down south the jungle began to thin out, but there were other things which were quite hairy. Like one time we had to advance through elephant grass, which is, you know, 10 feet tall, something like that. And you couldn't see the chap either side of you. You never knew who you were going to bump into. A few feet ahead might be a Jap with his gun pointing at you, you know. It was a really hairy experience, going through elephant grass in enemy country. But we got through it all right, thank goodness.

So how far south did you actually get?

Further than Mandalay. A place called Meiktila, below Mandalay. We was in that area for a while, and then we came out to start training for the invasion of Malaya. We flew out in Dakotas – United States Army Air Force – to Imphal, and then it was along the jeep track to Kohima and Dimapur, and west on the train to a place called Visapur, which was outside Poona. Took a party of officers one time while we was there to Bombay for a waterproofing exercise – you know, waterproofing of vehicles. For the invasion of Malaya.

But anyway the Bomb dropped, and so that was cancelled.

So being time-expired really, we mostly came home. Anyone that stayed behind was made up to Sergeant straight away. Which some did. But most of them came home.

Was it strange, coming back to the same job that you'd done before the war?

It was, yes. Drivers were ten a penny, and the wages weren't all that good. So I didn't intend to stay there really. But my boss asked me to go back, and I went back for a while to help him out. But then, you know, things happened. I got married, and then he bought this house for us to live in, and that's how it went on. So that's why I stayed.

Do you think your time in the Army was of benefit to you?

Yes [thoughtfully]. It taught you how to mix with people, you know. And not take them at their face value. In the service a lot of people were . . . well, you know, you tend to form opinions before you get to know someone. But we had a good battalion. There was a really great sense of comradeship during the war. That was what you missed when you came out, the comradeship, you know. Because you don't get it in civvy life. However many friends you have, you don't get the same feeling.

You get . . . I dunno . . . I suppose 'love' is a funny word for your mates and that. I lost my brother during the war, and yet the deaths of friends in my own unit hit me more than did my own brother. I could have cried, you know, but there wasn't that sort of feeling when my brother was killed.

When you get in the unit, it's like it becomes your family.

There was some of the same community spirit at home, of course. Everyone would do everything for anybody else, and there wasn't all this backbiting that there seems to be now. But then people got back to their old ways – you know, blow you, Jack, I'm all right. Yes, that's the one thing during the war that was really nice, you know. Everyone would help anyone else. And you hoped it would carry on after the war, but it didn't, unfortunately.

Human nature, I suppose. Human nature. Yes, I guess so.